MANCHESTER.

A BRIEF RECORD OF ITS PAST

AND

A PICTURE OF ITS PRESENT,

INCLUDING

AN ACCOUNT OF ITS SETTLEMENT AND OF ITS GROWTH AS TOWN AND CITY; A HISTORY OF ITS SCHOOLS, CHURCHES, SOCIETIES, BANKS, POST-OFFICES, NEWSPAPERS AND MANUFACTURES; A DESCRIPTION OF ITS GOVERNMENT, POLICE AND FIRE DEPARTMENT, PUBLIC BUILDINGS, LIBRARY, WATER-WORKS, CEMETERIES, STREETS, STREAMS, RAILWAYS AND BRIDGES; A COMPLETE LIST OF THE SELECTMEN, MODERATORS AND CLERKS OF THE TOWN AND MEMBERS OF THE COUNCILS, MARSHALS AND ENGINEERS OF THE CITY, WITH THE STATE OF THE VOTE FOR MAYOR AT EACH ELECTION; THE STORY OF ITS PART IN THE WAR OF THE REBELLION WITH A COMPLETE LIST OF ALL ITS SOLDIERS WHO WENT TO THE WAR; AND SKETCHES OF ITS REPRESENTATIVE CITIZENS.

WITH

THIRTY-EIGHT STEEL AND EIGHTEEN WOOD ENGRAVINGS OF ITS PROMINENT MEN AND BUILDINGS.

MANCHESTER, N. H.:
JOHN B. CLARKE.
1875.

Mirror Office: JOHN B. CLARKE,
MANCHESTER, N. H.

PREFACE.

THIS book is designed to answer the question, "What has Manchester been and what is it to-day?" It aims to record briefly the circumstances of its origin and growth as the background to a picture of its present life.

The credit of collecting and writing its contents, under my supervision, belongs to my nephew, Maurice D. Clarke. The sources have been many from which information has been obtained and the chance for inaccuracy has been therefore great. Records have been found to err, personal recollections have conflicted, but comparison of different authorities has been made when possible and accuracy has been sought if not reached.

The first twenty-four pages were condensed from Judge Potter's "History of Manchester" and the list of town and city officers had been prepared by Judge Isaac W. Smith when he revised the city ordinances. The writer acknowledges indebtedness, also, to the officers of the corporations, banks, churches and societies; to Ex-Gov. E. A. Straw, Ex-Gov. Frederick Smyth, Col. Phinehas Adams and the city clerk, Joseph E. Bennett, for valuable information; to Charles H. Marshall, librarian of the public library, for unusual privileges; to the Hon. Joseph W. Fellows, an acknowledged authority upon Freemasonry; to Sylvester C. Gould, whose large collection of documents bearing upon the city's early years has been the source from which much has been drawn; and, in general, to the Hon. Jacob F. James, Joseph G. Edgerly, Joseph L. Stevens, D. K. Mack, R. H. Hassam and very many others whom there is no space to enumerate.

John B. Clarke,

June, 1875.

ERRATA.

Page 30, line 14, read March for October.
Page 169, line 23, read Presbyterian for Congregational.
Page 193, lines 21, 29, 31, read Alphonso for Alpheus.
Page 273, line 14, read 1842 for 1852.
Page 273, line 20, read 1851 for 1841.
Page 327, line 19, read 1844 for 1845.

CONTENTS.

The Early History—1622–1751 9
Derryfield—1751–1810 15
Manchester—A Town—1810–1846 23
Manchester—A City—1846–1875 41
The City of To-Day 65
Schools 109
Religious and Benevolent Societies 127
Miscellaneous Societies 211
Post-Offices, Banks and Insurance Companies 249
Manufactures 267
Newspapers 323
Manchester in the Rebellion 339
Residences 471
Representative Men 373
Index 445

ILLUSTRATIONS.

Portrait of Col. Phinehas Adams to face page 10
William Amory................................ 16
Amoskeag Manufacturing Company's Mills—View from the West side of the River 24
Portrait of Charles E. Balch............................ 32
the Hon. Charles H. Bartlett.................... 40
Joseph E. Bennett............................ 48
Aretas Blood.................................. 56
Dr. W. W. Brown........................ 64
the Hon. David A. Bunton......... 72
Amoskeag Manufacturing Company—Dam and Gate-House.. 78
Court-House.......... 82
Public Library....... 88
Manchester Water-Works—Pumping Station.......... 94
Location of the Dam, Races, etc.. 104
Details of Penstock................ 112
Details of Dam.................. 120
Section of Pumping-Station and Pumps..................... 128
Plan of Pumping-Station and Pumps...................... 136
Details of Reservoir............. 144
Portrait of the Hon. G. Byron Chandler.................... 152
the Hon. P. C. Cheney.......................... 160
the Hon. Joseph B. Clark....................... 168
the Hon. L. W. Clark........................... 176
John B. Clarke............ 184
the Hon. William C. Clarke... 192
Dr. Josiah Crosby 200
the Hon. Moody Currier........................ 208
Col. M. V. B. Edgerly.................. 216

Portrait of the Hon. Moses Fellows........................ 224
the Hon. Herman Foster............... 232
the Hon. E. W. Harrington........................ 240
Gen. Natt Head.................................. 248
the Hon. John Hosley.......... 256
the Hon. Jacob F. James...................... 264
Amoskeag Manufacturing Company — Counting-House and Buildings on Upper Canal.......................... 272
Amoskeag Manufacturing Company's Mills—Lower Yard.... 280
Stark Mills 288
Portrait of the Hon. Warren L. Lane.... 296
Amoskeag Manufacturing Company — Machine-Shops and Lower Mill-Yard................................ 304
Amoskeag Manufacturing Company—Lumber-Yard, Mechanics' Row, Gate-House and Dam................. 312
Portrait of Col. B. F. Martin................. 320
the Hon. John P. Newell............ 328
A. P. Olzendam....... 336
the Hon. Nathan Parker........................ 344
the Hon. C. E. Potter. 352
Gen. William P. Riddle.................... 360
Residence of Ex-Gov. Frederick Smyth. 370
Portrait of Col. Waterman Smith........... 376
the Hon. Frederick Smyth..................... 384
the Hon. C. W. Stanley....................... 392
the Hon. E. A. Straw.............. 400
D. B. Varney.................................. 408
Residence of Col. B. F. Martin............................ 416
Portrait of the Rev. C. W. Wallace........................ 424
Residence of Col. Waterman Smith......................... 430
Portrait of the Hon. James A. Weston.................... 440

THE EARLY HISTORY.

1622—1751.

A RECORD of the City of Manchester may be written in one sentence, of which a history is the expansion. After an embryonic life of years it was born in 1751, attained its majority in 1846, and is in the prime of manhood to-day. The land on which it stands was shared with several towns till the beginning of its individual life, and the history of this territory is for some distance identical with that of the state of which it forms a part.

Among the speculators whom the discovery of a western continent produced in the old world were Sir Ferdinando Gorges and Capt. John Mason, who obtained from the English government in 1622 a grant of land which included the greater part of New Hampshire. They subsequently dissolved partnership and Mason became the sole proprietor of the land west of the Piscataqua river, deriving his title from the king of England, who professed to be the owner. On the other hand, the Rev. John Wheelwright of Braintree, Mass., obtained, May 17, 1629, from Passaconnaway, the head of the Pennacook Indians, and three other chiefs, whom he deemed the proprietors by right, a deed of the southern part of the state, which enclosed a large piece of Mason's grant, and, banished by the Puritans from Massachusetts on account of his religion, settled in Exeter. The dispute between these claimants descended to their heirs and was the seed of much strife.

The first settlement of Londonderry was made in 1719 by Scotch Irish people, who obtained from John, the grandson of the Rev. John Wheelwright, a deed dated October 20, 1719, which conveyed to them a tract of land ten miles square, in what was known as the "chestnut country" from the abundance of its chestnut trees, which also gave the name of "Nutfield" to Londonderry. To them in 1722 the governor of the province made a grant which was the third within the present limits of Manchester. The first was a gift in 1663 to the Indian chief, Passaconnaway, who had been reduced to poverty, and the second, which included nearly half of Manchester and was the ancient Chester, was made by the governor in 1720 to a number of men who, wrongly supposing the settlers of Londonderry to be Irishmen and Roman Catholics, were anxious to obtain beforehand the territory on which the latter had settled. Their plan was thwarted by their ignorance of civil engineering and their consequent inability to fit their deed to the land in question.

The Presbyterian settlers of Londonderry had played much the same part in Scotland as the Puritans in England. Persecuted by Episcopalians and Roman Catholics, they sought a refuge in the north of Ireland, and, after fighting for their religious rights and enduring the memorable siege of Londonderry, followed the Puritans to the new world, coming to Boston in 1718 and to Londonderry the next year, introducing in this country the cultivation of the potato and the spinning of flax. They were eminently men of energy, independence and a bluff honesty, and of them were the first settlers of Manchester in 1722.

Till then the territory of the latter town had been occupied by Indian tribes, of whom the Namaoskeags, who were subject to the Pennacooks, dwelt around Amoskeag Falls.

American Bank Note Co. Boston.

Phins Adams

Namaoskeag — the place of much fish — originally meant the series of falls and rapids from Concord to Nashua, in all of which fish had abounded, but the latter at length were found in plenty only at Amoskeag and the name was therefore restricted to that place. Here the Rev. John Eliot, the "Apostle to the Indians," preached about 1651; here, later, Simon Betogkom, a Christian Indian, exhorted his fellows; and here were supported by the converted savages the first preaching and school in the state north of Exeter. The river at this point overflowed, in the season, with salmon, shad, alewives and lamprey-eels going up the river to spawn; the alewives vanishing in the small rivulets above the Falls, the eels seeking the pebbly bottoms, the salmon and shad separating at the forks at Franklin to ascend, the one the Pemigewasset and the other the Winnipisseogee.

These fisheries the proprietors of Londonderry had meant to secure in their grant, but their ignorance of the country made their surveys faulty, and a strip of land between the then line of Chester and the Merrimack, a little over a mile wide and eight miles in length, extending from what is now Hooksett to Litchfield, was left outside of any provincial grant. This piece of land, on which the mills and stores of Manchester stand to-day, was called Harrytown.

In 1722, John Goffe, jr., and his brothers-in-law, Edward Lingfield and Benjamin Kidder, men from Massachusetts who were related to the Londonderry settlers, built for themselves houses on Cohas brook, being the first known inhabitants within the present city. Goffe lived on the north bank of the brook nearly opposite the falls to which he has left his name. As early as 1729 people from Massachusetts had made settlements upon the ungranted land near Amoskeag Falls and, to establish the right of Londonderry to the place, in 1733 Archibald Stark (the father of the Revolutionary hero), John McNeil and John Riddell (as the name was then spelt) went from that town to occupy lands near the Falls, Stark settling upon the "Stark place," McNeil upon the "Kidder farm," and Riddell upon the "Ray farm." These were the first known white settlers near Amoskeag Falls.

All the New Hampshire settlements had been usurped in 1658 by Massachusetts, but in 1679 New Hampshire was made a royal province. In 1686, however, it was united with the rest of the colonies into New England and made a province subordinate to Massachusetts authority. In 1733 seven tracts of land in New Hampshire were granted to soldiers in the Narragansett War of 1675 under the name of "Narragansett townships." The southeastern part of Narragansett No. IV included the village of Amoskeag and was the fourth grant of land within the limits of Manchester. Narragansett No. V included what is now Piscataquog village and was the fifth grant. In 1735 Massachusetts granted also a tract of land on the east side of the Merrimack, three miles wide and extending from Suncook to Litchfield, to Major Ephraim Hildreth, John Shepley and other soldiers who had fought the Indians in 1703 under Captain William Tyng, in whose honor the place was named Tyngstown. It included the old Harrytown and was the sixth grant within Manchester's limits. Major Hildreth, in 1735 or 1736, built upon the Cohas, a little east of Harvey's mills, a saw-mill, the first mill of any kind in Manchester. A settlement grew up there, and a meeting-house was built in the vicinity which was afterwards destroyed by sparks from burning woods. But the feuds between the New England Puritans and the Scotch Presbyterians prevented the permanent establishment of church or school.

During all this time there had been continual controversy as to the boundary line between New Hampshire and

Massachusetts, which was settled in 1740 by cutting off from Massachusetts twenty-six townships which she had claimed as hers, among which was Tyngstown. The next year New Hampshire was made a separate province and Benning Wentworth governor.

In the French and Indian War, which began in 1746 and was concluded by the treaty of Aix-la-Chapelle in 1748, the settlers took a worthy part, building a fort at the outlet of what is now Nutt's pond, a place central to the three settlements at Amoskeag, Goffe's Falls and what are now Webster's mills. At the latter place John McMurphy and his son Alexander had built in 1742 a saw-mill, with some idea that iron ore might be mined in that vicinity.

In 1746 Captain Mason sold his claim to a number of men, who gave up the title to their lands in incorporated towns, but the people of Harrytown and the Narragansett townships were obliged to pay them a small sum. About this time the settlers on this ungranted tract became desirous of living in a town of their own, and, as it was too small to make a township without additions, the latter were obtained by subtraction from others adjacent. So, at a meeting of the governor and council, September 3, 1751, a charter was granted, under the name of Derryfield, to a territory which enclosed eighteen square miles of the southwest part of Chester, nine square miles of the northwest part of Londonderry, and eight square miles of Harrytown, thirty-five miles in all, making a township of irregular shape and various soils. The north part of Harrytown, called Henrysburg or Henrysborough, was left ungranted but was annexed in 1792. The charter was written in the name of the king of England, George II, and signed by the governor, Benning Wentworth. The name of Derryfield is said to have been given to the new township because the people of Derry had been used to pasture their cows within it.

DERRYFIELD.

1751—1810.

THE first meeting of the inhabitants of the new-born town was held September 9, 1751, at the house of John Hall, a tavern-keeper living at what is now known as "Manchester Centre," and in that vicinity they continued to assemble till 1840. At that meeting were chosen five selectmen, a town-clerk, two auditors, a constable, two tithing-men, two surveyors of highways, two invoice men, two haywards, two deerkeepers, a culler of staves and a surveyor of lumber. Between the third day of March and the twenty-second of the next February eleven roads were laid out, of which eight were wholly or in part new.

The Seven Years' War, between the British and French, began in 1754 and lasted till 1761, and in it the men of Derryfield bore a prominent part, the "Rangers," under command of Col. John Goffe, Capt. Robert Rogers and Capt. John Stark, being especially noted. It is a curious fact that Col. Goffe's men, dressed in odd clothes, wearing their hair long or tied in queues, their heads protected by woolen nightcaps, suggested to Dr. Shackburg, a surgeon in the British regular army, the idea of writing to a tune called "Nankey Doodle," which had come down from Cromwell's time, a song in derision of these nondescripts, changing "Nankey" to "Yankey" and thus originating the title of the popular air of to-day.

At the close of this war a day of rest and prosperity, dawned upon the New England colonies, though its light was faint in Derryfield. Its settlers were enticed from their farms by the fisheries, the thrift which belongs to agriculture was wanting, and the Scotch Presbyterians and English Puritans, whose union the war had cemented, broke apart and quarreled. At the town-meeting in 1751 money had been appropriated to pay for preaching, but it does not appear that a preacher was hired. At a meeting in 1753 certain barns were designated as places of worship and a call was extended to Alexander McDowell, but he seems to have made no reply. In 1754 the town voted to build a meeting-house at the Centre. The frame was put up in 1758 and from that time till 1766 there was a continual quarrel about the support of preaching and the location of the house. The popular feeling was deeply stirred and the resolves of one meeting were vetoed at the next. This condition of affairs bore its natural fruit in a depopulation of the town, there having been a decrease of one-fifth of the polls in the year which ended with March, 1766.

At the town-meeting which was held on the third day of that month the party which favored the existing location of the meeting-house gathered in force with extreme punctuality and "went through the motions" in great haste, electing their own officers and then adjourning. When the other faction came upon the scene and learned what had happened, they also elected a full set of officers, claiming the previous proceedings illegal. This of necessity caused confusion, and the state legislature of that year, upon petition of a number of the citizens of Derryfield, passed a bill vacating the town-meetings of that year and ordering a special meeting on the thirteenth of August. At that time the party before victorious again triumphed, but, at a special meeting held December 22, their opponents carried the day and refused to vote money for preaching or for anything else.

W Allison

This added to the trouble, but at the town-meeting held March 2, 1767, a compromise was probably made and a reconciliation effected between the two factions. Even during this sorry quarrel preaching had been maintained a part of each year, and in 1773 it was voted to hire the Rev. George Gilmore, but he neglected to reply to the invitation. The meeting-house, which by this time had been partially finished, was repaired in 1790 and the pews were sold. In 1792 the space in the gallery was sold but pews were never built in it and the building was never finished for a meeting-house. When the village on the river, which the Amoskeag Company started, grew up, it was voted to hold the town-meetings there, and the old house, in which the town had so long held its religious and secular meetings, was sold and converted into a dwelling-house. It is still standing next to the burying-ground on the road through the Centre.

In 1771 New Hampshire was divided into five counties, and Derryfield was attached to one of them called Hillsborough in honor of Willis Hills, Earl of Hillsborough and a member of the privy council of George III. All the courts had hitherto been held at Portsmouth, but now Amherst was made a shire town, and courts of general sessions, common pleas and probate established. The Hon. Samuel Blodget of Derryfield, to be widely known afterwards as the projector and builder of the Blodget canal, was made a "justice of the court of common pleas of the peace for Hillsborough county."

Derryfield shared with the rest of the country the inspirations of tyranny and insult which aroused the colonists to the Revolutionary War in 1775, and endured, besides, provocations peculiar to itself and its vicinity. When the lands of New Hampshire were first granted, all the white pine trees, from fifteen to thirty-six inches in diameter, were reserved by the king to make masts for the royal navy. The trees which then grew in the valley of the Piscataquog river were well adapted for this purpose, one having gained in tradition the fame of such a size as to allow a yoke of oxen to be driven on its stump. The business of cutting and hauling them became so extensive that the "Mast road" was built up the Piscataquog, through Goffstown and Weare, branching into New Boston. The laws of the province compelled all land-owners, before they cut their timber, to have marked by the appointed officer the trees which belonged to the king. If this were neglected, all the timber they cut that year was forfeited, and thus men who were unable to pay the surveyor were deprived in a moment of the results of a winter's work.

When the news of the battle of Lexington in 1775 reached Derryfield, such was the state of popular feeling that the selectmen and thirty-four out of thirty-six men who were able to bear arms went at once to the war, leaving but two at home with the old and infirm. The records of the Revolutionary War relate the deeds of the men of Derryfield at Bunker Hill, Trenton, Princeton, Bennington, Saratoga, West Point and in various expeditions till the siege of Yorktown. Captain John Stark and his men were immortalized by their victory at Bennington, for which the former was made a brigadier-general by the Continental Congress. The signing of the articles of peace in 1783 was celebrated on the tenth of July by a general merry-making at Amoskeag Falls.

At the beginning of trouble in 1775 Gov. Wentworth, departing the province, left the people to govern themselves; and the inhabitants of Hillsborough county, meeting by delegates at Amherst, formed a system of government for the county, appointing men to act as justices of the peace and establishing a court of justice to be held at Amherst. Derryfield was governed under this system till the formation of the state government by a convention of delegates at Exeter in 1776. The latter was amended in different ways till the establishment of a permanent system in 1793. By this last Derryfield was classed with Litchfield for the choice of a representative to the legislature and at a joint meeting held March 25, 1793, Major John Webster of Derryfield was chosen the first representative and it was voted to hold the annual meetings in each town alternately, and in Derryfield at the present residence of John P. Moore.

The taxes which the war had imposed had been too burdensome to allow a large expenditure for preaching, but at its close returning thrift and regard for education and morality were marked at the March meeting in 1784 by a liberal appropriation for preaching and schooling, and it was voted to divide the town into four school districts. From that time till the mills were built on the Merrimack the town made a continual advance. The state assessed in 1791 a tax upon the towns for educational purposes, but not until 1795 was there a school-house in Derryfield, when one was built by private subscription on what was then the Falls road just in the rear of the present residence of the Hon. David Cross. In 1798 the town voted to buy that house and build two more, and in 1809 the districts were re-made and a house built at the Centre.

In 1788 Derryfield cast her vote, in common with the whole country, for George Washington for President of the United States. In 1792 a number of men formed a corporation as the proprietors of the Amoskeag bridge, and the bridge was completed in September of that year. It crossed the Merrimack at the foot of Bridge street and was known as "McGregor's bridge," from Robert McGregor who lived just across the river in Goffstown. The same year Henrysburg was annexed and the town was visited by the small-pox.

In 1793 the Hon. Samuel Blodget, who was born at

Woburn, Mass., April 1, 1724, who had been a sutler in the colonial wars and the Revolution, a judge of the court of common pleas and a merchant with extensive business connections, took up his residence on the east bank of the Merrimack near Amoskeag Falls. He had conceived the idea of building around the latter a canal through which might be carried to market vast quantities of lumber from the forests which grew on the banks of the river. He began work upon it May 2, 1794, building a basin from a point above the Falls to another nearly opposite the residence of Samuel B. Kidder, and extending the canal thence to a point near the upper end of the Amoskeag Company's machine-shop. He lost time and money in a vain attempt to make practicable a lock of his own invention, and it was not until May 1, 1807, having spent all his own fortune and what money he could raise by lotteries, that he saw his work done. He died on the first day of September of the same year, and his canal, passing into the hands of the proprietors of the Middlesex canal, was of great benefit till the railroad destroyed its usefulness and it went to decay.

Judge Blodget was a far-sighted man. He invited Boston capitalists to build in Derryfield the mills which others erected thirty years after, and, in anticipation of their construction, he bought the clay lands where the well known Hooksett brick are made to-day. It is well written on his monument in the Valley Cemetery that he was "the pioneer of internal improvements in New Hampshire."

In 1795 a number of citizens associated themselves to form a social library and in 1799 they were incorporated as "The Proprietors of the Social Library in Derryfield," when they had seventy-eight books, but the organization was subsequently dissolved.

The town voted in 1800 to build a pound at the south end of the meeting-house lot at the Centre, which was used till 1830. In 1804 town-meeting day was changed from the first Monday in March to the second Tuesday. In 1806 the town was divided into highway districts which remained the same till the adoption of the city charter in 1846.

It had been proposed to build locks on Cohas brook to make it possible to float through it, to the Merrimack, the lumber which grew around Massabesic pond, and in 1803 the town voted to petition the legislature for an act of incorporation to allow it to carry out the plan. The act was obtained, but in 1806 the town voted to leave the enterprise to private individuals, and the next year took five shares of stock in the enterprise, after which there is no record of it.

March 13, 1810, when the population of the town was six hundred and fifteen, and the first mill had just been built upon the river at Amoskeag, the town chose Thomas Stickney, John G. Moor and Amos Weston a committee to petition the legislature to change the name of Derryfield to Manchester, and the request was complied with at the June session of that year. The new name was chosen in compliment to Judge Blodget, who had said the town would become "the Manchester of America." Mr. Weston was the father of the present governor of the state and mayor of the city — the Hon. James A. Weston.

MANCHESTER—A TOWN.

1810—1846.

THE record has thus far been of the natural growth of a town from causes which it possessed in common with others, but is henceforth of such growth stimulated by foreign enterprise. In the early part of 1809 Benjamin Prichard, with Ephraim, David and Robert Stevens, built on the west side of Amoskeag Falls, in what was then Goffstown, a small mill, and, finding the burden too heavy for individual enterprise, formed the next year a joint stock company. This held its first meeting January 31, 1810, as "The Proprietors of the Amoskeag Cotton & Wool Factory," and was incorporated in June of that year as the "Amoskeag Cotton and Woolen Manufacturing Company." Its mill was forty feet square and two stories high. There was then no picker and the cotton was ginned in the neighborhood at four cents a pound. The machinery consisted only of spindles, and the yarns, at once the company's dividends, the officers' salaries and the operatives' wages, were either sold as they were spun or woven for the company by the housewives of the town.

The machinery ran till 1816 and then stood still till 1822, when Olney Robinson of Rhode Island bought the property and resumed business, being soon succeeded by Larned Pitcher and Samuel Slater of Pawtucket, R. I. In 1825 they sold three-fifths to Willard Sayles and Lyman Tiffany, of the firm of Sayles, Tiffany & Hitchcock,—now

Gardner Brewer & Co.,—Dr. Oliver Dean and Ira Gay. Dr. Dean became the agent of the company, coming to Amoskeag in 1826, when a new mill, called the "bell mill," and another on an adjacent island, were built. Thus began an enterprise which assumed definite shape in 1831 by the incorporation of the "Amoskeag Manufacturing Company." It bought the land for some distance on both sides of the river and subsequently gave it away or sold it to actual settlers, thus building a village. Controlling the water-power, it leased mill-sites to new corporations and thus added fresh stimulus to the growth already begun.

Manchester furnished its quota in the war of 1812, and in 1815, after having made one vain request in 1811, was allowed by the legislature to be represented in that body by itself, instead of being classed with other towns, and March 12, 1816, Isaac Huse was chosen as the first representative under the new allotment.

The year 1821 is remarkable for the first known murder committed by a citizen of Manchester and recognized by the judicial authorities. On the fourth day of October of that year Daniel D. Farmer of Manchester murdered a worthless woman of Goffstown named Anna Ayer, by striking her on the head in a sudden fit of anger. He was arrested and committed to jail, and, by the court at Amherst in October, was found guilty and sentenced to be hung. The sentence was executed January 23, 1822.

Major General John Stark, the hero of the Revolution, died May 8, 1822, aged nearly ninety-four years. He was buried in the presence of a large concourse of people, with military honors, in a private cemetery on the "Stark place," and the family erected over his remains a plain granite shaft. Thither the survivors of the late War of the Rebellion make annual pilgrimage when they decorate the graves of their departed companions in arms.

About this time the project of building the Mammoth

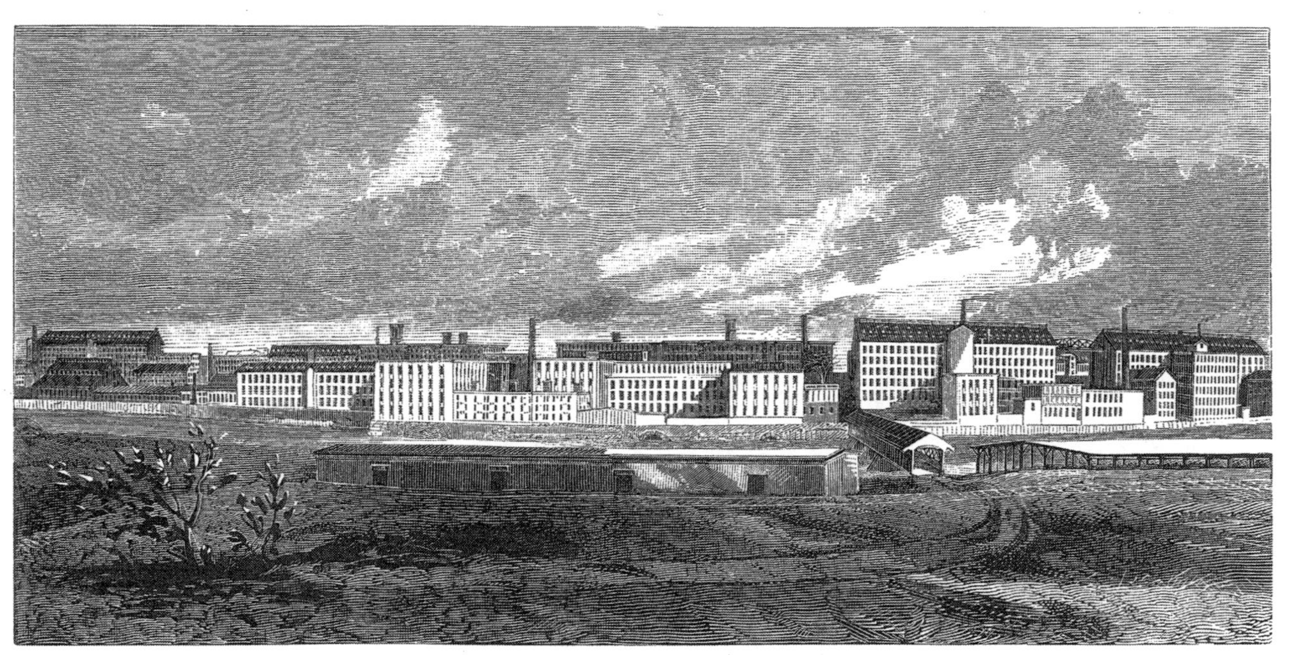

AMOSKEAG MANUF'G CO.'S MILLS.

VIEW FROM WEST SIDE OF THE RIVER.

road sprang into existence, and with it a controversy which delayed its completion almost till it was made of little comparative value by the construction of the Concord railway. It was intended for a more direct route from Concord to Lowell, was wanted by those towns, by several others and by the stage proprietors, but was opposed by Manchester and Londonderry because it would subject them to expense and would be of no benefit to them. The road was first suggested in town-meeting in 1823, when an article authorizing its construction was voted down. It was advocated again and again and was as often successfully opposed till 1830, when the court ordered the town to build it. It was not, however, till 1834, after the court had threatened summary measures, that the town complied.

In 1829 the town voted to divide the literary fund among the school districts and let each choose its own prudential committee. In 1834 the small-pox made some stir, and in 1836 the selectmen were authorized to convert the old meeting-house into a town-house.

On the twenty-fourth day of October, 1838, occurred the first of four public sales of land by which the Amoskeag Company disposed of its possessions to men who were the builders of the coming city. Some streets had been laid out already in this vicinity, but there were graded only Elm street from Central to Lowell, and Chestnut and Pine from Manchester to Lowell. The land which now is enclosed in Merrimack and Concord squares was reserved, and one hundred and forty-seven lots were sold between Elm, Lowell, Union and Hanover streets. The sound of hammer and saw was at once heard, and in January, 1839, Mrs. Anna Heyes of Londonderry built the first private house on the Company's land in the city proper, standing on the northwest corner of Concord and Chestnut streets. In this year and the next were built several of the blocks on Elm street, the Manchester House, the "Governor Bell house," the one which was once owned by the Stark Mills and occupied by its agent and now used as the Roman Catholic Orphan Asylum, the First Congregational church and several other buildings on Hanover street.

At the annual "Goffstown muster," September 24, 1839, Jeremiah Johnson, a member of the Manchester Rifle Company, was killed in a general quarrel by Elbridge Ford. The latter was tried the next year, found guilty of manslaughter and sentenced to the state prison for five years, but was pardoned at the end of three.

During the summer of 1839 the number of people and houses had largely increased on account of the Amoskeag Company's first sale, and prices at the second, which occurred October 8, 1839, were much higher. The land sold was included between Elm, Hanover, Union and Merrimack streets.

After this second sale the village assumed such proportions that it soon became patent that the old regulations were ill adapted to existing needs, and at a special meeting, October 26, 1839, it was voted to establish a system of police and a board of health, and to take measures for protection against fire. The "new village," as the settlement upon the Company's land was now called, was allowed to nominate the fire-wards. The latter organized and bought a fire-engine called "Merrimack No. 1," and the first engine-house was built on Vine street. There was already in town an engine which was owned by the Stark Mills, and, as early as 1818, one had been bought by Piscataquog village, then a part of Bedford.

In 1839 was established by John Caldwell "The Representative," the first newspaper published in Manchester. It was a Democratic paper and its first number was issued October 18, and it appeared on subsequent Fridays till 1842, when it was sold and merged with "The Manchester Democrat." In this year the first police officers were appointed, four in number.

The ill feeling between the dwellers in the old town and those in the new reached its height at the March meeting of 1840, when thirty constables had to be chosen to keep order before the other town officers could be elected. There were two sets of candidates, representing thus the old town and the new. The latter carried the day, and thereafter held the reins of government.

In 1840, the Lowell-street Universalist church, the First Baptist church (which stood on the corner of Manchester and Chestnut streets till swept off by the fire of 1870), a wooden chapel on Hanover street for the Second Methodist Episcopal society, and Granite bridge, were built; the Amoskeag Insurance Company was started; "The Memorial" newspaper, and the "Manchester Workman," a campaign paper, were established by J. C. Emerson; the town was divided by the selectmen into nine school districts; another small-pox excitement produced a general vaccination; and Elm, Bridge, Lowell, Concord, Amherst, Hanover, Manchester, Pine and Chestnut streets were laid out as far as they extended upon the Company's land. The population then was three thousand three hundred and twenty-five.

In 1841 the first town-meeting was held in the new village in a hall on Amherst street. During this year the town voted to accept a deed of the Valley cemetery from the Amoskeag Company and bought of the latter for twenty-four hundred dollars the lot on the corner of Elm and Market streets where the city hall now stands. The same year a town-house was built upon it at a cost of seventeen thousand dollars. There were erected this year a large number of buildings, including school-houses in districts number three and four and what is now the old high-school house on Lowell street, the Freewill Baptist church on the corner of Merrimack and Chestnut streets, and Union building on the corner of Elm and Market streets, which was the first one built by private individuals on the Company's land west of Elm street. There was bought this year for a town farm the land of Moses Davis, which forms a part of the present farm, and there were laid out Vine street, parts of Merrimack, Union and Orange streets, and several back streets.

In 1842 the first town-meeting was held in the new town-house, when it was voted to build reservoirs for fire purposes on the corner of Elm and Hanover streets and on Lowell street in front of Isaac Riddle's house. At this time the custom of printing the annual town reports was begun. In this year were built school-houses in districts number six and nine, a hook-and-ladder house where the Franklin street church now stands, and the Amoskeag Falls bridge; and the Second Methodist Episcopal society, which had sold to the Unitarian society its wooden chapel on Hanover street, built a brick church on Elm street. This year was marked also by an especially liberal appropriation for schools, by the organization of the Manchester Lyceum to provide annual lecture-courses, and by the trial-trip of the Concord railway, which occurred June 28, the road being opened to the public on the fourth of the next month. In this year was established by W. H. Kimball and Joseph Kidder "The Manchester Democrat," and several other newspapers were started this year and the next whose lease of life was shorter.

In 1843 there was a temperance agitation and the town appointed a liquor-agent and instructed the selectmen to prosecute all violators of the license law, but the interest in the matter was temporary and the prosecutions were few. This year the town voted to fit up a house on the town farm as a house of correction and decided to build the "Hooksett road." The Episcopal society built a wooden church, then known as St. Michael's, on the corner of Lowell and Pine streets, which has since given place to one of stone called Grace church.

The year 1844 was an important one in the town's life. The Manchester Atheneum — the nucleus of the public library — was organized; the legislature passed a bill to allow the October term of the court of common pleas to be held in the town; the custom of ringing the bell on the town-house as a summons to school was established; the Unitarian society, which had bought of the Methodists their chapel on Hanover street, moved it to the corner of Pine and Merrimack streets and there established worship; and on the twenty-sixth of September the third land sale of the Amoskeag Company took place, when the tract bounded by Elm, Merrimack, Union and Park streets was sold at prices in advance of those of the previous sales. On the twelfth of August the town-house was burned, and in less than three weeks the town voted to build another on the same spot. Carelessness kindled the fire, and, taught wisdom by its loss, the town voted to buy two new fire-engines, built new reservoirs and enlarged the old ones, fitted the ponds on Merrimack and Hanover squares for use in case of fire, and appointed a committee to consider the sources of water supply. This committee reported, thirty years before the completion of the present water-works, that there was no water available for fire purposes nearer than Massabesic pond. The water of the latter, however, could not be brought to the town without subjecting it to an expense at that time beyond its means.

In the year 1845 the town took extraordinary strides in growth, and public improvement kept pace. It gradually assumed greater dignity and was fast ripening into a city. The present city hall was built in October at a cost of thirty-five thousand dollars, after plans by Edward Shaw of Boston. In this year a committee was chosen at the town meeting to count the cost of a common sewer in Elm street, a board of engineers was established, the court of common pleas was held in the town for the first time, the

Hon. Ira A. Eastman presiding, and the first town-meeting was held in the present city hall. On the thirtieth of September occurred the fourth and last extensive land sale of the Amoskeag Company, when the land between Elm, Lowell, Union and Orange streets was put into the market and still higher prices were obtained. In this year were started "The Independent Democrat," which was moved to Concord subsequently, and the "Saturday Messenger," which was united with "The American."

But the event of all others in this year was known far and wide as the "Parker murder." Jonas L. Parker, who had been collector of taxes in 1844, was enticed from his house on Manchester street late in the evening of the twenty-sixth of October, 1845, by a man unknown to any one but Parker, on a plea that a lady wanted to see him in Janesville on urgent business. Between this village and the more thickly settled part of the town was a piece of woods, and in them, near what is now the corner of Manchester and Beech streets, Parker's body was found the next morning with the throat cut and other evidences of a murder. Most of the money he had with him was taken. The coroner, Joseph M. Rowell, summoned a jury, consisting of Daniel Clark, Dr. Charles Wells and Dr. D. J. Hoyt, who made a careful examination of great length. In 1848 Asa and Henry T. Wentworth, brothers, who had been connected with a Janesville tavern, were arrested in Saco, Maine, upon a suspicion of being the murderers, but they were discharged after an examination. In 1850, however, they were re-arrested, brought to Manchester and arraigned together with Horace Wentworth of Lowell and one William C. Clark. The two latter were discharged after a long hearing and the others were held to answer farther. At the October term of court, however, the grand jury failed to find a bill against them and they were discharged, and the murderer is to this day unknown.

In 1846 a sewer was built through Elm street from Bridge to Granite, and several more roads were laid out in the compact part of the town. So large an increase had there been in the number of people that the town was able to send eight representatives to the general court. At the town-meeting held on the tenth of March a committee was chosen, consisting of David Gillis, Samuel D. Bell, Isaac Riddle, William C. Clarke, John A. Burnham, Luther Farley and Walter French, to petition the legislature for a city charter when they deemed it wise. They saw no cause for delay, and on the first of June, in accordance with their petition, the legislature passed an act to incorporate the City of Manchester, which was accepted by the town on the first of August by a vote of four hundred and eighty-five yeas and one hundred and thirty-four nays.

The first election occurred August 19, when there were four candidates for mayor: — Hiram Brown, a Whig; William C. Clarke, a Democrat; Thomas Brown, who was the Abolition candidate; and William Shepherd. There were cast eleven hundred and seventy votes, and Hiram Brown, who received five hundred and sixty-nine, lacked seventeen of the required majority. At this meeting, however, there were chosen aldermen, members of the common council, school committee, overseers of the poor and assessors. On the first day of September a second election for mayor took place, when there were four candidates: — Hiram Brown, a Whig; Isaac C. Flanders, a Democrat; Thomas Brown, an Abolitionist; and John S. Wiggin. There were cast eleven hundred and fifty-four votes, and Hiram Brown, who received six hundred and two, was chosen by twenty-four majority. The city government was organized in the town-house, September 8, 1846, at ten o'clock in the forenoon, in the presence of a large number of citizens. Moses Fellows, chairman of the retiring board of selectmen, presided, and prayer was offered by the Rev. C. W. Wallace, the senior clergyman of the city, after which the oath of office was administered by the Hon. Daniel Clark to the mayor, and he in turn qualified the remaining members of the city government. After the delivery of an address by the mayor, the various boards met and organized by themselves. The Hon. Samuel D. Bell was appointed by the governor and council justice of the police court, and Isaac Riddle and Joseph Cochran, jr., special justices, and George T. Clark was appointed city marshal by the mayor and aldermen. At that time the valuation of the town was $3,187,726; the tax-list for 1846 was $22,005.95; the number of polls, 2056; the number of inhabitants, 10,125.

Chas. E. Balch

OFFICERS

OF THE

TOWN OF MANCHESTER.*

SELECTMEN.

1751.
John Goffe,
William Perham,
Nathaniel Boyd,
Daniel McNiel,
Eleazer Wells.

1752.
John Goffe,
Archibald Stark,
Alexander McMurphy.

1753.
William Perham,
Alexander McMurphy,
John Riddell.

1754.
William McClintock,
Alexander McMurphy,
John Hall.

1755.
Daniel McNiel,
Robert Anderson,
John Harvey.

1756.
Daniel McNiel,
Robert Anderson,
John Harvey.

1757.
Eleazer Robbins,
Robert Anderson,
Daniel McNiel.

1758.
William Perham,
William McClintock,
Abraham Merrill.

1759.
William Perham,
William McClintock,
Abraham Merrill.

1760.
William McClintock,
Hugh Sterling,
Abraham Merrill.

1761.
William Perham,
John Hall,
Thomas Russ.

1762.
William Perham,
John Stark,
John Moors.

1763.
John Stark,
William McClintock,
John Moors.

* Changed from Derryfield in 1810.

1764.
William McClintock,
John Stark,
John Moors.

1765.
William Perham,
William McClintock,
Abraham Merrill.

1766.
*Alexander McMurphy,
Ebenezer Stevens,
John Hall,
†David McKnight.

1767.
Eleazer Robbins,
Alexander McClintock,
Nathaniel Boyd.

1768.
John Hall,
John Goffe,
John Harvey.

1769.
William McClintock,
Alexander McMurphy,
John Moor.

1770.
William McClintock,
Alexander McMurphy,
John Moor.

1771.
William McClintock,
Alexander McMurphy,
John Moor.

1772.
Alexander McMurphy,
John Moor,
William McClintock.

1773.
John Stark,
Samuel Boyd,
James McCalley.

*Until Aug. 13.
†From Aug. 13.

1774.
James McCalley,
Samuel Boyd,
John Perham.

1775.
John Stark,
John Moor,
Joseph George.

1776.
David Starrett,
Ezekiel Stevens,
John Perham.

1777.
John Goffe,
Ebenezer Stevens,
Benjamin Crombie.

1778:
John Hall,
Benjamin Baker,
Samuel Boyd.

1779.
*David Starrett,
John Perham,
Samuel Moor,
†Jonathan Russ.

1780.
Jonathan Russ,
John Shelden,
Samuel Moor.

1781.
John Hall,
Samuel Moor,
Jonathan Russ.

1782.
Samuel Moor,
Jonathan Russ,
Joseph Sanders.

1783.
Samuel Moor,
Joseph Sanders,
Jonathan Russ.

*To July 16, 1779.
†From July 16.

1784.
Joseph Sanders,
John Goffe,
John Hall.

1785.
John Goffe, jr.,
William Perham,
Samuel Stark.

1786.
Joseph Fermor,
John Goffe, jr.,
Isaac Huse.

1787.
James Thompson,
Isaac Huse,
John Greene.

1788.
John Hall,
John Webster,
John Perham.

1789.
James Thompson,
John Green,
John Ray.

1790.
Isaac Huse,
Samuel Moor,
John Stark, jr.

1791.
Isaac Huse,
Samuel Moor,
John Stark, jr.

1792.
Daniel Davis,
Samuel Moor,
John Stark, jr.

1793.
John Goffe,
Isaac Huse,
John Webster.

1794.
John Stark, jr.
Daniel Davis,
Samuel Moor, jr.

1795.
Daniel Davis,
John Stark, jr.,
Samuel Moor, jr.,
John Ray,
John Perham.

1796.
Isaac Huse,
John Tufts,
John Stark, jr.

1797.
John Goffe,
Samuel Moor, jr.,
Samuel Blodget.

1798.
John Goffe,
Daniel Davis,
John Stark.

1799.
John Ray,
Joseph Moore,
Daniel Davis.

1800.
Samuel Moor, jr.,
John Ray,
Israel Webster.

1801.
Samuel Moor, jr.,
John Ray,
Israel Webster.

1802.
Samuel Moor, jr.,
Israel Webster,
John Ray.

1803.
Samuel Moor, jr.,
Israel Webster,
John Stark, 3d.

1804.
Samuel Moor, jr.,
Isaac Huse,
John Stark, 3d.

1805.
Samuel Moor, jr.,
Edward Ray,
Archibald Gamble.

1806.
Samuel Moor, jr.,
Edward Ray,
Amos Weston.

1807.
Samuel Moor, jr.,
Amos Weston,
Edward Ray.

1808.
Samuel Moor, jr.,
Amos Weston,
Samuel Hall.

1809.
Samuel Moor, jr.,
Isaac Huse,
John Stark.

1810.
Samuel Moor, jr.,
Thomas Stickney,
Isaac Huse.

1811.
John Stark, jr.,
Amos Weston,
Israel Webster.

1812.
Samuel Moor, jr.,
John Stark, jr.,
John Dickey.

1813.
Samuel Moor,
Job Rowell,
John Dickey.

1814.
Isaac Huse,
Israel Webster,
John G. Moor.

1815.
Isaac Huse,
Israel Webster,
Ephraim Stevens, jr.

1816.
Isaac Huse,
John Frye,
John Stark, 4th.

1817.
Isaac Huse,
John Stark, 4th,
John Dickey.

1818.
Isaac Huse,
John Dickey,
Nathaniel Moor.

1819.
Samuel Moor,
Ephraim Stevens, jr.,
John Stark, 4th.

1820.
Joseph Moor,
Ephraim Stevens, jr.,
Amos Weston, jr.

1821.
Amos Weston, jr.,
Ephraim Stevens, jr.,
John Proctor.

1822.
Amos Weston, jr.,
John Proctor,
Nathaniel Moor.

1823.
Amos Weston, jr.,
Nathaniel Moor,
John Proctor.

1824.
Amos Weston, jr.,
Nathaniel Moore,
Isaac Huse.

1825.
Amos Weston, jr.,
Isaac Huse,
Nathaniel Moore.

1826.
Frederick G. Stark,
Israel Merrill,
James McQueston.

1827.
Frederick G. Stark,
Amos Weston, jr.,
Franklin Moor.

1828.
John Gamble,
John Ray,
Nathaniel Moore.

1829.
Frederick G. Stark,
Archibald Stark,
James McQueston.

1830.
Amos Weston, jr.,
John Proctor,
Nathaniel Conant.

1831.
Frederick G. Stark,
John Proctor,
George Clark.

1832.
Amos Weston, jr.,
Frederick G. Stark,
George Clark.

1833.
Amos Weston, jr.,
John Proctor,
James McQueston.

1834.
James McQueston,
Gilbert Greeley,
Frederick G. Stark.

1835.
Frederick G. Stark,
Amos Weston, jr.,
Isaac Huse.

1836.
Frederick G. Stark,
Amos Weston, jr.,
Gilbert Greeley.

1837.
Amos Weston, jr.,
Gilbert Greeley,
Joseph M. Rowell.

1838.
Joseph M. Rowell,
Archibald Gamble, jr.,
Isaac Huse.

1839.
Joseph M. Rowell,
Archibald Gamble, jr.,
Isaac Huse.

1840.
Amos Weston, jr.,
J. T. P. Hunt,
Hiram Brown.

1841.
Amos Weston, jr.,
Isaac C. Flanders,
Isaac Huse.

1842.
Moses Fellows,
Andrew Bunton, jr.,
Abram Brigham.

1843.
Moses Fellows,
Andrew Bunton, jr.,
David Child.

1844.
Nathan Parker,
Warren L. Lane,
George Clark.

1845.
Nathan Parker,
George Clark,
Charles Chase.

1846.
Moses Fellows,
Andrew Bunton, jr.,
Edward McQueston.

MODERATORS.

1751. John Goffe.
1752–4. William Perham.
1755–6. John Goffe.
1757. Archibald Stark.
1758–60. William McClintock.
1761. William Perham.
1762–3. John Goffe.
1764. John Stark.
1765. Alexander McMurphy.
1766. John Hall.
1767. David Starrett.
1768. Thomas Russ.
1769. William McClintock.
1770–3. John Stark.
1774. John Goffe.
1775. John Stark.
1776–7. John Goffe.
1778. John Hall.
1779. John Goffe.
1780. John Harvey.
1781. John Hall.
1782. John Little.
1783. John Stark.
1784. John Hall.
1785. John Stark.
1786. John Hall.
1787. John Little.
1788. James Gorman.
1789. John Stark.
1790. Samuel Moor.
1791–2. John Stark.
1793. John Webster.
1794. John Stark.
1795–6. Daniel Davis.
1797. John Goffe.
1798. Samuel Blodget.
1799. Daniel Davis.
1800. Samuel P. Kidder.
1801. John Stark.
1802. Joseph Moor.
1803. John Stark.
1804. Joseph Moor.
1805. Samuel P. Kidder.
1806. John Stark.
1807–8. David Flint.
1809–11. John G. Moor.
1812. David Flint.
1813. William Hall.
1814. John G. Moor.
1815–16. John Dwinnells.
1817–18. John Stark.
1819. Samuel Moor.
1820. Nathaniel Moor.
1821. John G. Moor.
1822. John Stark.
1823–5. Nathaniel Moor.
1826. Ephraim Stevens, jr.
1827. John Stark, 3d.
1828. Nathaniel Moor.
1829. Ephraim Stevens, jr.
1830–2. Frederick G. Stark.
1833. Ephraim Stevens, jr.
1834. Gilbert Greeley.
1835. Ephraim Stevens, jr.
1836. Gilbert Greeley.
1837. Frederick G. Stark.
1838. Ephraim Stevens, jr.
1839–40. Charles Stark.
1841. James McK. Wilkins.
1842–3. Joseph Cochran, jr.
1844. George W. Morrison.
1845–6. Herman Foster.

TOWN CLERKS.

1751–3.	John Hall.	1799–1810.	Samuel Moor, jr.
1754.	Alexander McMurphy.	1811.	John Stark, jr.
1755–6.	John Goffe.	1812–13.	Isaac Huse.
1757–66.	John Hall.	1814.	Samuel Moor.
1767–74.	David Starrett.	1815–18.	John G. Moor.
1775.	John Hall.	1819–23.	Frederick G. Stark.
1776–9.	*David Starrett.	1824–5.	Amos Weston, jr.
1779–86.	†Asael Smith.	1826–8.	Franklin Moor.
1787.	John Russ.	1829–30.	Samuel Jackson.
1788.	John Hall.	1831–3.	Amos Weston, jr.
1789–93.	John Goffe.	1834–7.	John R. Hall.
1794.	John Stark, jr.	1838–40.	Samuel Jackson.
1795.	Isaac Huse.	1841.	Walter French.
1796.	Samuel P. Kidder.	1842–46.	John M. Noyes.
1797–8.	John Tufts.		

*To July 16, 1779.
†From July 16.

Chas. H. Bartlett.

MANCHESTER—A CITY.

1846—1875.

FROM that day to this the city's history is one of gradual but real progress. Its foundations had been well laid and it only remained for the walls to rise. The amendments to its charter by the legislature, which have been so many as to make the original nearly unrecognizable, are indices in part of the changes in the city. The surrender of the charter itself was proposed in 1848, after the legislature of that year had passed an act by which the representatives to the general court were made eligible from each ward of the city voting as a town, instead of being chosen by the city at large, as before. Upon the request of one hundred legal voters, a call was issued by the mayor and aldermen, in accordance with a provision of the charter, for a citizens' meeting. This was held in the city hall on the nineteenth of August, 1848. A moderator was chosen, and, after several motions made to delay business had been disposed of, the meeting voted by ballot, three hundred and ninety-five yeas and twenty-two nays, to surrender the city charter and adopt a town organization. A committee was appointed to consider what steps were necessary to accomplish such result, and, at an adjourned meeting on the second of September, made a long report recommending the surrender of the city charter and giving the opinion of the late chief justice, Samuel

D. Bell, that a town organization might legally be adopted. The opinion of Joel Parker, then chief justice of Massachusetts, which had been obtained, was also read, declaring the act of the legislature unconstitutional. The meeting was then adjourned to the sixteenth of October, at which time the records of the last meeting were read and an adjournment *sine die* was effected and that was the last of it.

The city was originally divided into seven wards but the act of 1848 reduced these to six, made one special justice of the police court instead of two, and caused several minor changes. By the original charter a majority of the votes cast was required for the election of a mayor, and this made necessary two elections in 1846, four in 1847 and three in 1848, and in 1849 it was not till the fifth trial, held in October, six months after the regular time, that a choice was made. This trouble was remedied in 1849 by an act of the legislature which made a plurality of votes suffice for an election. In 1851 the justice of the police court was made its clerk, itself becoming thus a court of record with power to naturalize foreigners and issue certificates. Jurisdiction in naturalization matters was repealed in 1855, restored in 1862, again repealed in 1868 and again restored in 1874, when a separate clerk was appointed. The justice was given in 1851 a salary of three hundred dollars together with the fees. In 1855 the salary was established at five hundred dollars and all fines and fees were required to be paid to the city marshal and by him to the city treasurer. In 1867 the salary was raised to one thousand dollars and in 1874 to fifteen hundred. The city marshal was at first the tax-collector, but the offices were separated by the legislature in 1851 and the act was approved by the city councils in 1852.

The villages of Piscataquog and Amoskeag, parts of Bedford and Goffstown respectively, were, to all practical intent, parts of Manchester, and were made so in deed by act of the legislature in 1853, accepted by the city councils the same year. The act was not passed without strenuous opposition from the towns of Goffstown and Bedford, though the villages themselves were anxious to enjoy the convenience of being a part of the city to which they were annexed. They became wards seven and eight and in 1855 the part of ward eight which lay south of the Piscataquog river was annexed to ward seven.

In 1855 the boards of mayor and aldermen and school committee were required to appoint a superintendent of public instruction. By the act of 1856, accepted by the voters of the city in that year, the annual meeting for the choice of city and ward officers, which had been held on the second Tuesday of March, the old town-meeting day, was appointed for the second Tuesday of December, and the municipal year was made to begin upon the first Tuesday of January instead of the third Tuesday of March. By the act of 1874 the old order of things was restored and the outgoing city councils were required to make the appropriation for the year ensuing. A plurality was made sufficient for the election of other city and ward officers, as well as mayors, by the act of 1856.

In 1858 the boundaries of several wards were changed by legislative enactment and of others in 1869 by the city councils. The wards were made anew and the number reduced to seven in 1874. In 1854 the city councils were authorized to establish a public library; in 1867 the regulation of the ward check-lists was transferred from the selectmen to the assessors and in 1874 returned to the selectmen; in 1868 the school districts were consolidated into one; and in 1871 the legislature authorized the construction of water-works at a cost of not over six hundred thousand dollars.

Noticeable in the city's history were the establishment of a high school by district number two in 1846; the acceptance by the city from the Amoskeag Company in 1848 of Concord, Merrimack and Tremont squares, upon condition of proper usage; the attention paid to sewerage, setting of shade-trees, and building of sidewalks; the care of the Valley cemetery and the purchase of a new one in 1855; the paving of Elm street and the erection of drinking fountains on the main thoroughfare; the construction of reservoirs for fire purposes; the appointment in 1854 of a superintendent of schools; the purchase of a steam fire engine in 1859; the consolidation of the school districts in 1868; the establishment of a free library in 1854 and the erection of a building for its use in 1871; the building of a court-house in 1868; and the completion of the water-works in 1874. The streets were first lighted by the city on condition that abuttors on street corners would put up a post and lamp. The fire cisterns, in the absence of any water-works, were supplied with water from the squares on the ponds.

The city celebrated the hundredth anniversary of its incorporation as a town by a meeting at the city hall in the afternoon and evening of October 22, 1851, when an address was delivered by the Rev. Cyrus W. Wallace, the senior clergyman of the city, a poem by William Stark was read by its author, and short speeches were made by the Hon. Richard H. Ayer, the Hon. Chandler E. Potter, Dr. William M. Parker, John B. Clarke, the Rev. Cyrus W. Wallace, the Rev. B. M. Tillotson, Charles A. Luce, John L. Kelly, Joseph C. Abbott, Albert Jackson and Joseph Kidder. An account of these proceedings, together with a history of Manchester, was published in 1856, by its author, the Hon. Chandler E. Potter.

OFFICERS OF THE CITY OF MANCHESTER,

FROM 1846 TO 1875.

MEMBERS OF CITY COUNCILS.

1846–7.

MAYOR.

HIRAM BROWN.

ALDERMEN.

1. Andrew Bunton, jr.
2. George Porter.
3. William G. Means.
4. David Gillis.
5. Trueworthy Blaisdell.
6. Edward McQueston.
7. Moses Fellows.

CITY CLERK.

John S. T. Cushing.

COMMON COUNCIL.

1. John S. Kidder,
   George W. Eaton,
   William Boyd.
2. Hervey Tufts,
   Daniel J. Hoyt.
   James M. Morrill.
3. Israel Endicott,
   Joel Russell,
   George P. Folsom.
4. David Cross,
   Abram Brigham,
   William M. Parker, *Pres't.*
5. Ebenezer Clark,
   Asa O. Colby,
   Nathaniel Herrick.
6. William Potter,
   Jacob G. Cilley,
   Frederick A. Hussey.
7. Sewell Leavitt,
   William W. Baker,
   Rodnia Nutt.

David Hill, *Clerk.*

1847–8.

MAYOR.

JACOB F. JAMES.*

ALDERMEN.

1. George F. Judkins.
2. Caleb Johnson.
3. James Wallace.
4. David A. Bunton.
5. Ebenezer Clark.
6. Edward McQueston.
7. Frederick Wallace.

CITY CLERK.

John S. T. Cushing.

COMMON COUNCIL.

1. Wm. Boyd,
   John S. Kidder,
   James McK. Wilkins.
2. Hervey Tufts,
   James M. Morrill,
   Wilber Gay.
3. Seth P. Ford,
   John H. Newman,
   Jacob Sawyer.
4. William M. Parker, *Pres't,*
   Charles Wells,
   Charles F. Warren.
5. David Brigham,
   Nathaniel Herrick,
   Jesse Anderson.
6. James O. Adams,
   William Potter,
   Moulton Knowles.
7. Sewell Leavitt,
   William W. Baker,
   Ebenezer Ross.

David Hill, *Clerk.*

* Elected May 22, 1847; sworn in May 25, 1847.

1848–9.

MAYOR.

JACOB F. JAMES.

ALDERMEN.

1. George F. Judkins.
2. Charles Wells.
3. Jacob Sawyer.
4. Eben C. Foster.
5. Ebenezer Knowlton.
6. William P. Newell.
7. John Calef.

CITY CLERK.

John S. T. Cushing.

COMMON COUNCIL.

1. Warren L. Lane,
Josiah M. Barnes,
George Aldrich.
2. William Hartshorn,
Frederick Smyth,
Nathaniel Marshall.
3. John H. Newman,
Warren Page,
George T. Mixer.
4. Charles F. Warren,
John G. Simpson,
Joseph W. Saunders.
5. David Brigham,
Retyre Mitchell,
Asa O. Colby.
6. James O. Adams, *President,*
Charles A. Luce,
Zebedee C. Gilbert.
7. William W. Baker,
Ebenezer Ross,
Isaac Huse.

David Hill, *Clerk.*

1849–50.

MAYOR.

WARREN L. LANE.*

ALDERMEN.

1. Henry T. Mowatt.
2. Daniel Balch.
3. Benjamin Kinsley.
4. Alonzo Smith.
5. Joseph E. Bennett.
6. Sewell Leavitt.

CITY CLERK.

Frederick Smyth.

COMMON COUNCIL.

1. Nathaniel Marshall, *Pres't,*
Theodore L. Hastings,
Holbrook Chandler.
2. David C. Batchelder,
Charles Currier,
Joseph Sawyer.
3. George W. Gilman,
George W. Eaton,
Joel Taylor.†
4. Thomas P. Pierce,
Reuben D. Mooers,
John H. Goodale.‡
5. Hilas Dickey,
Harry Leeds,
Joseph D. Emerson.
6. Isaac Huse,
James M. Webster,
Jacob Woods.

Benjamin F. Ayer, *Clerk.*

*Elected Oct. 3, 1849; sworn in Oct. 6, 1849.
† In place of Frederick Smyth, resigned.
‡ In place of Hibbard Stevens, resigned.

1850–1.

MAYOR.

MOSES FELLOWS.

ALDERMEN.

1. Amasa Waterman.
2. Daniel Balch.
3. John L. Bradford.
4. Isaac C. Flanders.
5. Samuel Dame.
6. William W. Baker.

CITY CLERK.

Frederick Smyth.

COMMON COUNCIL.

1. Holbrook Chandler,
   Theodore L. Hastings,
   Theodore T. Abbot.
2. David C. Batchelder,
   Charles Currier,
   William Reynolds.
3. Edward Hall,
   Lorenzo Dow,
   Joseph Wilson.
4. John H. Goodale,
   John L. Fitch, *President*,
   Reuben D. Mooers.
5. Harry Leeds,
   Hilas Dickey,
   Joseph D. Emerson.
6. Isaac Marshall,
   Lewis Bartlett,
   Charles G. Morse.

Benjamin F. Ayer, *Clerk*.

1851–2.

MAYOR.

MOSES FELLOWS.

ALDERMEN.

1. Amasa Waterman.
2. David Brigham.
3. George Clark.
4. George T. Mixer.
5. Joseph W. Saunders.
6. Peter Mitchell.

CITY CLERK.

Frederick Smyth.

COMMON COUNCIL.

1. Samuel Fish,
   Asa S. Trask,
   Erastus Danielson.
2. George M. Stevens,
   Nathaniel Smith,
   Daniel C. Bent.
3. Daniel W. Fling,
   Isaac W. Smith, *President*,
   James Mitchell, jr.
4. Francis Reed,
   Daniel Haynes,
   Henry Clough.
5. James McColley,
   Benjamin Currier,
   Cyrus Sanborn.
6. John L. Kelly,
   Daniel C. Gould,
   Israel Webster.

George A. French, *Clerk*.

1852-3.

MAYOR.

FREDERICK SMYTH.

ALDERMEN.

1. Amasa Waterman.
2. David Brigham.
3. Nahum Baldwin.
4. Robert Moore.
5. Isaac Tompkins.
6. Ira W. Moore.

CITY CLERK.

George A. French.

COMMON COUNCIL.

1. Samuel Fish,
   Asa S. Trask,
   Erastus Danielson.
2. George M. Stevens,
   John M. Harvey,
   Daniel C. Bent.
3. Isaac W. Smith, *President*,
   Daniel W. Fling,
   James Mitchell, jr.
4. Francis Reed,
   Henry Clough,
   John B. Goodwin.
5. James McColley,
   Benjamin Currier,
   Alpheus D. Burgess.
6. John L. Kelly,
   Stephen M. Baker,
   John P. Moore.

Enoch N. Abbott, *Clerk*.

1853-4.

MAYOR.

FREDERICK SMYTH.

ALDERMEN.

1. Amasa Waterman.
2. Stephen Palmer.
3. Daniel W. Fling.
4. Robert Moore.
5. Samuel Dame.
6. Ira W. Moore.

CITY CLERK.

George A. French.

COMMON COUNCIL.

1. Sampson Clatur,
   Francis W. Holbrook,
   Davis Baker.
2. John M. Harvey, *President*,
   John C. Lyford,
   Orin B. Robinson.
3. Horace Johnson,
   George Q. Johnson,
   Ephraim Stevens.
4. John B. Goodwin,
   David J. Clark,
   William Patten.
5. Amherst Kimball,
   George W. Merriam,
   Ninian Cochran.
6. Thomas Emerson,
   John P. Moore,
   Robert Baker.

Enoch N. Abbott, *Clerk*.*
Isaac W. Smith, *Clerk*.

* Resigned Oct. 11, 1853; Isaac W. Smith elected to fill vacancy.

Joseph E. Bennett

1854–5.

MAYOR.

FREDERICK SMYTH.

ALDERMEN.

1. Amasa Waterman.
2. John M. Harvey.
3. Daniel W. Fling.
4. George A. Barnes.
5. Isaac Tompkins.
6. Samuel B. Paige.
7. James Walker.
8. Charles F. Davis.

CITY CLERK.

George A. French.

COMMON COUNCIL.

1. Jesse F. Angell,*
Francis W. Holbrook,
Samuel J. Tilton.
2. John C. Lyford,
Orin B. Robinson,
Samuel Gould.
3. George Q. Johnson,
Jacob Peavy,
Hiram H. Kimball.
4. David J. Clark, *President*,
Gilman H. Kimball,
Benjamin F. Locke.
5. William E. Eastman,
Jewett B. Eastman,
Horace Pettee.
6. Nathaniel Baker, 2d,
Thomas Emerson,
Benjamin F. Mitchell.
7. Joseph B. Gage,
William B. Patten,
Philip Stark.
8. Enoch N. Ela,
Thomas S. Montgomery,
DeLafayette Robinson.

Isaac W. Smith,† *Clerk*.
Samuel D. Lord, *Clerk*.

1855–6.

MAYOR.

THEODORE T. ABBOT.

ALDERMEN.

1. Joseph Knowlton.
2. John M. Harvey.
3. John S. Yeaton.
4. Daniel C. Bent.
5. Nathaniel Herrick.
6. Justin Spear.
7. John Moulton.
8. Henry H. Fuller.

CITY CLERK.

George A. French.

COMMON COUNCIL.

1. Samuel J. Tilton,
Jesse F. Angell,
Ira Stone.
2. Samuel Gould, *President*,
James M. Howe,
Barnabas Hinds.
3. John R. Chandler,
John T. Spofford,
Frederick A. Morse.
4. John Prince,
John S. Folsom,
Andrew J. Butterfield.
5. Walter Neal,
Moses O. Pearson,
William Stearns.
6. William B. Bullard,
Ephraim S. Harvey,
Oliver Gould.
7. John B. Watson,
David Spofford,
William J. Fisher.
8. James K. Stevens,
Daniel A. Durgin,
William Todd.

Samuel D. Lord, *Clerk*.

*Jesse F. Angell was elected to fill the vacancy occasioned by the resignation of Sampson Clatur.

† Resigned. Samuel D. Lord elected to fill vacancy.

1856-7.

MAYOR.

THEODORE T. ABBOT.

ALDERMEN.

1. Joseph Knowlton.
2. William Reynolds.
3. John S. Yeaton.
4. James Wallace.
5. John M. Hill.
6. Justin Spear.
7. John Moulton.
8. Samuel H. Edgerly.

CITY CLERK.

†Joel Taylor.
Frank H. Lyford.

COMMON COUNCIL.

1. Jabez Besse,
John Hosley,
Ansel Buckminster.
2. William T. Evans,
Henry B. Moulton,
Abiel C. Flanders.
3. Frederick A. Morse,
John T. Spofford,
John R. Chandler.
4. John Prince,
John S. Folsom, *President*,
Andrew J. Butterfield.
5. Amos W. Sargent,
Elbridge G. Haynes,
Leonard Sanborn.
6. William B. Bullard,
Samuel D. Farrar,
Ephraim S. Harvey.
7. Charles K. Walker,
Chauncy C. Favor,
Thomas F. Moulton.
8. John Shaw,
Levi D. Heath,
James K. Stevens.

Elijah M. Topliff, *Clerk*.

1857.

MAYOR.

JACOB F. JAMES.

ALDERMEN.

1. Jonathan Morse.
2. William Reynolds.*
3. Moody Currier.
4. David Atwood.
5. Bradbury P. Cilley.
6. Justin Spear.
7. Andrew C. Wallace.
8. Daniel Farmer, jr.

CITY CLERK.

Frank H. Lyford.

COMMON COUNCIL.

1. John Hosley,
Jeremiah O. Pulsifer,
Benjamin Kinsley.
2. Daniel K. White,
Jonathan Horn,
William T. Evans.
3. Timothy Wiggin Little,
Frank A. Brown,
Benjamin F. Martin.
4. William S. Berry,
Elijah M. Topliff, *President*,
Joseph B. Sawyer.
5. Amos W. Sargent,
Elbridge G. Haynes,
Ruel Walker.
6. Samuel D. Farrar,
Alden W. Sanborn,
Nathan Johnson.
7. Chauncy C. Favor,
Charles K. Walker,
Edward C. Bryant.
8. John E. Stearns,
William H. B. Newhall,
John T. Nelson.

Amos B. Shattuck, *Clerk*.

* William Reynolds resigned February 17, 1857. James White was elected to fill the vacancy, and resigned June 4, 1857, and James H. Peabody was elected to fill the vacancy.

† Resigned April 15, 1856; Frank H. Lyford elected to fill the vacancy.

1858.

MAYOR.

ALONZO SMITH.

ALDERMEN.

1. Jonathan Morse.
2. Thomas S. Sargent.
3. William C. Clarke.
4. Samuel W. Parsons.
5. William E. Eastman.
6. Daniel C. Gould.
7. Andrew C. Wallace.
8. Daniel Farmer, jr.

CITY CLERK.

Joseph Knowlton.

COMMON COUNCIL.

1. Benjamin Kinsley,
   Moses O. Pearson,
   Charles Canfield.
2. Otis P. Warner,
   Alfred B. Soule,
   David M'Colley.
3. Benjamin F. Martin,
   William Richardson,
   Stephen D. Green.
4. Ebenezer H. Davis,
   Moulton Knowles,
   Elijah M. Topliff, *President.*
5. James A. Brigham,
   Ruel Walker,
   George W. Merriam.
6. Nathan Johnson,
   John B. Fish,
   Samuel A. Hackett.
7. Benjamin F. Wallace,
   Leonard Moore,
   Joseph N. Prescott.
8. George S. Chandler,
   William H. B. Newhall,
   Damon Y. Stearns.

Amos B. Shattuck, *Clerk.*

1859.

MAYOR.

E. W. HARRINGTON.

ALDERMEN.

1. Reuben Dodge.
2. Thomas S. Sargent.
3. Frank A. Brown.
4. George A. Barnes.
5. George H. Hubbard.
6. Samuel D. Farrar.
7. Ira Barr.
8. Daniel Farmer, jr.

CITY CLERK.

Joseph Knowlton.

COMMON COUNCIL.

1. Moses O. Pearson,
   Charles Canfield,
   George W. Thayer.
2. Daniel K. White,
   George S. Neal,
   Josiah A. Chamberlin.
3. William Richardson,
   Stephen D. Green,
   John B. Chase.
4. Moulton Knowles,
   James A. Brigham,
   John H. Maynard.
5. Thomas Baxter,
   Elijah Perry,
   Horace Bonney.
6. John B. Fish,
   Horace Pettee, *President,*
   Levi H. Sleeper.
7. Leonard Moore,
   Joseph N. Prescott,
   John Bartlett.
8. George S. Chandler,
   William G. Haynes,
   Nathaniel H. Martin.

Simeon D. Farnsworth, *Clerk.*

1860.

MAYOR.

E. W. HARRINGTON.

ALDERMEN.

1. Reuben Dodge.
2. James A. Tebbetts.
3. Benjamin F. Martin.
4. George A. Barnes.
5. George H. Hubbard.
6. Samuel D. Farrar.
7. John Moulton.
8. Daniel Farmer, jr.

CITY CLERK.

Joseph Knowlton.

COMMON COUNCIL.

1. George W. Thayer,
   George C. Gilmore,
   Henry A. Campbell.
2. Josiah A. Chamberlin,
   George S. Neal,
   George T. Cram.
3. John B. Chase,
   Albert H. Daniels,
   Albion Barker.
4. John H. Maynard,
   Seth Milliken,
   Eben French.
5. Thomas Baxter,
   Elijah Perry,
   Horace Bonney.
6. Horace Pettee, *President*,
   Levi H. Sleeper,
   Charles W. Adams.
7. John Bartlett,
   Willard P. Stratton,
   Daniel Mack.
8. George S. Chandler,
   Dennis Cassidy,
   Damon Y. Stearns.

Simeon D. Farnsworth, *Clerk*.

1861.

MAYOR.

DAVID A. BUNTON.

ALDERMEN.

1. George C. Gilmore.
2. James A. Tebbetts.
3. Henry C. Merrill.
4. James M. Bean.*
5. John Coughlin.
6. Elbridge G. Haynes.
7. John C. Smith.
8. Thomas S. Montgomery.

CITY CLERK.

Joseph Knowlton.

COMMON COUNCIL.

1. Henry A. Campbell,
   Elbridge G. Woodman, *Pres't*,†
   Jeremiah O. Pulsifer.
2. George T. Cram,
   Josiah Hackett,
   Charles W. Clement,
3. John H. Goodale, *President*,
   Albion Barker,
   Ephraim S. Peabody.
4. Seth Milliken,
   Eben French,
   William S. Palmer.
5. Hugh Burns,
   Daniel Connor,
   John Gillis.
6. Ezra Kimball,
   Benjamin C. Kendall,
   Charles W. Adams.
7. Daniel Mack,
   John H. Rand,
   Elbridge Hartshorn.
8. Dennis Cassidy,
   Edwin R. Warren,
   William Todd.

Simeon D. Farnsworth, *Clerk*.

* John H. Maynard elected in March to fill the vacancy occasioned by the death of Mr. Bean.

† Elected President in October, 1861, *vice* John H. Goodale.

1862.

MAYOR.

DAVID A. BUNTON.

ALDERMEN.

1. George C. Gilmore.
2. Henry B. Moulton.
3. Henry C. Merrill.
4. John H. Maynard.
5. John Coughlin.
6. Elbridge G. Haynes.
7. John C. Smith.
8. Thomas S. Montgomery.

CITY CLERK.

Joseph Knowlton.

COMMON COUNCIL.

1. Jeremiah O. Pulsifer,
   Elbridge G. Woodman, *Pres't*,
   Stephen P. Duntley.
2. Josiah Hackett,
   Charles W. Clement,
   Samuel Clark.
3. Ephraim S. Peabody,
   Henry P. Wilson,
   Thomas R. Hubbard.
4. William S. Palmer,
   Robert F. Moore,
   Nathaniel W. Cumner.
5. James Madden,
   William Little,
   Thomas Stack.
6. Benjamin C. Kendall,
   Ezra Kimball,
   Jeremiah L. Fogg.
7. John O. Parker,
   James W. Preston,
   Ebenezer Hartshorn.
8. Edwin R. Warren,
   John E. Stearns,
   Warren Stearns.

Orren C. Moore, *Clerk*.

1863.

MAYOR.

THEODORE T. ABBOT.

ALDERMEN.

1. John Hosley.
2. Henry B. Moulton.
3. Joseph H. Haynes.
4. George Holbrook.
5. Thomas Howe.
6. Ira W. Moore.
7. James W. Preston.
8. Thomas S. Montgomery.

CITY CLERK.

Joseph Knowlton.

COMMON COUNCIL.

1. Francis P. Sargent,
   Henry C. Tilton,
   Andrew J. Dickey.
2. Samuel Clark,
   Isaac H. Russell,
   John T. Robinson.
3. Thomas R. Hubbard,
   George W. Quinby,
   William C. Hazelton.
4. Robert F. Moore,
   Nath'l W. Cumner, *President*,
   George W. Gardner.
5. William Little,
   Thomas Stack,
   Michael Gillis.
6. Jeremiah L. Fogg,
   Jonathan Y. McQueston,
   Ebenezer G. Knight.
7. John O. Parker,
   John C. Head,
   David K. Boutelle.
8. John E. Stearns,
   Warren Stearns,
   Harmon S. Burns.

Orren C. Moore, *Clerk*.

1864.

MAYOR.

FREDERICK SMYTH.

ALDERMEN.

1. John Hosley.
2. Samuel Clark.
3. Joseph H. Haynes.
4. George Holbrook.
5. John Rourke.
6. Ira W. Moore.
7. Allen N. Clapp.
8. Thomas S. Montgomery.

CITY CLERK.

Joseph Knowlton.

COMMON COUNCIL.

1. Andrew J. Dickey,
 Amos Sargent,
2. John Gillis.
 Isaac H. Russell, *President*,
 John T. Robinson,
 Jeremiah Fisk.
3. George W. Quinby,
 William C. Hazelton,
 Thomas R. Hubbard.
4. Otis Barton,
 Hamilton M. Bailey,
 Hiram Hill.
5. Asa Place,
 Michael Gillis,
 Timothy D. O'Connor.
6. Jonathan Y. McQueston,
 Ebenezer G. Knight,
 George N. Andrews.
7. David K. Boutelle,
 John Patterson,
 Joseph N Prescott.
8. Harmon S. Burns,
 Richard W. Lang,
 William G. Everett.

Horace M. Gillis, *Clerk*.

1865.

MAYOR.

DARWIN J. DANIELS,*
JOHN HOSLEY.†

ALDERMEN.

1. John Gillis.
2. Samuel Clark.
3. Thomas R. Hubbard.
4. David A. Bunton.
5. John Rourke.
6. Ebenezer G. Knight.
7. Allen N. Clapp.
8. Thomas S. Montgomery.

CITY CLERK.

Joseph Knowlton,‡
Joseph E. Bennett.§

COMMON COUNCIL.

1. Amos Sargent,
 Harvey Huse,
 Daniel H. Maxfield.
2. Isaac H. Russell, *President*,
 William W. Wade,
 Christopher C. Colby.
3. Hiram Forsaith,
 Elbridge G. Fisk,
 Cyrus Dunn.
4. Otis Barton,
 Hamilton M. Bailey,
 Hiram Hill.
5. Timothy D. O'Connor,
 Asa Place,
 John Ryan.
6. Amos J. Wilson,
 James P. Eaton,
 Enos C. Howlett.
7. Joseph N. Prescott,
 John Patterson,
 Robert M. Shirley.
8. William G. Everett,
 Richard W. Lang,
 Dennis Cassidy.

Horace M. Gillis, *Clerk*.

* Died August 15.
† Elected to fill vacancy.
‡ Died May 31.
§ Elected to fill vacancy.

1866.

MAYOR.

JOHN HOSLEY.

ALDERMEN.

1. John Gillis.
2. Isaac H. Russell.
3. Samuel Hall.
4. John C. Young.
5. Daniel Connor.
6. Isaac Whittemore.
7. John Patterson.
8. Thomas S. Montgomery.

CITY CLERK.

Joseph E. Bennett.

COMMON COUNCIL.

1. Daniel H. Maxfield,
   Harvey Huse,
   Henry A. Campbell.
2. Christopher C. Colby,
   William W. Wade,
   Joseph W. Bean.
3. Hiram Forsaith, *President*,
   Cyrus Dunn,
   William P. Newell.
4. Charles E. Balch,
   George S. Holmes,
   Arthur L. Walker.
5. George W. Hunkins,
   John Ryan,
   John White.
6. Enos C. Howlett,
   Joseph Rowley,
   Thomas Emerson.
7. Robert M. Shirley,
   Chauncy C. Favor,
   Charles S. Fisher.
8. James K. Stevens,
   John Field,
   Alonzo L. Day.

Horace M. Gillis, *Clerk*.

1867.

MAYOR.

JOSEPH B. CLARK.

ALDERMEN.

1. William G. Perry.
2. Ezra Huntington.
3. Samuel Hall.
4. John C. Young.
5. Daniel Connor.
6. Isaac Whittemore.
7. John Patterson.
8. Daniel K. White.

CITY CLERK.

Joseph E. Bennett.

COMMON COUNCIL.

1. Henry A. Campbell,
   Henry C. Sanderson,
   John Plumer.
2. Joseph W. Bean,
   Granville P. Mason,
   John Pattee.
3. William P. Newell,
   Seth J. Sanborn,
   John Brugger.
4. Charles E. Balch,
   George S. Holmes,
   Arthur L. Walker.
5. George W. Hunkins,
   George Fox,
   Andrew Farrell.
6. Joseph Rowley,
   Alexander M. Corning,
   William F. Sleeper.
7. Charles S. Fisher,
   Isaac Lewis,
   Joseph H. Brooks.
8. John Field,
   George H. Gerry,
   David A. Messer.

Horace M. Gillis, *Clerk*.

1868.

MAYOR.

JAMES A. WESTON.

ALDERMEN.

1. William G. Perry.
2. Ezra Huntington.
3. William P. Newell.
4. Horace B. Putnam.
5. Daniel Connor.
6. Joseph Rowley.
7. Chauncy C. Favor.
8. George H. Gerry.

CITY CLERK.

Joseph E. Bennett.

COMMON COUNCIL.

1. Henry C. Sanderson, *Pres't*,
John Plumer,
William Bursiel.
2. John Pattee,
Henry A. Farrington,
Henry Lewis.
3. Seth J. Sanborn,
Peter K. Chandler,
Reed P. Silver.
4. Arthur M. Eastman,
Benjamin W. Robinson,
Jonathan B. Moore.
5. George Fox,
Andrew Farrell,
Michael Kelley.
6. William F. Sleeper,
Alexander M. Corning,
George H. Hubbard.
7. Joseph H. Brooks,
Isaac Lewis,
Samuel Brooks.
8. David A. Messer,
Albert A. Partridge,
Hiram Stearns.

Horace M. Gillis, *Clerk*.

1869.

MAYOR.

ISAAC W. SMITH.

ALDERMEN.

1. Daniel H. Maxfield.
2. Henry A. Farrington.
3. William P. Newell.
4. Horace B. Putnam.
5. Daniel Connor.
6. George H. Hubbard.
7. Chauncy C. Favor.
8. George H. Gerry.

CITY CLERK.

Joseph E. Bennett.

COMMON COUNCIL.

1. William Bursiel,
William H. Maxwell,
John P. Currier.
2. Henry Lewis,
Thomas R. Northrup,
William B. Underhill.
3. Peter K. Chandler, *President*,
Reed P. Silver,
Simon F. Stanton.
4. Arthur M. Eastman,
Benjamin W. Robinson,
Jonathan B. Moore.
5. Cornelius Healey,
Patrick Devine,*
John McKeon.
6. Dustin L. Jenkins,
John W. Johnson,
George E. Glines.
7. Samuel Brooks,
David O. Webster,
John K. McQueston.
8. Albert A. Partridge,
Hiram Stearns,
William G. Everett.

Horace M. Gillis,† *Clerk*.

* Resigned; John L. Kennedy elected to fill vacancy.
† Died July 7, 1869; Elbridge D. Hadley elected to fill vacancy.

Aretas Blood

1870.

MAYOR.

JAMES A. WESTON.

ALDERMEN.

1. Daniel H. Maxfield.
2. Henry A. Farrington.
3. Peter K. Chandler.
4. Horace P. Watts.
5. Cornelius Healey.
6. George H. Hubbard.
7. Samuel Brooks.
8. William G. Everett.

CITY CLERK.

Joseph E. Bennett.

COMMON COUNCIL.

1. William Bursiel,
William H. Maxwell,
John P. Currier, *President.*
2. Thomas R. Northrup,
William B. Underhill,
Henry W. Powell.
3. Simon F. Stanton,
Nehemiah S. Bean,
George R. Simmons.
4. William R. Patten,
Jacob B. Hartwell,
Joseph B. Sawyer.
5. John L. Kennedy,
Lawrence Foley,
Thomas Willis.
6. Dustin L. Jenkins,
John W. Johnson,
George E. Glines
7. David O. Webster,
John K. McQueston,
William M. Shepard.
8. Henry H. Fuller,
Harris J. Poor,
Albert A. Woodward.

Elbridge D. Hadley, *Clerk.*

1871.

MAYOR.

JAMES A. WESTON.

ALDERMEN.

1. George W. Thayer.
2. Henry Lewis.
3. William Flanders,*
Peter K. Chandler.†
4. James S. Cheney.
5. Daniel Connor.
6. John Hosley.
7. William N. Chamberlin.
8. William G. Everett.

CITY CLERK.

Joseph E. Bennett.

COMMON COUNCIL.

1. Israel W. Dickey,
Oscar M. Titus,
Sylvanus B. Putnam.
2. Henry W. Powell,
Dana D. Towne,
John C. Smith.
3. Nehemiah S Bean,
George R. Simmons,
Henry C. Reynolds.
4. William R. Patten, *President,*
Jacob B. Hartwell,
Joseph B. Sawyer.
5. Lawrence Foley,
John L. Kennedy,
Austin O'Malley.
6. Jacob J. Abbott,
Edwin Kennedy,
Jeremiah Hodge.
7. William M. Shepard,
James C. Russell,
Benjamin K. Parker.
8. Harris J. Poor,
Albert A. Woodward,
Silas A. Felton.

Elbridge D. Hadley, *Clerk.*‡

* Died February 7, 1871. † Elected March 14, 1871.

‡ Resigned December, 1871; Thomas W. Lane elected to fill vacancy.

1872.

MAYOR.

PERSON C. CHENEY.

ALDERMEN.

1. George W. Thayer.
2. Henry Lewis.
3. Nehemiah S. Bean.
4. Horace Pettee.
5. Lawrence Foley.
6. Ephraim S. Harvey.
7. William N. Chamberlin.
8. Albert A. Woodward.

CITY CLERK.

Joseph E. Bennett.

COMMON COUNCIL.

1. Israel W. Dickey,
   Oscar M. Titus,
   Levi L. Aldrich.
2. Dana D. Towne,
   John C. Smith,
   Leonard Shelters.
3. Henry C. Reynolds,
   Charles A. Smith,
   John L. Kelly.
4. Charles R. Colley,
   Jason Weston,
   Joseph L. Smith.
5. John L. Kennedy,
   Austin O'Malley,
   Patrick Harrington.
6. Jacob J. Abbott,
   Edwin Kennedy, *President*,
   Jeremiah Hodge.
7. James C. Russell,
   Benjamin K. Parker,
   Augustus G. Stevens.
8. Silas A. Felton,
   John Field,
   Frank D. Hanscom.

Thomas W. Lane, *Clerk*.‡

1873.

MAYOR.

CHARLES H. BARTLETT,*
JOHN P. NEWELL.†

ALDERMEN.

1. Israel W. Dickey.
2. Jonathan B. Moore.
3. Nehemiah S. Bean.
4. Horace Pettee.
5. John Sweeney.
6. Ephraim S. Harvey.
7. Luther E. Wallace.
8. Albert A. Woodward.

CITY CLERK.

Joseph E. Bennett.

COMMON COUNCIL.

1. Levi L. Aldrich,
   Sam C. Lowell,
   James L. Sweet.
2. Leonard Shelters,
   John W. Dickey,
   Frank S. Pushee.
3. Charles A. Smith, *President*,
   Rufus H. Pike,
   Robert G. Annan.
4. Charles R. Colley,
   Joseph L. Smith,
   Jason Weston.
5. John L. Kennedy,
   Patrick Cullity,
   John F. Cahill.
6. Henry B. Fairbanks,
   Amory Cobb.
   Charles K. Tucker.
7. William G. Dunham,
   Isaac W. Darrah,
   Isaac R. Dewey.
8. Silas A. Felton,
   Frank D. Hanscom,
   John Field.

Sylvanus B. Putnam, *Clerk*.

‡ Resigned May, 1872; Sylvanus B. Putnam elected to fill vacancy.
* Resigned February 18th, 1873. † Elected to fill vacancy.

1874–5.

MAYOR.

JAMES A. WESTON.

ALDERMEN.

1. Israel W. Dickey.
2. Jonathan B. Moore.
3. George R. Simmons.
4. Martin V. B Edgerly.
5. John L. Kennedy.
6. John M. Hayes.
7. James P. Walker.
8. Silas A. Felton.

CITY CLERK.

Joseph E. Bennett.

COMMON COUNCIL.

1. Sam C. Lowell,
   James L. Sweet,
   James Patten.
2. John W. Dickey,
   Frank S. Pushee,
   Jonathan Dodge.
3. Rufus H. Pike, *President*,
   Robert G. Annan,
   Thomas W. Lane.
4. Samuel F. Murry,
   Augustus F. Hall,
   John K. Piper.
5. Patrick Cullity,
   Patrick Riordan,
   Patrick J. O'Neil.
6. Isaac Huse,
   Jeremiah Abbott,
   David M. Goodwin.
7. William G. Dunham,
   Isaac W. Darrah,
   Isaac R. Dewey.
8. Madison Gerry,
   Warren K. Richardson,
   Lorenzo D. Colby.

Sylvanus B. Putnam, *Clerk*.

CITY TREASURERS.

1846. Thomas Hoyt.
1847–8. Jacob G. Cilley.
1849–50. James M. Berry.
1851–75. Henry R. Chamberlin.

CITY SOLICITORS.

1846–8. Daniel Clark.
1849–50. William C. Clarke.
1851. Daniel Clark.
1852–3. David Cross.
1854–5. Isaac W. Smith.*
1855–6. Samuel D. Lord.†
1857. Herman Foster.
1858–9. Joseph B. Clark.
1860. William W. Morris.
1861–4. Charles W. Johnson.
1865–6. Edward S. Cutter.
1867. Charles H. Bartlett.
1868–9. Cyrus A. Sulloway.
1870–2. Nathan P. Hunt.
1873. John H. Andrews.
1874. James F. Briggs.

* Resigned in July, 1855.

† Elected in July, 1855.

STATE OF THE VOTE FOR MAYOR AT EACH ELECTION.

Till 1850 a majority of all the votes cast was necessary for an election; after that a plurality. The second Tuesday of March was first appointed for the city election, but the day was changed in 1856 to the second Tuesday of December. In 1874 the original time was again appointed by the legislature.

1846.

August 19.

Hiram Brown (whig), 569
William C. Clarke (democrat), 442
Thomas Brown (temperance), 106
Scattering, 42
No choice.

September 1.

Hiram Brown (whig), 602
Isaac C. Flanders (dem.), 347
Thomas Brown (temp.), 109
Scattering, 51
Hiram Brown elected.

1847.

March 9.

Jacob F. James (whig), 797
Richard H. Ayer (dem.), 689
Thomas Brown (temp.), 155
Scattering, 20
No choice.

March 30.

Jacob F. James (whig), 553
Richard H. Ayer (dem.), 479
Thomas Brown (temp.), 256
Scattering, 53
No choice.

April 30.

Jacob F. James (whig), 472
George W. Morrison (dem.), 316
Thomas Brown (temp.), 145
Scattering, 103
No choice.

May 22.

Jacob F. James (whig), 644
George W. Morrison (dem.), 247
Thomas Brown (temp.), 78
Scattering, 64
Jacob F. James elected.

1848.

March 14.

Jacob F. James (whig), 886
Moody Currier (dem.), 603
Joseph Cochran, jr., (abolition), 266
Thomas Brown (temp.), 74
Scattering, 14
No choice.

April 7.

Jacob F. James (whig), 618
Moody Currier (dem.), 498
Joseph Cochran, jr., (abo.), 144
Scattering, 82
No choice.

April 29.

Jacob F. James (whig), 644
Moody Currier (dem.), 216
Joseph Cochran, jr., (abo.), 64
Scattering, 130
Jacob F. James elected.

1849.

March 13.

Mace Moulton (dem.), 676
Joseph Cochran, jr., (abo.), 661
Jacob F. James (whig), 308
Scattering, 21
No choice.

April 14.

Joseph Cochran, jr., (abo.), 367
Jacob F. James (whig), 344
Mace Moulton (dem.), 79
Scattering, 62
No choice.

May 5.

Joseph Cochran, jr., (abo.), 355
Jacob F. James (whig), 255
Walter French (dem.), 161
Scattering, 17
No choice.

June 2.

Joseph Cochran, jr., (abo.), 338
Jacob F. James (whig), 185
Walter French (dem.), 152
Scattering, 54
No choice.

October 6.

Warren L. Lane (dem.), 422
Thomas R. Crosby (whig), 268
Joseph Cochran, jr., (abo.), 17
Scattering, 9
Warren L. Lane elected.

1850.

Moses Fellows (whig), 936
Warren L. Lane (dem.), 803
Scattering, 6
Moses Fellows elected.

1851.

Moses Fellows (whig), 893
Walter French (dem.), 610
Alonzo Smith (abo.), 257
Scattering, 15
Moses Fellows elected.

1852.

Frederick Smyth (whig), 934
Walter French (dem.), 727
Alonzo Smith (abo.), 87
Scattering, 87
Frederick Smyth elected.

1853.

Frederick Smyth (whig), 1026
Stevens James (dem.), 604
Scattering, 9
Frederick Smyth elected.

1854.

Frederick Smyth (whig), 1344
William C. Clarke (dem.), 787
Scattering, 10
Frederick Smyth elected.

1855.

Theodore T. Abbot (know-nothing), 1995
Frederick G. Stark (dem.), 668
Scattering, 7
Theodore T. Abbot elected.

1856.

March 11.

Theodore T. Abbot (republican), 1104
George W. Morrison (dem.), 1041
Scattering, 7
Theodore T. Abbot elected.

1856.

December 9.

Jacob F. James (rep.), 1253
Isaac C. Flanders (dem.), 407
Scattering, 17
Jacob F. James elected.

1857.

Alonzo Smith (rep.), 809
Edward W. Harrington (dem.), 754
Jacob F. James (rep.), 368
Scattering, 5
Alonzo Smith elected.

1858.

Edward W. Harrington (dem.), 1100
Alonzo Smith (rep.), 1085
Scattering, 4
Edward W. Harrington elected.

1859.

Edward W. Harrington (dem.), 1335
Bradbury P. Cilley (rep.), 1303
Scattering, 1
Edward W. Harrington elected.

1860.

David A. Bunton (rep.), 1288
Bradbury P. Cilley (independent), 842
Scattering, 26
David A. Bunton elected.

1861.

David A. Bunton (rep.), 1052
James A. Weston (dem.), 800
Scattering, 3
David A. Bunton elected.

1862.

Theodore T. Abbot (rep.), 910
James A. Weston (dem.), 892
Theodore T. Abbot elected.

1863.

Frederick Smyth (rep.), 968
Scattering, 11
Frederick Smyth elected.

1864.

Darwin J. Daniels (rep.), 966
Joseph Kidder (dem.), 403
* Darwin J. Daniels elected.

1865.

John Hosley (ind.), 1035
Joseph B. Clark (rep.), 968
John Hosley elected.

1866.

Joseph B. Clark (rep.), 1320
Edward W. Harrington (democrat), 786
Joseph B. Clark elected.

1867.

James A. Weston (dem.), 1637
Joseph B. Clark (rep.), 1355
Scattering, 4
James A. Weston elected.

1868.

Isaac W. Smith (rep.), 1490
James A. Weston (dem.), 1467
Isaac W. Smith elected.

1869.

James A. Weston (dem.), 938
Isaac W. Smith (rep.), 792
James A. Weston elected.

1870.

James A. Weston (dem.), 1153
Andrew C. Wallace (rep.), 957
Peter K. Chandler (temp.), 162
Scattering, 3
James A. Weston elected.

* Died August 15, 1865. John Hosley (republican) elected by the City Councils.

1871.

Person C. Cheney (rep.), 1676
John Hosley (dem.), 1027
Person C. Cheney elected.

1872.

Charles H. Bartlett (rep.), 1316
Joseph Kidder (ind.), 935
†Charles H. Bartlett elected.

1873.

James A. Weston (dem.), 1580
John P. Newell (rep.), 1067
Charles C. Keniston (temp.), 173
James A. Weston elected.

†Resigned February 18, 1872. John P. Newell (republican) elected by the City Councils.

THE CITY OF TO-DAY.

THE Manchester of to-day is the wonderful outgrowth of a town which once had the name of being the poorest in the state. It is situated in latitude forty-two degrees fifty-three minutes north, in longitude seventy-one degrees thirty-one minutes nine seconds west, its meridian time being one minute and thirty-one seconds slower than that of Boston. It extends up and down both sides of the Merrimack river, is sixteen miles south from Concord, seventeen north from Nashua, forty-one west from Portsmouth, twenty-six northwest from Lawrence, fifty-two north-northwest from Boston. It contains twenty-one thousand seven hundred acres, about one quarter of which is improved land. On the east is Massabesic lake, the largest sheet of still water in the state south of Concord, through which passes the line between Manchester and Auburn. On the south are Litchfield and Londonderry, on the west Bedford and Goffstown, on the north Goffstown and Hooksett.

It was the first city incorporated in New Hampshire, is the largest and wealthiest, possesses one-tenth of the state's wealth and population, produces one-eighth of its manufactured goods, and is the fourth city in the United States in the value of its cotton and woolen manufactures. Thirty-five years ago it was tenanted by less than a thousand people, while to-day it counts thirty thousand inhabitants and has over six thousand two hundred ratable polls. The tax-list of 1874 was $312,835.95, of which the state tax was $36,428; the county tax, $20,637.18; and the municipal tax, $255,770.77. The resident tax was $311,717.-24; the non-resident tax, $1,008.71; the dog tax, $757. The rate of taxation was twenty-four dollars and sixty cents on a thousand dollars. There were fourteen hundred and three horses, valued at $111,854; five hundred and ninety-seven cows and oxen, valued at $17,342; forty-one sheep, valued at $116; carriages valued at $37,126; six hundred and twenty-five male and sixty-six female dogs. The money in the city at interest which was taxed was $33,660; the value of the stock in trade, $1,174,290; of stocks in banks, $301,540; of factories and machinery, $2,930,900; of real estate, $7,488,224; of the polls, $621,-000. The total assessed valuation was $12,716,892, which is about two-thirds of the actual value. The value of the city property, including the school property, is about $1,-350,000. The city has $50,000 invested in the Suncook Valley railway. Its debt is about nine hundred and forty thousand dollars, two-thirds of which is in bonds issued to meet the expense of its water-works, while the rest is in city bonds and individual notes.

Manchester is in congressional district number two, in councilor district number three, and is the whole of senatorial district number three, having, of course, within its limits, the state senator, the Hon. George B. Chandler. It is divided into seven wards, is entitled to about twenty-five state representatives, and had in March, 1874, nearly forty-two hundred legal voters. It is the residence of two ex-governors—the Hon. Frederick Smyth and the Hon. Ezekiel A. Straw; of the present governor — the Hon. James A. Weston, who is also mayor of the city; of the county treasurer — Daniel W. Lane. It is the home of the attorney general — the Hon. Lewis W. Clark; of an associate justice of the superior court of judicature — the Hon. Isaac W. Smith; of an associate justice of the circuit court — the Hon. Clinton W. Stanley; of an ex-judge of the court of common pleas — the Hon. Charles R. Morrison; of the judge of the United States district court in New Hampshire — the Hon. Daniel Clark; of two United States commissioners — the Hon. Charles H. Bartlett and the Hon. Clinton W. Stanley; of the clerk of the New Hampshire district court — the Hon. Charles H. Bartlett; of two ex-members of the United States Senate — the Hon. Daniel Clark and the Hon. Samuel N. Bell; of an ex-member of the United States House of Representatives — the Hon. George W. Morrison; of the collector of internal revenue for the second collection district — Elijah M. Topliff; of the deputy collector — Cyrus A. Sulloway; of the judge of probate for Hillsborough county — the Hon. Lucien B. Clough; of the late judge of probate — the Hon. David Cross; of one of the county commissioners — Col. George W. Riddle.

STREETS.

Manchester's centre of population and business is nearly half way from its northern and southern limits and on the east side of the Merrimack. Along the latter's east bank are stretched its manufactories, their canals running parallel with the river and bordered by the track of the Concord railway and a street of sixty feet in width which belongs to the corporations. Forty or fifty rods to the east of this and parallel with it, at an elevation of ninety feet from the surface of the river, extends the city's main thoroughfare, called Elm street, two miles and a half long, paved in part with granite blocks, bordered with brick or concrete sidewalks and shaded with trees. It was laid out as a public highway by the selectmen of the town on the fifth of

May, 1840, one hundred feet wide, twelve feet on each side for sidewalks and ten feet in the centre for ornamental trees. Some of the elms which gave it its name were left standing in the middle of the street till the gas from leaky pipes destroyed the last, in front of Smyth's block, in 1855.

Manchester is divided into thirteen highway districts, each under the charge of a superintendent annually elected by the city councils, of which district number two includes the city proper and contains six miles of sewers. In the space given on Weston's map, which includes somewhat more than the compact part of the city, there are fifty-seven miles of streets. Outside of that there are sixty more, making a total of about one hundred and twenty miles of streets already built and many more are projected and will be laid out before long. There was appropriated by the city in 1874 for repairs of highways $18,500; for paving and macadamizing $10,000; for new streets $7,000. Including paving and macadamizing, this would give $240 as the sum per mile expended on streets already built; exclusive of them, $155.

Within the compact part of the city the streets run nearly north and south, east and west, and are from fifty to sixty feet wide. On the west side of the river and in the suburbs of the city the highways conform to the old lines of travel. The soil is generally light and sandy, some portions, however, being productive and easy of cultivation. Granite ledges are found in the northern and eastern sections. Its surface is generally level, but there are several hills in a group in the northeast part, one of which, just to the east and making a division between the slopes to the river and the lake, overlooks the whole city and commands an extensive view of the surrounding country. There is a high bluff on the west side of the river, to which the name of Rock Rimmon was long since given and which time has corrupted into Rock Raymond.

STREAMS AND PONDS.

Manchester's largest stream, the Merrimack and Piscataquog rivers excepted, is Cohas brook, through which the waters of Massabesic lake run four miles, falling one hundred and twenty-five feet in that distance, and empty into the Merrimack river. The lake itself is about four miles from the city proper, contains twenty-three hundred and fifty acres and has a circumference of twenty-five miles. It is divided into two parts each about one mile wide and three miles long, connected by a narrow stream at what is called "Deer Neck," to one of which the frequency of small islands has given the name of Island pond.

There are several other ponds whose outlets, flowing across it from east to west, diversify the surface of the city. Stevens pond lies at the base of a hill in the eastern part of the city, contains twelve acres and empties into the Merrimack through Cemetery brook. Long pond lies south of Massabesic, and its outlet is the Little Cohas brook. It contains thirty acres. Mosquito pond contains eight or ten acres, is situated near the school-house in district number nine, and its waters flow into the Great Cohas. Nutt's pond, once called Fort pond because a fort was built near its western shore during the Indian wars, is in the southern part of the city. It contains about fifteen acres and its waters mingle at length with those of the Merrimack. There are a dozen brooks of greater or less size, of which the most important are Great and Little Cohas brooks, which flow respectively from Massabesic lake and Long pond into the Merrimack; Cemetery brook, once known as Amoskeag brook, which empties into the same river the waters of Stevens pond; Ray brook, which rises in Hooksett and flows into the Merrimack near Amoskeag Falls; Black and Millstone brooks, which are tributaries of the Merrimack on its western side in Amoskeag; and Mile brook, which flows, chiefly in culverts, through the most densely settled parts of the city, carrying the waters of the ponds on Hanover and Merrimack squares into the Cemetery brook.

VILLAGES.

The city has several villages which arose from geographical circumstance, viz.: Piscataquog, Amoskeag, Manchester Centre, Goffe's Falls, Bakersville, Hallsville, Janesville, Youngsville and Towlesville. Amoskeag was named from the falls — "the place of much fish;" Piscataquog from the river — "the place of much deer;" the Centre because it was the original town. Goffe's Falls obtained its designation from Col. John Goffe, who settled there in 1734, but took the name of Moore's village after the Goffe farm and mills passed into the hands of Capt. Samuel Moore who married a daughter of Col. Goffe. The place is now known, however, as Goffe's Falls. That name was originally given to the falls in Cohas brook, but is now applied to the rapids in the Merrimack just above the brook's mouth. Bakersville was so called from being built upon the farm of the late Joseph Baker. Hallsville was named for Joseph B. Hall, once a large real estate owner in that vicinity; Janesville for Mrs. Jane Southwark, wife of Taylor M. Southwark, whose maiden name was Jane Young and who inherited the land there; Towlesville for Hiram Towle who owned the territory on which the settlement stands; Youngsville for the Youngs who dwelt there. The last five were built on land beyond that which was included in the Amoskeag Company's purchases, and not many years ago were separated from the compact part of the city by woods. Hallsville and Janesville once had their tavern and stores, but they are all now only localities, their identity being slowly lost in the city's expansion. Manchester Centre, Amoskeag and Piscataquog have been each the centre of business and enterprise. Of these the Centre was entirely bereft by the railway, but Piscataquog, though no longer at the head of navigation on the river, is a thriving village, while Amoskeag has been till recently employed in the manufacture of shoes. Goffe's Falls, as well as the two latter places, supports stores of its own, and the Cohas brook supplies water power for hosiery, crash and cassimere mills. The trains on the Portsmouth railway stop at Hallsville and Massabesic pond; those of the North Weare at Piscataquog; while Manchester itself, Amoskeag and Goffe's Falls are stations on the Concord railway.

SEWERS.

The system of sewerage in the compact part of the city is based upon a survey and report made in 1856 by James Slade, a civil engineer in the employ of the city of Boston, in accordance with a vote of the city councils. By this system the city is divided, for purposes of drainage, into four sections, and large sewers were projected in Elm and Union streets and two others to the east, running north and south and connecting with the main sewer on Cedar street, running east and west, which was to empty into the Merrimack river below the lowest mill. From the large sewers branches of smaller size were to be built in the streets running east and west, and from these again other sewers still smaller to branch into the streets lying north and south of the latter. The general idea of this plan was adopted by the city and new sewers are built and old ones repaired in accordance with it. The original sewer still remains in Elm street and a new one, egg-shaped, of six times its capacity, has been built. The sewers in Union and Cedar streets have been partially built and the other large ones are not yet needed. They are at present discharged into Cemetery brook and thence into the lower canal. The smaller sewers are continually being replaced by new ones. Piscataquog village is drained by sewers in Main street, emptying into Piscataquog river, and in Granite street, emptying into the Merrimack. The largest sewers are generally of brick, though partially of brick and cement.

SQUARES.

To the Amoskeag Company Manchester is indebted for five public commons in the heart of the city, in addition to the private squares which surround its own blocks and those of other corporations and the lot in the northeast part of the city which encloses its reservoir. These commons are known as Merrimack, Concord, Tremont, Hanover and Park squares, and were given by the Company on condition that the city should never build upon them or allow roads through them, should keep them neat, plant trees and lay out walks within them.

Concord square was the first in the city, being laid out in 1839, before the Company's first land sale. It is bounded by Vine, Concord, Pine and Amherst streets, contains four and five-eighths acres, and was deeded to the city in 1848. It was stipulated in the deed that an iron fence should be built around it within three years, but this has not yet been done, though a stone edging will surround it in another year. Near its centre is a small pond supplied with water from the pond on Hanover square. Many of the old trees remain upon it and new ones have been planted.

Merrimack square is the largest of all, containing five and seven-eighths acres, and is situated between Elm, Merrimack, Chestnut and Central streets. It was given to the city in 1848 on condition of the construction of an iron

S. A. Bunton

fence about it within five years, and this condition has been complied with, though not within the time. There is a large pond on its northern side, supplied by a culvert which runs into it from Hanover square.

Tremont square is the smallest in the city, containing but two acres and a half, and is situated between Pine, Bridge, Union and High streets. This was made over to the city in 1848 and its old fence was replaced by one of wood. It is in a pleasant part of the city, though without water of any kind, and part of the original forest shades it.

Hanover square, the gift of the Company in 1852, is bounded by Union, Amherst, Beech and Hanover streets, and contains four acres. The Mile brook ran through it and was dammed up on Union street to make a pond. This supplies a number of reservoirs with water for fire purposes, besides feeding the ponds on Concord and Merrimack squares, and water from an excellent spring on its south bank is carried an eighth of a mile in pipes to rise in drinking-fountains on Elm street.

Park square, situated between Chestnut, Park, Pine and Cedar streets, contains three acres and a half, is very level, without water, and partially shaded.

CEMETERIES.

The city owns two large cemeteries, beautiful now and growing in beauty with age. The older of the two, known as the "Valley Cemetery," is situated on the southern verge of the compact part of the city, and the industry of business is encircling it with manufactories, though in 1840, when the Amoskeag Company gave it to the city, it was considered far out of town. It contains nineteen and seven-tenths acres, and is bounded by Auburn, Pine, Valley and Willow streets. The conditions of the deed are such that the land can be used for no other purpose than for a burying-ground and the Company reserved the right to flow the valley in it through which the Cemetery brook passes. The lots are now all taken up, and as early as 1855 the need of another resting-place for the dead became so apparent as to cause the purchase by the city in that year, from John S. Kidder and George M. Flanders, of two adjacent tracts of land about two miles and a half south of the city hall, between the Calef road and the River road. These contained about forty acres and were called the "Pine Grove Cemetery." The lack of natural irrigation has been here supplied by artificial water-works, and art has added to both burial-grounds what nature refused to supply.

In accordance with the provisions of the deed of the Valley a committee was appointed in 1841 to assume its charge and has been annually appointed since, the Pine Grove being also placed under its care. The committee first elected went to work with a will, and, having obtained from the citizens a subscription of two hundred and thirty-four dollars, spent it in building a fence, trimming the trees and laying out walks. The formal dedication occurred on the fifth of July, 1841, when the Sunday schools of the city, accompanied by many citizens and escorted by the Stark Guards, marched in procession to the spot. An address was delivered by the Rev. George W. Gage and the four thousand people present joined in religious services. Thereafter the town appropriated money to be used in its adornment, and in 1846 a thorn hedge was planted on two sides and twenty-five hundred plants set out. The Pine Grove was let for pasturage and remained unimproved till 1858. Each cemetery is in care of a superintendent. In 1853 the city bought of the Hon. David A. Bunton a lot of land upon the Calef road for a cemetery, but it was found unsuitable and the Pine Grove was bought. This lot was sold in 1860 to James Barrett, who mortgaged it to the city. The mortgage was foreclosed in 1866 and the land sold to William M. Rolfe.

There are also the old burying-ground at the Centre, which was extensively used till 1840; one at Goffe's Falls; one in Amoskeag; one in Piscataquog; one just upon the western limit of the city on the road to Amherst, occupied by the Roman Catholics; one near the school-house at Harvey's mills, known as the "Merrill cemetery;" one in the eastern part of the city, formerly known as the "Huse yard," and now as "Stowell's ground;" the "Ray cemetery" on the River road near Amoskeag Falls; "the Forest cemetery" on the old Weston farm in the south-eastern part of the city; and a small yard in the north part of the city. All of these but the Catholic burial-place are little used, and some are private and others are under the control of the city.

RAILWAYS.

The Concord railway was opened to the public from Nashua to Manchester on the fourth of July, 1842, and from Manchester to Concord on the first of the following September. An additional track, to accommodate its increasing business, was built in 1846, 1847 and 1848. The Manchester & Lawrence railway was opened to Manchester November 13, 1849. In 1850 a railway was built from Portsmouth to Candia, Suncook and Concord, called the Portsmouth & Concord railway. It did not pay expenses and in 1861 its name was changed to the Concord & Portsmouth, the track between Candia and Suncook was discontinued, a new track built from Candia to Manchester, and the Concord and Lawrence railways built jointly the piece from Hooksett to Suncook. The New Hampshire Central railway, now known as the Manchester & North Weare railway, was built in 1849 and 1850 from Manchester to Henniker, but the piece between North Weare and Henniker was torn up and never re-laid. The tearing-up, which made a great excitement at the time, was done on Sunday, October 31, 1858, by a gang of men who came from Concord with four locomotives, and the reason for it was that it suited the interests of the owners of the railway. The Suncook Valley railway was built from Hooksett to Pittsfield in 1869. In 1865, in accordance with a resolution of the city councils, a survey of a proposed route for the Manchester & Keene railway was made by the Hon. James A. Weston, but no farther steps have been taken by Manchester towards building it. The building now used as a car-house by the Concord railway was its first passenger station. It then fronted on Canal street and had a portico and pillars upon that side. The railway ran between that and the freight station which then occupied the spot where the present passenger station stands. The business of the corporation had increased so fast by 1853 that it outgrew its facilities, and its cars used to obstruct public travel by remaining on the track at the crossing of Granite street. The city brought a number of suits against it and meetings of the citizens of Manchester and Bedford were held to endorse the action. The corporation finally agreed to build the present station, which was completed in 1855, and the suits were withdrawn. A new freight station was erected south of Granite street. Charters have been granted, also, for railways from this city to Claremont and to Ashburnham, Mass., and a horse railway has been incorporated, but no attempts have been made to construct any of them.

The Concord railway runs through the western part of the city on the left bank of the Merrimack from north to south. The North Weare, the Lawrence, Portsmouth and substantially the Suncook Valley railways start from it. It is on a direct route to the White Mountain region, northern Vermont, New York, Montreal, Ogdensburg and the great lakes. Stages leave daily for Candia and Deerfield, by connecting with the Portsmouth train at Candia station, and for Amherst, Milford and New Ipswich on Tuesdays, Thursdays and Saturdays. The agent of the Concord railway at its station in Manchester is Major Josiah Stevens, who had been master of transportation at Concord but was appointed in 1869 to succeed W. Henry Hurlbut who was killed by an accident on the North Weare railway. The present ticket-seller, Lon Elliott, was appointed the same year. The station-agent at Goffe's Falls is L. P. Moore and at Amoskeag is Thomas L. Quimby. There are in the season of travel seven trains north daily; seven south; two to North Weare and return; two to Portsmouth and return; three to Lawrence and return; two to Pittsfield and return. It is estimated that two hundred thousand people annually buy tickets at this station. Allowing fifty to a car, they would require four thousand cars, and these, at sixty feet to a car, would make a line over forty-five miles long, or would cover the track from here to Portsmouth.

BRIDGES.

The first bridge of any importance within the limits of Manchester was built across the Cohas brook on the road leading from the Centre to Londonderry in 1738 at private expense. The first bridge over the Merrimack was built in 1792 at the foot of Bridge street by a corporation and was known as McGregor's bridge. This went to ruin about 1815 and was replaced in 1825 by another. Twelve years later it was bought by the Amoskeag Company and the toll on foot-passengers abolished. A freshet carried off two piers in 1848, but these were replaced and the bridge remained till 1851, when it was entirely swept away and has not been re-built. Granite bridge was built by a company at what was known as "Merrill's Falls" on the Merrimack in 1840. Granite street was built at the same time. In 1848 the toll was abolished and the bridge became the property of Manchester and Bedford. The ice-freshet of 1851 carried it off, and the present one was built by the two towns that year. When Piscataquog village was annexed, the bridge came entirely into the hands of Manchester. A bridge was built in 1842 over the Merrimack at Amoskeag Falls by a corporation. It was made a free bridge in 1852 and carried away by a freshet in March of the next year. The city of Manchester re-built it in 1854. Several bridges over the Piscataquog river were built in early days by the town of Bedford, the last one previous to the annexation of part of it to Manchester being a wooden one which was put up in 1843. This was burned in 1862 and an iron one immediately replaced it. This fell in February, 1873, under a loaded team, and the present wooden one was built to take its place. When the Concord railway was built in 1842 a single-track bridge was carried over the Merrimack at Goffe's Falls. This gave way in 1869 to a double-track bridge, which was built without the detention of a train. The bridge over the Merrimack on the Manchester and North Weare railway, originally built in 1850, was burned in 1871 and a new one was constructed that year. Meanwhile the trains ran as far as Piscataquog village, and the passengers were brought over to the city proper in carriages. Ferries which had long existed at different points upon the river were made useless by the building of the highway bridges and were discontinued.

MANUFACTURES.

The Amoskeag Falls have a fall of fifty-four feet and ten inches; those at Lowell have one of thirty feet and those at Lawrence of twenty-eight. The dam, by which the water is turned into the canals, cost sixty thousand dol-

AMOSKEAG MANUF'G CO.

DAM AND GATE HOUSE.

lars. The upper canal is two hundred feet more than a mile long, and the lower is a mile and sixteen hundred and twenty feet in length. At the northern end of the canals are situated some of the smaller manufactories of the city to which the establishment of the large corporations gave life, and the place is called Mechanics' Row. Its business is gradually forsaking it, drifting to the southern portion of the town in the vicinity of the railways and using steam power. From the Row the large mills extend, with slight intervals, to the lower end of the canals. These mills make *one hundred and forty-three miles* of cloth a day, set in motion nearly three hundred thousand spindles and seventy-six hundred looms, and have an aggregate monthly pay-roll of two hundred and thirty thousand dollars. By the census of 1870 the capital invested in the city in manufactures of all kinds was nearly ten million dollars; the number of men, women and children employed in them, nine thousand; the total yearly pay-roll, three million, six hundred and seventy-four thousand dollars; the value of the manufactures, eighteen million dollars. The city makes now five million dollars' worth more goods and employs a thousand more operatives.

INCIDENTALS.

There is one through express in Manchester, north and south, started when the Concord railway was built in 1842, the late Col. James S. Cheney being its first messenger and the first railway expressman in Manchester. There is, besides, one south to Boston, one to New Boston and Francestown, one to North Weare and Henniker and one to Candia and Deerfield. There are two telegraph offices, — the Franklin and Western Union. There are eight hotels, — the Amoskeag Hotel in Amoskeag village, the Merrimack House in Piscataquog village, the Massabesic House at

Massabesic lake, the Island Pond House at Island pond, the Manchester House, City Hotel, Haseltine House and National Hotel, in the heart of the city. Manchester has about forty lawyers, thirty doctors and twenty clergymen. It supports two daily newspapers—the "Mirror and American" and the "Manchester Daily Union"; three weeklies —the "Mirror and Farmer," the "Union Democrat" and the "Saturday Night Dispatch"; one monthly—the "New Hampshire Journal of Music." A recent estimate made thirty-two secret organizations in the city and allowed them seven-eighths of the citizens. The New Hampshire Agricultural Society and the New Hampshire Poultry Society have their headquarters in this city, where the treasurer of both, who is also treasurer of the New England Agricultural Society, resides.

THE REFORM SCHOOL.

In 1855 the state legislature passed an act which authorized the governor and council to appoint a board of three commissioners, empowered to buy a tract of land and erect buildings thereon, to provide a "house of reformation for juvenile and female offenders against the laws." The commissioners,—the Hon. Frederick Smyth of Manchester, the Hon. Matthew Harvey of Concord and Hosea Eaton of New Ipswich—were appointed that year and selected as the site for the house proposed the farm which was once the home of Gen. John Stark, two miles north of the city hall, on the Merrimack river, Concord railway and River road, containing about one hundred acres. The price paid was ten thousand dollars, and another piece of ten acres was bought soon after for a thousand dollars more. The building was commenced in the spring of 1856, finished in the autumn of 1857 and furnished in the spring of 1858. Its cost was thirty-four thousand dollars; the total cost, therefore, of building and land, was forty-five thousand dollars. The house was dedicated on the twelfth of May, 1858, and occupied at that time, when the first superintendent, Brooks Shattuck, was appointed. He was succeeded on the twentieth of April, 1866, by Isaac H. Jones. Upon his departure Edward Ingham was elected, the seventeenth of May, 1870. The present superintendent, John C. Ray, was appointed on the second of July, 1874. The institution is now known as the state reform school and is under the management of a board of nine trustees, by whom the superintendent is chosen, and who are appointed by the governor and council. The farm where the school is located is fertile and its culture affords employment to the inmates. Upon it are two unfailing springs of pure water. The number of inmates is about one hundred, all but a few of whom are boys. Besides the superintendent, matron, assistants and men in charge of the farm, there are teachers employed who give daily instruction to the inmates. A fire on the twentieth of December, 1865, nearly destroyed the building and the children were temporarily kept in the buildings known as the "Stark house" and "Gamble house," which had stood near by since the early settlement of the town. During their residence in it the Stark house was set on fire and consumed. As soon as possible after the fire, the old school building was repaired and the inmates returned to it. The institution is in annual receipt of interest from the legacies of James McKeen Wilkins of Manchester and Moody Kent of Pembroke, which amount to six thousand and three thousand dollars, respectively.

PUBLIC BUILDINGS.

The county jail had been located in Amherst since the establishment of the courts, but the railways made Manchester much more accessible and it was decided that its place should be changed. The new one was built by the city of Manchester in 1863, just south of the Valley cemetery, on a lot bought of the Amoskeag Company and containing one hundred and eighty-seven thousand square feet. It is a brick building and has accommodations for seventy inmates. Gilbert Hills had been its jailer in Amherst and continued in office till 1865, when Alfred G. Fairbanks was appointed, who was succeeded in 1874 by Nathan H. Pierce. The latter, Daniel L. Stevens, John L. Kennedy, Daniel F. Healey and Anson Merrill are the deputy sheriffs resident in the city.

The county court-house was built by the city in 1868, at a cost of forty thousand dollars, and is a two-story brick structure situated upon the corner of Merrimack and Franklin streets. The lot where it stands contains nineteen thousand square feet, and was bought of the Amoskeag Company in 1847 upon condition that no other building than one to be used for city or county purposes should be placed there. Two terms of the circuit court are held yearly in Manchester.

The city hall stands on the corner of Elm and Market streets and was built in 1845 at a cost of thirty-five thousand dollars. It was then thought to be the finest building in the state, but is now regarded contemptuously and will give place to another before many years.

The old town farm was bought in 1841 of Moses Davis for four thousand dollars. It contained one hundred acres and was situated upon Bridge street near the Mammoth road. In 1846 there was added to this a farm of about one hundred and thirty-five acres, situated upon the Mammoth road and adjacent to the old farm. It was formerly the property of Capt. Ephraim Stevens, jr., and passed from him into the hands of the Hon. Frederick G. Stark, who sold it to the city for six thousand dollars. The widow of Capt. Stevens was also paid a thousand dollars to relin-

Court House.

quish her right of dower. Some of the land has been sold and there now remains of both farms about two hundred and twelve acres. The poor, who had been kept on the Davis farm, were moved in 1846 to the building which is now used as a poor-house and house of correction and which was a large tavern when the stage-coaches ran daily over the Mammoth road. On the old farm is an unused pest-house and a pound. A new pest-house was built of brick in 1874 upon the old farm near the Mammoth road.

GOVERNMENT.

The government of the city is vested in a mayor, seven aldermen, one from each ward, and twenty-one members of the common council, three from each ward, all elected annually by the people. The mayor is chairman of the board of mayor and aldermen and the city clerk is the clerk of the board. The common council chooses a presiding officer from its members and appoints a clerk. The salary of the mayor is one thousand dollars, and the city clerk, whose duties are those of the clerk of any corporation with indefinite and numberless additions, receives the same wages with the fees added. The salary of the clerk of the common council is one hundred dollars. The aldermen and councilmen give their services to the city without pecuniary return. Seven assessors, one from each ward, elected annually by the people, are paid three dollars a day while at work upon the tax-list. One moderator, one ward-clerk and three selectmen are elected annually from each ward. The moderator is paid three dollars a year and the clerk and selectmen five dollars each. One overseer of the poor, with a salary of twenty-five dollars, is elected annually by the people of each ward. The city councils in convention elect the city clerk and the city treasurer, each with a salary of a thousand dollars; the city solicitor who receives one hundred dollars; the city physician whose salary is fifty dollars; the city messenger who is paid six hundred dollars; the superintendent of the poor-farm and keeper ot the house of correction, whose wages are five hundred dollars; the superintendents of highways, of whom the superintendent in district number two receives three dollars, and the rest two dollars, per day of actual service; and several minor officers. The board of mayor and aldermen appoints annually a collector of taxes with a salary of one thousand dollars, and a city liquor agent with a salary of one hundred dollars. The mayor annually appoints three health officers who receive twenty-five dollars each.

POLICE.

The police court was established with the city and its first justice was the Hon. Samuel D. Bell, who assumed the office in October, 1846. Upon his appointment as justice of the court of common pleas, he was succeeded in June, 1848, by the Hon. Chandler E. Potter, who served till July, 1855, when the Hon. Isaac W. Smith was appointed. Upon his retirement in February, 1857, the Hon. Samuel Upton succeeded to the office and continued in it till July, 1874, when the present justice, the Hon. Joseph W. Fellows, was appointed. The special justices during this time, of whom there were two in office at once till the amendment of the city charter in June, 1848, reduced the number by one, were Isaac Riddle, Joseph Cochran, jr., Warren L. Lane, George Bell, Amos B. Shattuck, Elijah M. Topliff, Henry E. Burnham and Newton H. Wilson. Judge Potter and Judge Smith, in whose time there was little room in the city hall to spare, held court in the rooms in the rear of the second floor of Riddle's building on the corner of Elm and Hanover streets. In 1857, during Judge Upton's administration, the hall of the city building, which had occupied the whole space from the second floor to the roof, was divided horizontally by a third floor, and in the space thus gained rooms were built to one of which the court was removed.

The officers of the court at present consist of a justice, a special justice to officiate in the former's absence, and a clerk. The justice is the Hon. Joseph W. Fellows and his salary is fifteen hundred dollars. The special justice is Newton H. Wilson, who receives two dollars for each day of actual service. The clerk is Roland C. Rowell and his salary is three hundred dollars. The criminal docket is called daily and the civil docket on the first Wednesday of each month. The court was made in 1874 a court of record and naturalization. The criminal cases of 1873 were nearly fifteen hundred and the amount of fines and costs nearly ten thousand dollars, which is one source of income to the city.

The police force consists of a city marshal, with a salary of nine hundred and fifty dollars; an assistant marshal with a salary of seven hundred and seventy-five dollars; a captain of the night watch, who receives two dollars and a half a day; two day policemen and twelve night watchmen who receive two dollars and twenty-five cents a day; six constables of whom the marshal and assistant marshal are two; besides a large number of special police officers. These are all appointed annually by the board of mayor and aldermen. The cost of the department to the city in 1873 was about nineteen thousand dollars.

FIRE DEPARTMENT.

The fire department consists of a chief engineer and four assistant engineers, four engine companies, to consist of not over fourteen members, one hose company and one hook and ladder company, to consist of not over thirty members each. The engineers are annually elected by the city councils. The salary of the chief is one hundred dollars, and of the assistants fifty dollars. The members of the department receive a salary of fifty dollars each, with higher wages for certain officers. The list of the companies is as follows: Amoskeag Steamer Company Number One, fourteen men, George R. Simmons foreman; Fire King Steamer Company Number Two, fourteen men, James F. Pherson foreman; E. W. Harrington Steamer Company Number Three, twelve men, John Patterson foreman; N. S. Bean Steamer Company Number Four, fourteen men, W. H. Vickery foreman; Pennacook Hose Company Number One, twenty men, Thomas W. Lane foreman; Excelsior Hook and Ladder Company Number One, thirty men, John N. Chase foreman. Pennacook is the name of the Indians who dwelt around the falls and Amoskeag the name the falls were given by them. Such titles as Fire King and Excelsior need no explanation and the other steamer companies were named in honor of former engineers.

This is the outgrowth of the vote of the town in 1839 to buy a fire engine and necessary apparatus. Others were bought as required and those which were owned by the manufacturing corporations were added to them, so that there were some eight or ten engine and hose companies under the city's control when the first steam fire engine, the first the Amoskeag Company ever made, was bought in 1859. From that time on, as more steamers were bought and the old hand engines discarded, a gradual reduction of the members of the fire department brought it to its present proportions.

The four steamers are all of the Amoskeag Company's make, two first-class and two second-class, three of which, with a hose carriage and hook-and-ladder wagon, are located in the brick engine-house on Vine street, while the other is situated in Piscataquog village. A hose carriage, from the Company's shop, has recently been added, and the one which was used by the Pennacooks will be put in charge of a new company not yet formed. There is, besides, a hose carriage at Goffe's Falls and one at Amoskeag. There are scattered all over the thickly settled part of the city two hundred and forty-seven hydrants supplied from the water-works and thirty-seven reservoirs and cisterns supplied from brooks and ponds. The department uses ten thousand feet of hose ; the total value of its engines, carriages, hose, etc., is not far from thirty-two thousand dollars ; and its cost in 1873 was nearly fourteen thousand dollars.

A fire alarm telegraph was constructed in 1872 at a cost of sixteen thousand dollars. It is a network of seventeen miles of wire, traversing the compact part of the city and reaching to Amoskeag and Piscataquog villages, Hallsville and Bakersville. There are thirty-three alarm boxes, whose keys are kept at houses or stores in their immediate vicinity, and five strikers, situated on the city hall, the Lincoln-street and Ash-street school-houses, the engine-house in Piscataquog village and a tower at the north end of the city. There are three large gongs, one at the Amoskeag machine shop and two at the engine-house, and eight small gongs upon the houses of the engineers and others.

Connected with the department is a firemen's relief association, a tax upon whose members is levied for the assistance of any one of them who is hurt at a fire. It was organized on the fourteenth of February, 1873, and has about one hundred members. Its president is B. C. Kendall; its vice-president, Joel Daniels; its secretary, J. E. Merrill; its treasurer, Horatio Fradd.

PUBLIC LIBRARY.

In 1795 a number of gentlemen of Derryfield and its vicinity established themselves as "The Proprietors of the Social Library in Derryfield." The association was continued till 1833 when it was dissolved and the books divided among the members. The "Manchester Atheneum" was established on the nineteenth of February, 1844. Its members formed a library, museum and reading-room. In 1846 it received from the Amoskeag Company a gift of one thousand dollars, and of five hundred from the Stark Mills, and the next year the Manchester Print-Works made a donation of five hundred dollars. In 1854 the library contained nearly three thousand volumes and in that year, after an act to authorize the transaction had been passed by the legislature, the property of the Atheneum was transferred to the city and the library was made free. By the conditions of the deed the city must make an annual appropriation of a thousand dollars for the purchase of books and provide for meeting the running expenses. The entire management of the library was to be vested in a board of nine trustees, of whom the mayor and president of the common council for the time being are *ex-officio* members, and the rest are chosen by the trustees and aldermen in convention. When first chosen they were to hold their office severally for one, two, three, four, five, six and seven years, and as one retired, his place was filled by another who was elected for seven years. The library prospered finely till 1856, when the fire of the fifth of February in Patten's block, where it was situated, nearly annihilated it. Its remains were taken to Smyth's block and thence to rooms in Merchants' Exchange, but, after the rebuilding of Patten's block, were removed to it in 1857. In July, 1871, it was located in a brick building erected for its use at a cost of thirty thousand dollars upon a lot on Franklin street which was given by the Amoskeag Company.

PUBLIC LIBRARY.

The first board of trustees elected consisted of Samuel D. Bell, Daniel Clark, David Gillis, William P. Newell, Ezekiel A. Straw, William C. Clarke, Samuel N. Bell. In 1862 David Gillis was succeeded by Samuel Webber, and he in 1865 gave place to Phinehas Adams. Upon the death of Samuel D. Bell in July, 1868, Waterman Smith was appointed and he in 1873 was succeeded by Nathan P. Hunt. Upon the death of William C. Clarke in April, 1872, Isaac W. Smith was chosen to fill the vacancy. The remaining trustees have been re-elected as often as their terms expired. Samuel N. Bell has been the treasurer of the board from its formation. William C. Clarke was its clerk up to the time of his death, the vacancy being filled by the election of Isaac W. Smith. Francis B. Eaton was the librarian from 1854 till October, 1863, when he resigned and Marshall P. Hall was appointed. He served till June, 1865, and was then succeeded by Ben: F. Stanton. The latter in April, 1866, gave place to Charles H. Marshall, the present incumbent.

There are now in the library about seventeen thousand seven hundred volumes, in which are reckoned about nine hundred pamphlets and eighteen maps. With it is connected a reading-room, supplied with sixty periodicals, and both are open eight hours, day and evening, six days in the week, throughout all but six weeks of the year. The late Dr. Oliver Dean, who was so prominent in connection with the early manufacturing interests of the city, left the library five thousand dollars, whose income must be devoted to the purchase of books. In 1872 it was given by the late Hon. Gardner Brewer of Boston a collection of six hundred and eighty-three volumes, many of them valuable works, and which is known as the "Brewer Donation." The salary of the librarian is eight hundred dollars, and the annual cost of the library, outside of the necessary appropriation of a thousand dollars, is not far from two thousand dollars. During the two hundred and forty days in which the library was open in 1873 for the delivery of books the number drawn was thirty-five thousand one hundred and eighty, a daily average of one hundred and forty-six, and of these only four were missing at the end of the year.

WATER-WORKS.

It has been mentioned that, startled by the burning of the town-house in 1844, the town chose a committee, one of whose members, the Hon. E. A. Straw, is the president of the present board of water commissioners, to examine the sources of water supply for the town. It had been supposed that the brooks which crossed it would furnish all the water that was needed at a moderate cost, but the committee, after making the necessary surveys, reported that Massabesic pond was the only sufficient source. The cost of bringing it thence was an insurmountable obstacle, and the citizens contented themselves with small reservoirs. But the matter was continually coming up in one way and another. Private enterprise attempted what the town shrank from doing. In 1845 the Manchester Aqueduct Company was chartered by the legislature; in 1852 the Manchester Aqueduct obtained a charter, as did a company of the same name in 1857; the last organization of the kind was in 1865 when the City Aqueduct was incorporated. The city was asked to take stock in the latter but refused. All three organizations failed of their mission, being generally unwilling to undertake a work of so much magnitude and whose results were doubtful. In 1860 the Hon. James A. Weston, the Hon. Jacob F. James and the Rev. William Richardson made a large number of surveys and reported upon them. Another report was made by J. B. Sawyer in 1869. In 1871 the city councils appointed a committee to conduct an examination of the sources of water supply to be made by a competent engineer. The committee selected William J. McAlpine of Pittsfield, Mass., for that purpose, and he, after a personal examination of the neighborhood, delivered a public lecture upon the subject and made a report which was published at the time, recommending Massabesic pond as the most available source of supply.

It had at length been discovered that the construction and control of water-works would be better conducted by the city than by private enterprise, and in 1871 the city councils requested of the state legislature authority for the undertaking. That authority was granted by the act of the thirtieth of June, 1871, and on the first day of August an ordinance, in accordance with the act, was passed by the city councils. The city was empowered by the legislature to construct water-works at a cost of not over six hundred thousand dollars to be raised by loan or taxation, and to appoint a board of seven commissioners to have them in charge, of which the mayor is an *ex-officio* member. There were elected by the mayor and aldermen, in whom the choice was vested, the Hon. E. A. Straw, the Hon. E. W. Harrington, the Hon. William P. Newell, Aretas Blood, Alpheus Gay, A. C. Wallace. The Hon. S. N. Bell was chosen their clerk by the board. By the terms of the act these were to hold office one, two, three, four, five and six years respectively, the length of each commissioner's term of office to be determined by lot, and thereafter upon the retirement of each member one was to be chosen for the term of six years. The retiring members have thus far been re-elected.

The commissioners were directed by the city councils to examine carefully different systems of water-works, especially the direct-pressure system, so called, and they visited for this purpose Ogdensburg, N. Y., Montreal, P. Q., Norwich, Conn., Worcester, Mass., and other places where water-works were in operation. They employed Col. J. T. Fanning, who had superintended the construction of water-works at Norwich, to make surveys of water-sheds in the vicinity, and his report favored the adoption of Massabesic lake as a source of supply. Among the different sources which had been considered were Merrimack and Piscataquog rivers, Dorr, Chase, Burnham, and Stevens ponds, Maple Falls brook and Sawyer pond combined, and Massabesic lake. In April, 1872, a public hearing was given by the commissioners to all persons interested and then a vote was taken to determine what source should be used. The result of the ballot was, five in favor of Massabesic lake, one in favor of Burnham's pond and one in favor of the latter as a present source of supply. After the choice had thus been made, it was decided to adopt hydraulic power as a means for pumping the water, and to locate the pumping station near the old Haseltine mill-site, the dam across Cohas brook near the Clough & Foster saw-mill and the distributing reservoir upon the summit of the hill at Manchester Centre near the "old parsonage." After these preliminaries had been settled and Col. Fanning had been appointed chief engineer of the water-works, the necessary plans were drawn and contracts made for the supply and laying of the pipes, the necessary machinery, etc. Land which might be flowed by the dam at the lake was acquired from the owners. The work was begun in July, 1872, and finished, substantially, in the fall of 1874, occupying over two years in all, and costing about the amount allowed by the legislative act, — six hundred thousand dollars. In Judge Potter's history of Manchester, published in 1856, the hope is expressed that the water of Massabesic lake may be brought into the city at no distant day. "It is estimated," says he, "that by a dam at these falls (the present location of the water-works dam) the water of the Massabesic can be brought into the city for eighty thousand dollars." Water was pumped from the lake into the city on the fourth of July, 1874.

Massabesic lake, which has thus been irrevocably fixed as the source of supply for some time to come, lies easterly of the city, has an area of twenty-four hundred acres, a water-shed of forty-five square miles and a circumference of twenty miles on the shore line. Dr. S. Dana Hayes, state assayer of Massachusetts, has made an analysis of its water and declares it "remarkably pure, being preferable to that now supplied to any of the large cities in the United States." The amount of its flow is estimated to be not less than forty million gallons a day. At its outlet by Cohas brook a dam has been built of granite masonry and hard earth embankments to a height of twenty-four feet from the lake's level. The water flows through gateways from the pent-up brook into a canal of fourteen hundred feet in length and through a wooden cylinder called a "penstock," six hundred feet long, to the wheels which it drives and the pumps which it feeds. Thence it is driven through the force-main, seven thousand feet long and twenty inches in diameter, to the reservoir at Manchester Centre, whence it issues to radiate through twenty miles of pipe in the city proper, reaching Elm street in a distance of thirteen thousand five hundred feet through twenty-inch pipe laid in the highway through Massabesic and Park streets. The Amoskeag Company's reservoir was used by the water-works after their distribution pipe had been laid, and after the pumping machinery had been set the lake's water was pumped into it till the completion of the reservoir at the Centre. That has a capacity of sixteen million gallons. It is one hundred and fifty-two feet above Elm street at the city hall, one hundred and eighty-eight feet above the level of Canal street at the Concord railway passenger station, and one hundred and thirteen feet in vertical height from the pumps which supply it.

The house which contains the pumping machinery and a tenement for the use of the man in charge of it is located a short distance from the lake. It is seventy feet long and forty-five feet wide and is built of brick with granite trimmings. A broad avenue extends from the reservoir to the pumping station, ending in a driveway along the penstock and canal and over the dam. The pumps and wheels are worked under a fall of forty-five feet, equal to five hundred horse-powers, having the capacity to pump and furnish water for a city of one hundred and twenty-five thousand inhabitants. There are two turbine wheels of three feet diameter each, and two pairs of upright pumps of the class known as "bucket and plunger." They are double-acting, forcing the water toward the reservoir with both up and down strokes. The shafts and gearing are so arranged that either turbine can be made to drive either pair of pumps at full speed, or either turbine may be made to drive both pairs of pumps at a slower speed. The four pump cylinders have a diameter of sixteen inches and the stroke of the pumps is forty inches.

The pumps can be run at a maximum speed of thirty strokes a minute, and at this speed each pair will deliver one thousand nine hundred and eighty gallons of water a minute, or two million eight hundred and fifty-one thousand two hundred gallons in twenty-four hours. This would be equal to supplying sixty gallons a day to each of forty-seven thousand five hundred persons. Both pairs of pumps will together deliver five million seven hundred and two thousand four hundred gallons in twenty-four hours, or a supply of sixty gallons a day for upwards of ninety thousand persons. The distribution pipes are made of wrought iron, cement-lined. The force-main and supply-main are each twenty inches in diameter, while the other pipes are, respectively, fourteen, twelve, ten, eight, six and four inches. The pipes and machinery were made and set by contract;

Manchester Water-Works—Pumping Station.

the reservoir was built directly by the commissioners. The annual income from the works, arising from the fees of consumers and the rates paid by the city for hydrants, was in 1873 about eighteen thousand dollars or about three per cent. of the cost of the works, and at the close of 1874 had reached a rate of twenty-five thousand dollars annually.

FIRES.

Manchester has had its share of fires, though it has never been the victim of one of those conflagrations, so common of late years, which consume a city in a night. The earliest fire of much consequence was that which, May 14, 1840, destroyed the Amoskeag Company's mill upon an island in the river at Amoskeag Falls, which was built for a machine-shop, and used subsequently for the manufacture of tickings and was known as the "Island mill."

In 1844, on the twelfth of August, occurred the fire which consumed the town house, to which reference has already been made. The attic was then occupied as an armory by the "Stark Guards" and the "Granite Fusileers." There the fire was started by a lighted paper carelessly thrown upon the floor, and there it burned unnoticed till it gathered such headway as to be beyond control. The post-office was then kept in the building, and its contents, together with those of the stores which occupied the lower story, were saved. J. C. Emerson, who had been the publisher of several newspapers, had a printing-office in the third story, and that, with the effects of the military companies, was destroyed. The loss to the town and individuals was about thirty thousand dollars.

There were still left at Amoskeag Falls in what was then Goffstown two wooden mills built by the Amoskeag Company or its predecessors in the early days, which occupied the spot where the paper-mill of P. C. Cheney & Co. now stands and which were known as the "old mill" and the "bell mill." They were heated by twenty-eight old-fashioned box-stoves for burning wood, and one man built the fires in each of them every day. Early in the morning of March 28, 1848, sparks flew from a fire already kindled, while the man was starting others, and set fire to the wood work. The mills were but fourteen feet apart, saturated with oil, and were consumed at once. The loss was estimated at seventy thousand dollars. Till then the famous "A. C. A." tickings had been made there.

March 16, 1850, a fire broke out in the north end of what was then called number two mill, belonging to the Stark corporation, and burned the roof and upper story, causing a loss of thirty thousand dollars. Wooden pulleys were then used for the belting to run over, as it went up through the floors, and the heat generated by the friction was intense. As long as the machinery was in motion, the current of air it excited kept the lint from contact with the hot wheels, but when that ceased and the pulleys happened to be over-heated, the blaze was quickly spread. At that time the operatives came into the mill at five o'clock and worked two hours before going out to breakfast. They left at once when the machinery stopped and were out of the building when the fire was discovered.

July 5, 1852, Baldwin & Co.'s steam-mill on Manchester street, which stood where D. B. Varney's brass-foundry now is, was burned, together with several buildings adjacent and across the street. It was feared at one time that the fire would reach to Hanover street. The wind was high and shingles heated to live coals were blown as far as the old high-school house on Lowell street. The house on the "Harris estate," on the corner of Hanover and Pine streets, occupied by Col. Phinehas Adams, the agent of the Stark Mills, was set on fire by sparks.

About five o'clock in the morning of September 22, 1853, a fire broke out in the drying-room of the printing department of the Manchester Print-Works, where then the cloths were hung in great quantities on frames to dry. The facilities for putting out fires were then of small acccunt and the main building of the printery was consumed, other buildings being saved only by the greatest exertions. The loss was about two hundred and sixty-five thousand dollars.

In the night of the fifteenth of July, 1855, occurred the fire which destroyed the south half of number one mill owned by the Manchester Print-Works. The lamp in a watchman's lantern fell, as he was passing through the carding-room in the lower story, into a pile of yarn. The first application of water checked the flames, and, the fire being considered extinguished, the people who had gathered set out to return home, when the breaking out of the fire anew called them back. The blaze mounted directly to the attic and it was impossible to quench it. The mill, up to the brick wall which divided it midway, was destroyed, causing a loss of about two hundred and seventy thousand dollars. One unfortunate circumstance helped the flames. The water from the Amoskeag Company's reservoir on Harrison street, especially provided for use in case of fire, strangely failed in a little while and the cause was not discovered till some time after the fire. The water was brought through the mill-yards by a pipe of eight inches in diameter which was laid just in front of the buildings. Eleven years before a gate had been put in the pipe, where it ran through the yard of the Stark Mills, to stop the water temporarily. The rod which moved it up and down was fastened to it by a nut and screw. When the need for stopping the water had ceased, the gate was lifted up, fastened and left. In process of time the iron rusted, the nut came off and the gate fell, with no one's knowledge, shutting off all the water but a little which flowed underneath the gate where a chance stick kept it from entirely closing. The pipe, of course, was full all the way, and, when this fire broke out, there was an apparent plenty of water, but the supply was soon exhausted and the mill was burned. There is now a pipe of fourteen inches in diameter which was laid beneath the track of the Concord railway and has no gate in it but at the reservoir.

While this was still raging, an alarm was sounded from the main street, a fire having broken out between Manchester and Hanover streets, just back of Elm, which threatened to sweep the whole square. After this had been burning an hour, the Hon. T. T. Abbot, then mayor of the city, came to the mills to implore help, fearing that the fire would cross Hanover street and go northward. At that time there were seven hand-engines in the city, of which the city owned four and the corporations the rest. The latter, however, were at the city's service except when needed at the mills. Waterman Smith was then agent of the Manchester Mills, Charles H. Dalton of the Print-Works, David Gillis of the Amoskeag New Mills and Phinehas Adams of the Stark Mills. The first three remained to look after the fire in the mill, while Mr. Adams took one engine to help the city. He ransacked the Stark Mills for hose and stretched a line of it from a hydrant in the mill-yard up to Hanover street, where it did good service. This later fire was started in a paint-shop on the back street between Manchester and Hanover streets and a little east of Elm street. It consumed a good deal of property in the heart of the square, burned all the wooden buildings on Elm street which then occupied the spot where Merchants' Exchange now stands, but did not cross Hanover, Manchester or Chestnut streets, though the First Congregational church and other buildings on the north side of Hanover street were scorched.

About five o'clock in the morning of February 5, 1856,

fire was discovered in the building known as "Patten's block," which stood on Elm street, just north of the city hall, taking up the rest of that square. It was occupied in part by stores, in part by the public library and lawyers' offices, and in part by the three establishments of the "Daily Mirror," "Daily American" and "Weekly Union." Nothing could check the flames and the building was consumed, nearly all the volumes in the library being burned. The loss was estimated at seventy-five thousand dollars.

In the afternoon of September 3, 1856, a fire broke out near Elm street between Concord and Lowell streets. It burned a house belonging to William Patten (the owner of Patten's block), stores and stables, and injured a house owned by E. P. Offutt where the flames were stayed. A line of hose was stretched from the yard of the Stark Mills up Spring street to the fire, and this was kept in use all night long, a channel being dug to lay it in beneath the railway track, so that the cars would not cut it. The loss at this fire was about ten thousand dollars.

A fire at Janesville, June 3, 1857, which destroyed Baldwin & Co.'s steam-mill, there being no water to extinguish it, was remarkable for the death of Charles Horr, who was killed by the falling of a brick wall expanded by the heat, upon the building he was in, crushing it to the ground and burying him beneath it.

May 19, 1862, a fire broke out on Manchester street, about halfway between Chestnut and Elm, which burned across to Hanover street, destroying a number of tenement-houses, causing a loss of fifteen thousand dollars.

On the fifth of the next June a fire burned the brewery and steam-mill belonging to Joseph A. Haines and A. C. Wallace, situated in Piscataquog village on the south bank of the Piscataquog river. The sparks set fire to the wooden bridge which crossed the river there, and it was consumed. The loss was about twelve thousand dollars.

December 20, 1865, a fire broke out in the state reform school on the river road about two miles from the city hall. One steam fire engine reached there after some delay and, when it was found that another was needed, the one in Piscataquog village was sent for, it not being thought advisable to take from the city proper the two engines which were there. The greater part of the building was burned to the ground.

On the first of March, 1867, at three o'clock in the morning, fire destroyed an old frame building at Amoskeag village, belonging to the Amoskeag Company and occupied by D. K. White for a grocery store and by Crain, Leland & Moody for the manufacture of shoes. A building which stood near by was partly burned. The loss amounted to twenty-five thousand dollars, much stock and machinery being ruined.

August 29, 1869, a fire, which started in the carding-room of the stocking-mill occupied by John Brugger in Mechanics' Row, burned fifteen thousand dollars' worth of stock and machinery.

A little before three o'clock on the morning of July 8, 1870, broke out the largest fire which ever occurred in the city outside of the mills. It is supposed to have caught from a steam-boiler in premises occupied by S. C. Merrill on Manchester street near Elm. Thence it spread with great rapidity and could not be checked till it had burned over nearly the whole territory bounded by Hanover and Chestnut streets, Manchester south back street and Elm east back street. The water which came from Hanover square pond failed at a critical moment, and it was feared at times that the Manchester House would be burned and that the flames would go east of Chestnut and north of Hanover streets. The First Congregational church again suffered, its surface being scorched and the old trees which stood in front of it being ruined. There was then no fire alarm telegraph, and it was a long time before the engine in Piscataquog village could be obtained; there were no water-works and the supply of water was wholly inadequate. The engines of the Manchester Print-Works and the Amoskeag Company rendered valuable aid in subduing the flames. Among the buildings burned were the First Baptist church on the corner of Manchester and Chestnut streets, the Masonic Temple, a hotel, printing-offices, stores, shops and tenement-houses. The loss was set at two hundred thousand dollars. The wind blew a gale that night, and large sparks flew as far as Col. Franklin Tenney's residence at the corner of Elm and Myrtle streets. The fire at one time threatened to burn the whole city and there was talk of blowing up buildings to arrest its progress.

In the afternoon of June 6, 1871, the bridge over the Merrimack river belonging to the Manchester & North Weare railway was destroyed by a fire which is supposed to have caught from sparks from a locomotive engine. It burned very quickly and in a few minutes fell into the river.

MARSHALS AND ASSISTANT MARSHALS.

FROM 1846 TO THE PRESENT TIME.

1846.

Marshal—George T. Clark.
Assistant Marshals { Daniel L. Stevens, James Wallace.

1847.

Marshal—Daniel L. Stevens.
Assistant Marshal—Joseph M. Rowell.

1848.

Marshal—Robert Means.
Assistant Marshal—Henry G. Lowell.

1849.

Marshal—Robert Means.
Assistant Marshal—Henry G. Lowell.

1850.

Marshal—Joseph M. Rowell.
Assistant Marshal—George P. Prescott.

1851.

Marshal—Daniel L. Stevens.
Assistant Marshal—Henry G. Lowell.

1852.

Marshal—Daniel L. Stevens.
Assistant Marshal—William H. Hill.

1853.

Marshal—William H. Hill.
Assistant Marshal—Isaac Tompkins.

1854.

Marshal—William H. Hill.
Assistant Marshal—Henry Clough.

1855.

Marshal—Samuel Hall.
Assistant Marshal—Albert P. Colby.

1856.

Marshal—Henry G. Lowell.
Assistant Marshal—Isaac W. Farmer.

1857.

Marshal—Henry G. Lowell.
Assistant Marshal—I. W. Farmer.

1858.

Marshal—Henry G. Lowell.
Assistant Marshal—William B. Patten.

1859.

Marshal—I. W. Farmer.
Assistant Marshal—William B. Patten.

1860.

Marshal—John L. Kelly.
Assistant Marshal—Justin Spear.

1861.

Marshal—William B. Patten.
Assistant Marshal—Benjamin C. Haynes.

1862.

Marshal—William B. Patten.
Assistant Marshal—Benjamin C. Haynes.

1863.

Marshal—John S. Yeaton.
Assistant Marshal—Daniel R. Prescott.

1864.

Marshal—John S. Yeaton. Died April 27, 1864.
Henry Clough, *vice* Yeaton.
Assistant Marshal—Daniel R. Prescott, continued in office from 1863.
Daniel W. Fling, elected April 27, 1864.

1865.

Marshal—Benjamin C. Haynes.
Assistant Marshal—Daniel R. Prescott.

1866.

Marshal—Henry Clough.
Assistant Marshal—Daniel R. Prescott.

1867.

Marshal—William B. Patten.
Assistant Marshal—Eben Carr.

1868.

Marshal—William B. Patten.
Assistant Marshal—Eben Carr.

1869.

Marshal—William B. Patten.
Assistant Marshal—Eben Carr.

1870.

Marshal—William B. Patten.
Assistant Marshal—Eben Carr.

1871.

Marshal—William B. Patten.
Assistant Marshal—John D. Howard.

1872.

Marshal—William B. Patten.
Assistant Marshal—John D. Howard.

1873.

Marshal—Gilman H. Kimball.
Assistant Marshal—Daniel R. Prescott.

1874.

Marshal—Darwin A. Simons.
Assistant Marshal—Daniel R. Prescott.

1875.

Marshal—Darwin A. Simons.
Assistant Marshal—Daniel R. Prescott.

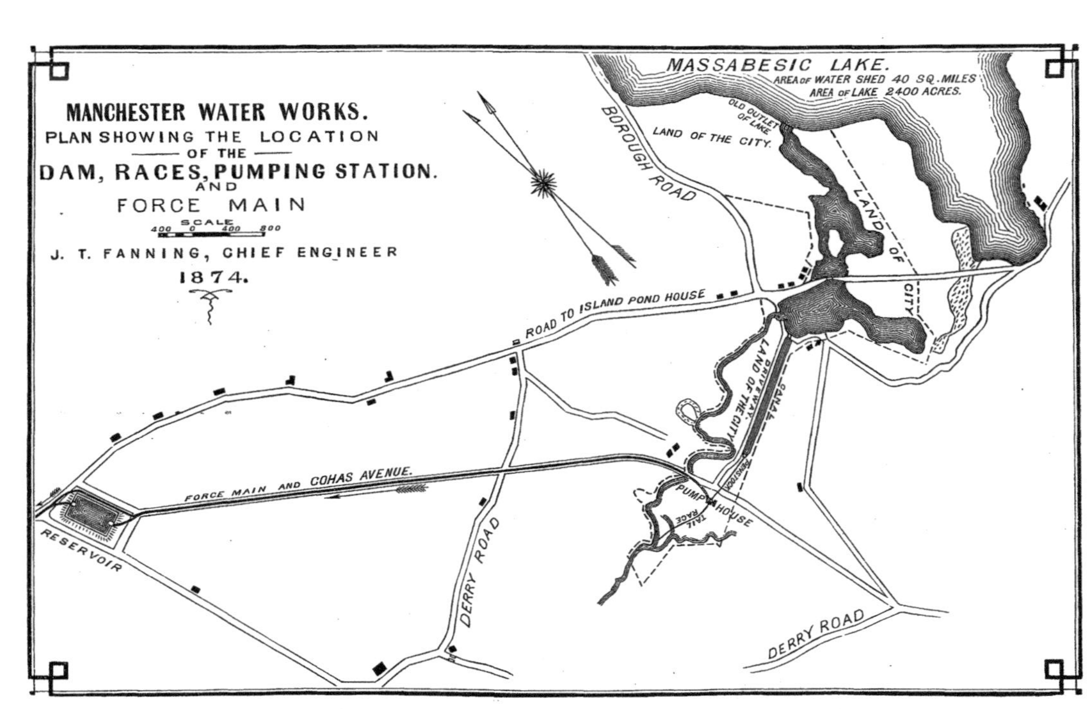
MANCHESTER WATER WORKS.
PLAN SHOWING THE LOCATION
OF THE
DAM, RACES, PUMPING STATION.
AND
FORCE MAIN
SCALE
400 0 400 800
J. T. FANNING, CHIEF ENGINEER
1874.
MASSABESIC LAKE.
AREA OF WATER SHED 40 SQ. MILES
AREA OF LAKE 2400 ACRES.
OLD OUTLET OF LAKE
LAND OF THE CITY.
BOROUGH ROAD
LAND OF CITY
ROAD TO ISLAND POND HOUSE
LAND OF THE CITY
DRIVEWAY
CANAL
PENSTOCK
PUMP HOUSE
TAIL RACE
FORCE MAIN AND COHAS AVENUE.
RESERVOIR
DERRY ROAD
DERRY ROAD

ENGINEERS OF THE FIRE DEPARTMENT,

FROM 1846 TO THE PRESENT TIME.

1846.

Chief Engineer—William C. Clarke.
Assistant Engineers—William Shepherd, Jonathan T. P. Hunt, Walter French, Ezekiel A. Straw, John P. Adriance, Henry G. Lowell.

1847.

Chief Engineer—William C. Clarke.
Assistant Engineers—Ezekiel A. Straw, Henry G. Lowell, Jonathan T. P. Hunt, John P. Adriance, Joseph Mitchell, William P. Newell.

1848.

Chief Engineer—William C. Clarke.
Assistant Engineers—John P. Adriance, Jonathan T. P. Hunt, Ezekiel A. Straw, Frederick A. Hussey, Caleb Duxbury, George W. Tilden.

1849.

Chief Engineer—Isaac C. Flanders.
Assistant Engineers—Cyrus Baldwin, Frederick Smyth, Samuel W. Parsons, John Twombly, Charles A. Luce, Samuel P. Greeley.

1850.

Chief Engineer—Warren L. Lane.
Assistant Engineers—Jacob F. James, Samuel W. Parsons, Frederick Smyth, Charles A. Luce, Daniel L. Stevens, Cyrus Baldwin.

1851.

Chief Engineer—Jacob F. James,* Daniel Clark.†
Assistant Engineers—Samuel W. Parsons,* Charles A. Luce, Harry Leeds, James A. Stearns, Frederick Smyth, Cyrus Baldwin,* Ezekiel A. Straw,† Samuel H. Ayer,† David Gillis,† Alonzo Smith.†

1852.

Chief Engineer—Daniel Clark.
Assistant Engineers—James A. Stearns, Alonzo Smith, Harry Leeds, Jonathan T. P. Hunt, John H. Maynard, Phinehas Adams, Caleb Duxbury.

*Resigned February 4, 1852. †Appointed February 4, 1852.

1853.

Chief Engineer—John H. Maynard.

Assistant Engineers—Charles H. Brown, John B. Clarke, James A. Stearns, Caleb Duxbury, Harry Leeds, William B. Webster, John Q. A. Sargent, Reuben D. Mooers, John L. Kelly.

1854.

Chief Engineer—John H. Maynard.

Assistant Engineers—Caleb Duxbury, William B. Webster, John Q. A. Sargent, Charles H. Brown, John L. Kelly, John B. Clarke, Reuben D. Mooers, Harry Leeds, Andrew C. Wallace.

1855.

Chief Engineer—Jacob F. James.

Assistant Engineers—Alden W. Sanborn, Charles H. Brown, Francis H. Lyford, Peter S. Brown, Nathaniel Baker, 2d, Charles Bunton, George W. Riddle, Ephraim T. Corey, Henry T. Mowatt, Alpheus Gay, jr.

1856.

Chief Engineer—John H. Maynard.

Assistant Engineers—Charles H. Brown, John L. Kelly, John Q. A. Sargent, Harry Leeds, Reuben D. Mooers, Caleb Duxbury, Orison Hardy, Edward W. Harrington, Phinehas Adams.

1857.

Chief Engineer—Peter S. Brown.

Assistant Engineers—Phinehas Adams, Charles H. Brown, John L. Kelly, Israel Dow, Orison Hardy, Eben French, Samuel W. Parsons, Jonathan T. P. Hunt, Alfred G. Fairbanks, Alpheus Gay, jr.

1858.

Chief Engineer—Peter S. Brown.

Assistant Engineers—John L. Kelly, Charles H. Brown, Alpheus Gay, jr., Edward W. Harrington, Phinehas Adams, Sidney Smith, Samuel G. Langley, Eben French.

1859.

Chief Engineer—Jonathan T. P. Hunt.

Assistant Engineers—Phinehas Adams, John Moulton, Samuel W. Parsons, John L. Kelly, Benjamin F. Martin, Samuel G. Langley, Eben French, William T. Evans, Albe C. Heath, Daniel W. Fling.

1860.

Chief Engineer—Jonathan T. P. Hunt.

Assistant Engineers—Daniel W. Fling, Alpheus Branch, Israel Dow, John C. Young, Charles H. G. Foss, Albe C. Heath, Brown S. Flanders.

1861.

Chief Engineer—Albe C. Heath.
Assistant Engineers—Daniel W. Fling, Israel Dow, Charles H. G. Foss, Brown S. Flanders, Andrew J. Butterfield, John C. Young.

1862.

Chief Engineer—Daniel W. Fling.
Assistant Engineers—Charles H. G. Foss, Israel Dow, Edward W. Harrington, Nehemiah S. Bean.

1863.

Chief Engineer—Daniel W. Fling.
Assistant Engineers—Charles H. G. Foss, Israel Dow, Albe C. Heath, Nehemiah S. Bean.

1864.

Chief Engineer—Albe C. Heath.
Assistant Engineers—Ezra Huntington, Israel Dow, Moses O. Pearson, Daniel W. Fling, Nehemiah S. Bean, Freeman Higgins.

1865.

Chief Engineer—Nehemiah S. Bean.
Assistant Engineers—Daniel W. Fling, Israel Dow, Charles H. G. Foss, Freeman Higgins, Benjamin C. Kendall, Ezra Huntington.

1866.

Chief Engineer—Nehemiah S. Bean.
Assistant Engineers—Daniel W. Fling, Israel Dow, Freeman Higgins, Ezra Huntington, Benjamin C. Kendall.

1867.

Chief Engineer—Israel Dow.
Assistant Engineers—Edwin P. Richardson, Elijah Chandler, Benjamin C. Kendall, Gilman H. Kimball.

1868.

Chief Engineer—Israel Dow.
Assistant Engineers—Benjamin C. Kendall, Edwin P. Richardson, Elijah Chandler, Wilberforce Ireland.

1869.

Chief Engineer—Edwin P. Richardson.
Assistant Engineers—Benjamin C. Kendall, Wilberforce Ireland, Andrew C. Wallace, Elijah Chandler, George Holbrook.

1870.

Chief Engineer—Edwin P. Richardson.

Assistant Engineers—Benjamin C. Kendall, Wilberforce Ireland, Andrew C. Wallace, Elijah Chandler.

1871.

Chief Engineer—Benjamin C. Kendall.

Assistant Engineers—Wilberforce Ireland, Andrew C. Wallace, Elijah Chandler, William T. Evans.

1872.

Chief Engineer—Benjamin C. Kendall.

Assistant Engineers—Wilberforce Ireland, Andrew C. Wallace, Albion H. Lowell, William T. Evans.

1873.

Chief Engineer—Benjamin C. Kendall.

Assistant Engineers—Wilberforce Ireland, Andrew C. Wallace, Albion H. Lowell, Freeman Higgins.

1874.

Chief Engineer—Benjamin C. Kendall.

Assistant Engineers—Wilberforce Ireland, Andrew C. Wallace, Albion H. Lowell, Freeman Higgins.

1875.

Chief Engineer—Albion H. Lowell.

Assistant Engineers—Freeman Higgins, Wilberforce Ireland, Andrew C. Wallace, Benjamin C. Kendall.

SCHOOLS.

POPULAR education met with little favor in Derryfield's early days. Though voluntary subscriptions for school purposes had kept its children from growing up in total ignorance, it was not till 1781, when the town voted to hire a school-master for nine months of the next year, that a successful attempt was made to furnish the town with a public school. There were at that time no school-houses and the selectmen designated private dwellings in different parts of the town where school should be kept. In 1783 the selectmen, by making four divisions of the town for school purposes, originated the school-district system which continued eighty-five years. Subsequent changes made the number of districts three in 1798; five in 1808; seven in 1818; and later eight. But in 1840 the town was divided anew into nine, increased to eleven by the annexation of parts of Bedford and Goffstown in 1853, which remained very much the same till their abolishment in 1868, when the city assumed control of the schools as a whole. The first teacher whose name has been preserved was Jonathan Rand.

All but five of the present school buildings were built under the district system. District number two included the compact part of the city and the rest are indifferently designated now by their old numbers or by some circumstance of situation. In the suburban districts the houses have been built since 1840, and many of them have since been exchanged for less antique structures. In the compact part of the city the earliest houses were small, wooden, one-story structures, built thus in accordance with the advice of the late Chief-Justice Bell, that, as the city grew, permanent structures should take their place at the centres of population and they be removed to less thickly settled localities to await another change.

The dates of erection and the estimated value of the school-houses now standing, follow: The old high-school house, on the corner of Lowell and Chestnut streets, was built in 1841 and is valued at $6,500: the unused wooden house on the corner of Bridge and Union streets, in 1847, and is worth $500; the house on Park street near Elm, in 1847, and is worth $8,000; the wooden house at Webster's Mills, not far from that time, and is valued at $600; the house on Spring street near Elm, in 1848, and is worth $14,000; the house on the corner of Manchester and Chestnut streets, in 1853, and is worth $8,000; the Wilson-hill house was built of wood in 1855, valued at $3,300; in 1856 were built the house on the corner of Merrimack and Union streets, valued at $15,000, the house on Centre street in Piscataquog and the south house in the same village, both of wood, valued at $5,000 and $2,800 respectively; the house on the corner of Franklin and Pleasant streets in 1857, worth $18,000; the house on Blodget street in 1859, valued at $3,000; in 1860, or about that time, were built the wooden house near Massabesic pond, worth $1,400, the wooden house near Mosquito pond, worth $1,000, and the house at Amoskeag village, worth $3,700; the wooden house at Bakersville, in 1863, worth $3,500; the house near Harvey's mills, in 1865, worth $2,500; the wooden house at Hallsville, in 1866, worth $3,500; the present high-school house, on the corner of Lowell and Beech streets, in 1867, valued at $45,000; in 1870 were built the house on Main street in Piscataquog village, worth $12,000, and the house at Goffe's Falls, worth $3,-

600; in 1871 were built the house in the Stark district, worth $3,000, and the house on the corner of Lincoln and Merrimack streets, valued at $50,000; the last house built was in 1874, on the corner of Ash and Bridge streets, and is valued at $60,000. The last two are called as fine buildings as any in the state. Where no material has been specified, it is to be understood that brick was used. The total value of school property is $279,675.

The "old Falls school-house," which once stood on the "old Falls road" near the residence of the Hon. David Cross, was set on fire in August, 1859, and the Blodget-street house was at once built. When Amoskeag village was made a part of Manchester in 1853, the old wooden school-house, which now stands on the west side of the river on the road to Piscataquog, was annexed with it and was used for school purposes till 1860, when the brick house was built farther north. It then went into the hands of the Amoskeag Company, having since been used as a school-house, with their permission, from 1868 till 1873. When Piscataquog village was annexed, Bedford bequeathed with it to Manchester several old buildings which have given place to the present ones. A wooden school-house was built in 1842 on Amherst street near Janesville and moved in 1850 to the corner of Lowell and Jane streets. In 1871 it was taken to Spruce street to be used as a ward-room in ward six, and school has since been kept in it at times. Two wooden houses were built on Bridge street, a little west of Elm, in 1842 and 1843, respectively, and moved in 1845 to the lot on Spring street where a grammar-school house was subsequently built. In a year they were taken to the lot on the corner of Merrimack and Franklin streets where the court-house now stands, and moved thence in 1849 to the lot on the corner of Concord and Beech streets upon which the Unitarian church has since been built. They were subsequently sold to be made into dwellings, and were moved, one to Maple street between Concord and Lowell and the other to that neighborhood. A lot on the corner of Union and Concord streets, where the residence of John B. Varick now stands, had been bought on which to build a high-school house, but the dwellers in that neighborhood were opposed to it and the lot was sold four years afterward. A wooden house on the corner of Merrimack and Union streets gave way to a new building in 1856, being moved to Laurel street and made into a dwelling-house. A wooden house was built on the corner of Manchester and Chestnut streets in 1842, which gave place in 1853 to the present building and was moved to the lot on the corner of Pleasant and Franklin streets and subsequently disposed of. The Amoskeag Company has either given or sold at half-price the land used for school purposes in the compact part of the city.

In 1853 an act was passed by the state legislature to allow the city to consolidate the school-districts into one and to appoint a superintendent of schools, but other measures were incorporated in the bill, and when it was submitted to the people, as provided, it was rejected by them. Two years later, however, the boards of mayor and aldermen and of school committee were required by legislative enactment to appoint a superintendent of public instruction, but it was not till 1868 that the complete control of the schools was vested in the city as a unit, by act of the legislature, the measure not being submitted to the people. By the original charter the school committee were to be elected annually, one from each ward, but by the act of 1874 the school board is constituted of two from each ward to serve two years when the plan has been started, eight of whom shall be elected annually. By the act of 1870 the mayor of the city and the president of the common council were made *ex-officiis* members of the board.

The old high-school building, on the corner of Lowell

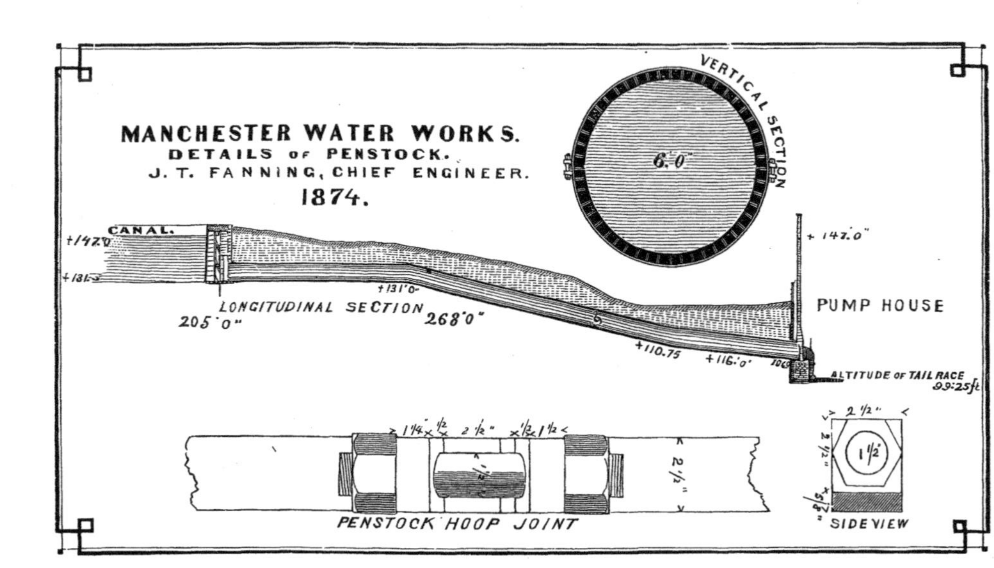
MANCHESTER WATER WORKS.
DETAILS OF PENSTOCK.
J. T. FANNING, CHIEF ENGINEER.
1874.
VERTICAL SECTION
6.0"
CANAL.
+147.0
+131.5
+131'0"
LONGITUDINAL SECTION
205'0"
268'0"
+147.0"
PUMP HOUSE
+110.75
+116.0"
ALTITUDE OF TAIL RACE
99.25 ft
PENSTOCK HOOP JOINT
SIDE VIEW

and Chestnut streets, was erected in 1841, at a cost of three thousand dollars, for a district school-house by district number two. The first master of the school was David P. Perkins, who was given a salary of two hundred and sixty-seven dollars. Mr. Perkins, was succeeded in 1843 by Joseph H. Wood, and he in 1844 by John G. Sherburne. The next year John W. Ray was elected master at a salary of five hundred dollars, which was increased by three hundred in 1848, and a high school was established. In 1849 Mr. Ray was succeeded by Amos Hadley, whose salary, at first six hundred dollars, was made eight hundred in 1853. Two years later John P. Newell became the principal, and he was followed in 1853 by Jonathan Tenney, who was given a salary of a thousand dollars the next year. Upon Mr. Tenney's resignation in 1854, Samuel Upton, who was then an assistant teacher, was promoted to the mastership, continuing in office one term. He was unwilling to remain longer in that position and Mr. Newell returned in 1855 to receive a salary of eleven hundred dollars. He taught till 1862, when he was succeeded by William W. Colburn at a salary of nine hundred dollars which was gradually increased to two thousand. He resigned in 1874 and was succeeded by Albert W. Bacheler at a salary of two thousand dollars. The district voted in 1850 to build a new high-school house at a cost of ten thousand dollars, but subsequently reconsidered its action, and it was not till seventeen years later that the plan was carried out. The school has grown rapidly within a few years and numbers over two hundred pupils. In its classical department several boys are annually prepared for admission to college.

The South grammar school was originally kept in a chapel on Concord street which had been used by the Episcopal society, from which it was moved in 1847 to the brick building on Park street which had been built for its use. A. M. Caverly was elected its principal in 1845 and taught till the spring of 1853, when Joseph E. Bennett was placed in temporary charge, being succeeded that year by William A. Webster who taught till the spring of 1861. Meanwhile, in 1857, the school had been transferred to its present location on the corner of Franklin and Pleasant streets. Josiah G. Dearborn became its master in 1861 and taught till 1866 when he was succeeded by Isaac L. Heath. Upon Mr. Heath's resignation in 1872, the present master, Daniel A. Clifford, was appointed.

The North grammar school was begun in 1848 in the brick building on Spring street, its first master being Moses T. Brown who taught till 1853, when Joseph E. Bennett had charge of it a few weeks till the appointment of William H. Ward. The latter was succeeded in 1857 by Henry C. Bullard who taught till the spring of 1865, when C. M. Barrows took charge. He resigned in December of that year and Francis W. Parker was appointed. He taught till the fall of 1868, being then succeeded by Jacob Eastman who taught till February, 1869. The term was finished by Elbridge D. Hadley, and that spring John S. Hayes was appointed, who taught two terms. In December, 1869, William E. Buck was elected master, who remained in charge till his removal, in September, 1874, together with part of the school, to the one in the northeast part of the city, known as the Ash-street grammar school, leaving the North grammar without a male teacher and with but a partial grammar grade.

The East grammar school was begun in 1867 in the new high-school house with two divisions gathered from the North and South grammar schools. The Wilson-hill school was then composed in part of scholars of a grammar grade. In the fall of 1868 another division was added to the East grammar and in the spring of 1869 it was moved to the old high-school building, where a first division was added and its first master, Lewis H. Dutton, appointed. He was succeeded in 1870 by Benjamin F. Dame, who was transferred with it to its present location on the corner of Lincoln and Merrimack streets. He resigned January 1, 1875, and was succeeded by Sylvester Brown.

The Park-street grammar school was organized as a public school in the spring of 1863. The building in which it was kept had been occupied by the South grammar school till 1857. From that time till 1861 it was unused. In the latter year the Roman Catholics obtained its use from district number two, and established in it a grammar school. Two years later the school was adopted by the city, with Thomas Corcoran as its master, and remained a public school till December, 1869, when it was discontinued. The Catholics still have the use of the building rent free.

With Piscataquog village in 1853 was annexed its present grammar school, which was taught by men in winter and women in summer till the spring of 1858, when James W. Locke became its master and continued in office two terms. He was followed in December by Joseph E. Bennett who taught one term. In the spring of 1859 Francis W. Parker taught one term, and in the fall Joseph G. Edgerly took charge of the school. He was succeeded in the spring of 1862 by Miss Marcia V. McQueston who taught one year. Her place was supplied by Miss Philinda P. Parker in the spring of 1863, who taught till the summer of 1867. Charles J. Darrah came in the fall and taught two terms, being succeeded in the spring of 1868 by Miss Annette McDoel, who taught one year. Lorenzo D. Henry taught from the spring of 1869 till the fall of 1870, when he was succeeded by Harry C. Hadley who taught one year. In the fall of 1871 Allen E. Bennett became the master. He continued in that position till the fall of 1873, when he was succeeded by Sylvester Brown. The latter was transferred, January 1, 1875, to the Lincoln street school, and A. M. Heath took his place. The school had always been kept in the Centre street building till 1874, when it was moved to the building on Main street.

Amoskeag village was annexed at the same time as Piscataquog, and its grammar school was kept after the same fashion till December, 1865, when Henry M. Putney became its teacher, continuing as such one year. Amos Wright succeeded him in December, 1866, and taught till the spring of 1868, when Lewis H. Dutton was elected and taught two terms. Then came Daniel A. Clifford in the winter of 1868 and taught one year. Alpha Messer taught from December, 1869, till the fall of 1871, when he was succeeded by Charles F. Morrill, who remained till the spring of 1873. He was followed by George P. Hadley, 2d, who taught one term. Miss Sarah B. Hadley taught the school from the fall of 1873 till January, 1874, when she was succeeded by the present teacher, Miss Emma A. H. Brown.

The intermediate school, organized as an ungraded school to afford instruction to those whom necessity or inclination kept from regular attendance throughout the school year, was first kept in the Museum building and similar places till January, 1854, when the brick house on the corner of Manchester and Chestnut streets was built for its use. Charles Aldrich, its first master, taught till the spring of 1858. The school was then closed for two terms, but re-opened in the winter of 1858, when Josiah G. Dearborn taught one term. He was succeeded in the spring of 1859 by Martin L. Stevens, who taught till the fall of 1861. Then William Harvey kept it two terms, and in the spring of 1862 Joseph G. Edgerly was transferred to it from the Piscataquog grammar school. He taught a few weeks and was then given leave of absence to enter the postal service of the Union army at Fortress Monroe. During his absence his place was filled by Orren C. Moore. He returned in the fall of 1862 and taught till the spring of 1864. Then Miss Emeline R. Brooks was placed in charge for two terms, Mr. Edgerly returning in the winter of 1864 and teaching one term. Wendell P. Hood followed him in the spring of 1865 and taught one term. Isaac L. Heath came in the fall of that year and taught till the spring of 1866, when he was transferred to the South grammar. Temporary teachers managed the school till December, 1866, when Mr. Edgerly again took it for one term, being succeeded in the spring by Elbridge D. Hadley who taught one term. In the fall of 1867 Samuel W. Clark took it and remained one year. The school was closed during the fall term of 1868, but opened in the winter, when Lewis H. Dutton taught one term, till his removal to the East grammar. In the spring of 1869 William E. Buck succeeded Mr. Dutton and taught two terms, till his removal to the North grammar. In December, 1869, Daniel A. Clifford took charge of it and continued its teacher three years, when he was appointed master of the South grammar. His place was taken in January, 1873, by Alfred S. Hall, who taught one term. The next term Sylvester Brown was its teacher, Mr. Hall returning in the fall of 1873 and teaching one year. The school was removed in the fall of 1874 to the old high-school building and Herbert W. Lull became its master.

The complete control of the schools and school-houses is vested in the school board, consisting at present of two members from each ward, half elected annually, who receive an annual compensation of ten dollars apiece. From the incorporation of the city till 1875 only one member was chosen from each ward. In 1871 the mayor and the president of the common council were made members *ex officiis*. The personal supervision and immediate government of the schools belong, under their direction, to the superintendent of public instruction, who is chosen once in two years by the mayor and aldermen and school committee in convention, and whose salary is eighteen hundred dollars. The salary of the master of the high school is two thousand dollars; of his first assistant eight hundred dollars; and of the others, five hundred. The masters of the grammar schools are paid fifteen hundred dollars, while their assistants and the teachers of the middle and primary schools receive three hundred and fifty dollars the first year, three hundred and seventy-five the second, four hundred the third and four hundred and fifty the fourth. The principal of the higher department of the school for instruction in the science of teaching receives six hundred dollars, and the principal of the lower department five hundred dollars. The music-master is paid fifteen hundred dollars, and an officer, with a salary of six hundred dollars, is annually appointed, whose sole business is to compel the attendance of truants.

There are in the city forty-four public schools, all but eight of which, located in the suburban districts, are graded. They are attended by over twenty-five hundred scholars, are kept in twenty-two different school-buildings and seventy-five school-rooms, and give employment to sixty-nine regular teachers and a permanent music-teacher, besides occasional writing and drawing-masters. Their cost in 1873, exclusive of construction and repairs, was about fifty thousand dollars, against three thousand one hundred dollars in 1844. The length of the school year is forty weeks, divided into one term of sixteen weeks and two terms of twelve weeks each. The school week is five days and the school day is six hours, in two sessions of three hours each, except in the primary schools whose afternoon session is but two hours long.

Among the schools is one which is used at once for the instruction of middle and primary scholars and the preparation of teachers. Young ladies who graduate from the high school may enter this as assistants and teach under the direction of the regular teachers, themselves becoming pupils in the science of instruction. Quite a number annually avail themselves of this opportunity and thus there is formed a permanent source of supply for educated teachers. There are naturally in Manchester many who are unable to attend day-schools and some of whom are thus forbidden an education they are eager to acquire. This matter provoked interest as early as 1854, when district number two established in Patten's block a free evening-school to educate in the common branches those who could not make use of the opportunities already theirs. This action seems to have had but a spasmodic force, as it was not till fourteen years afterward that another evening-school was begun. In the winter of 1868 the plan was resumed and has been continued yearly since, schools having been kept in the intermediate building, in the wooden houses on the corner of Bridge and Union streets and of Concord and Beech streets, in the police-court room and in the old high-school building. In 1873, besides the one which was kept in the latter house, another was organized in Piscataquog village. Each employs a principal and several assistants. They are begun in the fall, are kept four or five months and are attended with very gratifying results. The aggregate attendance in the two schools in 1873 was three hundred of both sexes and all ages above fifteen, and the number increases annually.

Several glee clubs in the schools are the natural outgrowth of the attention which is given to music. An alumni association connected with the high school has had an existence at intervals and was re-organized in January, 1873. There is an association of the teachers of all the schools which was begun in 1859 and has been kept up intermittently since. The last organization was formed in 1872. It meets fortnightly to discuss educational matters and is valued as a means of information and inspiration.

The association of the teachers of the state, in whose annual exercises the Manchester teachers bear a prominent part, was begun in the city hall in May, 1854.

The Roman Catholic population had supported some private schools in district number two previous to 1861, but in that year the district voted to give them the use of the Park-street building, and schools were kept there at the expense of the Catholics and under the superintendence of the Rev. William MacDonald, pastor of St. Ann's (Roman Catholic) church till 1863. In March of that year the school board voted to take charge of them and from time to time established others, so that in 1868 there were some half a dozen Roman Catholic schools, whose teachers were elected upon nomination by Mr. MacDonald and who wore in school the dress peculiar to nuns of Roman Catholic convents. These, besides the grammar school in the Park-street building, taught by Thomas Corcoran, a man of the same religious faith, were all supported at the city's expense. It became at last so patent that these schools were in fact controlled by one religious denomination, acting through the proper authorities, and that sectarianism was becoming an element in the public education, that at the election of teachers in 1868 by the school board those who wore the nun's dress were dropped from the list and their schools were discontinued. This action provoked a bitter controversy in the board and very great excitement in the city, but was not revoked. Mr. Corcoran continued in the pay of the city till December, 1869, when his name was dropped from the roll and his school was discontinued. The city has not, however, deprived the Roman Catholics of the use of the building which was given them in 1861 by district number two, and Mr. Corcoran still teaches there under their auspices.

The Roman Catholics support four schools, which are free to children of that denomination, the members of

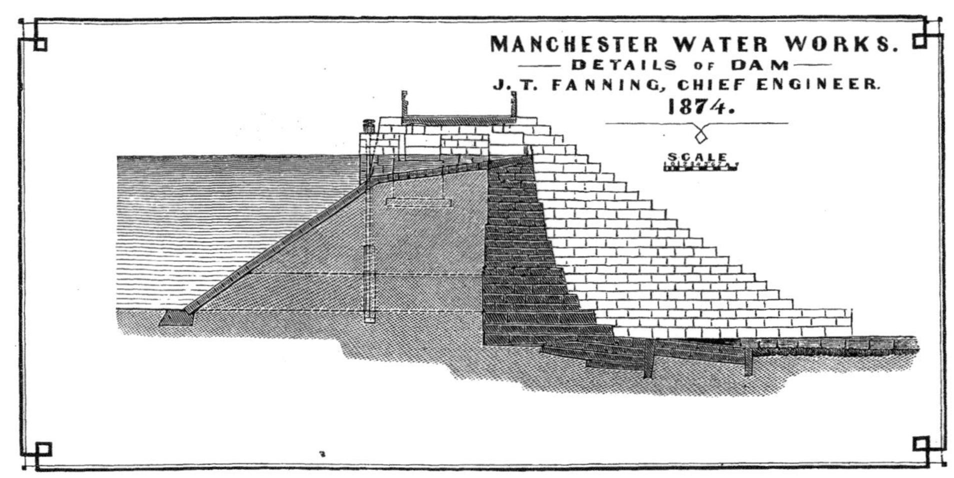
MANCHESTER WATER WORKS.
DETAILS OF DAM
J. T. FANNING, CHIEF ENGINEER.
1874.
SCALE

their churches being taxed to support them. The first of them was started fifteen years ago. The Rev. William MacDonald is their superintendent. The principal of the grammar school receives fourteen hundred dollars a year. The rest of the twenty teachers are all nuns, wearing the convent dress, and are paid three hundred dollars each. This makes an annual cost of seven thousand dollars for salaries, and this, together with the money needed for furniture, repairs and incidentals, is contributed by the churches of the denomination in the city.

The largest of their schools is the one on Park street, whose principal is Thomas Corcoran, assisted by several nuns, which contains eight rooms and has one hundred and thirty grammar scholars, one hundred and twenty middle scholars and two hundred primary scholars. On the corner of Lowell and Birch streets are kept four schools, primary and middle, employing four teachers and having two hundred and fifty scholars. In the vestry of St. Joseph's church are two schools, primary and middle, employing four teachers and having two hundred scholars. And on the corner of Union and Laurel streets is a school of the same size as the one on Birch street. An institution which teaches the higher branches, called Mount St. Mary's Academy, with which a primary department is, however, connected, is also supported by the denomination, but its doors are open to any one who will pay the tuition fees. The teachers, all nuns, are eight in number and there are on an average one hundred pupils.

SCHOOL OFFICERS.

SUPERINTENDENTS,

FROM THE ESTABLISHMENT OF THE OFFICE, AUGUST, 1855, TO THE PRESENT TIME.

1855–59. James O. Adams.
1859–60. John W. Ray.
1860–67. James O. Adams.
1867–75. Joseph G. Edgerly.

SCHOOL COMMITTEES,

FROM 1846 TO THE PRESENT TIME.

1846.

Archibald Stark,
Nathaniel Wheat,
Joseph Knowlton,
Moses Hill,
James McColley,
W. W. Brown,
C. H. Eastman.

1847.

Ephraim Stevens, jr.,
J. G. Sherburne,
Thomas Brown,
Moses Hill,
John S. Elliott,
W. W. Brown,
C. H. Eastman.

1848.

Ephraim Stevens, jr.,
John B. Clarke,
A. M. Chapin,
Archelaus Wilson,
James Hersey,
W. W. Brown,
William Grey.

1849.

A. M. Chapin,
Josiah Crosby,
Sylvanus Bunton,
David P. Perkins,
John S. Elliott,
J. Y. McQueston.

1850.

William G. Means,
Josiah Crosby,
Chandler E. Potter,
David P. Perkins,
John S. Elliott,
J. Y. McQueston.

1851.

A. M. Chapin,
Josiah Crosby,
J. C. Tasker,
F. B. Eaton,
A. B. Fuller,
Amos Abbott.

1852.

James O. Adams,
D. C. Bent,
J. C. Tasker,
F. B. Eaton,
J. E. Bennett,
C. H. Eastman.

1853.

James O. Adams,
William Grey,
Sylvanus Bunton,
Justin Spaulding,
A. G. Tucker,
C. H. Eastman.

1854.

T. T. Abbot,
William Sage,
J. C. Tasker,
John H. Goodale,
E. A. Jenks,
T. P. Sawin,
B. F. Wallace,
J. B. Quimby.

1855.

Reuben Dodge,
H. M. Bacon,
Jonathan Tenney,
E. M. Topliff,
Benjamin Currier,
S. D. Lord,
John O. Parker.

1856.

Reuben Dodge,
A. C. Heath,
Jonathan Tenney,
J. D. Patterson,
Benjamin Currier,
S. D. Lord,
B. F. Wallace,
D. P. Currier.

1857.

Seth T. Hill,
Ephraim Corey,
William L. Gage,
J. E. Bennett,
J. B. Hoitt,
J. Y. McQueston,
B. F. Wallace,
Thomas S. Montgomery.

1858.

Seth T. Hill,
E. B. Merrill,
F. B. Eaton,
Moses T. Brown,
J. B. Hoitt,
J. Y. McQueston,
George A. Bowman,
Thomas S. Montgomery.

1859.

Seth T. Hill,
E. B. Merrill,
Justus D. Watson,
Amos W. Sargent,
George H. Hubbard,
J. Y. McQueston,
James P. Walker,
Thomas S. Montgomery.

1860.

Seth T. Hill,
Waterman Smith,
Justus D. Watson,
Amos W. Sargent,
George H. Hubbard,
James O. Adams,
{ B. F. Wallace, resigned,
{ S. Webber, *vice* Wallace,
Thomas S. Montgomery.

1861.

John Hosley,
Waterman Smith,
James B. Straw,
Hiram Hill,
John Coughlin,
James O. Adams,
Samuel Webber,
Daniel Farmer, jr.

1862.

John Hosley,
Waterman Smith,
James B. Straw,
Hiram Hill,
John Coughlin,
George Pierce,
Samuel Webber,
Daniel Farmer, jr.

1863.

Seth T. Hill,
Waterman Smith,
Benjamin F. Bowles,
Holmes R. Pettee,
William Little,
George Pierce,
Samuel Webber,
Daniel Farmer, jr.

1864.

Seth T. Hill,
Waterman Smith,
Benjamin F. Bowles,
Holmes R. Pettee,
William Little,
George Pierce,
{ Samuel Webber, resigned,
{ J. P. Whittle, *vice* Webber,
John E. Stearns.

1865.

William G. Perry,
Waterman Smith,
Benjamin F. Bowles,
Isaac W. Smith,
William Little,
Ignatius T. Webster,
John M. Ordway,
John E. Stearns.

1866.

William G. Perry,
Waterman Smith,
Benjamin F. Bowles,
Isaac W. Smith,
William Little,
Ignatius T. Webster,
John M. Ordway,
Thomas L. Thorpe.

1867.

Henry T. Mowatt,
Waterman Smith,
Moody Currier,
George W. Weeks,
William Little,
J. Y. McQueston,
James P. Walker,
Thomas L. Thorpe.

1868.

Henry T. Mowatt,
Marshall P. Hall,
Moody Currier,
George W. Weeks,
William Little,
Daniel C. Gould, jr.,
James P. Walker,
Thomas S. Montgomery.

1869.

Henry T. Mowatt,
Marshall P. Hall,
Daniel Clark,
Samuel Upton,
William Little,
Elbridge D. Hadley,
James Dean,
Thomas S. Montgomery.

1870.

Henry C. Sanderson,
Marshall P. Hall,
Thomas Borden,
Samuel Upton,
Patrick A. Devine,
Ephraim S. Peabody,
James Dean,
DeLafayette Robinson.

1871.

James A. Weston, } *ex officiis.*
William R. Patten, }
Henry C. Sanderson,
Marshall P. Hall,
Thomas Borden,
Samuel N. Bell,
Patrick A. Devine,
William P. Merrill,
James Dean,
DeLafayette Robinson.

1872.

Person C. Cheney, } *ex officiis.*
Edwin Kennedy, }
Henry C. Sanderson,
Marshall P. Hall,
Daniel Clark,
Samuel Upton,
Daniel C. Gould, jr.,
James Dean,
DeLafayette Robinson.

1873.

Charles H. Bartlett, resigned, }
John P. Newell, *vice* Bartlett, } *ex officiis.*
Charles A. Smith,
Henry E. Burnham,
Marshall P. Hall,
Daniel Clark,
Nathan P. Hunt,
Frank J. Murray,
{ Frank G. Clark, resigned,
{ Edwin Kennedy, *vice* Clark,
George P. Rockwell,
George H. Colby.

1874.

James A. Weston, } *ex officiis.*
Rufus H. Pike, }
Henry E. Burnham,
Marshall P. Hall,
John G. Lane,
Nathan P. Hunt,
Frank J. Murray,
Edwin Kennedy,
{ George P. Rockwell, resigned,
{ John K. McQueston, *vice* Rockwell,
John E. Stearns.

RELIGIOUS AND BENEVOLENT SOCIETIES.

IT was not till some years after Derryfield had become Manchester that there was aroused among its citizens a lasting interest in religious matters. The settlers of New England could never forsake entirely the faith which had provoked them to cross the sea, and the men who were Derryfield's first settlers kept up religious services, of a desultory character indeed, in spite of their quarrels. Before the suggestion of Derryfield had been made, the savage tribes who were wont to flock to Amoskeag Falls in the fishing season received from the Rev. John Eliot, the well-known translator of the Bible into the aboriginal tongue of New England, religious instruction, and, after his departure, his work was continued by Simon Betogkom, a convert to the faith which Eliot held. Later, when the white men were attracted to the Falls by the abundance of the fish, religious services were occasionally held on Sundays. It is known that before and after 1743 the Rev. Mr. Seccomb of Kingston, an apostolic fisherman, preached on Sundays when he came to the Falls to pursue his favorite pastime.

There is no record of other preaching till after the incorporation of the town. In 1753 the Rev. Alexander McDowell was invited by the town to preach, but there is no farther record of the matter. Barns had been the churches hitherto, but in 1754 the town voted to build a meeting-house near the Centre. Its location displeased a faction, and the next year thirty citizens petitioned for a town-meeting, to which the law entitled them and which the selectmen refused to call. The petitioners, however, made request to Joseph Blanchard and Matthew Thornton, justices of the peace, who ordered a meeting, at which the vote to build the meeting-house was reconsidered.

In 1758, however, the town voted to build a house and the frame was put up in that year. But the men who opposed its erection would not pay the assessment laid upon them, and no more was then done. But in succeeding years doors and windows were put in and the house came to a state of partial completion, in which it continued some time. The quarrel which its location provoked continued all the while, now one party triumphant and now the other, and at length the original cause of dispute was nearly lost sight of in personal enmity. In 1766 the party which had located the house at first assembled in town-meeting and elected their candidates for town officers before the rest came. Upon the arrival of the latter they organized and chose others. Such confusion was thus produced that the legislature of that year, upon petition of a number of the inhabitants, declared the town-meetings void and ordered a new one, when the same party was victorious. The dispute was finally settled by a compromise.

Preaching had generally been kept up during this time, and in 1773 the Rev. George Gilmore, who had occasionally been hired by the town, was invited to become its permanent preacher, but there is no record of his reply. The Revolutionary War was begun two years later, and while that lasted there was little preaching or care for any. The house went to decay and was not repaired till 1783. In 1790 the "pew-ground" was sold, the buyers paying "two-thirds of the purchise in Glass, Nailes, or marchant-

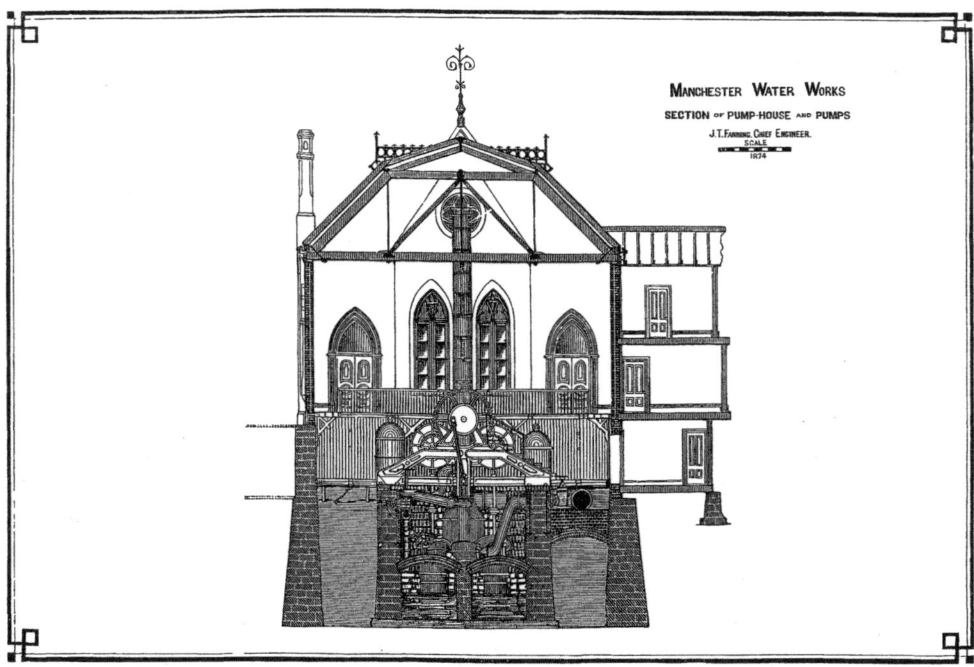
MANCHESTER WATER WORKS
SECTION OF PUMP-HOUSE AND PUMPS
J. T. FANNING, CHIEF ENGINEER.
SCALE
1874

able Clabboards or Putty," and the rest in cash. In 1792 farther repairs were made and the pew-ground in the galleries was sold, but the pews were never built and the house remained incomplete, never being finished for a meeting-house. Part of the inhabitants found more convenient places of worship in Londonderry and Bedford, and the others were unable to have stated preaching or make their house suitable for worship. It was kept barely fit for town-meetings, the rain and wind finding easy access and swallows building their nests within it. The Rev. William Pickels, preaching in it in 1803, effected some improvement by telling his hearers the devil would carry them off through the cracks if they were not closed. In 1840 it was forsaken entirely, the town voting to hold its meetings at the newly created village near the river. Thirteen years later it was bought by H. T. Wilson and B. H. Cheney, moved a few rods and converted into a dwelling-house.

After the departure of the Rev. Mr. Pickels in 1804 David Abbott, who had come into the town the previous year and was of the Baptist faith, began holding meetings at different houses, which were continued till 1812, when a Baptist church was organized with fourteen members. It flourished under Mr. Abbott's care for some years till at length some unknown cause divided it and its life departed. This has the honor of being the first church organized in the town.

The first meeting-house in the town was built about 1736 near the burying-ground on the old Weston farm known as the "Forest cemetery," by the English settlers to whom the land was granted on condition that a church should be built. After having been used some years it was destroyed by fire from burning woods. Of the meeting-houses which have come down to us, the old town-house, still standing at the Centre, was the first one built; the old church in Piscataquog village was the first one that was built by private enterprise within the present limits of Manchester; while the house belonging to the First Methodist Episcopal society and located at the Centre was the first ever built by a religious society within the original town. The first permanent church building in the compact part of the city was erected in 1839 by the First Congregational society. In the same year the First Freewill Baptist society built a wooden chapel on Concord street, which was used successively by them, by the Episcopalians and by the Second Congregational society, and for the general purposes of a hall, and, being moved to Central street, was occupied by the Wesleyan Methodists and also used for a school-house. It is standing on that street, the fifth house west from Chestnut, number fifty-nine, and is occupied as a store.

Though the germs of the Universalist, Congregational and Calvinistic Baptist churches were planted in Amoskeag village, there never was any meeting-house there and services were held in halls. In 1839 they all forsook Amoskeag and began worship in the new village across the river, establishing in feebleness the institutions of religion in a city which now maintains fifteen different churches and in which four others have been organized and disbanded. The approximate number of members in the Protestant churches is two thousand, and the approximate value of Protestant and Roman Catholic church property half a million dollars.

FIRST CONGREGATIONAL CHURCH.

On the twenty-first of May, 1828, a Presbyterian church was organized at Manchester Centre by an ecclesiastical council and Daniel Watts was appointed clerk. It never had a house of its own and a pastor was never settled over it. For a few months after its formation its pulpit was supplied by the Rev. William K. Talbot. In 1833 Benjamin F. Foster was ordained as an evangelist and he for some time furnished occasional preaching. Those of its members who united with the Amoskeag church to form another at the new village in Manchester were: Moses Noyes, Lucy Noyes, Robert P. Whittemore, Hannah Jane Whittemore, Jennet Dickey, Elizabeth Hall, Sally Whittemore, Eliza A. Moor, Jerusha Griffin, Maria Noyes, Elizabeth Stark, Abby Stark, Mrs. F. G. Stark.

At Amoskeag village in Goffstown, across the river and three miles from the Presbyterian church, a Congregational church was organized, December 2, 1828, at the house of Col. Daniel Farmer. Like the Presbyterian church it was without a house or a pastor of its own. Among those who occupied its pulpit were the Rev. B. F. Foster, who divided his time between this church and the one at the Centre, the Rev. Mr. Noble, the Rev. Mr. French, the Rev. Mr. Stone, afterwards a missionary in Siam, and Cyrus W. Wallace, who began his labors with it on the last Sunday in April, 1839, and who afterwards became its pastor. About that time the church began to hold meetings at the new village in Manchester with the approval of the church at the Centre, sustaining thus the first regular Sunday services in what is now the compact part of the city. At the time when it ceased to exist as a separate church its members were: Daniel Farmer, George Berry, Samuel Poor, Henry Peacock, Nahum Baldwin, Betsey Farmer, Mrs. Samuel Poor, Mrs. Nahum Baldwin, Lettice McQueston, Betsey Flanders, Mary Rodgers, Lydia Drew, Harriet Jones, Mary C. Perry, Catherine French, Mrs. Pollard.

It had become by this time patent that a union of these two churches would be a gain to each and that the place for the new church was at the village which the manufacturers were building on the east bank of the Merrimack. The union was effected August 15, 1839, by a council which met first at the house of Phinehas French in Amoskeag village and then adjourned to Franklin Hall, and the church thus formed was called the "First Congregational Church in Amoskeag," a house of worship being built for its use at the new village in 1839. The name was afterwards changed to that of the First Congregational Church in Manchester. Cyrus W. Wallace, then a licentiate of the Londonderry Presbytery, had already, as has been said, commenced his labors with the Amoskeag church, but did not preach as a candidate for settlement. He supplied the pulpit till November of that year and then received a call to be settled as the pastor of the church and society. He accepted the invitation and was ordained, January 8, 1840, being the first minister ever ordained and installed in the town.

At the time of the union of the two churches, Moses Noyes was the deacon of the Presbyterian church and Daniel Farmer of the Congregational church, and by mutual agreement they became the deacons of the new church, continuing in office till death removed them, the one in October, 1860, and the other, October 30, 1865. In 1850 Nahum Baldwin and Hiram Brown were made deacons. They resigned upon their departure from town, the one in 1871 and the other in 1869. In 1848 Henry Lancaster and Holbrook Chandler were chosen deacons. The former resigned in 1858 and was then succeeded by Ebenezer C. Foster, who was taken away by death February 18, 1865. Mr. Chandler resigned in 1857 upon his removal from town. Daniel C. Gould became a deacon in 1858 and held the office till his death, November 3, 1872. In 1862 Theodore T. Abbot was elected deacon, but resigned in 1874 when he removed from the city. In 1866 Henry Clough, Peter K. Chandler and Leonard French were added to the list of deacons. The two latter continue in office; the former fell dead on the evening of November 17, 1872, at a meeting of a temperance society connected with the church. December 10, 1872, three more were chosen deacons — John P. Newell, Horace Pettee, S. S. Marden. June 19, 1874, the system of church government was re-organized. By request, all the deacons resigned and were at once re-elected, to serve for a definite term instead of for life as before. P. K. Chandler was chosen for one year; Leonard French, two years; John P. Newell, three years; Horace Pettee, four years; S. S. Marden, five years.

At the first meeting of the church after its foundation in 1839 George Perry was chosen its clerk, holding the office till his death in 1841. From that time there is no record of the election of a clerk and the records were in the main kept by the pastor till June 23, 1854, when William Hartshorn was chosen clerk. He was succeeded, May 5, 1860, by George W. Pinkerton, and he, January 4, 1863, by Charles A. Daniels. Thomas B. Brown was chosen clerk May 31, 1864, and treasurer in 1867. He was succeeded, June 19, 1874, by John D. Patterson as clerk, and by Jasper P. George as treasurer.

Dr. Wallace, who had been the pastor of the church since its formation and whose uninterrupted service with one church far exceeded in length that of any other clergyman ever settled in Manchester, sent his resignation to the church January 11, 1873, and it was accepted by the latter to take effect the last of August. Edward G. Selden accepted a call to succeed Dr. Wallace and was ordained, December 16, 1873. By a vote of the church, "as an expression of their affectionate regard," Dr. Wallace was made "pastor *emeritus*" of the church, on the first of January, 1874. The church has a membership of about four hundred and seventy-five and the Sunday-school connected with it numbers about five hundred. Of the latter Holmes R. Pettee is superintendent, and Peter K. Chandler assistant superintendent.

A meeting of persons interested in forming a Congregational society was held at Amoskeag, April 4, 1838. These were organized as the "First Congregational Society in Amoskeag village," and at an adjourned meeting on the twenty-seventh adopted a constitution and chose Daniel Farmer, president; George W. Kimball, secretary; Nahum Baldwin, Samuel Poor and George Perry, directors. The next year Moses C. Greene was chosen secretary and appointed treasurer, and Joseph Moody and David A. Bunton became directors in place of Messrs. Poor and Perry. In 1840 David A. Bunton was chosen president, and J. Appleton Burnham, Daniel Farmer and James Wallace, directors. The next year Paul Cragin, jr., succeeded Mr. Greene as secretary and treasurer. In 1842 William G. Means was chosen secretary and treasurer, and Hiram Brown and Foster Towns succeeded Messrs. Burnham and Farmer as directors. Mr. Towns died within the year and William Hartshorn was elected to fill the vacancy. These officers continued through the next year, and in 1844 Hiram Brown was made president and his place in the board of directors was filled by Abram Brigham, who was succeeded in 1845 by David Hill.

The society failed to hold the annual meeting of 1846 at the appointed time, and a special meeting was called by the Hon. Samuel D. Bell as justice of the peace, on request of Messrs. Means, Hartshorn and Bunton, when the officers of the year before were re-elected, continuing through 1847. In 1848 Frederick Wallace and Francis Reed were chosen to succeed David Hill and James Wallace as directors, being themselves succeeded the next year by David A. Bunton and Joshua Deane. In 1850 Samuel Fish succeeded Mr. Deane and in 1851 Holbrook Chandler took Mr. Bunton's place. There was no change in 1852 and but one in 1853, Jacob G. Cilley being elected a director in place of Mr. Fish. The next year Hiram Brown, who had been present of the society since 1844, was succeeded by Nahum aldwin; William G. Means, who had been secretary and easurer since 1842, gave place to William Hartshorn; and olbrook Chandler, Jacob G. Cilley and William Patten ere elected directors, Mr. Patten being succeeded in 1855 y Ebenezer C. Foster. There was no change in 1856, and 1857 William Patten was re-elected director in Mr. Chanler's place, being himself succeeded the next year by eorge W. Pinkerton.

The officers of 1858 were re-elected in 1859, and in 1860 avid A. Bunton was again chosen a director, in place of Ir. Foster. In 1861 Horace Pettee succeeded Mr. Pinkrton as a director; in 1862 there was no change; and in 863 Moulton Knowles became a director in Mr. Bunton's ace. The next year Nahum Baldwin, president of the ociety for ten years, gave place to Peter K. Chandler; Villiam Hartshorn, secretary for the same length of time, as succeeded by John P. Newell, upon whose resignation ithin the year Jacob G. Cilley was elected, and Thomas . Brown took Mr. Cilley's place on the board of directors. hese officers continued through 1865, 1866 and 1867. In 868 John P. Newell was elected president, and Joseph B. awyer, secretary and treasurer, both of whom have served p to the present time; and Henry Clough, Horace Goron and Henry C. Reynolds were chosen directors. There as no change in 1869 and 1870, Daniel Farmer succeedig Mr. Reynolds in 1871. The directors of 1872 were aniel Farmer, George P. Rockwell and Stephen P. Chase; f 1873, Peter K. Chandler, Stephen P. Chase and Horce P. Watts; of 1874, Horace P. Watts, Charles R. Morison and Thomas S. Sargent.

Shortly after the formation of the society a vote was assed to form the "Amoskeag Joint Stock Company" for e purpose of building a church in Amoskeag village. his vote was rescinded, other plans and places were discussed and in 1839 it was decided to build the present house of worship on Hanover street near Elm. The Amoskeag Company gave the land and the Stark Mills gave five hundred dollars to help build the church. Other means were obtained by making shares of stock which were soon taken up. The house was begun in the spring, finished in the autumn and dedicated in November, of 1839. It then contained one hundred and twenty-two pews and would accommodate six hundred and fifty persons. During the process of building, the society, which had already left Amoskeag, worshiped in Franklin hall on Amherst street, nearly in the rear of the present church. In 1852 the house was enlarged, the congregation worshiping meanwhile in the city hall. About 1842 a vestry or chapel was built just back of the church. The property is now estimated to be worth about eighteen thousand dollars.

About 1846 the society forsook its original name and took that of the First Congregational Society in Manchester. January 9, 1865, it having been twenty-five years since the settlement of the Rev. Dr. Wallace, the event was celebrated by the society and other friends by a gathering at Smyth's hall, Peter K. Chandler, then president of the society, in the chair. Dr. Wallace preached a commemorative sermon, and addresses were made by the Rev. Thomas Savage of Bedford, a member of the council convened to settle Mr. Wallace, the Rev. Henry E. Parker of Concord, the Rev. Nathaniel Bouton, D. D., of Concord, the Rev. Henry M. Dexter of Boston and the Rev. William H. Fenn of Manchester, former pastors of the Franklin-street society, William G. Means of Andover, Mass., secretary and treasurer of the First society from 1842 to 1854, and John B. Clarke of Manchester. Dr. Wallace was made the recipient of several articles in testimony of the regard of his people.

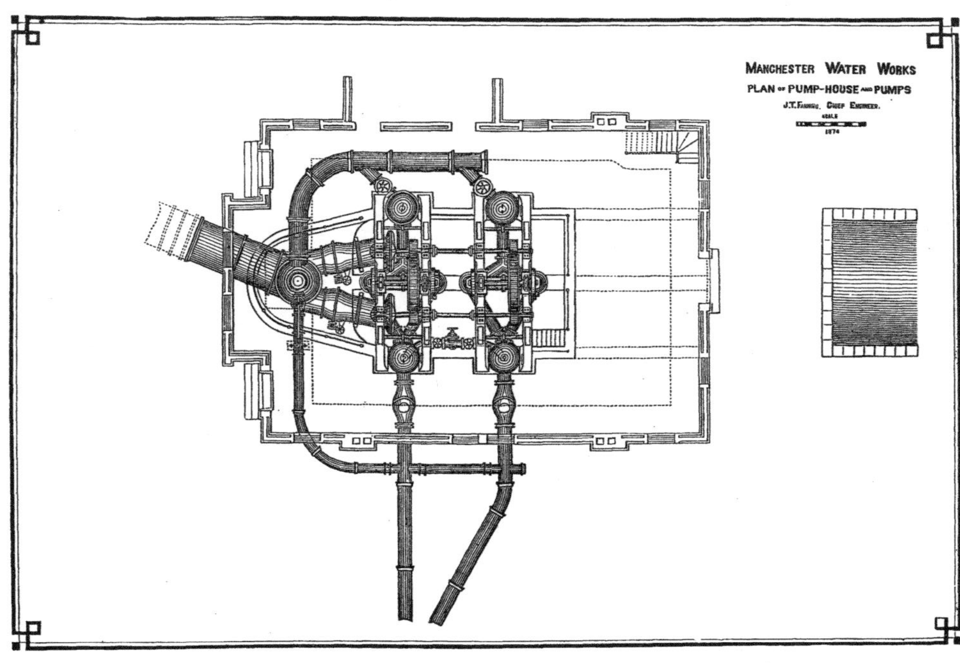

MANCHESTER WATER WORKS
PLAN OF PUMP-HOUSE AND PUMPS
J.T. FANNING, CHIEF ENGINEER.
SCALE
1874

FIRST METHODIST EPISCOPAL CHURCH.

Methodism was first introduced to Manchester about 1827, and its first apostles were the Rev. Orlando Hinds, the Rev. E. Peaslee, a local preacher named B. Haskell, and others. In 1828 and 1829 the Rev. John Broadhead was made preacher in charge, assisted by the Rev. Caleb Lamb, of a circuit of eight or ten towns among which Manchester was included. A church was organized September 27, 1829, and in that year under Mr. Broadhead's labors eighty members were added to it. Among its first members were Daniel Webster, John G. Webster, Joseph B. Hall and Isaac Merrill. At that time the Centre was the town, there being but three or four dwelling-houses where now is the city proper, and at the Centre in 1829 was begun by this church the erection of the first meeting-house ever completed in the original town and the first begun by a society. It was completed the next year at a cost of two thousand dollars.

The first pastor of the church was the Rev. Matthew Newhall, appointed in 1829 and re-appointed in 1830. The Rev. Mr. Gridley is supposed to have been stationed over it the next two years. In 1833 the preacher in charge was the Rev. Silas Greene; in 1834, the Rev. Caleb Dustin; in 1835, the Rev. William S. Lock; in 1836 and 1837, the Rev. Converse L. McCurdy; in 1838, the Rev. William J. Kidder. In 1839 the Rev. Matthew Newhall, the first resident preacher, was returned to his old charge and continued with it that year and the next, being succeeded in 1841 by the Rev. Joseph Hayes. In 1842 the Rev. Elihu Scott was made the preacher in charge of this church and of the Second Methodist church which had been organized in 1839 at the new village, but he did not preach at the Centre. The Rev. William S. Lock supplied the pulpit and continued with the church nearly three years, being succeeded in 1845 by the Rev. Charles H. Eastman, who was re-appointed the next year, but whose want of health compelled him to retire from ministerial work.

In 1847 and 1848 the Rev. Horatio W. Taplin was the pastor of the church, being succeeded in 1849 by the Rev. Henry Nutter, who remained two years. In 1851 the Rev. Isaac W. Huntley was appointed, and re-appointed in 1852, but died before the close of the year. In 1853 the pastor was the Rev. Elijah R. Wilkins; in 1854, the Rev. Robert S. Stubbs: and in 1855 the Rev. H. W. Hart. The latter, for want of health, preached but little, and the pulpit was supplied by a student from the theological school at Concord. In 1856 the Rev. Henry Nutter returned to the church as its pastor after six years' absence, being succeeded the next year by the Rev. L. H. Gordon. In 1859 and 1860 the Rev. A. B. Buzzell was the pastor; in 1861, the Rev. J. P. Stinchfield; in 1862, the Rev. Elijah R. Wilkins, who had just come back from service as chaplain in the War of the Rebellion. In 1863 the Rev. William Hews was appointed but preached only a few times and then resigned the charge, the pulpit being supplied the rest of the year by the Rev. Mr. Wilmot. In 1864 and 1865 the pastor was the Rev. H. A. Mattison; in 1866 and 1867, the Rev. W. L. Chase; in 1868, the Rev. James Dean; in 1869, 1870 and 1871, the Rev. J. Mowry Bean. He was succeeded in 1872 by the Rev. Thomas Tyrie, who left before the end of the year to join the Freewill Baptist church. The present pastor, the Rev. C. W. Taylor, was appointed in 1873 and re-appointed in 1874. The church has seventy-five members and the Sunday-school connected with it has one hundred and ten. The superintendent is P. W. Sanborn, and the assistant superintendent, A. S. Lamb. The first parsonage was replaced in 1870 by a new one. The value of the church property is estimated to be six thousand dollars.

FIRST UNIVERSALIST CHURCH.

The germ of what is now the First Universalist Society in Manchester was started in 1825 at Amoskeag village by Dr. Oliver Dean, then the agent of the manufacturing company out of which the Amoskeag Company grew. The first pastor was the Rev. Frederic A. Hodsdon. In 1839 the society was transferred to Manchester, and a brick building for its use—the present church—was erected in the summer and fall of that year on Lowell street near Elm, on land given by the Amoskeag Company. It was dedicated in February, 1840, and the Rev. N. Gunnison was settled in May and resigned in October of that year. George W. Gage was ordained over the church and society in June, 1841, but was dismissed in April, 1844, being succeeded at that time by the Rev. B. M. Tillotson, who resigned October 10, 1859. The Rev. B. F. Bowles became the pastor June 27, 1860, and was dismissed in 1866. The Rev. S. L. Roripaugh was installed June 26, 1867, and resigned October 3, 1868. He was succeeded on the first day of the new year by the Rev. Thomas Borden, who remained till December, 1871. The Rev. G. L. Demarest began his labors September 1, 1872, and continued as pastor till February 1, 1875, when his resignation was accepted. Shortly after the Rev. Mr. Gage's dismissal, some disaffection arose in the First church and some of its members organized a "Second Universalist Church" with him for a pastor, which held meetings in a hall in Merrimack block, opposite the Manchester House, but whose existence was brief.

No records of the society for the years previous to 1851 have come down to these times. In that year Samuel W. Parsons was its president; Isaac C. Flanders, vice-president; Warren L. Lane, secretary; and John S. Kidder, treasurer. The next year Mr. Flanders became president and his vacant place was filled by the election of Alonzo

Smith as vice-president. With these exceptions the officers remained the same till 1858 when Alonzo Smith was elected president; John H. Maynard, vice-president; Abel M. Keniston, clerk; and Joseph Kidder, treasurer. In 1859 Mr. Kidder was succeeded by Thomas P. Pierce, and in 1860 Darwin J. Daniels was chosen vice-president, and Daniel W. Lane, clerk. The next year Mr. Daniels became president; George C. Gilmore, vice-president; and George B. Chandler, treasurer. These continued in office during 1862, but in 1863 William H. Elliott was chosen president; Thomas B. Eastman, vice-president; Hiram Hill, clerk; Gilman B. Fogg, treasurer. The president, clerk and treasurer remained in office five years. In 1865 Jeremiah Fisk became vice-president, to be succeeded the next year by P. B. Putney, who gave place a year later to A. J. Lane.

In 1868 N. E. Morrill was chosen president; William N. Chamberlin, vice-president; J. L. Smith, clerk; and J. F. Woodbury, treasurer. The next year William H. Elliott again became president; S. C. Forsaith, vice-president; William F. Robie, clerk; and William G. Hoyt, treasurer. In 1870 Mr. Forsaith was elected president; John B. McCrillis, vice-president; W. S. Hill, clerk; and N. E. Morrill, treasurer. In 1871 J. L. Smith again became clerk. The next year Mr. McCrillis was chosen president; William B. Johnson, vice-president; and A. H. Weston, treasurer. In 1873 Joel Daniels succeeded Mr. Smith as clerk, and Hiram Hill took Mr. Weston's place as treasurer. In 1874 Samuel W. Parsons, who had held the office in 1851, was chosen president; George C. Gilmore, vice-president; and A. H. Weston, treasurer. In 1875 Thomas W. Lane succeeded Mr. Parsons as president; John B. McCrillis became vice-president; Alexander H. Downs, clerk; and N. E. Morrill, treasurer.

The church records are begun as follows: "On the fourth day of September, 1833, the following persons associated themselves together as the 'First Universalist Church of Bedford and Goffstown,' and partook of the sacrament of the Lord's Supper:—Frederic A. Hodsdon, John Stark, 3d, George Daniels, Hiram A. Daniels, John Mullet, Edwin Smith, David Fiske, Nehemiah Preston, Mary Parker, Mrs. Pattee, Moses Gage, John V. Wilson and Caleb Johnson."

On the twentieth of November the church met at the school-house in Amoskeag village and chose the Rev. Frederic A. Hodsdon moderator, and George Daniels clerk, of the meeting. After adopting a declaration of faith and a constitution, the church chose George Daniels its clerk and treasurer, and Wilbur Gay a deacon. The meetings thereafter were generally held at Amoskeag hall. On the twenty-second of December of the same year John McAllaster was chosen as a second deacon. In 1834 Hiram A. Daniels became clerk, and Wilbur Gay, treasurer. The former, who was chosen as a third deacon November 18, 1835, continued as clerk till November 16, 1836, when he was succeeded by Darwin J. Daniels. At the same time it was voted to change the name of the church to that of the "First Universalist Church of Amoskeag." The last record which is dated at Amoskeag was made November 21, 1838.

The next year the society was removed to the village of Manchester across the river, but it was not till three years later that a church was organized. April 28, 1842, several members of the society, according to notice previously given, met at the residence of the pastor, the Rev. George W. Gage, "for the purpose of consulting on the subject of church organization." A committee — the Rev. George W. Gage, Deacon Caleb Johnson and Ira Ballou — was chosen to report a resolution to express the sense of the assembly. At a meeting held May 3, the resolution, which advocated the immediate formation of a church, was adopted, and a committee, consisting of Deacon Wilbur Gay, Deacon Caleb

Johnson, Hiram A. Daniels, Dr. Zaccheus Colburn, Ira Ballou, Isaac C. Flanders and the Rev. George W. Gage, was chosen to report a declaration of belief and a form of government, which were adopted on the tenth. On the fourteenth of the following September J. M. Barnes was elected secretary, and Ira Ballou, treasurer; and in November Charles Pierce and Hiram A. Daniels were made deacons.

May 12, 1844, another deacon, Leonard Dakin, 2d, was chosen. In 1849 the secretary, J. M. Barnes, was made treasurer also. January 25, 1852, Caleb Johnson was elected deacon; February 22, 1852, Justus Fisher and J. C. Hill; July 5, 1854, Archibald Dow; July 1, 1855, Luther Smith and Zebina Perry; November 1, 1857, Henry J. Dow; May 4, 1862, Alonzo Smith. Upon the latter's death, Gilman B. Fogg was chosen, May 7, 1865, to take his place. Mr. Fogg resigned and the vacancy was filled by the election of Horace Stearns, May 2, 1869. July 6, 1856, Luther Smith was chosen clerk and treasurer, but the record was mainly kept by the pastor, Mr. Tillotson, till 1858, when Luther H. French was elected. John B. McCrillis succeeded him in 1862, but the record was kept by the pastor, Mr. Bowles. N. Maria Woods was elected clerk in 1864, and Mrs. Ella A. Elliott, in 1866. The latter was succeeded the next year by Sylvanus B. Putnam, the present clerk and treasurer.

The church building was enlarged in 1850 and has since been materially altered. The property is estimated to be worth eighteen thousand dollars. The church has a membership of about fifty, and the Sunday-school, which is under the care of Sylvanus B. Putnam, numbers about one hundred and twenty-five.

FIRST BAPTIST CHURCH.

On the twenty-sixth of July, 1835, the Baptist church in Goffstown voted to recognize ten persons, viz.: Elder John Peacock, Daniel Gooden, John Stevens, Mary R. Peacock, —— Stevens, Hopy Tewksbury, Betsy Tewksbury, Elizabeth McIntire, Zilpha Gould and Abigail Rider, as the "Amoskeag branch of the Goffstown church." They met for the first time, five days later, at the house of Daniel Gooden in Amoskeag village and chose John Peacock pastor and clerk of the church. They first held public worship on the second of August in a hall and thereafter met at Hull's hall and at the houses of the members. January 3, 1836, Daniel Gooden was chosen deacon. At a meeting held at the house of Deacon John Plumer, December 1, 1836, the branch resolved to ask a dismissal from the Goffstown church and invited a council to assist them in becoming a distinct organization. The council met, January 4, 1837, at Roger Williams hall, and recognized the branch as an independent church, the late Andrew T. Foss, well-known as one of the anti-slavery agitators, preaching the sermon of recognition. The church held its first meeting the next day at Daniel Gooden's house.

This church was affected, like the rest in Amoskeag village, by the natural tendency to the new town across the river, and in 1840 a brick building was built for the uses of the church on a lot of land given by the Amoskeag Company and situated on the corner of Manchester and Chestnut streets. Thither the church removed in that year and voted to be known as the First Baptist Church in Manchester on the twenty-second of September. Elder Peacock, who had been dismissed from the pastorate of the church and left town in 1837, returned in 1842 and began preaching at Amoskeag village, the church in Manchester passing a vote in approval "of efforts of brethren at Amoskeag to sustain preaching there." September 25, 1842, about twenty persons were recognized at their request as the "Amoskeag branch of the Manchester Baptist church," and supported services of their own at Amoskeag village. Edwin Baldwin was chosen their clerk, treasurer and deacon. Their pastor was Mr. Peacock, who left them in April, 1842, and they voted, September 24, 1843, "to close up the meetings of the branch and unite with the Manchester church in worshipping the Lord."

In 1838, the year after the first pastor, the Rev. John Peacock, was dismissed, the Rev. E. K. Bailey received and accepted a call. He was succeeded in 1842 by the Rev. James Upham, who was followed in order by the Rev. Joseph Storer, the Rev. Benjamin Brierly, who remained till 1847, the Rev. Thomas O. Lincoln, and the Rev. Isaac Sawyer, whose resignation was accepted May 28, 1854. The Rev. Benjamin F. Hedden began his labors with the church October 8, 1854, and relinquished them in November, 1856. The Rev. George Pierce became pastor April 5, 1857, and remained such eight years, his resignation being accepted October 1, 1865. He was succeeded, March 21, 1866, by the Rev. N. C. Mallory, who remained till July 1, 1870. The present pastor, the Rev. A. C. Graves, was installed February 7, 1871.

The Rev. Mr. Peacock, as has already been stated, was chosen the first clerk, being succeeded in 1837 by Andrew J. George. Two years later Henry Kimball was elected, and in 1840 Charles P. Crockett succeeded him. Upon the latter's dismissal, June 9, 1842, David P. Perkins was chosen clerk. The first volume of the records of the church after it came to Manchester is lost and there is therefore no indication of what the church did between 1842 and 1853. The second volume begins December 26, 1853, with a record of the annual meeting of the church, at which Joseph E. Bennett was chosen clerk, and George M. Stevens treas-

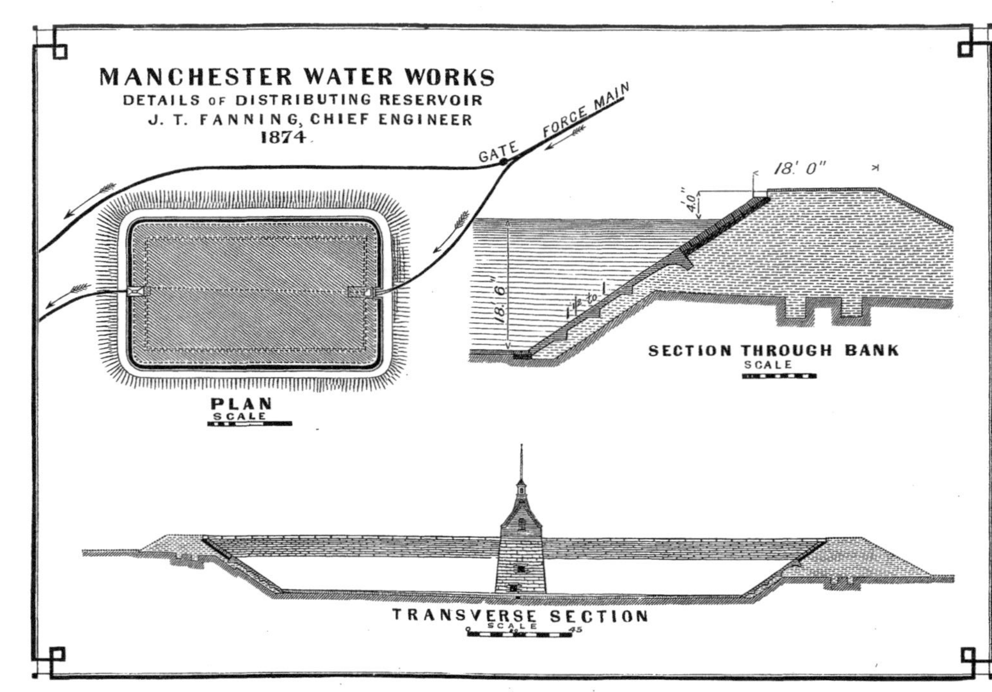
MANCHESTER WATER WORKS
DETAILS OF DISTRIBUTING RESERVOIR
J. T. FANNING, CHIEF ENGINEER
1874.
GATE
FORCE MAIN
18' 0"
4.0"
18' 6"
1½ to 1
SECTION THROUGH BANK
SCALE
PLAN
SCALE
TRANSVERSE SECTION
SCALE
0
45

urer. In 1855 Benjamin Currier became treasurer. Although Mr. Bennett was clerk, George Kimball was chosen clerk *pro tempore* and kept the records from May, 1857, to January, 1859. In 1860 Benjamin Currier was chosen clerk, and John Paige treasurer. In 1864 Mr. Currier was succeeded by the present clerk, Henry L. Kimball, the son of Henry Kimball who was clerk of the church in 1839 while it was still at Amoskeag village. In 1866 Benjamin Currier was again elected treasurer and has held the office ever since.

The first record of the choice of a deacon is found under date of January 3, 1836, when Daniel Gooden was elected. He was dismissed in 1845 to form with others the Second Baptist church. January 8, 1841, John Plumer and Charles P. Crockett were chosen, both being dismissed the next year. It would appear from the records that at the time the second volume was begun, in 1853, among the deacons were George M. Stevens and O. B. Robinson, who were dismissed in 1854, John Paige, who was dismissed in 1867, Joseph E. Bennett, who resigned in 1864, Benjamin Currier, Ebenezer Clark, Daniel Balch and Trueworthy Blaisdell. Deacon Clark was dismissed in 1848 to join the Second church, but was in 1850 again received into the First. George Kimball and Seth J. Sanborn were added to the number January 3, 1858. The former resigned in 1866 and the latter was removed by death in 1872. April 4, 1866, James Baldwin and Orison Hardy were elected deacons. The church has a membership of three hundred and twenty-five, of whom about two hundred are resident; there are three hundred and seventy-five in the Sunday school, which is under the charge of Henry H. Huse, the superintendent, and Francis A. Hawley, assistant superintendent.

At the request of George A. Barnes and others a meeting was called, January 27, 1855, at Mr. Barnes's store, "to organize a society for the purpose of conducting the financial interests of the First Baptist church in Manchester." A few articles of agreement were signed by George A. Barnes, Ebenezer Clark, E. B. Merrill and others. Joseph B. Clark was chosen clerk, and the society was organized as the "First Baptist Religious Society of Manchester." At a meeting held February 19, a committee was chosen to prepare a proper constitution, which was reported and adopted February 26, when the following officers were chosen: Otis Barton, president; Joseph B. Clark, clerk; Ebenezer Clark, treasurer; Joseph E. Bennett, Orison Hardy, George A. Barnes, A. D. Burgess, Peter S. Brown, C. W. Baldwin, Charles Brown, directors. To this society the church voted, March 15, 1855, to transfer its property. Joseph E. Bennett was elected president for 1856 and Joseph H. Peabody was elected treasurer. Mr. Clark continued clerk till 1862. In 1857 Mr. Bennett was succeeded as president by Peter S. Brown, and he by Benjamin Currier in 1858, when Orison Hardy became treasurer. The latter was treasurer also in 1860, Joseph B. Clark holding the office in 1859 and 1861. In the latter year Peter S. Brown was elected president, being re-elected the next year, when Daniel R. Prescott was chosen clerk, and Henry R. Chamberlin treasurer, the latter holding his office till 1874.

In 1863 Joseph E. Bennett was chosen president; in 1864, Justin Spear; and in 1865 there was no change. In 1866 Orison Hardy was chosen president, and J. B. Prescott clerk. In 1869 Otis Barton succeeded Mr. Hardy, and in 1870 Frederick C. Dow took Mr. Prescott's place as clerk. There was no change till 1873, when Mr. Hardy again became president. The next year Mr. Dow became treasurer and Uriah A. Carswell was chosen clerk. Edson Hill succeeded Mr. Hardy as president in 1875. The following have been members of the board of directors without being elected to any other office, and so not mentioned above:

E. B. Merrill, Charles Brown, John Paige, Ephraim S. Peabody, Ruel Walker, S. C. Merrill, George Kimball, J. Simons, Seth J. Sanborn, Isaac Sanborn, James Baldwin, D. F. Smith, John Hamilton, Cyrus Puffer, Lewis W. Clark, S. P. Duntley, Hiram Simpson, James K. Taylor, Storer Nason, James A. H. Grout, Jeremiah L. Fogg, J. Irving Whittemore, William H. Wilson, Francis A. Hawley, Samuel Martin, Henry H. Huse.

July 5, 1870, the society voted to repair its meeting-house at an expense of five thousand dollars, and three days later it was burned, being consumed by the great fire of Friday morning, July 8, 1870. The next day a meeting was held in the common-council room in the city hall and a committee appointed to devise plans for future action. Services were first held in Music hall (then the Elm-street Universalist society's meeting-house) and afterwards in Smyth's hall. Meanwhile, in accordance with a plan which had been proposed and adopted by the society, a new church was being built on the corner of Union and Concord streets, which was dedicated April 30, 1873, the society having previously held services in the vestry, which was first completed. The value of the church and land is set at seventy-five thousand dollars.

FIRST FREEWILL BAPTIST CHURCH.

Members of the Freewill Baptist denomination began holding meetings in Manchester in a school-house the last of the year 1838. Elder Lemuel Whiting came from Lowell once a fortnight and preached for several months. The Rev. John L. Sinclair came to this city in September of the next year and from his coming dated definite action. Timothy Foss, Winthrop James, Nehemiah Chase and others met at the house of Winthrop James, September 9, 1839, to consider the subject of forming a Freewill Baptist society and building a meeting-house. Timothy Foss was chosen moderator, and Smiley Gordon clerk. A committee was chosen to take the matter into consideration, and, September 13, a constitution was adopted and the society was organized as the First Freewill Baptist Society in Manchester, and the first officers were chosen October 7, as follows: Timothy Foss, president; Nehemiah Chase, vice-president; Smiley Gordon, clerk and treasurer; Ezra T. Rumery, David Ricker, Leonard Jackson, Henry D. Colby, Samuel A. Simpson, Francis H. Watson, Winthrop James, directors. Soon afterwards a few members of the society built a small hall on Concord street to rent to the society for a house of worship, and the latter used it as such till increasing numbers and strength encouraged them to build a meeting-house for themselves. In January, 1842, the Amoskeag Company gave them a lot of land on the north-east corner of Chestnut and Merrimack streets, and in the same year they built upon it the church which now stands there and forsook their first meeting-place, which has since been occupied by various societies, and, having been removed to Central street is now used for a store. In 1840 the society elected the following officers: president, Leonard Jackson; vice-president, Daniel Haines; clerk and treasurer, Smiley Gordon; directors, Jerome B. Rumery, David Ricker, Jehoah Tuttle, Timothy Foss, Ezra T. Rumery, Samuel A. Simpson, Nehemiah Colby.

January 11, 1841, Smiley Gordon resigned as clerk and treasurer and the Rev. John L. Sinclair, the pastor, was chosen to fill the place. March 31, 1841, members of the society met and formed a legally incorporated society under the same name. They adopted a new constitution April 19 and chose, as president, Leonard Jackson; vice-president, Albert B. Chamberlin; secretary, John L. Sinclair; treasurer, Jerome B. Rumery; prudential committee, Daniel Haines, David Ricker, Francis H. Watson. The first annual election under the new constitution was held in December of that year, when Leonard Jackson was re-elected president, continuing to hold that office till 1848; Liberty Raymond was chosen vice-president; A. B. Chamberlin, clerk and treasurer; Alpha Currier, Henry D. Colby, Ebenezer P. Sawin, prudential committee. The next year Jerome B. Rumery was chosen vice-president, and Daniel Haines, Stevens James and Timothy Foss, prudential committee. In April, 1843, Joseph L. Ames was chosen clerk and treasurer. At the election in December, 1843, Daniel Haines was chosen vice-president; Henry D. Colby, treasurer; Edson Hill, Jeremiah Wheeler and Daniel Haines, prudential committee. In 1844 Joseph Knowlton was elected treasurer, and Leonard Jackson, Stevens James and Liberty Raymond, prudential committee. In 1845 Jeremiah B. Hoitt was elected secretary; John S. Folsom, treasurer; John S. Folsom, Joseph D. Emerson, Andrew J. Butterfield, prudential committee. In 1846 Hiram W. Savory succeeded Mr. Folsom as treasurer, while Andrew J. Butterfield, Samuel Page and Joseph Fogg were chosen prudential committee. In 1847 the offices of secretary and treasurer were combined in Jeremiah B. Hoitt, and the prudential committee consisted of Daniel Haines, Osgood Paige and Jonathan Smith.

In 1848 Samuel Gould became president; Hiram W. Savory, vice-president; J. B. Hoitt, secretary; Daniel Haines, treasurer; Liberty Raymond, H. W. Savory, Osgood Paige, prudential committee. In 1849 H. W. Savory was chosen president; L. P. Ware, vice-president; J. B. Hoitt, secretary and treasurer; John S. Folsom, David Ricker and Stevens James, prudential committee. In 1850 J. S. Harriman was elected to succeed Mr. Hoitt as secretary and treasurer, and Daniel Haines, Liberty Raymond and Stevens James were chosen prudential committee. In 1851 Samuel Gould was elected president; H. W. Savory, vice-president; J. S. Harriman, secretary; Liberty Raymond, treasurer; John S. Folsom, Samuel Gould, James M. Berry, prudential committee. In 1852 these were re-elected, and in 1853 Justin Spear succeeded Mr. Harriman as secretary, and James M. Bean was chosen to take Mr. Raymond's office. In 1854 John W. Severance was chosen president; William B. Dana, vice-president; S. P. Chase, secretary; James M. Bean, treasurer; H. W. Savory, Justin Spear, Jonathan Horn, prudential committee. In April of the next year Samuel Gould succeeded Mr. Chase as secretary. The annual meeting, which had hitherto been held in December, was now held in January and the officers for 1856 were: president, John W. Severance; vice-president, W. B. Dana; secretary, Silas Hamilton; treasurer, Jefferson Knowles; prudential committee, James M. Bean, John S. Folsom, W. B. Dana. These were re-elected the next year. In 1858 W. B. Dana was chosen president, and J. S. Harriman, vice president, George W. Quinby succeeding Mr. Folsom as a member of the prudential committee. H. W. Savory was elected to the office of treasurer in April. The last election was held in 1859, when Jacob Clark was chosen president; J. B. Daniels, vice-president; Jacob Clark, M. E. George, A. J. Butterfield, prudential committee.

November 14, 1839, a meeting was held at the hall of the Freewill Baptist society by those who were interested in forming a church, the Rev. John L. Sinclair presiding. A committee, consisting of John L. Sinclair, Leonard Jackson and Nehemiah Chase, was chosen to report articles of faith. Another meeting was held two days later, when a covenant was adopted, the church was organized and the Rev. John L. Sinclair was chosen its first pastor. He was dismissed, March 4, 1843, and the Rev. Daniel P. Cilley was chosen in his place. After a pastorate of seven years he resigned, April 1, 1850, and the Rev. Joseph B. Davis succeeded him. He left in September, 1855, and the Rev.

F. W. Straight was chosen pastor on the first of December of that year. Mr. Straight left in the summer or fall of 1857, after which H. F. Snow supplied the pulpit till June 10, 1858, when he was ordained. The Rev. J. M. Bailey began his labors March 31, 1859, and continued with the church till the separation in the fall, mentioned below, becoming pastor of the Pine-street church in December.

The first clerk of the church was David Ricker, who was succeeded in 1840 by Leonard Jackson. Neither of them performed the duties of the office, and the Rev. John L. Sinclair, who had kept the records from the first, was chosen clerk in 1842. He was succeeded in January, 1843, by J. B. Rumery, who served till 1845, when Daniel Haines, who had been made treasurer the year before, was chosen clerk. In 1849 Hiram W. Savory was elected clerk and treasurer, being succeeded by Joseph C. Dyer in May, 1855, who retained the office till September, when Charles W. Eaton was chosen. In 1856 Samuel Gould succeeded him, and in 1857 George S. Holmes was chosen, who kept the records up to the dissolution of the church. Timothy Foss and Daniel Haines were chosen deacons, October 2, 1840; Osgood Paige, May 25, 1844; Samuel Lougee, Charles F. Stanton and Moses S. Boynton, March 10, 1849; Samuel Gould, Liberty Raymond and Hiram W. Savory, January 11, 1854; J. W. Severance, September 26, 1855; Jonathan J. Straw, August 12, 1857.

The society, which had become embarrassed by lack of funds, conveyed its property, January 28, 1859, to the "Union Association," an organization of members of the society, and thus obtained money to discharge its obligations. This association exchanged in the fall their meeting-house for the one then owned by the First Unitarian society and which stands on the corner of Pine and Merrimack streets, and the Freewill Baptist society, which had been hiring the old house of this association, voted, December 16, 1859, to use the one obtained of the Unitarians. This is the last record of the First Freewill Baptist society. The church connected with it voted, August 27, 1859, the record asserts, to disband, and though the church afterwards known as the Elm-street, and now as the Merrimack-street Freewill Baptist church, has proven that the meeting at which the church is alleged to have been dissolved was an illegal one and has established before the Rockingham Quarterly Conference, to which it belongs, its right to the title of the First Freewill Baptist Church, it has never seen fit to adopt it since it assumed a different name. Trouble arose in the fall of 1859 and a separation took place, a part, consisting mostly of members of the church and retaining the church records, going to a church on Elm street and being organized, January 11, 1860, as the Elm-street Freewill Baptist Church, and the rest, including a majority of the society and keeping the society records, moving to the old Unitarian chapel and being formed, December 21, 1859, into the Pine-street Freewill Baptist Church. An ineffectual attempt to unite them was made in 1871.

ST. PAUL'S METHODIST EPISCOPAL CHURCH.

The Methodists had been the first to own a meeting-house in the original town of Manchester, having built one in 1829 at the original centre of business and population. And ten years later, when the manufacturing industries had made the town anew and moved the point around which the city was to crystallize westward to the river, the Methodists were on the spot and were supporting occasional preaching. At length the Second Methodist Episcopal Church was organized, December 16, 1839, and in June of the next year the Rev. John Jones was appointed pastor. In that year they built a chapel on the corner of Han-

Geo. Byron Chandler

over and Chestnut streets, where the residence of the Hon. Nathan Parker now stands, and worshiped there till 1843, when, having outgrown it, they sold it to the First Unitarian society, who moved it to the corner of Pine and Merrimack streets. To take its place they built the brick church on Elm street, between Market and Merrimack, which afterwards passed out of their hands, they retaining a lease of the property. Upon their removal to Elm street, they assumed the name of the Elm-street Methodist Episcopal church.

In 1855 twenty-three members left it and were organized on the nineteenth of May of that year as the North Elm-street Methodist Episcopal church. Their first pastor was the Rev. Elisha Adams, who was stationed in 1853 and 1854 over the church out of which this was formed. He remained but part of one year and the Rev. C. N. Smith filled out his term. The latter was succeeded by the Rev. George W. H. Clark, who was the pastor in 1856 and 1857. The next year the Rev. Charles Young was appointed and continued through 1858 and 1859. The Rev. George S. Dearborn was pastor in 1860 and a part of 1861, the Rev. Mr. Owens filling out the year, remaining till the union of this with the parent church in 1862. They held services in Smyth's hall and the city hall.

"It had long been thought," writes the Rev. J. M. Buckley, pastor of the Elm-street church in 1861, in recording its consolidation with the seceding church, "that a union of the two churches was desirable, and the attempt had been made to form it, but from various causes it had failed. About the time of the assembling of the New Hampshire Annual Conference, April, 1862, the depression of business in the city and the consequent reduction in the numbers and funds of the societies, which was increased by the departure of between thirty and forty members of the church for the seat of war, rendered it obvious that the time had come when the interests of both societies would be promoted by their consolidation into one. Members of both churches assembled in the Elm-street vestry on Monday evening, April 7, 1862, there being present twenty-one of the Elm-street and eighteen of the North Elm-street church. The Rev. J. M. Buckley of the former church was chosen chairman, and Nathaniel Herrick of the latter, secretary. A proposition was then brought before the convention to dissolve the present organization and form out of the whole number of members of both churches a new church and society upon an equal basis. This proposition, being placed in the form of a resolution, was adopted by a vote of thirty-nine, which included the entire delegation of both churches present."

The Rev. Osmon C. Baker, then bishop, recognized the union at the Conference then in session at Sanbornton Bridge, named the new organization St. Paul's Methodist Episcopal Church of Manchester, stationed over it the Rev. J. M. Buckley, and, in conjunction with the Rev. James Pike, then presiding elder of the district, appointed the following trustees to manage the affairs of the church: Nathaniel Herrick, Waldo Whitney, Benjamin H. Piper, James Mitchell, jr., Hilas Dickey, Levi H. Sleeper, E. W. Copp, Artemas Jackson, E. W. Bartlett. To these trustees was conveyed the property of the Elm-street church. The present church has a membership of four hundred and thirty, and the Sunday-school connected with it numbers five hundred and seventy-five. Of the latter Joseph A. Foster is superintendent, and R. M. Couch assistant superintendent.

The following have been the pastors of the church from its formation as the Second church to the present time:

1840.	John Jones.	1853–4.	Elisha Adams.
1841.	Silas Greene.	1855–6.	Henry H. Hartwell.
1842.	Elihu Scott.	1857.	Richard S. Rust.
1843–4.	James W. Morey.	1858–9.	Henry Hill.
1845.	Osmon C. Baker.	1860.	John Currier.
1846–7.	John Jones.	1861–2.	James M. Buckley.
1848.	Samuel Kelly.	1863–4.	Jonathan Hall.
1849.	Lorenzo D. Barrows.	1865–6.	William H. Thomas.
1850.	Charles N. Smith.	1867.	Hiram L. Kelsey.
1851.	Silas Quimby.	1868–9.	Daniel C. Babcock.
1852.	Justin Spalding.	1870–1–2.	E. A. Smith.
	1873–4. James Pike.		

GRACE CHURCH.

In June, 1841, a desire having been expressed to the diocese of New Hampshire that Episcopal services might be held in Manchester, the Rev. P. S. Ten Broeck of St. Paul's church, Concord, performed services in the old high-school-house on Lowell street on the second Sunday of the following July. These services were followed during that month and the next by others held in the same place and conducted by the Rev. Theodore Edson of Lowell, Mass.

The first meeting with reference to a church was held July 19, at the residence of William A. Burke, when a committee, consisting of John A. Burnham, William A. Burke, Henry C. Gillis, B. F. Hathorne and Samuel P. Greeley, was appointed to take the matter into consideration. They subsequently made a report which was unfavorable to immediate action. After July there were no services till the third of October, when they were resumed in a room called "Chapel hall," in Union building on the southern corner of Elm and Market streets. The Rev. Edward Livermore was the first to officiate, being followed in October and November by the Rev. Moses B. Chase of Hopkinton, the Rev. A. McCoy of Lowell, Mass., the Rev.

Theodore W. Snow of Roxbury, Mass., and the Rev. Ferdinand Putnam of Methuen, Mass. Near the close of November the Rev. William H. Moore of New York city, a recent graduate of the General Theological Seminary, visited Manchester by invitation and officiated on the twenty-eighth in the hall in Union building. The attendance being encouraging, an invitation was extended to all who wished to form a church after Protestant Episcopal usage, to meet the next Monday evening, November 29, 1841, at the same place. A number of gentlemen met at that time, organized a church to be known as St. Michael's, and elected the following officers: William A. Burke, senior warden; John S. T. Cushing, junior warden; J. Appleton Burnham, Oliver W. Bayley, Robert Read, Henry C. Gillis, vestrymen; Samuel F. Wetmore, secretary. Robert Read subsequently declined to serve, and Samuel P. Greeley was chosen in his stead. The gentlemen present at the meeting were the Rev. William H. Moore, J. Appleton Burnham, William A. Burke, John S. T. Cushing, Henry C. Gillis, Samuel P. Greeley, Samuel F. Wetmore, Daniel Savage, Charles D. Horr, John M. Hyland. A constitution and by-laws were subsequently adopted.

At the annual meeting at Easter in 1842, Daniel Savage was elected one of the vestry in place of Mr. Gillis. The next year Mr. Greeley was succeeded by Samuel F. Wetmore and William B. Webster was chosen secretary in Mr. Wetmore's place. In 1844 Joshua M. House and George T. Clark were elected vestrymen to succeed Messrs. Savage and Wetmore. In 1845 John S. T. Cushing and Samuel F. Wetmore were elected wardens; John A. Burnham, Oliver W. Bayley, George T. Clark and Thomas R. Crosby, vestrymen. In 1846 Mr. Wetmore was succeeded by T. Wiggin Little, and in 1847 Mr. Clark by Thomas Hoyt. In October, 1847, Mr. Burnham resigned and S. L. Wilson was chosen in his stead. In 1848 Oliver W. Bayley and

Charles T. Durgin were elected wardens; Thomas R. Crosby, S. L. Wilson, William A. Putney and Thomas D. Bradley, vestrymen. In October James Collins was chosen to take Mr. Bradley's place.

In 1849 John S. T. Cushing and David Ames were elected wardens; Oliver W. Bayley, James Collins, Caleb Duxbury and T. Wiggin Little, vestrymen. These were re-elected at the annual meeting of 1850, but in November Mr. Cushing was succeeded by S. L. Wilson. In 1851 Davis Baker was elected a warden to succeed Mr. Ames, and Charles T. Durgin was chosen a vestryman to succeed Mr. Collins. These continued in office through the next three years, except that Mr. Baker was succeeded in 1853 by William Langford, and Mr. Wilson in 1854 by R. H. French. Joel Taylor took the latter's place the next year, and Mr. Langford resigning soon after, William C. Young was chosen to fill the vacancy. In 1856 Justus D. Watson succeeded Mr. Duxbury and George L. Andrews was chosen secretary, the latter being also chosen warden the next year in Mr. Young's stead.

In 1858 Mace Moulton and Justus D. Watson were elected wardens; Thomas Hoyt, T. Wiggin Little, Davis Baker, Joel Taylor, Andrew G. Tucker and Charles Wells, vestrymen; Justus D. Watson, secretary. In 1859 Mr. Little was elected warden to succeed Mr. Moulton, and William B. Webster and George A. French took the place of Messrs. Little and Taylor in the vestry. These were re-elected in 1860 and George A. French was chosen secretary in place of Mr. Watson. There is no record of an election in 1861.

By an act of the legislature, passed at the June session of 1861 and accepted by the parish June 2, 1862, the name of "St. Michael's" was exchanged for "Grace," and the latter's records begin in 1862, when Joel Taylor and James E. Pollard were elected wardens; William B. Webster,

Thomas Hoyt, Justus D. Watson, J. B. Bradley, vestrymen; T. W. Little, clerk. In 1863 William B. Webster succeeded Mr. Pollard as warden and John Truesdale and A. A. Dunk took the places of Messrs. Webster and Hoyt among the vestrymen. In 1864 Messrs. Watson and Bradley were succeeded as vestrymen by James McEvoy and G. W. Stratton, and Horatio Fradd was chosen clerk. There was no change in 1865, and in 1866 L. B. How was elected warden to succeed Mr. Webster.

In 1867 John Cayzer was chosen warden in place of Mr. How; John Truesdale, Benjamin F. Martin, William L. Killey, J. B. Bradley and George A. French were chosen vestrymen; and Horatio Fradd continued as clerk. In 1868 the places of Messrs. Killey and Bradley in the vestry were filled by the election of James M. Varnum and D. P. Hadley. In 1869 William B. Webster was chosen to succeed Joel Taylor as warden and there has since been no change in that office; Lucien B. Clough was chosen a vestryman to succeed Mr. Truesdale. In 1870 Martin V. B. Edgerly took Mr. Varnum's place in the vestry and Charles H. Hill was chosen clerk. There was no change in 1871. In 1872 Charles Wells was elected a vestryman in place of Mr. Clough, the latter being chosen clerk the next year and Mr. Wells being then succeeded by A. H. Sanborn, all the officers being re-elected in 1874.

A house on Concord street which had been built and used by the First Freewill Baptist society was hired and fitted becomingly, and the congregation removed thither in June, 1842. There they remained till they outgrew the place and an effort was made to build a church. By the exertions of the congregation, donations from abroad and the gift of a lot of land from the Amoskeag Company, situated on the northwest corner of Lowell and Pine streets, this purpose was accomplished, and the new church was consecrated December 28, 1843, by the Right Reverend

Manton Eastburn of the diocese of Massachusetts. This house was of wood and was displaced by the present one of stone, which was consecrated December 4, 1860. The old one was cut in two and moved, one half to the south side of Merrimack street, between Beech and Maple, where it now stands, and the other half to Hanover street, to be burned in the fire of 1870. The real estate, including the parsonage, is valued at fifty thousand dollars. The system of free seats was adopted at Easter, 1864.

The first rector was the Rev. William H. Moore, who entered upon his duties December 25, 1840. Want of health compelled his resignation, April 23, 1848, and he was succeeded, June 18, 1848, by the Rev. John Kelly, a graduate of Trinity college, Hartford, Conn., who remained till April 1, 1852. The Rev. I. G. Hubbard, the next incumbent, took charge of the parish May 16, 1852, but he was forced to resign at Easter, 1866, by physical infirmity. During his rectorship the parsonage, on the northeast corner of Pine and Orange streets, was built. He was succeeded, June 3, 1866, by the Rev. William J. Harris, who remained till January 1, 1869, being followed in November of that year by the present rector, the Rev. Lorenzo Sears. The church has a membership of one hundred and forty, and the Sunday-school connected with it, of which the rector is the superintendent, has a hundred members.

FIRST UNITARIAN CHURCH.

The first preaching in this city of the doctrine belonging to the Unitarian faith was given in March, 1841, by the Rev. S. Osgood, then of Nashua, when a considerable number of persons united in a subscription for the support of religious services, which were continued about four months. On account of the unfavorable situation of the rooms which were obtained for services, it was thought best to suspend them till the town hall was finished, and then, in March, 1842, they were resumed. The Rev. Charles Briggs, the agent of the American Unitarian Association, preached the first Sunday and the Rev. Oliver H. Wellington continued services through the month of April.

"April 24, 1842, at a meeting of those persons who were interested in the support of Unitarian preaching in the town of Manchester, held at the house of William Shepherd, John D. Kimball was chosen chairman and E. A. Straw, secretary. There were also present James May, M. G. J. Tewksbury, William Shepherd, James McKeen Wilkins, H. F. Richardson, B. F. Osgood, Edwin Bodwell, Herman Foster and J. H. Kimball." E. A. Straw and Daniel Clark were chosen a committee to draft a constitution and by-laws, which were adopted at a meeting held on the twenty-seventh of April, when E. A. Straw was chosen clerk and treasurer of the society. May 1, J. D. Kimball was chosen president, and William Shepherd and B. F. Manning, directors. These continued in office till 1847, except that Mr. Straw was succeeded as clerk and treasurer, November 11, 1844, by Isaiah Winch, and he, March 22, 1845, by Charles F. Warren.

In 1847 Richard H. Ayer was elected president; William Shepherd and George Hall, directors; and A. G. Tucker, clerk and treasurer. The latter was succeeded the next year by F. A. Hussey; in 1849 Luther Farley took Mr. Hall's place as a director; and B. F. Manning was chosen, September 9, 1849, clerk and treasurer. In 1850 Daniel Clark was chosen president; William Shepherd and Samuel H. Price, directors; F. A. Hussey, clerk and treasurer. Messrs. Shepherd and Price were succeeded the next year by John H. Moore and Frank A. Brown, and Mr. Hussey by Charles L. Richardson. E. A. Straw became president in 1853; Daniel Clark became a director in 1854 in place of Mr. Brown; in 1855 Samuel P. Jack-

Engd by A. H. Ritchie

L. C. Cheney

son succeeded to Mr. Moore's place, himself being followed in October by F. A. Brown.

In 1857 A. W. Sargent was elected president; Daniel Clark and F. A. Brown, directors; A. P. Gilson, clerk and treasurer. In 1858 F. A. Brown became president, and Charles F. Warren and Charles L. Richardson, directors. In 1859 Moody Currier was elected president, and William A. Webster, clerk and treasurer. The next year J. B. Chase and R. N. Batchelder were added to the board of directors. In 1861 Samuel Webber became president; John Hosley and George W. Thayer succeeded Messrs. Warren and Richardson as directors; and Isaac W. Farmer was elected clerk and treasurer. In 1862 Edwin P. Richardson and Moses W. Oliver were chosen directors in place of Messrs. Chase and Batchelder. In 1863 Herman Foster was elected president; Moses W. Oliver, Moody Currier, George G. Shute and Emil Custer, directors. The next year David B. Varney was chosen a director to succeed Mr. Shute, and James B. Straw, clerk and treasurer, to succeed Mr. Farmer. In 1865 Moody Currier became president, and Thomas R. Hubbard and John Brugger took the place of Messrs. Currier and Custer as directors.

In 1866 John L. Kelly was elected president; Alfred F. Perry, Horatio H. Ladd, George W. Weeks and Noah S. Clark, directors; and the next year Mr. Straw was succeeded as clerk and treasurer by Horace M. Gillis. In 1868 Albert Mallard became president; George B. Chandler, J. M. Howe, Person C. Cheney and Henry A. Farrington, directors; and George W. Weeks was chosen clerk and treasurer the next year. In 1870 Clinton W. Stanley was elected president; David B. Varney, Nathaniel W. Cumner, Abraham P. Olzendam and E. M. Tubbs, directors; and in 1871 Charles L. Richardson became clerk and treasurer. There was no change in 1872, but in 1873 Person C. Cheney was chosen president; William Perkins, George

F. Judkins, John M. Chandler and John Gillis, directors; Henry A. Farrington, clerk and treasurer. In 1874 George W. Weeks was elected president; Emil Custer, John M. Chandler, Joseph L. Stevens and George H. True, directors; Henry A. Farrington, clerk and treasurer. These were re-elected in 1875.

On the afternoon of July 19, 1842, the day on which the first pastor, Mr. Wellington, was ordained, "according to appointment a discourse was delivered by the Rev. William H. Channing of Nashua, before an assembly met for the purpose of organizing a church. After the discourse, the covenant agreed upon and the names of those who had signed it was read and a declaration made that by this act of faith a new branch of the church of Christ was now planted. The members of the church from this and other societies then partook of the Lord's Supper." The names of the signers of the covenant are these: Benjamin F. Osgood, S. Manning, Esther Parker, Melinda Osgood, Mehitable Eastman, Oliver H. Wellington, C. A. K. Wellington, Susan Manning, John Caldwell and H. M. A. Foster. The pastors acted as clerks of the church. September 26, 1852, during Mr. Fuller's ministry, A. W. Sargent and Thomas Ordway were chosen deacons, and Charles Aldrich and Isaac W. Farmer were subsequently elected to that office.

The first pastor of the society was Oliver H. Wellington, who was ordained July 19, 1842, by a council which met at the Manchester House. The pastors of all the churches in the city were invited to be present and assist in the services, but all of them, except the pastor of the Universalist church, declined. Mr. Wellington's labors with the society ceased April 1, 1844, and he was succeeded by the Rev. A. Dumont Jones, who was installed July 10, 1844, his connection with the parish ceasing at the end of March, 1845. "At the close of Mr. Jones's ministry the society found itself enfeebled and remained destitute of a pastor, its pulpit, however, being generally supplied by various clergymen. For some eight or ten Sundays the Rev. Mr. Gage, formerly of Nashua, preached to good acceptance. Mr. Edward Capen was likewise engaged subsequently for an equal length of time, but this was the nearest approach to a permanent ministry till the latter part of December, 1846, when the Rev. M. I. Motte, formerly of Boston, was engaged to preach for one year. * * * * While the city, however, had increased to a population of fourteen thousand in the brief period since its founding, it being only nine years since one house alone could be found in the place, yet the society had not increased, but was found feeble and in debt at the close of Mr. Motte's engagement. A motion was made to dissolve the society, which was, however, negatived and it was resolved that another effort should be made." Arthur B. Fuller, a brother of the celebrated Margaret Fuller, the Countess D'Ossoli, then a recent graduate of the divinity school, accepted a call and was ordained March 29, 1848, remaining with the society till June 1, 1853.

The next pastor was the Rev. Francis LeBarron, who took charge of the society without a formal installation, August, 1853. His resignation was accepted October 14, 1855. "At the close of his ministry the society was for several months without a pastor, unable to settle upon any of the many candidates they heard. The Sunday-school was reduced to one class, which was taught through the winter of 1855–56 by Miss Susan Manning. Still preaching was maintained and the society kept out of debt."

William L. Gage was ordained June 25, 1856, resigning the first Sunday in April, 1858, and being succeeded by the Rev. Sylvan S. Hunting, who was installed September 29, 1858, and left about November, 1861. A. W. Stevens was ordained November 5, 1862, and left the society the last of October, 1865. The Rev. Augustus M. Haskell was his successor, being installed September 12, 1866, and resigning March 30, 1869. The Rev. Charles B. Ferry was installed December 9, 1869, and took his departure in the summer of 1874. The Rev. Henry Powers began his labors with the society November 1, 1874, declining a formal installation.

The society's first place of worship, after it left the city hall, was a small wooden chapel built in 1841 on the corner of Hanover and Chestnut streets, where Nathan Parker's house now stands, by the Second Methodist Episcopal society. In 1843 when the Methodists built their brick church on Elm street, they leased this chapel to the Unitarians at an annual rent of six per cent. upon its cost, and Mr. Wellington first preached in it July 2, 1843. That month, however, the society bought it and moved it to a lot on the corner of Merrimack and Pine streets, the gift of the Amoskeag Company, and enlarged it. During Mr. Fuller's ministry the capacity of the chapel was still farther increased and its appearance improved.

In 1852 the Hon. Richard H. Ayer left the society in his will a house on the corner of Chestnut and Central streets, which was used subsequently for a parsonage and sold in 1864 to John Ryan. About this time a new church was talked of and the lot on the corner of Elm and Bridge streets was one of the sites proposed, but the idea was given up. In 1859 the society exchanged its house for the one built by the First Freewill Baptist society on the corner of Chestnut and Merrimack streets, then in the hands of a "Union Association," giving them three thousand five hundred dollars besides. This they sold in 1871 to Col. Waterman Smith, and in 1872 they dedicated a new house of worship on the corner of Beech and Concord streets. This, with the lot on which it stands, is valued at forty thousand dollars. A large congregation worships there, and the Sunday-school, of which George W. Weeks is superintendent, has one hundred and fifty members.

FRANKLIN-STREET CHURCH.

After the annual meeting, April 27, 1844, of the "First Congregational society in Amoskeag village," by which name the First Congregational or Hanover-street society was still known, was dismissed, William G. Means called to order those who remained and a resolution which declared the formation of a second society advisable was offered and discussed. Another meeting was held on the third of May, when a committee, consisting of the Rev. C. W. Wallace, Asa O. Colby, Abram Brigham, Andrew Moody and William G. Means, which had been appointed to make farther inquiries, reported in favor of the plan and the resolution of the previous meeting was passed. May 7, a constitution was adopted and signed by sixteen individuals and the Second Congregational society of Manchester was thus formed.

The first officers were: Josiah Crosby, president; Abram Brigham, clerk and treasurer; William C. Clarke, Thomas Carleton, Walter T. Jaquith, directors. These were re-elected the next year. In 1846 Joseph E. Smith and George T. Mixer succeeded Messrs. Carleton and Jaquith as directors. In 1847 the president was David Brigham; clerk and treasurer, Abram Brigham; directors, George T. Mixer, Aldus M. Chapin, Albe C. Heath. In 1848 Asa O. Colby became president, and Messrs. Mixer and Heath were succeeded as directors by David Gillis and William W. Brown. In 1849 William C. Clarke and William Richardson were chosen directors in place of Messrs. Brown and Chapin. The next year Josiah Crosby was again chosen president and the rest were re-elected. These continued in office till 1855 with hardly a change, Phinehas Adams being chosen in 1852 to succeed Mr. Gillis, and A. M. Chapin in 1854 to take Mr. Richardson's place. In 1855 William W. Brown was made president; William C. Clarke, David J. Clark and Reuben Dodge, directors.

The next year Frederick Smyth became president, Ephraim Corey took Mr. Clarke's place among the directors, and Abram Brigham, who had been clerk and treasurer of the society from its formation, resigned and his place was filled by Albert H. Daniels. In 1857 Isaac W. Smith, Alfred G. Fairbanks and Abram Robertson were elected as the board of directors. In 1858 Josiah Crosby was again chosen president; the offices of clerk and treasurer were separated, Francis B. Eaton being chosen as the former and Frederick Smyth as the latter; and Albert H. Daniels, David Gillis and William C. Clarke were chosen directors. The next year Albert H. Daniels succeeded Mr. Smyth as treasurer, and John M. Harvey took Mr. Daniels's place among the directors. In 1860 George S. Neal was chosen a director in place of David Gillis, and there was no change the next year. In 1862 Charles Morrill and Samuel Upton were elected directors in place of Messrs. Harvey and Neal, and the two next elections made no change except that Mr. Daniels was succeeded as treasurer by Isaac W. Smith in 1864.

In 1865 John M. Ordway was chosen president; Albert H. Daniels, clerk; Isaac W. Smith, treasurer; Samuel Upton, A. M. Chapin and J. S. Sanborn, directors. In 1866 Robert M. Shirley succeeded Mr. Sanborn as director, and in 1867 William W. Brown took Mr. Ordway's place as president. In 1868 William W. Brown was president; Daniel C. Gould, jr., clerk; Marshall P. Hall, treasurer; Samuel Upton, Albert H. Daniels and George W. Dodge, directors. In 1869 William P. Newell and Alden W. Sanborn succeeded Messrs. Daniels and Dodge as directors, and James A. Weston was chosen treasurer and has been annually re-elected since. In 1870 Isaac W. Smith was chosen president and John M. Hill became a director in place of Samuel Upton. The next year Mr. Sanborn was succeeded by David Cross, and in 1872 John B. Clarke succeeded Mr. Newell, and Marshall P. Hall was chosen clerk.

In 1873 there was no change and in 1874 George W. Riddle was elected a director in place of Mr. Hill. The legislature, at the June session of 1859, passed an act authorizing the society, which had built some years previously a house of worship on Franklin street, to assume the name of the Franklin-street society and the society voted on the twenty-fifth of April of the next year to accept the act.

Their first religious services were held in the town hall on the first Sunday in June, 1844. There they worshiped till the burning of the town house on the twelfth of August, when they removed to a chapel on Concord street which had been first used by the First Freewill Baptist society and then by St. Michael's (now Grace) church, but was at this time vacant. In December they took possession of the hall in Patten's block and worshiped there till the completion of the new town house in 1845. This they occupied till the completion of their present church on the southeast corner of Franklin and Market streets, which was dedicated December 22, 1847.

On the twentieth of May, 1844, a committee had been appointed to consider the expediency of organizing a church in connection with this society, and on the twenty-seventh of June the Second Congregational church was formed by a council which met at the house of the Rev. C. W. Wallace, then pastor of the First church. The following persons united in its formation: Mr. and Mrs. Henry Lancaster, Mrs. Elizabeth Gordon, Mr. and Mrs. Richard Trow, Mr. and Mrs. Asa O. Colby, Miss Abby S. Robertson, all of the First church; Miss Mary Libbey and Mrs. Susan H. Moody of a church in Lowell, Mass.; Elizabeth Page and Mary Emerson of the church at Goffstown; Ira Merrill of that at Plymouth; Rodney L. Huntington of that at Francestown; Nicholas Youngman of that at Saugerties, N. Y.; Josiah Crosby, Mrs. Olive L. Crosby, Harriet McClary, Abram Brigham and Alma Brigham of that at Meredith Bridge.

The following became members of the church at its first meeting: Andrew Moody of a church at Lowell, Mass.; Mr. and Mrs. Walter T. Jaquith of the church at Milford; Mr. and Mrs. David W. Grimes, David Brigham, Mr. and Mrs. Thomas Carleton of the First church; Sarah J. Emerson of the church in Candia; Joshua Avery of the church at Meredith Bridge. In accordance with a vote of the members, December 17, 1847, it assumed the name of the Franklin-street church.

The Rev. Mr. Wallace held the office of moderator till the settlement of a pastor and David Brigham was chosen as clerk and treasurer. He resigned the latter office March 26, 1857, when Alfred B. Soule was chosen to fill his place, and was also succeeded by Mr. Soule as clerk, September 9, 1858. Mr. Soule resigned both offices November 29, 1858, and H. C. Bullard was his successor. When the latter's place became vacant by his removal from the city, Aldus M. Chapin was elected, January 5, 1866, to fill it. He resigned May 7, 1871, when Albert H. Daniels was chosen clerk, and Isaac W. Smith, treasurer, both of whom have continued in office to the present time.

Shortly after the formation of the church David Brigham was chosen a deacon, and, a little later, Thomas Carleton received an election to the same office. December 18, 1845, Walter T. Jaquith was chosen deacon, and May 14, 1846, George T. Mixer. December 24, 1847, Aldus M. Chapin was elected to succeed Mr. Jaquith, who had left the city. Deacon Carleton resigned January 4, 1849, and Erastus Danielson was chosen March 29, 1849, to take his place. Mr. Brigham resigned his deaconship March 26, 1857, and Albert H. Daniels was chosen in his stead. April 16, 1857, Deacons Mixer and Chapin having left the city, Alfred B. Soule was elected to the office. Francis B. Eaton was made deacon November 11, 1858. Deacon Danielson left the city in 1858 and Deacon Soule in 1859, and

Joseph B. Clark

November 1, 1860, Aldus M. Chapin, having returned, was re-elected to his former office. Henry T. Mowatt was chosen deacon April 6, 1866, and resigned April 2, 1874. In 1871 Deacon Chapin again left the place, and July 9, 1872, George Murdough and Ira Barr were elected, making four deacons now in office.

The first pastor was Henry M. Dexter, who was ordained November 6, 1844. He was dismissed March 14, 1849, and was succeeded, September 26, 1849, by the Rev. Henry S. Clarke. The latter remained till July 1, 1852, and, November 3, 1852, the Rev. Samuel C. Bartlett was installed. He was dismissed February 18, 1857, and his successor, the Rev. Aaron C. Adams, was settled on the twenty-second of July of the same year. He left September 22, 1858, and William H. Fenn became pastor of the church February 10, 1859. He remained over seven years, being dismissed July 17, 1866. He was followed by William J. Tucker, who was ordained January 24, 1867. In the summer of 1874 interest in Mr. Tucker's preaching had drawn so many to the Franklin-street church that there were no pews unrented, and many were seeking accommodation in vain. Mr. Tucker, in declining a call to become the pastor of the Madison-avenue Congregational church in New York city, where the salary is at least ten thousand dollars, drew the attention of the church and society to the need of a larger house of worship, and a committee was raised to have the matter in charge and obtain, if possible, fifty thousand dollars by subscription, the estimated cost of a new building. A partial effort was made at that time to this end, and there the matter rested till February 21, 1875, when Mr. Tucker read to the congregation from the pulpit a communication in which he offered his resignation, stating in substance that his usefulness was crippled by the want of accommodation for those who wished to enjoy the privileges of worship in the Franklin-street church. This announcement was received with general surprise and regret, and a meeting of the congregation was held that afternoon, when twenty thousand dollars was pledged for the building of a new church. This sum was afterwards raised to thirty-seven thousand dollars, but no further increase could be made. Other plans were proposed but failed of execution, and Mr. Tucker, deeming it inconsistent with the interests of the church and society to withdraw his resignation, publicly re-affirmed it March 14, intending to close his labors with the church after the first Sunday in May.

The church property is estimated to be worth eighteen thousand dollars. The church has a membership of about three hundred, and the Sunday-school numbers nearly six hundred. Of the latter Samuel Upton is superintendent, and Albert H. Daniels assistant superintendent.

MERRIMACK-STREET BAPTIST CHURCH.

"Early in the year 1845 the pastor of the First Baptist church in Manchester, in contemplating the rapidly increasing population of the place and the fact that the church numbered more than three hundred communicants, and that sufficient accommodations could not be obtained for more than one-half of the inhabitants if all the places of public worship were filled, felt that the cause of Christ and the interests of religion demanded of the First church to make an effort to establish and sustain a second interest."

"May 2, 1845, the subject was brought before the church by the pastor, the Rev. Benjamin Brierly, and after a free and full discussion it was voted that Brethren David P. Perkins, John B. Goodwin, Daniel Gooden, Deacon Samuel Weston and the Rev. Andrew T. Foss be a committee to ascertain what can be done in relation to the subject of organizing a second church and report at a future meeting."

May 26, the committee made a report favorable to the enterprise, which was adopted, and, June 2, the church voted that it was expedient to organize a second church at once.

"October 27, 1845, the First Baptist church in Manchester met for business, when the following brethren and sisters presented their request to be dismissed from this church for the purpose of forming a second church in this town, agreeably to a vote of the church passed June 2, 1845, viz.: Andrew T. Foss, Samuel Weston, Elviress Parmenter, Daniel Gooden, John B. Goodwin, David P. Perkins, Alfred George, Thomas George, John Buzzell, Henry G. Buzzell, Jonathan Rand, John Rider, M. M. Foss, Eliza Weston, Electa Parmenter, Marinda Gooden, Caroline S. Goodwin, Abigail Brooks, Ann W. Parmenter, Sarah Emerson, Betsey Conner, Esther P. Rand, Betsey Buzzell, Rosanna Buzzell, Milla R. Parker, Elizabeth Night, Ann E. Weston, Mary Ann George, Lydia George, Lydia George, 2d, Caroline George, Sarah Rand, Clorinda Rider and Abigail Rider, and Isaac Manning and Ann E. Manning by letter."

October 31, 1845, those who were purposing to form the church met at John B. Goodwin's house and chose the Rev. A. T. Foss moderator and David P. Perkins clerk of the evening. Upon motion of Deacon Samuel Weston it was voted to organize as the Second Baptist Church in Manchester, and David P. Perkins was chosen its clerk. The church was publicly recognized as such by a council December 3, 1845.

The first pastor was the Rev. A. T. Foss. He was dismissed at his own request July 11, 1847, and was succeeded, December 26, by the Rev. J. C. Morrill, who left July 15, 1849. The next minister was the Rev. O. O. Stearns, who remained not quite a year and was followed in January, 1851, by the Rev. Isaac Woodbury. After his withdrawal in January, 1853, the Rev. John Peacock, formerly pastor of the old Amoskeag Baptist church, supplied the pulpit till the middle of April and then different clergymen officiated for two or three months. In July, 1853, the Rev. J. M. Coburn became the pastor. His resignation was accepted October 8, 1855, but seven weeks later he was invited to again become pastor of the church and accepted the invitation. His resignation was again offered and accepted December 5, 1858, and the Rev. King S. Hall was recognized as pastor March 30, 1859. He left September 4, 1862, and the Rev. A. W. Chaffin succeeded him June 10, 1863. He remained till February 2, 1868, when his resignation was accepted. The Rev. Alden Sherwin, the present pastor, was recognized as such November 18, 1868.

The first clerk of the church was David P. Perkins, who was chosen upon its formation. Upon his dismissal in 1847 Daniel Gooden acted as clerk till July 2, 1849, when Caleb Gage was chosen. George Holbrook acted as clerk from January, 1851, to July, when the Rev. Isaac Woodbury, who had been chosen clerk in April, took the records, being succeeded, January 24, 1853, by Pliny Allen. George Holbrook was chosen clerk January 2, 1854, and has held the office ever since. The first treasurer was Daniel Gooden, who was elected November 9, 1845, and was succeeded January 1, 1851, by Caleb Gage, the present treasurer.

At the organization of the church Samuel Weston, Elviress Parmenter and Daniel Gooden were chosen deacons, Deacon Weston being dismissed in 1847. January 8, 1849, Ebenezer Clark, Caleb Gage and Jerry Felt were added to the number, Deacon Clark leaving in 1850 to join the First church from which he had come two years before, and Deacon Felt being dismissed in 1854. Savory T. Burbank, Lyman Wood and Calvin Boynton were chosen deacons October 29, 1855, and, March 2, 1856, George Holbrook and Timothy S. Jacobs.

The meetings of the church were first held in Classic hall and afterwards in Temple hall in Patten's block, but during Mr. Morrill's pastorate services were held for a short time in the chapel on Central street which was moved from Concord street, where it had been occupied in succession by the First Freewill Baptist society, St. Michael's church and the Second Congregational society. Thence the church moved to the city hall, which it occupied till February 22, 1849, when the brick church on the southwest corner of Elm and Pleasant streets was occupied for the first time. This was built by Daniel Gooden with a view to its possession by the church, to which he sold the second story, with the understanding that the third might be bought whenever the church desired. With Mr. Gooden were afterwards associated John V. Gooden and Stephen D. Green, and subsequently the property fell into the latter's hands. The church voted, December 14, 1853, to adopt the name of the Elm-street Baptist church.

March 27, 1854, the following associated themselves to form a corporation under the name of the Elm-street Baptist Church, for the purpose of holding the property: Jesse M. Coburn, Daniel Gooden, Stephen M. Bennett, William H. Gilmore, Caleb Gage, John B. Goodwin, Alfred George, Thomas H. Stevens, Elviress Parmenter, Oliver Gould, Gilman Stewart, Silas F. Dean, George Holbrook. They re-elected the officers of the church. One payment had been made upon the building, but the church declined to make another and, after remaining there till February, 1857, they left and worshiped with the First church and in Smyth's hall and the city hall till the dedication of their present house of worship, October 27, 1857. This was built by a society which had been formed in June of that year and which bought of John H. Maynard and George W. F. Converse the lot on Merrimack street between Pine and Union on which the church stands. It had been proposed to disband two years before they left the house on Elm street, but the church resolved to cling together and at length outlived their troubles. The name of the church was changed, January 31, 1859, to that of Merrimack-street Baptist Church. December 11, 1870, the church celebrated the twenty-fifth anniversary of its existence with appropriate ceremonies. It has now two hundred and fifty members, one hundred and fifty resident. The Sunday-school, of which John C. Balch is superintendent and George Holbrook assistant superintendent, has one hundred and fifty members.

The Merrimack-street Baptist Society was formed June 1, 1857, by Caleb Gage, Calvin Boynton, John B. Goodwin, William H. Gilmore, Elviress Parmenter, Lyman Wood, Wallace W. Baker, Gilman S. Stewart and George Holbrook. The corporation was first organized as the Merrimack-street Baptist Church, but the name of "church" was changed the next day to that of "society." At the first meeting Wallace W. Baker was chosen president; George Holbrook clerk, and Caleb Gage treasurer; and these were elected at the annual meeting in January, 1858, together with a board of directors, consisting of Lyman Wood, John B. Goodwin, C. W. Barker, Savory T Burbank, Elviress Parmenter, W. H. Gilmore and James Holbrook. In 1857, as has once been mentioned, the society bought a lot and built upon it a meeting-house. About 1860 the "Domestic Benevolent Society," an association of women connected with the church, raised the necessary funds and built a chapel in the rear of the house. The value of the whole property is estimated at ten thousand dollars.

Mr. Baker was succeeded as president by Caleb Gage in 1863, who remained till 1866, when Joseph Simonds took his place. In 1868 John L. Davis was chosen, and he was succeeded in 1870 by W. H. Gilmore who now holds the office. Mr. Holbrook has been the society's clerk ever since its formation. Mr. Gage continued treasurer till 1869 when Timothy S. Jacobs was elected. His place was taken the next year by Charles W. Barker, who was succeeded in 1871 by the present treasurer, Douglas Mitchell. The following, who have not been included among the officers mentioned above, have been directors at one time and another since the formation of the society: Robert Gilmore, Oliver Gould, Abram Putnam, Leander Gage, William A. Vincent, Charles Wheeler, Jason White, William Heap, John C. Balch, Edwin C. Stevens, John H. Wales, Henry I. Caswell, George Dickinson, George W. Davis.

FIRST WESLEYAN METHODIST CHURCH.

March 13, 1849, the following persons united to form a church which should be governed by the usages of the Wesleyan Methodist church of America: John Jones, Francis Monroe, Prudence B. Jones, Charles E. Mills, Catherine Mills, Joseph Bartlett, Harriet N. Bartlett, John L. Trefran, Stephen Wiggin, Hannah M. Wiggin, James T. Hardy, Elbridge Dearborn, John C. Wadleigh, Jesse F. Wiggin, John Templeton, Margaret Robertson, Lucia A. Morrill, Melissa Morrill.

These were mainly seceders from the Second Methodist Episcopal church and their first pastor was the Rev. John Jones, the first preacher stationed over the church whence they had come, having been its minister in 1840 and again in 1846 and 1847. He was succeeded in October, 1851, by the Rev. Jonas Scott, who remained till some time in 1852, when the Rev. Thomas M. Latham took his place. In 1854 the latter was succeeded by the Rev. R. C. Stone and in that year or the next the church was dissolved, the records ending abruptly in the middle of a sentence.

The first clerk of the church was James T. Hardy. He

was succeeded by J. C. Wadleigh, and he by R. G. Eaton, and then Mr. Wadleigh was again chosen and succeeded by Langdon Munroe. The treasurers were William Root and Jeremiah D. Jones. The church held services in the city hall, in Patten's and Granite halls, in the chapel on Central street which had been moved thither from Concord street, and finally in the old meeting-house in Piscataquog village, where the church broke up.

MANCHESTER CITY MISSIONARY SOCIETY.

In the spring of 1847 the Rev. J. L. Seymour was employed as a city missionary by individuals interested in the cause of religion, who paid his salary and hired a hall where he opened a Sunday-school and conducted religious services. In this way the idea of a free church was suggested and the building now used for that purpose, on the northwest corner of Merrimack and Beech streets, was built in 1850 and dedicated on the twenty-third of October of that year. The land on which it stands was given by the Amoskeag Company and the money which built it was the contribution of individuals in the city and of the Congregational and Presbyterian churches in the state. The property is worth about six thousand dollars and is held in trust, on condition that the seats in the church shall be free and that public worship shall be maintained, by the Manchester City Missionary society, which was legally organized April 24, 1850, at a meeting in the vestry of the First Congregational church. George T. Mixer was chosen chairman and David Brigham secretary, and a constitution was adopted which defines the object of the society to be to sustain a missionary or missionaries for the religious instruction of those who do not usually attend public worship. This was amended in 1870 so as to make the distribution of charity an additional object. The society numbers about a hundred members.

Lewis W. Clark

At the first meeting for choice of officers Moulton Knowles was elected president; George T. Mixer, vice-president; David Brigham, secretary; Henry Clough, treasurer; Stephen Smith, Archelaus Wilson, William G. Means, Frederick Smyth, Aldus M. Chapin, executive committee. In 1851 David Gillis was chosen president and Nahum Baldwin vice-president. In 1852 William G. Means was made president; Aldus M. Chapin, vice-president; and James O. Adams succeeded Mr. Brigham as secretary. In 1853 Mr. Chapin was relieved by George T. Mixer, and Abraham Robertson became treasurer in place of Mr. Clough. The next year James Hersey succeeded Mr. Means as president, and in 1855 Ephraim Corey was elected vice-president and William H. Ward secretary. In 1856 Mr. Corey was chosen president and Jonathan Tenney was elected to the place thus left vacant. In 1857 Henry T. Mowatt was chosen president; Moulton Knowles, vice-president; David Hill, secretary. Within the year the latter was succeeded by Charles Aldrich, and Abraham Robertson, who had been treasurer since 1853, was succeeded by Horace Pettee.

In 1858 George W. Pinkerton became vice-president; in 1859 there was no change; and in 1860 Mr. Pinkerton was elected president; John Harvey, vice-president; Sylvanus Bunton, secretary; Holmes R. Pettee, treasurer. In 1861 Horace Pettee was chosen president and Theodore T. Abbot vice-president. There is no record of a meeting in 1862, and the next year William Bailey became vice-president and Thomas B. Brown secretary. These officers were re-elected in 1864 and 1865 with the exception of Mr. Bailey, who was succeeded by Charles Currier in 1865, and there was no change in 1866, 1867 and 1868. In 1869 Henry W. Herrick was elected president; Alden W. Sanborn, vice-president; and John G. Lane secretary, who has held the office ever since. In 1870 Orison Hardy became vice-president and Joseph H. Peabody secretary. In 1871 Henry Clough was elected president; James T. Frost, vice-president; and William F. Childs, treasurer, who has been re-elected annually since. In 1872 Storer Nason succeeded Mr. Frost as vice-president and in 1873 Albert H. Daniels succeeded Mr. Clough as president, since when there has been no change. The executive committee of 1874 consisted of Alden W. Sanborn, Marshall P. Hall, Alfred G. Fairbanks, Horace Pettee and Moses E. George.

The Rev. Mr. Seymour continued his labors as missionary after the church had been built and in April, 1851, was succeeded by the Rev. T. P. Sawin, who remained till about the same time in 1856. He was followed by the Rev. Lyman Marshall, who remained till 1860. For six years thereafter the enterprise languished, no missionary was hired and religious services were not sustained. In 1866, however, the Rev. T. P. Sawin returned to assume the duties of missionary and remained three years, leaving in May, 1869, and being followed in October of that year by the Rev. Frank G. Clark. He resigned in April, 1873, to become pastor of a church in Rindge, and the present missionary, the Rev. William H. Rand, began his labors in September. Miss M. E. Spear served as assistant missionary in parts of 1869 and 1870, and, after she left, Mrs. George P. Woodman performed her duties a part of the time till the appointment of Miss Sarah J. Fitzpatrick—now Mrs. Thomas Bailey—in April, 1872. She held the office till May, 1874, when she resigned, and in September Mrs. Daniel S. Adams was appointed and now serves.

The society's annual income is derived from several different sources. From the start it had received one hundred and fifty dollars a year from the state missionary society, but this ceased about 1870, when the mission in this city enlarged its sphere of action. The sum of sixty dollars accrues as interest upon a thousand dollars bequeathed in

1851 by the late Thomas D. Merrill of Concord; the interest of eighty-eight dollars is received from a fund left in trust for the society's uses: and the two Congregational churches in the city make an annual appropriation of three hundred dollars each. About 1870, when the society combined charitable with religious work, the Amoskeag, Stark, Manchester and Langdon corporations agreed to pay for the support of the mission a sum equivalent to one hundredth of one per cent. upon their capital stock, amounting in all to six hundred and fifty-five dollars. Voluntary contributions at the services in the free church add about one hundred dollars, making a stated income of about fourteen hundred dollars. From this is paid the missionary's salary of twelve hundred dollars and the current expenses, and the surplus is used, so far as it goes, to support an assistant city missionary for a longer or shorter time.

The needs of the poor had become so apparent after the war that subscriptions were raised at irregular times, and Mr. Sawin, who was then missionary, spent a part of his time in the relief of the destitute. The result of this has already been referred to in the recognition by an amendment to the society's constitution of the distribution of charity as a part of the missionary's work and the annual contribution of over one-half his salary by the corporations. The relief fund is kept in a separate account and was begun by the raising of five hundred dollars at a levee five or six years ago. This was spent in about three years and Mr. Clark, then the missionary, raised three hundred dollars more by subscription, which has gradually been spent, and the society relies upon individual subscriptions of money, clothing and other necessaries for means to carry on its charitable work, none of the stated income being spent in that way. The society, while it was engaged solely in religious work, was solely a Congregational society, but when it began to relieve the suffering, an effort was made to enlist the sympathies of other denominations in the city, and for a year or two nearly all made contributions for its support. The interest, however, was but temporary and aid from other than Congregational churches has ceased, though other denominations are represented in its officers.

Shortly after the free church was built it seemed desirable to those who attended service there or who took part in the Sunday-school, that a church should be regularly organized to worship there, and, December 7, 1852, in accordance with a notice previously given, a few persons assembled to take the matter into consideration. They decided to proceed and chose Abraham Burton clerk. The church was formally organized December 30, 1852, by an ecclesiastical council, under the name of the "Christian Mission Church." The city missionary was always the pastor of the church. Joseph T. Ayer was chosen treasurer March 5, 1853, and, December 31, 1853, James Brooks and Abraham Burton were elected deacons. Deacon Burton resigned his clerkship in 1857 but continued to keep the books. The last record was made in 1859 and about that time the church fell to pieces. A Sunday-school had been supported there till the closing of the church in 1860. While it remained unopened, a mission-school was organized in the vestry of the First Congregational church and transferred thence to the free chapel, when worship was resumed there. The school has now about two hundred and fifty members. John G. Lane is the superintendent and Daniel S. Adams assistant superintendent.

SECOND UNIVERSALIST CHURCH.

The Second Universalist society was formed by men who separated from the First society and who met and adopted a constitution December 10, 1859. They were followers of the Rev. B. M. Tillotson, who had been pastor of the First church, but had resigned its charge the previous October. They met again the first day of the next year at Smyth's hall and elected Lewis Simons president, Charles H. Chase vice-president, Ira A. Bowen secretary, and John D. Bean treasurer. In March of that year the Rev. B. H. Davis accepted an invitation to become pastor of the society and remained till February, 1861. In January, 1861, Charles H. Chase became secretary and Luther Smith succeeded him as vice-president, but before the month was out, all the officers resigned, and John Gillis was elected president, P. D. Howe vice-president, J. D. Jones secretary, and E. P. Pearson treasurer. On the fourteenth of December, 1861, the Rev. B. M. Tillotson, whose services the society had endeavored to obtain at the outset, began his labors with it. In 1862 Lewis Simons again became president; E. P. Pearson, vice-president; W. P. Rundlett, secretary; and J. D. Bean, treasurer. These continued through the next year. January 11, 1863, the society voted to take the name of the Elm-street Universalist Society. Till that year worship had been held in Smyth's hall, but then the society moved to what is now Music hall, which had been built with a view to its occupancy by the society. In 1864 Eleazer Martin was chosen president; John Gillis, vice-president; Ira A. Bowen, secretary; and John D. Bean was re-elected treasurer. The next year Allen Partridge was chosen vice-president and Darwin A. Simons treasurer, Mr. Martin and Mr. Bowen being re-elected, but upon the former's death in June, Thomas Maskey was elected to take his place. In 1866 Charles H. Chase became secretary and there was no change till after the annual election of the next year had passed.

It was deemed wise to form a legally incorporated society, and, February 27, 1867, Thomas Maskey, Lewis Simons, George H. Dorr, Charles H. Chase, H. L. Drew, Darwin A. Simons and George E. Glines were associated as the

Elm-street Universalist Society, proper notice of the fact being given. In April Thomas Maskey was chosen president; Allen Partridge, vice-president; Charles H. Chase, clerk; and Darwin A. Simons, treasurer. The next year Lewis Simons became president and George H. Dorr vice-president. In 1869 George E. Glines succeeded Mr. Dorr. In 1870 A. C. Osgood became clerk and George E. Wilson treasurer. In 1871 H. L. Drew was elected president; B. K. Parker, vice-president; A. C. Osgood, clerk; and A. B. Chase, treasurer. In March of that year the Rev. B. M. Tillotson left the pastorate of the society, and preaching was supplied by the Rev. A. P. Folsom from May till November, on the twenty-seventh of which month the society voted to dissolve.

The Elm-street Universalist Church was formed in June, 1860, and disbanded in the fall of 1871, eighty-seven members having been connected with it. Its clerk was John Gillis; its treasurer, J. C. Hill; and its deacons, J. C. Hill, Amasa Waterman, John Gillis, Lewis Simons, Columbus Wyman. In connection with it a Sunday-school was organized in 1860, which had a hundred and sixty members. Its superintendents were J. C. Hill, George H. True and the several pastors.

FIRST PRESBYTERIAN CHURCH.

Prior to the year 1820 there was no house of worship in Manchester except the old town-house at the Centre. At that time the inhabitants of Piscataquog village, then a part of Bedford, feeling the need of better religious privileges, took measures to build a meeting-house. A company was organized and the stock, divided into thirty-three shares of one hundred dollars each, subscribed for, and, though there were then but ten houses in Piscataquog, all the money was raised in the village. A very desirable lot of land, situated on the river road on the hill which rises from the south bank of the Piscataquog, was given, and a large part of the stock was taken, by the heirs of William Parker, a wealthy merchant of the village, then lately deceased. Work was begun on the house in the spring of 1820 and it was finished and dedicated on the fifteenth of November of that year. The building committee consisted of James Patten, Jonathan Palmer and William P. Riddle.

It had been hoped that on the completion of the house an arrangement might be made with the Presbyterian church at Bedford Centre, by which the pastor of that church might divide his labors and occupy the pulpit of the new house a part of the time. It is worthy of remark that the Presbyterian doctrine was taught in Piscataquog and at Manchester Centre, and that Presbyterians were many in the vicinity of the meeting-house which was built in 1736 in the southeast part of the town, while Congregationalism, in which the kindred denomination has now been lost, as far as Manchester is concerned, emanated from Amoskeag village. As this arrangement with Bedford could not be made, and as the people of the village were unable of themselves to sustain preaching, no stated and regular services, except occasionally for a few months at a time, were held in the house till its occupation by the Wesleyan Methodists in 1855. However, soon after its dedication the Rev. Mr. Long was engaged to teach the district school and preach on Sundays, and after his retirement the Rev. Mr. Pomeroy, a fresh graduate from the theological seminary at Andover, supplied the pulpit for some time and an unsuccessful effort was made to settle him as a colleague with the Rev. David McGregor of Bedford. Just before the revival of 1831 a Mr. Saulsbury preached acceptably and in the spring of 1839 an old minister named Miltimore occupied the pulpit for a time.

In 1842 the proprietors decided to dispose of the house and it was accordingly sold for about three hundred dollars to a company, which, six years later, was incorporated under the name of "The Piscataquog Village Academy," the grantees being William P. Riddle, Jonas B. Bowman, James Walker, Daniel Mack, Mace Moulton, Frederick G. Stark, Henry C. Parker, Samuel Brown, Andrew J. Dow, James Harvell and Ephraim Harvell. The upper part of the building was fitted for school purposes, the lower part being still retained for public worship, and in the fall of 1842 the house was opened to the public as an academy. The first principal was Dr. Leonard French, now of this city. He was succeeded by Hiram Wason, and he by Charles Warren. In March, 1845, Benjamin F. Wallace, afterwards an elder in the Presbyterian church which was formed in the village, took charge of the school and remained its instructor till its discontinuance, with the exception of one year when it was taught by the Rev. Amos Abbott, once a missionary in India.

In the summer of 1855 the First Wesleyan Methodist church, which had been meeting for several years in various halls in the city proper, obtained permission to occupy the house and sustained religious services for a short time and then withdrew. The pastor, the Rev. R. C. Stone, succeeded, however, by making a strong personal effort among the people, in raising sufficient funds for his support, and continued his ministrations during the fall.

In the spring of 1856, by advice of the Londonderry Presbytery and with the aid of the Presbyterian Board of Missions, the Rev. George A. Bowman was employed and he continued to supply the pulpit till July, 1866. During his ministry, a committee of the Londonderry Presbytery, appointed for that purpose at Windham in October, 1858, met, November 9, 1859, at Piscataquog village, which had become a part of Manchester three years before, and organ-

John B. Clarke.

ized the "First Presbyterian Church in Manchester" with the following members: Mr. and Mrs. Samuel McQueston, B. F. Wallace, Marion Wallace, Mrs. Sarah French, Celia N. French, Ellen B. French, Robert H. French, Mrs. Betsey P. Walker, Mrs. James Harvell, Jonas B. Bowman, Asenath L. L. Bowman, Margaret McQueston, Mrs. Adeline Livingston. The church held a meeting the same day and elected Deacon Samuel McQueston and Benjamin F. Wallace elders and the latter was ordained to the office of elder, being also chosen clerk. At different times during its existence a number of persons were added, but in 1867, the year after Mr. Bowman's departure, it was disbanded and its last record was made December 20, 1867, by the Rev. Arthur Little, pastor of the church at Bedford, who granted, by authority of the Presbytery, letters of dismission to Ira Barr, Mrs. Lucinda S. McQueston, Miss Margaret McQueston and Mrs. Sarah C. Harvell, who joined the Franklin-street church, and Mr. and Mrs. Ebenezer Hartshorn, who went to the First Congregational church.

In 1870 Mrs. Mary P. Harris, a native of Piscataquog village and the daughter of William Parker, having expressed a desire to repair the church and put it in the hands of the Young Men's Christian Association, the proprietors voted to give it to her for that purpose with the understanding that the Association would always keep it in repair. In accordance with this vote Mrs. Harris accepted the house, and, having thoroughly renewed it, transferred it to the Association, by which it is held in trust, the latter agreeing on its part to keep the building in good condition and to maintain "evangelical" preaching in it. It was dedicated April 21, 1872, with appropriate religious exercises, different clergymen of the city taking part and the Rev. Dr. Wallace giving a brief history of religious worship in Piscataquog. A Sunday-school was then organized and has continued since in a flourishing condition, first under the superintendence of Col. Francis W. Parker and then, successively, of Edward Taylor and Charles A. Davenport. It has now about one hundred members. The city clergymen supply the pulpit in succession Sunday afternoons.

PINE-STREET FREEWILL BAPTIST CHURCH.

"December 21, 1859, in compliance with the request of some Freewill Baptist brethren in Manchester a council, consisting of the Rev. S. Curtis, A. R. Bradbury, E. M. Tappan and J. P. Nutting, convened in this city for the purpose of re-organizing a church," and, by the advice and assistance of this council, the Pine-street Freewill Baptist church was formed. The Rev. J. M. Bailey, who had been pastor of the First Freewill Baptist church from which this had arisen, was installed the same day as pastor. He closed his labors in November, 1861, and, September 10, 1862, Reuben V. Jenness was ordained. He resigned June 1, 1863, and was succeeded by the Rev. Nahum Brooks. The latter resigned May 12, 1869, and the Rev. N. L. Rowell accepted an invitation to become pastor of the church. In November, 1873, he resigned and the Rev. Harrison F. Wood was installed May 22, 1874.

At the organization of the church Silas Hamilton was chosen clerk and treasurer. He resigned October 3, 1862, and H. W. Savory succeeded him, continuing in office till April 30, 1873, when Mr. Hamilton resumed his former office. December 30, 1859, H. W. Savory and J. J. Straw, who had been deacons in the old church, were elected to the same office in this, and July 8, 1868, Samuel Gould was added. December 28, 1870, J. B. Daniels and F. P. Smith were also elected deacons. The church has now about two hundred and twenty-five members, probably one hundred and fifty resident, and the Sunday-school numbers two hundred and seventy-five. Of the latter James S. Berry is superintendent, and Harvey B. Sawyer assistant superintendent.

The "Union Association" was formed for the purpose of assuming the debts of the First Freewill Baptist society, January 8, 1859, meeting at the residence of Jonathan Cilley. Its members were J. M. Bean, George W. Quinby, William B. Dana, H. W. Savory, Jonathan J. Straw, A. J. Butterfield, Liberty Raymond, Silas Hamilton, Francis G. Bean and Jonathan Cilley. They elected, as president, William B. Dana; vice-president, Francis G. Bean; secretary and treasurer, Silas Hamilton; directors, J. M. Bean, Liberty Raymond, H. W. Savory. A constitution and by-laws were subsequently adopted.

As has already been stated, this association, having bought of the First Freewill Baptist society its church and exchanged it for the one then occupied by the Unitarians, rented the latter to the Pine-street church. Their first officers continued through 1860 and there was but one change in 1861, when J. M. Bean resigned his office as director on account of want of health and was succeeded by J. J. Straw. The same year George W. Quinby sold his stock to F. P. Smith, who thus became a member of the association. These officers were re-elected in 1862, but the next year, upon Mr. Hamilton's departure from the city, H. W. Savory was chosen to succeed him as clerk and treasurer and F. P. Smith took Mr. Savory's place in the board of directors.

The property was held by this association till August 30, 1865, when the Pine-street Freewill Baptist society was formed to take its place, its members meeting in the vestry of the church and being called to order by Nahum Brooks. They adopted a constitution, and, at a meeting held September 6, 1865, chose True Dudley secretary and treasurer, and Joseph Bean, Moses E. George and John Kittredge, wardens. These were re-elected at the first annual meeting in December of that year, but in 1866 Joseph Bean, Joseph Peabody and C. S. Boynton were chosen wardens, being succeeded in 1867 by Joseph Bean, David Ricker and J. B. Daniels. A revised constitution was adopted that year by which the title of wardens was changed to that of prudential committee and a president and vice-president were added to the list of officers, Samuel Gould being chosen as the former and B. W. Robinson as the latter.

The society voted, September 25, 1868, to accept the act of incorporation passed by the legislature of that year. The grantees were: Nahum Brooks, J. J. Straw, A. J. Butterfield, Joseph Peabody, H. W. Savory, F. P. Smith, David Ricker, Samuel Gould, Joseph Bean, True E. Dudley, Lyman Batchelder and Moses A. Hunkins. The officers chosen that year were: Moses E. George, president; B. W. Robinson, vice-president; Harvey B. Sawyer, secretary and treasurer; David Ricker, Lyman Batchelder and Moses A. Hunkins, directors. In 1869 Joseph Peabody succeeded Mr. Ricker as a director and during the next year F. P. Smith was elected to take Mr. Hunkins's place. At the election of 1870 J. B. Daniels, J. L. Dearborn and M. C. Clark were elected prudential committee, the two latter being succeeded the next year by A. A. Ainsworth and James S. Berry.

The annual election had heretofore been held in December and the officers elected in one year had served in the next, but now the time of meeting was changed to January and the year of election made coincident with the year of service. In 1873 Nahum Brooks was elected president; David Ricker, vice-president; Harvey B. Sawyer, secretary and treasurer; James S. Berry, I. D. Palmer and David Ricker, prudential committee. In 1874 A. A. Ainsworth succeeded Mr. Ricker as vice-president, and I. D. Palmer,

Moses E. George and Silas Hamilton were chosen prudential committee. In 1875 George T. Bailey was chosen clerk, Mr. Sawyer continuing treasurer, and Charles E. Cox, David H. Burbank and Nahum Brooks were chosen prudential committee. The value of the society's property is about eight thousand dollars.

MERRIMACK-STREET FREE BAPTIST CHURCH.

Those members of the First Freewill Baptist church who kept the records and claimed the name met for the first time for business January 11, 1860, in the brick church on the corner of Elm and Pleasant streets, formerly occupied by the Second (Calvinistic) Baptist society. George S. Holmes, who was the church clerk when the house on Merrimack street was occupied, was chosen clerk and treasurer March 21, 1860. In October of that year it was voted to adopt the name of the Elm-street Freewill Baptist Church. The Rev. J. B. Davis occupied the pulpit for a few months, and, March 27, 1861, the Rev. J. A. Knowles was installed as pastor, continuing such till the first of March, 1871.

J. W. Severance, Samuel Gould and Stephen H. Randlett were chosen deacons March 21, 1860, and on the first of August Joseph E. Walker was added to their number. B. J. Robinson was elected April 3, 1861; Stevens James, February 11, 1863; and John S. Folsom, January 1, 1868. Mr. Holmes, the first clerk and treasurer, continued to act in that capacity till August 1, 1866, when Samuel Gould succeeded him. William H. Cate took his place January 2, 1867, and was succeeded in January, 1871, by Timon M. Morse, who had acted as clerk since the previous March. Upon Mr. Morse's departure from town, George S. Holmes was chosen, December 31, 1874, to take his place.

The financial affairs of the church were conducted by an association, like that which was formed in the other Freewill Baptist church, till February, 1864, when the members of the congregation met to consider the propriety of forming a religious society. Samuel Gould was chosen chairman, and William H. Cate, secretary, and John W. Severance, Samuel Gould and Stevens James were appointed to draft a constitution. This was adopted February 22, 1864, and the following officers chosen: Samuel Gould, president: Stevens James, vice-president; William H. Cate, secretary; John S. Folsom, treasurer; S. H. Randlett, D. D. Goodwin and Jeremiah Russell, prudential committee. The name of the "Randall Freewill Baptist Society" was first taken, but it was voted, December 21, 1864, to change the name to that of "Elm-street Freewill Baptist Society."

In 1865 Stephen H. Randlett was chosen vice-president; James M. Nutt, secretary; Benjamin J. Robinson, William H. Cate and Charles Davis, prudential committee. In 1866 Benjamin J. Robinson succeeded Mr. Nutt as vice-president, and Joseph W. Bean, Stevens James and L. W. Nourse were elected prudential committee. The next year John S. Folsom became vice-president and D. D. Goodwin succeeded Mr. Nourse as a member of the prudential committee. In 1868 Joseph W. Bean was chosen vice-president and W. H. Cate became a member of the prudential committee in place of Mr. Goodwin, and there was no change in the next year. In 1870 C. C. Frost was elected president; Oscar M. Titus, vice-president; Will C. Morse, secretary; John S. Folsom, treasurer; C. C. Frost, Timon M. Morse and Oscar M. Titus, prudential committee.

The last record of this society is dated March 29, 1871, and on that day it was succeeded by the Merrimack-street Freewill Baptist Society, the same organization with a change of name induced by the removal of the church and society about this time to their old house of worship on the corner of Merrimack and Chestnut streets. Their officers were elected March 31, as follows: C. C. Frost, president;

Timon M. Morse, vice-president; James M. Clough, secretary; Oscar M. Titus, treasurer; Charles Davis, George A. Bailey and George H. Kenniston, prudential committee. The latter were succeeded in 1872 by B. J. Robinson, George S. Holmes and Charles Davis. There was no change in 1873, and in 1874 C. C. Frost was chosen president; Timon M. Morse, vice-president; Joseph E. Merrill, secretary; George A. Bailey, treasurer; Charles Davis, George S. Holmes and Timon M. Morse, prudential committee. In 1875 Joseph W. Bean was elected vice-president; Will C. Morse, treasurer; Charles Davis, Joseph W. Bean and Benjamin J. Robinson, prudential committee.

The church remained but a few months in the old house and then declined, holding irregular meetings at the houses of the members, till 1873, when regular service was begun in the hall of the Young Men's Christian Association in Masonic Temple. The Rev. Samuel McKeown was installed as pastor July 2, 1873. In 1874, gathering numbers and strength, they returned once more to their first home and in April of that year bought the house and lot of Col. Waterman Smith, who had acquired them from the Unitarians. The church had assumed the name of the Merrimack-street Freewill Baptist Church in 1871, and in 1874, in conformity to a new usage, changed the title of Freewill Baptist to that of Free Baptist. Mr. McKeown resigned July 1, 1874, and the Rev. George M. Park became pastor in November of that year. The church has about fifty members, and the real estate is estimated to be worth twelve thousand dollars. There are one hundred and twenty-five members of the Sunday-school, of which George S. Holmes is superintendent, and Joseph E. Walker assistant superintendent.

SECOND ADVENT CHURCH.

Believers in the doctrine of what is known as the "second advent" probably held services in Manchester as early as 1843 and have continued them nearly all the time since, worshiping in Granite hall, Merrimack hall, in halls in the Museum building and in Merchants' Exchange, in other places and now in Martin's hall. They can hardly be said to have had any settled pastor, and not till 1870 any organization. On the first of August of that year, after a preliminary meeting in July, they formed a society on the basis of a belief in the speedy coming of Christ and the adoption of the New Testament as a rule of life, making Christian character the only test of membership.

At a meeting held August 8, 1870, a committee, which serves the purposes of a board of directors, was chosen, consisting of Andrew J. Mayhew, Elisha Slager and Orlando Proctor. James W. C. Pickering was elected treasurer and Enos C. Howlett and William A. Lovejoy were created deacons, Marshall J. Kendrick being joined with them in the office, June 3, 1872. All these officers continued through 1871 and 1872. At the annual meeting in 1873 L. H. Summers was chosen as secretary and treasurer and John Wilson took Mr. Proctor's place as a member of the committee. April 2, 1873, M. B. Harvey was elected a member of the committee to succeed Mr. Slager. At the annual meeting of 1874 Andrew J. Mayhew, S. S. Hatch and Henry J. Hicks were chosen the committee, and the latter became secretary and treasurer. In 1875 these were succeeded as members of the committee by Elisha Slager, William A. Lovejoy and S. S. Hatch. There is a Sunday-school of seventy-five members connected with the church, of which Albert J. Sawyer is superintendent and Benjamin Flanders is assistant superintendent.

Wm. C. Clarke.

FIRST CHRISTIAN CHURCH.

On Wednesday evening, September 21, 1870, those who were interested in the formation of a society according to the faith of those who deem the name "Christian" sufficiently indicative of religious belief met, according to previous notice, in Whitney's hall in Ferren's building, and were called to order by J. W. Wallace. It was decided to form a society, and G. W. Hancock, W. H. Cate and J. W. Wallace were chosen to draft a constitution and by-laws. On the nineteenth of the next month they met again and were organized as the First Christian Society of Manchester, adopting a constitution and choosing W. H. Cate president, J. M. Nutt vice-president, J. W. Wallace secretary and treasurer, and Cyrus Fenderson, Joseph Alsop and Noah Kenaston a prudential committee. The next year Elijah Rollins was chosen president, and Noah Kenaston vice-president. W. H. Cate was made treasurer and has continued such till the present time, while J. W. Wallace remained secretary and Mr. Kenaston's place on the prudential committee was filled by Alanson Walker. In 1872 the only change was in the prudential committee, Mr. Fenderson and Mr. Wallace giving place to J. M. Nutt and Alpheus Crosby. In November, 1872, however, upon the decease of Mr. Rollins, J. M. Nutt was appointed president. He continued in office in 1873, and Albert Gregory was elected vice-president; Abraham Alderson, secretary; and J. W. Wallace, Edward Cogswell and John B. Bickford, prudential committee. Mr. Alderson resigned July 15, 1873, and was succeeded by the present secretary, N. A. Robinson. In 1874 J. M. Nutt was chosen president; Alpheus Crosby, vice-president; and Samuel Amsden, J. A. Carr and Frank E. Mason, prudential committee. In 1875 Alpheus Crosby became president; John B. Bickford, vice-president; James M. Nutt, secretary; John A. Carr, C. A. McKelvie and Milton Proctor, prudential committee.

Men and women interested in what is technically known as the "Christian" belief held meetings for religious purposes in Whitney's hall from August, 1870, till October, 1871, being supplied during that time by occasional preachers. January 15, 1871, some of them, meeting in the hall for the purpose, adopted a constitution and were organized as the First Christian Church of Manchester, W. H. Cate acting as clerk. At a meeting held January 25, he was elected clerk and treasurer and remains such still. On the fifteenth of the next month Noah Kenaston and James M. Nutt were chosen deacons. The Rev. O. J. Hancock was the first settled pastor, coming to the charge of the church August 6, 1871. The next month the latter had outgrown its first quarters and began worship in the city hall. Mr. Hancock left the church August 28, 1872, becoming, a few months later, superintendent of the Young Men's Christian Association of this city. He was succeeded January 5, 1873, by the present pastor, the Rev. Elisha H. Wright. The society owns no real estate, but leases the city hall as a place of worship. The church has a membership of one hundred and two, while the Sunday-school has a total attendance of two hundred. The superintendent of the latter is W. H. Cate, and the assistant superintendent Alfred B. Richardson.

ROMAN CATHOLIC CHURCHES.

In July of 1844 the Rev. William McDonald came to Manchester to assume the charge in spiritual matters of the six hundred Roman Catholics in the city. They began worship the next year in Granite hall, and four years later began the erection of a brick church on the southeast corner of Merrimack and Union streets, known as St. Ann's. After they had begun to hold services in it, it was found to be unsafe and they were compelled to take it down and rebuild it. The property, including a parsonage, is now valved at sixty thousand dollars. Mr. McDonald still remains the priest of St. Ann's and is at present assisted by the Rev. John Powers.

With succeeding years the numbers of the denomination were multiplied and the Rev. John O'Brien became an assistant to Mr. McDonald. At length the increase justified the forming of another congregation and in 1869 St. Joseph's church was built on the southeast corner of Lowell and Pine streets, being dedicated April 18, 1869. The church and the parsonage are valued at eighty thousand dollars. Mr. O'Brien has continued as priest of the congregation.

Among the features of the city's growth has been the increase of its Canadian-French inhabitants, who are attracted by the prospect of work in the manufactories. They are in general of the Roman Catholic faith, and they were organized by themselves in 1871 under the charge of the Rev. J. A. Chevalier, and two years later, after occupying the church on the corner of Merrimack and Chestnut streets for a time, they built a church on the southwest corner of Beech and Spruce streets, called St. Augustine's, which, with the parsonage, is considered worth sixty thousand dollars. It was dedicated November 27, 1873. Mr. Chevalier has continued with the church since its formation.

There is also supported by the Roman Catholics what is known as the "Convent of the Sisters of Mercy," which occupies a brick building on the corner of Union and Laurel streets and was instituted in July, 1858. Mary Francis Xavier Warde is the "mother superior," and there are connected with it about forty nuns. Within its enclosure was started in April, 1870, an orphan asylum, which was moved after four years to the "Harris estate," which occupies nearly the whole square bounded by Pine, Hanover, Amherst and Union streets, and was bought for fifty thousand dollars.

About fifty orphans are generally supported there, employing seven nuns in their care.

The Roman Catholics of Manchester own three churches and parsonages, the orphan asylum and lot, two schoolhouses and lots, besides the convent and other buildings on the square bounded by Union, Laurel, Beech and Merrimack streets, nearly all of which is theirs, a lot on the corner of Merrimack and Chestnut streets and two other pieces of land in the southern part of the city proper. The land and buildings aggregate in value, at a rough estimate, over three hundred and fifty thousand dollars.

THE ARCHITECTURE OF THE CHURCHES.

The church buildings, as a general thing, were erected not far from 1839 and 1840, when religion was in haste to get a foothold upon the soil which was being so rapidly occupied by secular enterprise, and, though well adapted to the needs of that day, are not remarkable for grace and beauty. Some of them are too small, others correspond ill with the present condition of the societies which own them, and the general appearance of nearly all of them points to the past. Five, however, are of more modern date.

Of these the oldest is Grace church, on the northwest corner of Lowell and Pine streets, which was built of stone to take the place of one called St. Michael's, which was owned by the same Episcopal parish and which stood upon the same spot. It is a model in architectural proportions and was built chiefly through the instrumentality of the Rev. I. G. Hubbard, then rector of the church, a man of great energy and thorough devotion to the Episcopal faith. The corner-stone was laid on the fifth of June, 1860, and the church was consecrated on the fourth of December of the same year. The building committee consisted of the Rev. I. G. Hubbard, B. F. Martin, T. Wiggin Little and

George A. French. It is one hundred feet long, on Lowell street, and forty-five feet wide, on Pine street; forty feet high, from floor to ridge; with a tower one hundred and twenty feet high. It is built in the Gothic style, of uncoursed stone-work, with slated roof, and furnished with ornamental bronze-plated doors, made after designs by R. H. Slack of Boston, and has capacity for seating five hundred persons. The organ-room is in the tower, on the southeast corner, and the robing-room is just across the chancel. The original plans, drawn by Richard Upjohn of New York, contemplated a chapel on the northern side, which has never been built. The church is furnished throughout with windows of stained glass, has an apsidal chancel with three double lancet windows of cathedral glass, and is finished inside with black walnut. The interior has been handsomely frescoed in polychrome, the chancel in 1872, through the liberality of Col. B. F. Martin and the Hon. George B. Chandler, and the nave in 1874 at the expense of Col. Martin alone, who also gave the church its costly chandeliers.

Curiously, the next church built was St. Joseph's, just across the way, on the southeast corner of Lowell and Pine streets. It was dedicated April 28, 1869, is the largest church in the city and the largest and most costly Roman Catholic church in the state. The church is built of brick, one hundred and thirty-seven feet long and seventy feet wide, with a vestry on the north-east corner, twenty-three feet in width and twenty-five in length, and a chapel on the southeast corner, twenty-three feet wide and fifty feet long. Its total length is thus about one hundred and sixty feet and the rear part is a hundred feet in length from north to south. The latter is two stories high and thus affords rooms for the Sunday-school and for general use. The height of the church, from floor to ridge, is thirty-five feet. In front is a tower, twenty-five feet square at the base, one hundred and sixty-five feet high, and surmounted by a gilded cross. The roof is supported by twelve pillars with carved rafters. On each side of the house are twelve duplicate windows of stained glass, besides dormer windows in the roof, and eight in the chapel, in addition to others. At the eastern end, behind the elegant altar, is a triple chancel colored window; elaborately pictured, whose central figure is the Virgin Mary, while on the right are the Holy Family and on the left the mother of the Saviour teaching her child the Scriptures. The walls and ceiling are handsomely frescoed and the former are hung with pictures. The church contains two hundred and twelve pews, thus affording seats for thirteen hundred people, outside of the gallery in the front, while the chapel has seats, in sight of the altar, for three hundred more. The church and land cost about seventy-five thousand dollars, besides the organ, which cost five thousand. The architect was P. C. Keeley of New York.

The First Unitarian society dedicated, May 1, 1872, a house of worship to take the place of the one which they obtained by exchange with the Freewill Baptists in 1859, and which they had outgrown. It is situated on the northwest corner of Concord and Beech streets, and is built of brick in the English decorated style and in the form of a cross. The audience-room is seventy-six feet long, seventy feet across through the transept and forty-five feet through the nave, with a chapel in the rear, sixty-five feet long and thirty-five feet wide, connected with which are the ladies' parlor, the pastor's study and a kitchen. The interior of the church is ornamented with columns, from whose capitals arches spring nearly to the apex of the roof. The whole is finished in ash and walnut, the organ-case and desk being of solid black walnut, and the windows are of stained glass. The total cost of the church, exclusive of land, was thirty-five thousand dollars. The architect was George E. Dickey of this city and the building committee consisted of Ezekiel A. Straw, Elijah M. Tubbs, Clinton W. Stanley, Abraham P. Olzendam, David B. Varney, Charles L. Richardson and Nathaniel W. Cumner.

The fire of July 8, 1870, which entailed loss upon so many people, was to none so great a blessing as to the members of the First Baptist society. Their church, then thirty years old, was burned to the ground, but in less than three years another, which far surpassed it in convenience, elegance and value, arose to take its place. Its corner-stone was laid July 15, 1871, and it was dedicated April 30, 1873. It is situated on the southwest corner of Concord and Union streets, upon land bought of George W. Morrison and David P. Perkins for three thousand dollars. It was built in the pure Romanesque style of architecture, of brick trimmed with white granite, and is one hundred and fourteen feet long, seventy-four feet wide, and eighty feet from floor to ridge. On the southeast corner is a ventilating-tower one hundred feet high, and on the northeast corner a bell-tower, twenty-two feet square at the base and one hundred and seventy-five feet high, surmounted by a large cross. The windows are of ground glass with stained borders and the roof is slated, with ornamental railings running on the tops of the ridges. On the first floor is the vestry, with parlors and kitchen. On the second is the audience-room, eighty feet long and sixty feet wide, with black walnut pews which contain seats for a thousand persons. Back of the desk is a recess for the organ, on one side of which is a room for the use of the choir and on the other the pastor's study, and there is a gallery at the eastern end. The interior is becomingly frescoed, and the ceiling is in the form of a segmental arch. The church cost not far from sixty-one thousand five hundred dollars; the organ, which contains thirteen hundred and seventy-two pipes, cost forty-five hundred dollars: and the bell, which weighs about a ton, cost a thousand dollars and is inscribed with the names of its givers—Deacon Seth J. Sanborn and Deacon Orison Hardy. The architect of the church was William H. Myers and the building committee consisted of Joseph B. Clark, William H. Wilson, Ephraim S. Peabody, Joseph E. Bennett, Charles Brown and Otis Barton.

In 1873 the French Roman Catholics, who had been worshiping in buildings which they rented of others, had increased to such an extent, under the ministrations of the Rev. Mr. Chevalier, that it was resolved to build a church of their own. The resolution was carried into effect and the church was dedicated November 27, 1873. It is built of brick, in the English Gothic style, in the form of a cross, and is situated on the southwest corner of Spruce and Beech streets. It is one hundred and twenty-five feet through the nave, fifty-six feet through the transept, with a tower one hundred and sixty feet high. It contains a handsome altar, the walls are frescoed and the chancel is adorned with the usual pictures. It contains one hundred and seventy pews, affording seats for about a thousand people. The windows are of stained glass and each one contains the picture of a saint. These were the gifts of individuals of the congregation. The cost of the church was about forty thousand dollars and the architect was George E. Dickey of this city.

YOUNG MEN'S CHRISTIAN ASSOCIATION.

On the twenty-fourth of February, 1854, the young men of the several "evangelical" churches of the city were invited to meet on the third of the next month to consult and take action in reference to "making systematic Christian effort to help young men and uniting in a closer bond Christians of different denominations." The call was signed by the following: Samuel Gould, Abram Brigham,

Josiah Crosby

Alfred B. Soule, John C. Tasker, Samuel C. Bartlett, John M. Sawyer, William Grey, Davis Baker, William C. Kimball, Edward A. Jenks, Samuel A. Hood, Nathaniel Herrick, James O. Adams, John Paige, Charles Hosmer, C. C. Keniston, George W. Stevens, I. G. Hubbard, W. D. Buck, C. P. Bradbury, William Hartshorn.

In accordance with that invitation a meeting was held at that time at the vestry of the First Congregational church and was called to order by Samuel Gould. Abram Brigham was chosen chairman, and John M. Sawyer secretary. It was voted to form an association for the purposes named in the call and a committee was chosen to draft a constitution. At a meeting held March 17, in the vestry of the Franklin-street church, this was adopted and officers were chosen as follows: William G. Means, president; John E. Tasker and E. B. Merrill, vice-presidents: J. S. Harriman, recording secretary; J. M. Coburn, corresponding secretary; Alfred B. Soule, treasurer; J. D. Jones, librarian; besides one director from each of the "evangelical" churches in the city. At the first annual meeting, May 15, 1854, these were re-elected.

The association held meetings at the vestries of several churches till June, when it occupied the hall in Patten's block for a place of meeting and a reading-room. January 20, 1855, it met for the first time in a hall in Smyth's block, which had just been built by William Patten, Frederick Smyth and Daniel W. Fling. The hall was in the third story and next to Spring street.

In 1855 Elisha Adams was elected president; J. C. Wing and Abraham Burton, vice-presidents; Samuel Upton, recording secretary; Samuel C. Bartlett, corresponding secretary; Alfred B. Soule, treasurer; Sylvanus Bunton, librarian.

The next year the president was John P. Newell; vice-presidents, W. H. Gilmore and J. U. Farnham; recording secretary, Justus D. Watson; corresponding secretary, E. B. Merrill; treasurer, John M. Sawyer; librarian, Sylvanus Bunton. In 1857 Samuel Upton was chosen president; Justus D. Watson and George Holbrook, vice-presidents; J. U. Farnham, recording secretary; Lyman Marshall, corresponding secretary; Sylvanus Bunton, treasurer and librarian.

In 1858 the officers were: Justus D. Watson, president; George Holbrook and D. B. Nelson, vice-presidents; H. C. Bullard, recording secretary; Henry Hill, corresponding secretary; Sylvanus Bunton, treasurer and librarian. The next year Silas Hamilton was elected president; D. W. Davis and Wallace L. Rogers, vice-presidents; George E. Fisher, recording secretary; George A. Bowman, corresponding secretary; Samuel Upton, treasurer; Sylvanus Bunton, librarian.

In 1860 the president was John G. Lane; vice-presidents, Anson C. Coult and George S. Marshall; recording secretary, John M. Sawyer; corresponding secretary, John P. Newell; treasurer, Holmes R. Pettee; librarian, Eben Ferren. During that year the association gave up its rooms in Smyth's block and moved to what is now Whitney's hall in Ferren's building. A new constitution was adopted and a new election was held in September, which resulted in the choice of the existing officers with the exception of vice-presidents and librarian; W. O. Abbott and H. C. Bullard being elected to the former office, and J. N. Childs to the latter.

The last election was held in 1861, when James Stoop and J. McAllister succeeded to the office of vice-president, T. P. Kinsley to that of recording secretary and J. Nowell to that of treasurer, the rest of the officers being re-elected. The coming on of the War of the Rebellion hastened the decrease of the association, though the lack of means had already crippled it. At length, March 3, 1862, the association held its last meeting, when it appointed J. M. Sawyer, J. S. Abbott and G. W. Rogers a committee to close its affairs and report to its officers. The latter met on the last day of March and appointed George W. Rogers, Holmes R. Pettee, James Stoop, J. C. Follansbee and John D. Patterson a board of trustees to have charge in trust of the property of the association. Some of it was sold to pay debts, some was kept and delivered to the association which was formed six years later, some of the papers were sent to the soldiers, its library was loaned to the city library till the new association was formed and obtained it, and its records remain in the hands of John D. Patterson, who was appointed at a meeting of the board of trustees, November 3, 1862, to assume charge of all the association's effects and settle all its bills.

Six years later the idea of a Young Men's Christian Association was revived and a meeting of those who were interested in its formation was held March 30, 1868, in the vestry of the Franklin-street church. It was called to order by John D. Patterson, and Marshall P. Hall was chosen secretary. A committee was appointed to draft a constitution, which was reported and adopted the next month, and on the thirteenth the following officers were elected; Francis W. Parker, president; Richard J. P. Goodwin, vice-president; Charles L. Bailey, secretary; Jasper P. George, treasurer; John P. Newell, librarian; George Holbrook, auditor; and a board of directors, one from each church. The first annual election was held in May when John P. Newell was chosen vice-president; Marshall P. Hall, corresponding secretary, and Eben F. Brown, librarian, the rest continuing in office.

In 1869 John P. Newell was elected president and has held the office ever since; William H. Cate was chosen vice-president; Marshall P. Hall, corresponding secretary; A. B. Putnam, recording secretary; H. B. Sawyer, treasurer; Frank Buckminster, librarian; George Holbrook, auditor. There were but two changes the next year, Holmes R. Pettee becoming recording secretary, and Henry B. Fairbanks treasurer. In 1871 the vice-president and the auditor changed places and George C. Kemp became librarian. In 1872 Mr. Pettee was succeeded as recording secretary by Warner J. Barton. In 1873 the office of corresponding secretary was abolished, and Charles A. Adams was elected secretary; W. H. Cate, treasurer; and John C. Balch, auditor. In 1874 C. A. Davenport was elected secretary, but subsequently resigned and was succeeded by James M. McIntosh. Holmes R. Pettee became treasurer and Charles A. Adams auditor.

The association's rooms were at first in Merchants' Exchange over the office of the Hon. Daniel Clark, but, upon the rebuilding of Masonic Temple after the fire of 1870, the association moved thither. In 1872 the Rev. O. J. Hancock, who had just resigned the pastorate of the Christian church, was appointed superintendent of the association, devoting all his time to its work. He held the office but a little while and in May of the next year, when the office of corresponding secretary was abolished, a new officer was appointed, under the name of general secretary, to take the place of a superintendent, and C. P. Wellman was elected to that position. He resigned in July, and the next February George Murdough, the present general secretary, was chosen to his office. The association has now about three hundred members and is supported by the contributions of the churches and the proceeds of an annual lecture-course. It has a free library and reading-room, sustains religious services in its rooms, at the jail and reform school, and in the suburban districts. The old church in Piscataquog village was bequeathed to it in trust by Mrs. Mary P. Harris, and under its auspices services are conducted there on Sundays by the clergymen of the city.

YOUNG WOMEN'S CHRISTIAN ASSOCIATION.

There had long been established an association designed to be of service to the young men of the city, when, in 1872, the idea was conceived, by some of the women connected with the Franklin-street church, of a similar society, to be composed of young women and whose object should be to prove beneficial to persons of the same sex. Accordingly, September 23, 1872, such a society was formed, to be known as the Young Women's Christian Association. At the first meeting there were elected, for president, Mrs. William J. Tucker; vice-president, Mrs. David Cross; secretary and treasurer, Miss Josie A. Bosher; auditor, Miss Alice A. Abbott; directors, Mrs. William W. Brown, Miss Emma J. Lincoln, Mrs. Henry B. Fairbanks, Miss Jennie Paige, Miss Ellen McCarrol, Mrs. Frederick Smyth.

The officers were continued through the next year, but in 1874 Mrs. William J. Tucker was elected president; Mrs. David Cross, vice-president; Miss Josie A. Bosher, secretary; Miss Alice A. Abbott, treasurer; Miss Sarah P. Howard, auditor; Mrs. William W. Brown, Miss Fannie E. Butman, Miss Mary Emma White, Mrs. E. M. Wadleigh, Miss Anna E. Willard, Mrs. A. M. Scott, directors. One of the vestries of the Franklin-street church was obtained for the use of the association, and, by the efforts of the members, the contributions of funds and appropriations from the church, the room has been supplied with books and made attractive with pictures, a number of newspapers and periodicals being regularly taken and kept on file there. The room is open every evening and all young women in the city are invited to make it their home for the time. Miss Sarah J. Fitzpatrick — now Mrs. Thomas Bailey — was appointed to take charge of the rooms and continued as superintendent till June, 1874, when she was succeeded by Mrs. M. J. Buncher. Since the latter's accession to the office, a small circulating library has been set in operation for the convenience of those who prefer to carry books home to read. The room is very pleasant and affords an attractive resort for young women who are strangers in the city or who have no other home than a boarding-house.

PISCATAQUOG AID SOCIETY.

Out of a "sewing-circle," which had enjoyed for a number of years the life of sewing-circles in general, the women of Piscataquog village formed, January 27, 1860, the Piscataquog Aid Society, with eighty or ninety members, whose objects were defined to be the "promotion of social and friendly feeling and amusement and the raising of funds to aid the cause of benevolence." It was controlled entirely by women, though men were admitted to membership. Its meetings were held at the old academy and at the houses of the members, and its funds were devoted, now to the benefit of the church, and now to the relief of the poor. During the war it did good service in making clothing for the soldiers at the front and those in the hospital in this city.

Its first president was Miss Philinda P. Parker; vice-president, Mrs. E. M. Riddle; secretary, Miss Ellen B. French; treasurer, Mrs. C. S. Fisher. In 1861 Mrs. C. S. Fisher became president; Mrs. Ira Barr, vice-president; Miss Mary A. Parker, secretary; and Mrs. Daniel K. Mack, treasurer. These were re-elected the next year. In 1863 Mrs. Ira Barr was elected president; Mrs. Daniel K. Mack, vice-president; Miss Lucy M. Rundlett, secretary; and Miss Philinda P. Parker, treasurer. These, also, were re-elected to serve for another year. In 1865 Mrs. Charles K. Walker was chosen president; Mrs. D. B. Eastman, vice-president; Miss Emilie Parker, secretary; and Mrs. Edward Bryant, treasurer.

Meetings were held throughout this year, but there is no record beyond January 5, 1866, and the society's life was temporarily suspended, to be re-awakened in 1872, when the meetings were once more begun and have since been kept up. At the time of revival Mrs. John Smith was chosen president; Mrs. John O. Parker, vice-president; Miss Lucy M. Rundlett, secretary; Mrs. Allen N. Clapp, treasurer. In 1874 Mrs. Smith was succeeded as president by Mrs. D. K. Mack, and Mrs. Parker as vice-president by Mrs. N. T. Folsom. In 1875 Mrs. N. T. Folsom was elected president; Mrs. Mary A. Hartshorn, vice-president; Miss Ellen P. Walker, secretary and treasurer.

The society has now about one hundred members and combines, as before, benevolence with social recreations. Social meetings are held every fortnight and the society meets twice a week in the winter for work. It derives its funds from assessments upon its members and the proceeds of entertainments. Its beneficiaries are the poor of Piscataquog village, a large number of its inhabitants being operatives in the mills across the river and out of work in times of dull business. It supplies to that village the aid which other societies afford to other parts of the city, and does a praiseworthy work.

MANCHESTER WOMEN'S AID AND RELIEF SOCIETY.

The depression of business in 1873 and 1874 threw many in Manchester out of employment and thus added to the number of the destitute, so that at the close of 1874 there was more suffering from poverty in the city than for many years before. No organization for purely charitable purposes existed and the only approximation to relief for the poor was afforded by the city missionary, the time and means at whose command were totally inadequate to immediate needs. The Rev. Mr. Tucker, the pastor of the

Franklin-street society, enlisted the sympathies of some of the women of the society in the matter, who made a canvass of the city and thus revealed to what extent and in what extremity destitution prevailed.

Their labors discovered that no one society was competent for the relief of all the needy, and in view of this fact and in pursuance of a belief that something ought at once to be done, a circular was sent, under date of January 19, 1875, to representatives of all the Protestant religious societies of the city, inviting them to meet two days later at the residence of Mrs. J. G. Cilley to assist in the formation of a women's society for charitable purposes. In answer to the call a large number of persons met at the place appointed, adopted a constitution and formed an organization under the name of the Manchester Women's Aid and Relief Society, electing the following officers: president, Mrs. B. F. Martin; vice-presidents, Mrs. P. C. Cheney, Mrs. Phinehas Adams, Mrs. John S. Kidder, Mrs. William L. Killey, Mrs. Henry C. Reynolds, Mrs. Edson Hill, Mrs. Israel Dow, Mrs. George S. Holmes, Mrs. H. F. Wood, Mrs. A. R. Wright, Mrs. James Dean; secretary, Miss Olive Rand; treasurer, Mrs. Aretas Blood; directors, Mrs. James A. Weston, Mrs. Lucien B. Clough, Mrs. W. W. Brown, Mrs. John B. Clarke, Mrs. D. B. Varney, Mrs. Frederick Smyth, Mrs. Bradbury P. Cilley, Mrs. J. G. Cilley, Mrs. George B. Chandler, Mrs. Moody Currier, Mrs. A. H. Daniels, Mrs. Frederick C. Dow, Mrs. George A. French, Mrs. Samuel P. Jackson, Mrs. William B. Johnson, Mrs. Orison Hardy, Mrs. George Holbrook, Mrs. Aaron Ferren, Mrs. Allen N. Clapp, Mrs. H. W. Herrick, Mrs. Joseph F. Kennard, Mrs. R. M. Miller, Mrs. William B. Webster, Mrs. John E. Stearns, Mrs. George W. Riddle, Mrs. James Baldwin, Mrs. Thomas Dunlap, Mrs. A. J. Lane, Mrs. Samuel Webber, Mrs. John F. Kennard.

The eleven vice-presidents are chosen, one from each of

Moody Currier

the religious societies of the place. The payment of fifty cents annually constitutes any woman a member of the society. Any person may become an honorary member by the annual payment of five dollars, and any person may become a life member upon payment of fifty dollars. The income of the society is derived from these sources and the life-membership fees are invested for a permanent fund. The society has divided the city into nineteen districts and assigned directors to each to have them in special charge and to explore them for cases of destitution. In the first fortnight of its existence the society had obtained, with no special effort, nearly five hundred dollars, and now rests upon a firm footing. It supplies a want which has always existed in the city but never in such proportions as at the present time.

MISCELLANEOUS SOCIETIES.

MANCHESTER is a city adapted by the conditions of its birth and growth to the element of secret societies, and they had here an early start and have grown vigorously since. The more prominent secret orders are considered by themselves in this chapter. Different temperance associations early took root but have withered away, with the exception of those recently started. Military organizations, of one kind and another, have always been sustained. Of other societies there is no limit, each year adding to the number, and each nationality crystallizing by inherent tendencies into associations peculiar to itself.

FREE MASONS.

The history of Free Masonry in Manchester begins in the year 1845, when Lafayette Lodge was removed from Bedford, the place of its nativity, to this side of the river, and a room was fitted for its occupancy in the attic of Dunck-lee's block over the "old family store," now kept by John M. Chandler. Within two years it had so prospered as to require a larger and better hall, which was found in the next story, and was dedicated in December, 1847, by the Grand Lodge. A dinner was served at the Manchester House and an oration was delivered by Sylvanus Cobb of Boston. This was the only Masonic body in the city till September, 1847, when Mount Horeb Royal Arch Chapter began its existence.

In September, 1853, Trinity Commandry, which had its birth in Hanover and after some years came to its death in Lebanon, found its resurrection in Manchester. These three Masonic bodies continued to hold meetings in the hall in Duncklee's block till April, 1856, when they occupied a hall and other rooms in a building on Hanover street, to which this circumstance gave the name of Masonic Temple. The burning in February of that year of the hall occupied by the Odd Fellows gave the Masons an opportunity to offer them the use of their own, a courtesy which was accepted, and which was returned when the great fire of 1870 swept away Masonic Temple.

In September, 1856, a new body arose under the name of Adoniram Council, and in January of the next year Washington Lodge began to work under a dispensation. In May, 1863, another body was organized under the title of Winslow Lewis Lodge of Perfection, John D. Patterson being its Thrice Illustrious Grand Commander, but it was found best to surrender its charter and the lodge was consolidated with Aaron P. Hughes Lodge of Nashua. This lodge was named in honor of Dr. Winslow Lewis of Boston, a very prominent Mason and especially in connection with the "Scottish rites." No event of special prominence occurred in the Masonic history of Manchester till July, 1870, when the Masonic Temple was burned to the ground, little of the property of the order being saved. But another soon arose upon the same spot to take its place and in it the Masons now find excellent accommodations.

The latest addition to the Masonic orders in the city was made in May, 1873, when Labarum Council of Knights of the Illustrious Order of Knights of the Red Cross of Rome and of Constantine was organized.

Members of the fraternity in Manchester formed, April 14, 1874, an organization under the name of the Masonic Relief Association, whose object was to provide for the families of members after the death of the latter. It affords, practically, a system of life insurance for a small amount, with simple and inexpensive machinery, a person previously designated by a member receiving, upon his death, as many dollars as there are members of the association. When the first death occurred, the sum due from the association was provided by the initiation fees which all had paid upon joining, and an assessment of a dollar was at once levied upon each member, thus providing the sum needed when the second death happened. In this way the sum due, when a death occurs, is kept on hand in readiness for immediate payment.

It has been said that Lafayette Lodge had its birth in Bedford. The first record of the steps which led to its formation is that of a meeting of several Masons of Bedford and vicinity, held at the house of Thomas Rundlett in Bedford, March 4, 1824. Mr. Rundlett, who was afterwards Master of the Grand Lodge of the state, lived at that time upon the River road, not far from what is now known as the "McGaw place." There were present at that meeting Joseph Colley, Jonathan Dowse, Samuel Chesman, John Martin, Adam Smith, jr., James Darrah, jr., Thomas Harris, Thomas Rundlett, Otis Batchelder, John Goffe, Adam Gilmore, Jesse Richardson, Mace Moulton, William P. Riddle, Lewis F. Harris, Diocletian Melvin, James McKean Wilkins, William Wallace, John Langley, Josiah Gordon, John Moore, William McDoel Ferson, and Robert Dunlap. A few of these men were not Master Masons at the time, but had taken, some one and some two degrees in Bible Lodge in Goffstown. There are of these but two now living—Gen. William P. Riddle of Bedford, and John Langley.

It was voted at this meeting to annul the doings of all former meetings, whatever they may have been, and Robert Dunlap was chosen the first Master of the proposed lodge ;

Thomas Rundlett, first Senior Warden; and John Moore, first Junior Warden. At the same time it was voted to accept a petition to the Grand Lodge of the state, prepared by James McK. Wilkins, asking for the establishment of a lodge in Bedford, to be known as Lafayette Lodge, Number Forty-one. The name was adopted in honor of the Marquis DeLafayette, who was just then making his last visit to this country. The petition was signed by all present, with the exception of Samuel Chesman, Adam Smith, jr., Thomas Harris, John Goffe, Adam Gilmore and John Langley, and with the addition of Joseph A. E. Long, James Harvell and Thomas Pollard, jr.

The petition, endorsed by Bible Lodge in Goffstown, Benevolent Lodge in Milford and Blazing Star Lodge in Concord, was presented to the Grand Lodge at its session in June of that year, and a letter of dispensation, bearing date June 9, 1824, was granted, under which a lodge was formed and "opened in the first degree" on the succeeding Monday. At that time the election of officers was proceeded with and it was voted to hold succeeding meetings in a hall over a store in Piscataquog village, owned by Gen. William P. Riddle, and which stood where the Amoskeag brewery is now situated. On the first day of September of the same year the lodge was formally consecrated by the Grand Lodge, its officers installed and its charter received. A procession was formed which marched from the hall to the meeting-house on the hill, where a sermon was preached by the Rev. Joseph A. E. Long, who was probably at that time supplying the Presbyterian church there.

For four years the lodge prospered, but in 1828, when the war against Masonry arose, this lodge, in common with the rest, felt its effects, no man being initiated into its mysteries for seventeen years. However, the lodge held its meetings, elected and installed its officers at the regular intervals, and preserved its life till its removal to the new town across the river in August, 1845. From that time till the present its record has been one of prosperity, and little has occurred to distinguish its life from that of the other Masonic bodies in the city. At a special meeting in December, 1848, Okah Tubbee, otherwise known as William Chubbee, a chief of the Choctaw tribe of Indians residing on the borders of Arkansas, took the first three degrees of Masonry under a dispensation for that purpose. The lodge has now about three hundred members.

The following have been Masters of the lodge since its formation:

1824-5.	Robert Dunlap.	1850.	James Collins.
1826.	John Moore.	1851.	Thomas Rundlett.
1827.	Joseph Colley.	1852.	John C. Lyford.
1828.	Diocletian Melvin.	1853-4.	Albert P. Colby.
1829.	Otis Batchelder.	1855.	John F. Duncklee.
1830-31.	Thomas G. Peckham.	1856.	John B. Fish.
1832.	Thomas Rundlett.	1857-8.	Henry T. Mowatt.
1833.	Robert Dunlap.	1859.	John B. Fish.
1834.	John Wells.	1860.	Ezra Huntington.
1835.	Joseph Colley.	1861.	John B. Fish.
1836-8.	William McD. Ferson.	1862-4.	Rufus L. Bartlett.
1839-43.	Jonathan Dowse.	1865-6.	Joseph E. Bennett.
1844-5.	Robert Dunlap.	1867-8.	Charles F. Warren.
1846.	James McK. Wilkins.	1869.	William B. Lane.
1847.	Daniel Balch.	1870-1.	David O. Furnald.
1848.	David S. Palmer.	1872-3.	Alpheus Gay.
1849.	Monroe G. J. Tewksbury.	1874.	Frank T. E. Richardson.

Mount Horeb Royal Arch Chapter, Number Eleven, is the next in order of institution, beginning its existence September 1, 1847, when nine Royal Arch Masons of this city held a preliminary meeting and chose Daniel Balch High Priest, receiving a dispensation November 15, 1847, and being regularly chartered September 7, 1848. The petition for the charter was signed by Charles W. Adams, Daniel C. Gould, Ira Bliss, Daniel Balch, William Shepherd, James A. Gregg, David S. Palmer, Leonard Dakin, Ammon Platt and James H. Fowler. It derives its name from allusions in the chapter ceremonies to the Mount

Horeb of the Holy Land. It has now about two hundred and twenty members, and the following gives the names of its chief officers, with the title of Most Excellent High Priest, and the dates of their installation:

Daniel Balch,	September 7, 1848.
Theodore T. Abbot,	September 28, 1850.
Isaac C. Flanders,	September 15, 1852.
Albert P. Colby,	September 15, 1854.
George W. Morrison,	September 28, 1855.
Edward W. Harrington,	September 20, 1856.
Zebina Perry,	October 9, 1858.
Daniel C. Gould,	September 28, 1859.
John B. Fish,	October 3, 1860.
Nathaniel W. Cumner,	October 8, 1862.
John D. Patterson,	October 19, 1864.
Asahel A. Balch,	October 10, 1866.
George H. True,	April 8, 1868.
Joseph E. Bennett,	April 21, 1870.
Joseph Kidder,	April 23, 1872.
Alpheus Gay,	April 16, 1874.

Trinity Commandry of Knights Templars was the first commandry in the state and the year of its first organization antedates that of Lafayette Lodge, though it was not instituted at Manchester till 1852. The commandries are more intimately associated than any other of the Masonic orders, in their history and ceremonies, with the Christian religion; the Crusades, in which the Knights Templars bore so prominent a part, being undertaken to gain possession of the sepulchre of the founder of that faith; and in accordance with this religious idea the commandry in Manchester derives its name. It was first chartered as Trinity Encampment, March 24, 1824, when the petitioners were James Freeman Dana, James Poole, Timothy Kenrick, Amos Bugbee, Ammi B. Young, Alpheus Baker, George W. Culver, Henry Hutchinson and George E. Wales. It was first located at Hanover, and, several years later, was removed to Lebanon. There it continued in existence till about 1836, when it sunk in the general depression of the Masonic interest. At the last meeting of which any record remains, May 30, 1830, Alpheus Baker was

elected Commander. Its own records show that Timothy Kenrick, who had been elected Commander in 1827, was re-elected in 1828, but it appears from the meagre records of the Grand Encampment that Amos Bugbee was Trinity's Commander in 1829. Its own records make no mention of any occurrence in 1829, but declare Alpheus Baker elected Commander in 1830. There is no means of knowing who held the office in 1831, but in 1832 Timothy Kenrick was present in the Grand Encampment as the Commander of Trinity, and by the returns made to that body in 1833 Alpheus Baker was named as commander. It was represented in the Grand Encampment by an inferior officer in 1834, that body holding no meeting the next year, and in 1836 and 1837 certain of its members were chosen officers of the Grand Encampment, and there the record ends.

This encampment, together with DeWitt Clinton and Mount Horeb Encampments, then respectively of Portsmouth and Hopkinton, which had been already organized, formed in 1826 the Grand Encampment of the state. At a meeting of the latter in 1827 it was resolved to designate each encampment by numbers according to priority of formation, the encampment in Hanover thus becoming Trinity Encampment Number One. It retained this title till 1873, when designation by numbers was abolished by the Grand Encampment.

In the fall of 1851, at a meeting in Manchester of former members of the encampment, the subject of re-organization was discussed and subsequently a petition was drawn up and sent to the General Grand Generalissimo of the United States, asking permission to revive the deceased encampment and to hold it in the city of Manchester. The petition was signed by George E. Wales, Jacob Carter, Charles W. Adams, Joshua Blaisdell, Daniel C. Gould, Timothy Kenrick, Calvin Benton, Brackett L. Greenough, Duty Stickney and Elias Frost. It was received, March 22,

1852, by the officer to whom it was sent, who held that he had no authority to revive a deceased encampment, but he granted the petitioners a dispensation to open and hold an encampment in Manchester under the name of Trinity Encampment Number One, which they accordingly did, expecting that their original charter would be revived at the next meeting of the General Grand Encampment of the United States. When this body met, however, it issued a new charter under date of September 19, 1853, which Trinity Encampment at first refused to accept, and subsequently took under protest. In 1856 it assumed the name of Commandry in conformity with an order of the supreme body, by which all subordinate encampments were thus designated. Four years later, in accordance with the commandry's wishes and in conformity with what was then deemed the policy of the order, the Grand Master of the United States declared the original charter revived and restored by an order dated March 23, 1860. Thus, from that time on, the commandry has been held by virtue of the restored charter, the charter of 1853 being preserved by the commandry as proof of its right to an existence from 1853 to 1860. It has now about one hundred and eighty members. Its Commanders and the dates of their installation, so far as the records give them, follow:

James F. Dana,	May 18, 1824.
Timothy Kenrick,	April 25, 1827.
Alpheus Baker,	May 3, 1830.
Amos Bugbee,	
	—— ——
Daniel Balch,	March 22, 1852.
Charles W. Adams,	October 16, 1856
Daniel C. Gould,	November 12, 1857.
Theodore T. Abbot,	October 14, 1859.
John S. Kidder,	November 22, 1860.
Isaac C. Flanders,	November 6, 1862.
Edward W. Harrington,	November 2, 1864.
John D. Patterson,	November 28, 1866.
John S. Kidder,	November 20, 1868.
Daniel F. Straw,	November 9, 1869.
John N. Bruce,	November 22, 1872.
Albert Jackson,	November 11, 1873.

By the year 1856 the Masons had increased to such an extent that the institution of a second lodge seemed advisable, and in accordance with this feeling a petition for a new lodge was presented to the Grand Lodge of the state, signed by John S. Kidder, Isaac C. Flanders, Edward W. Harrington, Samuel G. Langley, Samuel W. Jones, Ebenezer H. Davis, Charles Moore, Caleb Duxbury, Wilbur Gay, William H. Hill, James S. Cheney, Edson C. George, James S. Cogswell, David B. Kibby, George W. Morrison, Charles W. Adams, DeLafayette Robinson, Nathaniel W. Cumner, Daniel C. Gould, Andrew W. Thompson, George B. Chandler, Samuel H. Edgerly, Ira Bliss, Jesse F. Angell, Ira Stone, Samuel B. Kidder and Daniel W. Fling. A dispensation was granted for the desired purpose by the Grand Master on the first of January, 1857, and the first meeting of the lodge was held on the tenth of the same month, when John S. Kidder was chosen Master. It was granted a charter under the name of Washington Lodge, Number Sixty-one, June 9, 1857, when Mr. Kidder was succeeded as Master by Edward W. Harrington. As the first lodge in the city had been named in honor of the French hero, Lafayette, it was deemed fitting that the second should be called Washington Lodge in honor of Lafayette's friend and companion in arms. It has now about two hundred and seventy-five members. Below are given its Masters and the years of their installation.

1857.	John S. Kidder.	1866.	Daniel F. Straw.
1857.	Edward W. Harrington.	1867.	Clinton W. Stanley.
1858–9.	Samuel G. Langley.	1868.	Isaac W. Smith.
1860–1.	John S. Kidder.	1869.	Joseph Kidder.
1862–3.	Nathaniel W. Cumner.	1870–1.	Andrew Bunton.
1864.	Charles Bunton.	1872–3.	Charles H. Bartlett.
1865.	Lewis W. Clark.	1874.	Daniel A. Clifford.

Adoniram Council Number Three, Royal and Select Masters, which acquires its name from a legendary connection of the order with the Adoniram mentioned in the Old Testament, was granted a dispensation, September 11, 1856, by

Grand Puissant Alexander Hamilton of Connecticut. It was chartered, September 27, 1857, by the Grand Council of Connecticut, the original charter members being Daniel Balch, Ira Bliss and Moses O. Pearson. Upon the formation of the Grand Council of New Hampshire, a new charter was given, under date of June 11, 1862. The number of members is about two hundred. The following, with the title of "Thrice Illustrious Grand Master," have been its highest officers:

1857–61.	Daniel Balch.	1867–69.	John Gillis.
1862–63.	Moses O. Pearson.	1870–71.	George H. True.
1864–66.	George H. True.	1872–73.	John M. Hayes.
	1874–75.	Henry Lewis.	

Labarum Council of Knights of the Illustrious Order of Knights of the Red Cross of Rome and of Constantine, Number Ninety-four, was chartered May 14, 1873, and is the only one in the state. There are Grand Councils of the order in New York, Pennsylvania and Illinois, and the number of subordinate councils is slowly increasing in the country at large. The charter members of Labarum Council are: Joseph W. Fellows, John D. Patterson, Joseph G. Edgerly, Nathaniel W. Cumner, Manchester; John A. Harris, Abel Hutchins, Samuel B. Page, Concord; William Barrett, Nashua; Joseph W. Welch, Dover; Solon A. Carter, Keene. Several others have since been added. Its chief officer is Joseph W. Fellows, with the title of Grand Sovereign, who is also deputy in this state for the Grand Imperial Council in London, England, from which body the charter was granted directly. The head of the order is Earl Bective, with the title of Grand Imperial Sovereign, who is a member and ardent supporter of the Masonic fraternity. This is a "Christian" order of Knighthood, conferred upon Knights Templars, and is founded upon the legend that the Roman emperor Constantine saw in the sky a cross, circumscribed with the words, "In Hoc Signo

Vinces," on the eve of the battle at Saxa Rubra, in which the emperor was victorious and on which the fate of Christianity for the time being hung. The technical name for the symbol which Constantine saw is "labarum," whence this council derives its name.

ODD FELLOWS.

The introduction of Odd Fellowship into Manchester occurred in 1843 and may not unjustly be ascribed to Isaiah Winch, who kept a store in the Methodist-church block. He had become interested in the order, and, without the knowledge of any one in Manchester, went to Massachusetts and was there initiated into its secrets. The first lodge of Odd Fellows in this state was instituted at Nashua, September 11, 1843, and was named Granite Lodge, Number One. After the germ of the order had thus been planted in New Hampshire, Mr. Winch interested himself in the formation of a lodge in Manchester and advocated the plan among his friends with such success that four men—Walter French, Charles Wells, Josiah M. Barnes, Jacob G. Cilley—went to Nashua and became members of the newly created lodge there. Taking cards of clearance from the Nashua lodge and returning to Manchester with only the initiatory degree, they received the five degrees at the hands of a District Deputy from Boston on the afternoon of Thursday, December 21, 1843, in a hall over the Second Methodist church on Elm street, becoming the charter members of the second lodge instituted in the state, to which was given the title of Hillsborough Lodge Number Two. In the evening the officers were elected and installed as follows: Walter French, Noble Grand; Charles Wells, Vice Grand; Isaiah Winch, Secretary; Josiah M. Barnes, Treasurer; Jacob G. Cilley, Warden. Of these but two are now living—Isaiah Winch, who resided for some time in Meredith

Village, N. H., but who has since removed to Fernandina, Florida, and Charles Wells, an esteemed physician of this city. Walter French died in 1853; Josiah M. Barnes, in 1855; and Jacob G. Cilley, in 1870. The same evening a large number of members were initiated, the necessary officers of the lodge were appointed and the organization was completed.

The order quickly spread in the city, over a hundred men becoming members of the lodge within a year. An encampment was instituted the next year, and another lodge, in the year succeeding that. The hall in the attic of the Methodist-church block, where the lodge was organized, was fitted up by the members of the order at their own expense, and, being leased by them for a term of years, acquired the title of Odd Fellows Hall. It was considered at that time a neat and convenient lodge-room. After a while, however, either because the church objected to leasing the hall for such gatherings or because the Odd Fellows needed better accommodations, or for both reasons, the latter leased of Col. William Patten a hall in the third story of the block he had built on Elm street, just above the city hall, and removed to it about 1847. That then succeeded to the title of Odd Fellows Hall.

From that they were driven by the fire of February 5, 1856, which destroyed all their property with trifling exceptions, the records of the secretaries being wholly lost. The Masons, then occupying a hall in Duncklee's block, at once put it at the disposal of the Odd Fellows, who gratefully accepted it. The two orders occupied it in common till April, when rooms were obtained in a new building on Hanover street and leased by the fraternities jointly for ten years. At the expiration of that time both orders had attained such development that it was thought advisable to separate, and the Odd Fellows leased rooms in Martin's block, on the corner of Elm and Lowell streets, occupying them till the completion of their own building on Hanover street. In 1866 a third lodge was organized, and in 1871 a second encampment, and it will not be surprising if a fourth lodge is instituted within a year.

The building above referred to is a testimonial to the substantial growth of the fraternity of Odd Fellows, and is the first which was owned by a secret order in the city. The land on which it stands, on the south side of Hanover street, near the corner of Chestnut, was bought in 1870 by the three lodges, the youngest lodge being obliged to issue bonds to obtain the funds. The building was begun in 1871 and was at first in charge of a committee of one from each lodge—Simeon S. Marden, Seth T. Hill and Nathan P. Hunt. But it was discovered that for the financial success of the undertaking some other system was necessary, and, in accordance with a plan which was adopted by the lodges, a company under the name of the Odd Fellows' Building Association was chartered by the legislature at the June session of 1871, and the lodges chose three members each to act under the charter. These drew lots to determine the length of their terms of office, the three members from each lodge remaining for one, two and three years respectively. By this arrangement three members retire annually and three are elected to take their places. This association issued bonds to the amount of thirty-five thousand dollars, due in five, ten or fifteen years, bearing interest at seven per cent. and guaranteed by a mortgage of the land and buildings by the lodges, which were all taken by the lodges and members of the order. The building, which is three stories high and of brick, was completed in the spring of 1872, costing, with the land, about forty-five thousand dollars. It was dedicated on the twenty-sixth of April, 1872, that being the fifty-third anniversary of the introduction of Odd Fellowship into America.

A lodge for the purpose of conferring degrees was instituted April 10, 1874, under the name of Union Degree Lodge, Number One, and has about one hundred and twenty-five members. Frank L. Rundlett was its Degree Master till 1875, when Parker W. Hanaford succeeded him. The Odd Fellows' Relief Association, whose plan is identical with that of the Masonic Relief Association already referred to, was organized in April, 1870, and has about six hundred and forty members. Its benefits were so highly appreciated as to lead to the organization, June 27, 1874, of another association under the name of the Odd Fellows' Mutual Life Insurance Company, which is based upon the same plan, but which includes, besides members of the order, their wives and widows. It has about a hundred and twenty members. The three lodges together contain about eight hundred and fifty members, and with the encampments have funds amounting to about twenty-two thousand dollars.

Hillsborough Lodge, Number Two, was instituted December 21, 1843, its charter members being Walter French, Charles Wells, Isaiah Winch, Jacob G. Cilley and Josiah M. Barnes. It has now about three hundred members and funds amounting to about eight thousand dollars. The "Noble Grands," or highest officers of the lodge, since its formation, are given below. Till 1847 each was in office but three months, but since that time six months has constituted a term. The first chief officer—Walter French—served from the twenty-first of December, 1843, till the first of April, 1844.

1844. Walter French, Charles Wells, Isaiah Winch, Isaac C. Flanders.
1845. John S. Kidder, John B. Fish, Luther Smith, Daniel J. Hoyt.
1846. Jacob G. Cilley, William M. Parker, Edward McQueston, Lucius B. Packard.
1847. Moses Hill, Jacob F. James.
1848. Henry T. Mowatt, Warren L. Lane.
1849. Flagg T. Underhill, Jonathan Horn.
1850. Henry Kimball, Nicholas G. York.

Moses Fellows

1851. Sylvanus Bunton, Justus Fisher.
1852. Joseph Kidder, Moses W. Oliver.
1853. Luther H. Brown, Benjamin M. Tillotson.
1854. John Hosley, Samuel B. Kidder.
1855. Walter Neal, James D. Wells.
1856. John H. Rand, Joel Taylor.
1857. Alpha Currier, Henry A. Gage.
1858. Christopher C. Colby, Arthur L. Walker.
1859. True O. Furnald, Lemuel Colby.
1860. Charles Abels, George S. Holmes.
1861. William B. Lane, Harvey D. Cutting.
1862. Ira G. Williams, Samuel B. Hope.
1863. Benjamin F. Bowles, Darwin A. Simons.
1864. Jacob Morse, Francis W. Nichols.
1865. Henry J. Tirrell, Seth J. Sanborn.
1866. John Gillis, Horace R. Philbrick.
1867. John L. Avery, John Shirley.
1868. George R. Vance, Andrew J. Holmes.
1869. Sylvester C. Gould, William G. Marden.
1870. Andrew J. Butterfield, Ephraim T. Hardy.
1871. Silas B. Woodbury, Luther M. Clark.
1872 David M. Goodwin, Edward O. Hill.
1873. James M. Clough, George A. Bailey.
1874. Calvin L. Walker, Parker W. Hanaford.
1875. Oscar F. Bartlett.

Wonolanset Encampment, Number Two, like Hillsborough Lodge, the second organized in the state, was instituted September 6, 1844, in less than a year after the formation of the lodge. Its charter members were: Walter French, Charles Wells, Isaiah Winch, Jacob G. Cilley, Isaac C. Flanders, Jonathan T. P. Hunt, Josiah M. Barnes. It has now about two hundred and thirty members, and funds amounting to about nine hundred dollars. The chief officer of an encampment is styled the "Chief Patriarch," who, at the close of his term of office, is eligible to the Grand Encampment. Another officer, styled the "High Priest," acquired nearly equal importance by being also admitted to the Grand Encampment till 1874, when the custom was discontinued.

The following have been the encampment's Chief Patriarchs from its organization:

1845. Jonathan T. P. Hunt, John B. Fish.
1846. Luther Smith, Edward McQueston.
1847. John C. Lyford, Albe C. Heath.

1848. Nicholas G. York, Jonathan Horn.
1849. Alvia Houghton, Nathaniel Smith.
1850. Jeremiah Preston, Barnabas Hinds.
1851. Leonard Demary, Isaac N. Haines.
1852. Samuel B. Kidder, Enoch Watson.
1853. George W. Weeks, Stephen Palmer.
1854. Charles H. Brown, Otis P. Warner.
1855. Joseph Kidder, Charles T. Durgin.
1856. George C. Gilmore, James D. Wells.
1857. James C. Wing, Stephen H. Crockett.
1858. Nathaniel E. Morrill, Joseph S. Hunkins.
1859. Horace M. Gillis, Walter Neal.
1860. Daniel Pulsifer, George S. Neal.
1861. James J. Baldwin, Henry B. Moulton.
1862. Christopher C. Colby, Rufus L. Bartlett.
1863. Darwin A. Simons, Jacob F. James.
1864. Henry J. Tirrell, Russell O. Burleigh.
1865. John U. Farnham, Seth J. Sanborn.
1866. John T. Robinson, Stephen H. Randlett.
1867. Frederick B. Balch, Jonathan B. Moore.
1868. Jeremiah Hodge, Harvey L. Currier.
1869. Horace R. Philbrick, Henry A. Farrington.
1870. Joel Daniels, Frank J. Poor.
1871. Uriah A. Carswell, Frank L. Rundlett.
1872. Edward D. Hill, Leonard Shelters.
1873. John Gillis, Seth T. Hill.
1874. Charles H. G. Foss, Henry S. Kolseth.
1875. Andrew J. Dickey.

The following is a list of the High Priests since the institution of the encampment:

1845. Isaac Flanders, Daniel J. Hoyt.
1846. Benjamin M. Tillotson, Benjamin M. Tillotson.
1847. Thomas S. Jones, Sylvanus Bunton.
1848. David C. Batchelder, Charles Currier.
1849. Charles T. Durgin, James M. Berry.
1850. Otis P. Warner, Charles H. Brown.
1851. Leonard Sanborn, Henry T. Mowatt.
1852. Moses W. Oliver, Granville P. Mason.
1853. Abraham Robertson, Nathaniel Herrick.
1854. Edward McCoy, John B. Fish.
1855. Charles Currier, John B. Fish.
1856. Joseph Kidder, Joel Taylor.
1857. Alpha Currier, John D. Patterson.
1858. Arthur L. Walker, James C. Wing.
1859. John D. Patterson, Granville P. Mason.
1860. Charles Currier, James C. Wing.
1861. Thomas B. Eastman, John B. Fish.
1862. Charles H. Brown, Daniel Pulsifer.
1863. Horace M. Gillis, Rufus L. Bartlett.
1864. Charles Currier, Robert B. Neal.

1865. Leonard Colby, Russell O. Burleigh.
1866. John Gillis, Seth J. Sanborn.
1867. Abiel C. Flanders, Gilman Stearns.
1868. John T. Robinson, Stephen H. Randlett.
1869. Frank T. E. Richardson, John C. Balch.
1870. Charles H. Osgood, Charles H. Osgood.
1871. William G. Marden, George R. Vance.
1872. John T. Robinson, John T. Robinson.
1873. Edward O. Hill, Frank L. Rundlett.
1874. Thomas C. Cheney, Charles C. Keniston.
1875. Charles C. Keniston.

Mechanics Lodge, Number Thirteen, the second in the city in point of age, was instituted November 25, 1845, with the following charter members: John S. Yeaton, Horace Gordon, John C. Lyford, Albe C. Heath, Otis P. Warner, Charles Currier, Nathaniel Smith. It has now about three hundred and fifty members, and funds amounting to about nine thousand dollars. The following have been the Noble Grands since the existence of the lodge, the first, Horace Gordon, holding the office from November 25, 1845, to April 1, 1846, and three months constituting a term till 1847.

1846. Horace Gordon, John C. Lyford, John S. Yeaton, Charles Currier.
1847. Albe C. Heath, Otis P. Warner.
1848. Nathaniel C. Smith, David C. Batchelder.
1849. William D. Buck, Charles H. Brown.
1850. Jeremiah Preston, jr., Abraham Robertson.
1851. Abel M. Keniston, Barnabas Hinds.
1852. Charles C. Keniston, John M. Harvey.
1853. Charles T. Durgin, George W. Weeks.
1854. Enoch Watson, George C. Gilmore.
1855. Bartlett A. Morse, James M. Howe.
1856. Charles Currier, Stephen H. Crockett.
1857. David Alden, James C. Wing.
1858. John D. Patterson, Jonathan Dodge.
1859. Daniel Pulsifer, George S. Neal.
1860. Charles H. G. Foss, Granville P. Mason.
1861. Samuel Upton, Henry B. Moulton.
1862. Evander G. Merrill, John G. Lane.
1863. Edward Garner, John U. Farnham.
1864. Lang Munroe, James Wilkins, jr.
1865. Abiel C. Flanders, Seth T. Hill.
1866. John T. Robinson, Russell O. Burleigh.
1867. John Prince, Joel Daniels.

1868. Gilman Stearns, Thomas C. Cheney.
1869. Stephen H. Rundlett, William G. Garmon.
1870. Leonard Shelters, Charles H. Osgood.
1871. Henry W. Powell, James M. House.
1872. James L. Sweet, John K. Piper.
1873. Henry S. Brown, Jacob Morrill.
1874. John C. Smith, Jeremiah D. Jones.
1875. James F. Pherson.

Wildey Lodge, Number Forty-five, is the last lodge organized in this city, being instituted August 8, 1866, with the following charter members: Henry A. Farrington, Jonathan B. Moore, Daniel R. Prescott, Uriah A. Carswell, Hazen K. Fuller, Francis L. Porter, David Cutter, Harvey L. Currier, John V. Sullivan, Edwin N. Baker, John D. Powell, James M. Moore, John N. Chase, Stephen Woodward. It has now about two hundred members and funds amounting to about four thousand dollars. The following is a list of its chief officers since its institution:

1866. Henry A. Farrington.
1867. Jonathan B. Moore, Daniel R. Prescott.
1868. Uriah A. Carswell, Hazen K. Fuller.
1869. John D. Powell, John C. Balch.
1870. Frank L. Rundlett, James M. Moore.
1871. George F. Elliott, Lyman W. Colby.
1872. Nathan P. Hunt, Hiram Hill.
1873. David P. Norris, Henry B. Gillette.
1874. Henry E. Burnham, Joseph G. Edgerly.
1875. William H. Stearns.

Mount Washington Encampment, Number Sixteen, was the second encampment in Manchester, being instituted March 2, 1871, with the following charter members: Joseph Kidder, George W. Weeks, John C. Balch, Charles H. Osgood, Nathan P. Hunt, John D. Powell, Sylvester C. Gould, Benjamin F. Hartford, George A. Clark, John A. Collins, Charles F. Hunt, Louis E. Phelps, David P. Norris, Charles W. Temple, Marden E. Barnard, Brackett B. Weeks, Henry A. Farrington. It has now over a hundred members and funds amounting to about two hundred dollars. The Chief Patriarchs of Mount Washington Encampment since its formation have been as follows:

1871. Joseph Kidder, John D. Powell.
1872. Nathan P. Hunt, David P. Norris.
1673. Daniel R. Prescott, Henry E. Burnham.
1874. Sylvester C. Gould, Benjamin F. Hartford.
1875. William G. Garmon.

The High Priests have been as follows:

1871. Charles H. Osgood, Brackett B. Weeks.
1872. Marden E. Barnard, George A. Clark.
1873. Louis E. Phelps, E. B. Worthen.
1874. L. H. Caldwell, William G. Garmon.
1875. Charles W. Temple.

KNIGHTS OF PYTHIAS.

The Knights of Pythias, an order of more recent origin than the associations of Free Masons and Odd Fellows, but which has now seventeen lodges and a thousand members in New Hampshire, was introduced to this state in 1870, and to this city in the same year. Early in March of that year Henry F. Carey, an operative in the Amoskeag Company's employ, having received a copy of the constitution of one of the Pythian lodges and thus become interested in the order, attempted to form a lodge here, but was unsuccessful. Through his instrumentality, however, a number of men, among whom were Timothy W. Challis, Frank E. Hart, Joseph L. Dow, Galen Eastman, Silas C. Clatur, Franklin W. McKinley, Samuel W. Shepherd and Silas R. Wallace, had caught something of his interest and they held several meetings during the month of March at which some progress was made towards the formation of a lodge. Pioneer Lodge, Number One, had already been instituted at Newmarket, on the second of March, and thus the order had gained a foothold in the state.

The first meeting here of which any records were kept was held March 31, 1870, at the old "Labor League" rooms in Smyth's block, when Timothy W. Challis was elected "Worthy Chancellor," the officer now entitled "Chancellor Commander" being then known by that name.

The next meeting was held April 2, in the Grand Army hall in Brown's block, and at an adjourned meeting held in the same place April 6, the list of officers was completed. There being then no Grand Lodge in the state, an application for recognition as a lodge by the jurisdiction of Massachusetts was made and favorably received, and the officers elect were notified that the installing officers of the Grand Lodge of Massachusetts would be in attendance to organize the lodge April 8, 1870. Accordingly a special meeting was called for that purpose on the evening of that day and at that time the lodge, under the name of Granite Lodge, Number Three, was instituted in form, with thirty-two members, and the officers were duly installed. The Massachusetts officers had instituted the previous evening at Exeter the second lodge in the state, under the name of Swamscott Lodge, Number Two. The membership of Granite Lodge rapidly increased, and on the eighteenth of April a number of members asked leave to withdraw to form a new lodge. The request was granted and accordingly Merrimack Lodge, Number Four, was instituted May 6, 1870. Both lodges worked under a dispensation till October 21, 1870, when a charter in form was granted to each by the Grand Lodge of this state, which had been formed the previous day in Manchester by representatives from six lodges, Rising Sun Lodge, Number Seven, of Rochester, although instituted, not being represented.

The charter members of Granite Lodge were Stephen C. Amsden, Timothy W. Challis, Frank E. Hart, Joseph L. Dow, James P. Carpenter, Gula A. Craig, Silas C. Clatur, Franklin W. McKinley, A. A. Wells, Silas R. Wallace. The present membership is about one hundred and thirty-five. Its Chancellor Commanders, or highest officers, for each year, follow:

1870. Timothy W. Challis, Frank E. Hart.
1871. Franklin W. McKinley, Levi L. Aldrich.
1872. William E. Moore, Alden E. Metcalf.

1873. Silas R. Wallace, Sidney J. Ela.
1874. Moses O. Pearson, Samuel Amsden.
1875. Jonathan M. Sanborn.

The charter members of Merrimack Lodge were: Samuel W. Shepherd, William R. Patten, Joseph B. Judkins, Samuel F. Murry, Albert Story, Daniel S. Holt, Edwin B. Cutler, Hazen Davis, Frank H. Hickok, Oliver B. Elliott, Robert A. Challis, John Wingate, Perkins C. Lane, Leroy J. French. The present membership is about one hundred and twenty. The Chancellor Commanders for the several years are given below.

1870. William R. Patten, Samuel F. Murry.
1871. Albert Story, Perkins C. Lane.
1872. Roland C. Rowell, John D. Patterson.
1873. Frank H. Hickok, Charles W. Temple.
1874. Samuel W. Shepherd, Hiram H. Gove.
1875. Hiram H. Gove.

The lodges held their stated meetings in the hall in Brown's block for nearly a year and then secured and fitted up a new and spacious hall in Globe block on Hanover street, in which the first meeting was held March 6, 1871, and which they have since occupied. It is used by both lodges, which own the property, free from incumbrance, in common, and work harmoniously together. Each lodge has five hundred dollars on hand and invested. A "Pythian Relief Association," which has now a hundred and fifty members, was formed in May, 1872, upon the same plan as the similar associations among the Masons and Odd Fellows.

TEMPERANCE SOCIETIES.

Among the earliest societies in the city organized upon the basis of temperance were those which succeeded the "Washingtonian" movement of 1840, and of these the first was known as the "Manchester Washington Total Abstinence Society," which was organized August 3, 1841, which had two thousand members, and one of whose presidents was Dr. Thomas Brown, who was an active advocate of temperance. In October of the next year a movement was begun among the women of the place which resulted in the formation of the " Martha Washington Temperance Society," of which Mrs. Benjamin Kinsley was at one time president. Another organization about that time was the " Manchester Young Men's Temperance Society," with William Mace at its head, and still another was the " Young Ladies' Temperance Benevolent Society" which was organized August 22, 1843. These associations, and others, if they existed, were generally organized by the influence of some traveling lecturer and often in connection with some particular church. They had no proper financial basis, held infrequent meetings, and resulted chiefly in obtaining spasmodically signatures to temperance pledges in which abstinence from the lighter intoxicants was not definitely named.

These were dissolved in five or six years, to be succeeded by an order called the "Sons of Temperance," which, an advance upon Washingtonianism in several features, was started in this country in 1842, as a possible plan of organization for the more effectual promotion of the temperance cause. Its pledge included abstinence from " malt liquors, wine, ale and cider," as well as from more potent spirits. It retained its members largely by the system of money benefits in case of sickness and death, and, though later years modified many of its social and pecuniary features, it was the means of much good.

The first division of the order in this state was organized at Portsmouth and the second at Nashua, while the third, under the name of Manchester Division Number Three, was instituted in this city July 13, 1846. Among those who held the office of " Worthy Patriarch " — the highest in the division — were Dr. Thomas Brown, John B.

Herman Foster

Fish, James Collins, Harrison Soule, Horace L. Eaton, O. R. Pratt, Edward McQueston, Charles Fish, David P. Perkins, J. A. D. Gregg and Edson Hill. The Grand Division of the state was organized March 11, 1847, at Portsmouth, and was located at Manchester. Among its chief officers were Dr. Thomas Brown and the Rev. Henry M. Dexter of this city.

Another division was organized in Manchester October 26, 1847, under the name of Excelsior Division, Number Eight. Among its highest officers were the Rev. Henry M. Dexter, Albert Jackson, the Rev. John W. Ray, Daniel W. McCaine, Alfred G. Fairbanks, Alfred B. Soule, J. B. Sawyer and C. W. Eaton. A higher order, under the name of Granite Temple of Honor, Number One, was instituted February 28, 1848. In the latter part of 1848 another division was organized, with the name of Niagara Division, Number Nineteen, which had but a brief existence. The "Daughters of Temperance," whose members were women, and the "Cadets of Temperance," a juvenile association, were cotemporaneous orders, existing to the same end. The subordinate bodies of the former were called "unions." Blackmar Union, Number Four, was instituted December 30, 1847; Union Number Six, April 8, 1848; and the Grand Union of the state, located in this city, was formed April 10, 1848. The subordinate bodies of the Cadets were called sections, and Manchester Section, Number Four, was instituted February 28, 1848. Four years later Excelsior Division was the only one of all these which survived, and that afterwards was dissolved. These bodies met in Sons of Temperance Hall in the first Patten's block.

Subsequently, however, a new interest in the order arose, and resulted in the institution, November 16, 1860, of Manchester Division, Number Nineteen. The charter was granted to John B. Fish, J. B. T. Baker, Aaron Jackson, Joseph G. Edgerly, Frank T. E. Richardson, H. H. Sum-

15

mers, James M. Clough, Charles F. Livingston, John G. Lane, T. E. Barker, G. S. Dearborn, M. L. Stevens, W. H. H. Crawford, L. B. Gould, John Verity, Francis Switser, R. F. Moore and D. S. Russell. They met in Ferren's building and afterwards in Mystic hall in Merchants' Exchange. It is probable that the Rebellion interfered with their prosperity, and their last session was held May 22, 1863.

The place in the country which the Sons of Temperance left vacant was occupied by the "Good Templars," who had their origin in 1851. Their basis was different from that of any preceding organization. They combined in one order the "Sons," "Daughters," and "Cadets," admitted women on the same basis as men and with equal eligibility to all offices, and are radical in all phases of the reform. They ignored the beneficiary system, thus largely reducing the fees and dues, and offered no motive to persons to join them except to be reclaimed from intemperance, if fallen into the habit, or to be kept from it or to keep others from it. They have plain and impressive ceremonies and the members assume, upon entering, a pledge of total abstinence for life. The "Good Templars" form the largest temperance society in the world, the membership averaging, of late years, over half a million persons, scattered wherever the English tongue is spoken. Since 1851 nearly three million persons in the United States and Canadas, and about one million in foreign countries, have been connected with the order.

The order reached Manchester about the close of the Rebellion, Stark Lodge, Number Four, being instituted May 31, 1865. Its charter was granted to A. J. Butterfield, A. O. Dillingham, G. L. P. Corliss, J. W. Wilkins, John Verity, Aaron Jackson, William G. Garmon, James M. Clough, L. W. Nourse, W. R. Call, S. L. Lewis, Aaron W. Stevens, Benjamin M. Tillotson, G. W. Rogers, Nathaniel Herrick,

Villiam H. Thomas, John A. Knowles, Joseph W. Fellows, Irs. J. W. Wilkins, Sarah M. Call, Sarah A. Davis, Lucreia Call.

Merrimack Lodge, Number Five, was instituted December , 1866. The charter members were: Daniel R. Prescott, Seth J. Sanborn, William F. Childs, S. C. Cunningham, J. '. Durgin, Charles G. Blake, Uriah A. Carswell, Joseph C. Bennett, E. W. Smith, Hattie D. Fuller, Mrs. J. L. 'rescott.

There is also a Union Degree Lodge and a Temple of Honor. The Templars met at first in the vestries of the Jnitarian and Pine-street Freewill Baptist churches, but soon occupied what is now Mirror hall in Merchants' Exchange in common with a "Machinists and Blacksmiths' Jnion." In 1870 they furnished a hall on Manchester street, which was destroyed, as were the rooms of the Masons and Knights of Pythias, in the great fire of 1870. They now meet in Pythian hall in Globe block on Hanover street. The lodges are yet thriving and have invariably ıeld their weekly meetings. Since their institution nearly wo thousand persons have been connected with them, the nembership of both combined averaging lately between hree and four hundred, and several thousand dollars, accruing from the small fees and dues, have been expended n their work.

At one time and another there have been other temperance associations, generally of a temporary character. Among them were the "Bands of Hope" which were started about 1858, and a women's temperance society ten years later, of which Mrs. Frederick Smyth was president. There are now societies for the promotion of temperance connected with several of the churches. A juvenile association under the name of the "Cold Water Temple" was organized in October, 1874, by the Rev. Harrison F. Wood, pastor of the Pine-street Freewill Baptist church, which has six hundred members; and a "Women's Temperance League," of which Mrs. H. F. Wood is president, was formed in November, 1874, with the purpose of creating an interest in the temperance cause. It has about seventy-five members.

Of several temperance societies found among the Roman Catholic population "St. Paul's Total Abstinence Mutual Benefit Society" is the oldest, having been organized in August, 1872, in connection with St. Joseph's church. It has now one hundred and sixty members and its president is James Dray. With it is connected a society of youth under the name of "Temperance Cadets," which was formed in May, 1873, and which contains one hundred and fifty boys and is superintended by Patrick A. Devine. February 18, 1874, another society was formed, in connection with St. Ann's church, under the name of "St. John's Total Abstinence Mutual Benefit Society," of which the Rev. John Powers is president, and which has about a hundred members. In April, 1875, a similar association was formed in connection with the remaining Roman Catholic church—St. Augustine's. These three societies last named are branches of a state organization, which in turn is part of the "National Catholic Total Abstinence Union" of the United States.

MILITARY ORGANIZATIONS.

The earliest of the military companies in Manchester whose existence reached to its incorporation as a city was the Manchester Rifle Company, which was organized in 1825 under Captain James McQueston. Among succeeding commanders were Nathaniel and Ira Moore and David Young, and it was dissolved about 1848. Next in order of formation were the Stark Guards, which were organized August 16, 1840, under Captain Walter French, who was followed by E. W. Harrington, George W. Morrison, E. A. Bodwell and others. They had an armory in the city hall and in Patten's block and kept up their organization a little over ten years, being a famous company in their time.

The Granite Fusiliers were organized August 10, 1842, under Captain Samuel W. Parsons, and assumed the name of City Guards in 1847. Among the commanders were George T. Clark, S. G. Patterson, J. C. Ricker, S. G. Langley, J. R. Bagley, Micajah Ingham and Francis H. Lyford. They occupied for armories rooms in the city hall, Granite block and Wells' block, and went out of existence about 1860. Other and smaller companies, which have no longer an existence, were the National Guards, organized August 17, 1863, with an armory in Wells' block, and who did service at Fort Constitution in Portsmouth harbor during the War of the Rebellion; and the Smyth Rifles, who were organized in August, 1865, and who had an armory in Wells' block.

The Amoskeag Veterans is the only one of the military organizations now existing in the city which can look back upon a life of over ten years, and is an independent company, while the rest form part of the state militia. It is the oldest "veteran" corps in New England with the exception of the Ancient and Honorable Artillery Company of Boston. Its formation was suggested by a visit which a company known as the Boston Association of Veterans paid to the citizens of Manchester in October, 1854. A paper was drawn up by the Hon. C. E. Potter and circulated for signatures, the subscribers agreeing thereby to become members of an association under the name of the Stark Veterans. The first meeting of the signers was held in the city hall, November 6, 1854. The Hon. Hiram Brown was chosen chairman, and the Hon. C. E. Potter clerk, and committees on officers, constitution and uniform were appointed, whose reports were afterwards adopted. At a subsequent meeting the name of Amoskeag Veterans was assumed. The first officers elected are given below:

William P. Riddle, Colonel.
William Patten, First Lieutenant.
Samuel Andrews, Second Lieutenant.
Hiram Brown, First Major.
E. T. Stevens, Second Major.
Samuel W. Parsons, First Sergeant.
Jacob G. Cilley, Second Sergeant.
S. M. Dow, Third Sergeant.
Reuben D. Mooers, Fourth Sergeant.
James Wallace, First Corporal.
Phinehas Adams, Second Corporal.
E. G. Guilford, Third Corporal.
Thomas Rundlett, Fourth Corporal.
John S. Elliot, Surgeon.
William W. Brown, Surgeon's Mate.
Benjamin M. Tillotson, Chaplain.
James Hersey, Treasurer.
Frederick G. Stark,
Daniel C. Gould,
John S. Kidder,
George Porter,
Theodore T. Abbot,
} Executive Committee.

Their first parade and ball occurred February 22, 1855, and the celebration of Washington's birthday has since been continued as an annual custom. At one o'clock in the afternoon of that day they marched to the Manchester House and escorted the Hon. Nathaniel B. Baker, then governor of the state, and other invited guests, to the city hall and were reviewed by the governor. At four o'clock an oration was delivered by the Hon. C. E. Potter of Manchester, followed by addresses by Governor Baker and the mayor of the city, the Hon. Frederick Smyth. In the evening a banquet was served in Patten's hall, and the evening's exercises were concluded with dancing in the city hall.

The organization was continued in this form till August 4, 1855, when an act of incorporation which had been granted by the legislature in June was accepted by the company, and the latter was then established as a corporate body. It still kept in view the objects which were aimed at in its formation, defined by the constitution to be military parades, the protection of life and property, the preservation of the peace and social enjoyments. Their first armory was in the Museum building, from which they removed to Granite block in 1869; they took possession of their present quarters in Towne's block in 1871. The association includes the most prominent and influential men in Manchester, and at first its members were nearly all from this city, but there are now in its ranks prominent citizens of Concord, Hooksett, Derry, Nashua, Keene, Portsmouth, Franklin, Bedford, Suncook, Enfield, Claremont and other places. It has had over four hundred members and there are now about one hundred active members enrolled.

The commanders of the company since its organization are given below, with the date of their election:

Gen. William P. Riddle, November 25, 1854.
Col. Chandler E. Potter, October 3, 1855.
Col. Theodore T. Abbot, October 21, 1857.
Col. Thomas Rundlett, October 19, 1860.
Col. Henry T. Mowatt, October 22, 1862.
Col. Chandler E. Potter, October 19, 1864.
Col. David Cross, October 31, 1866.
Gen. Natt Head, November 18, 1868.
Col. Martin V. B. Edgerly, February 22, 1873.
Col. George C. Gilmore, March 25, 1875.

In June, 1855, the Veterans made their first excursion, visiting at that time Boston, Bunker Hill and Lowell. In December of the same year they made the most extensive journey of all during their existence as a company. They left Manchester on the thirteenth for an excursion to Washington and Mount Vernon. On their way they were cordially received and hospitably treated by the military organizations and official representatives of the cities of New York, Philadelphia and Baltimore, banquets being given in their honor at each of these places. At Washington they were the recipients of marked courtesy and were the especial guests of the President of the United States — Gen. Franklin Pierce — a New Hampshire citizen. They did not reach home till the twenty-second, after an absence of nine days.

They visited Newburyport, Mass., in 1866; Hartford, Conn., Springfield and Worcester, Mass., in 1867; New York, as the guests of the famous Ninth Regiment, under command of Col. James Fisk, in 1870; and in 1873 visited Providence, R. I., and participated in a parade and union festival with the Ancient and Honorable Artillery Company of Boston, the Newburyport Veteran Artillery Association, the Putnam Phalanx of Hartford, the First Light Infantry and the Light Infantry Veteran Association of Providence.

Five companies of the First Regiment New Hampshire Volunteer Militia belong in Manchester, together with the colonel, William H. Maxwell; the adjutant, B. L. Hartshorn; and the quartermaster, Nathan P. Kidder. The companies have not far from fifty members each. The Head Guards, Company C, were organized July 25, 1865, were named for Gen. Natt Head of Hooksett, and have an armory in Lafayette hall. Their captain is Charles H. Reed. The Straw Rifles, Company E, John J. Dillon, captain, were organized March 17, 1873, were named in honor of Ex-Gov. E. A. Straw of this city, and have an armory in Merchants' Exchange. The Haines Rifles, Company F, were organized as the Clark Guards January 1, 1868, and subsequently assumed their present name in honor of Gen. John M. Haines of Chichester, then Adjutant-General of the state. Their armory is in Granite block and their captain is Jonas S. Everett. The Sheridan Guards, Company G, were organized in August, 1865, and named in honor of Lieutenant-General Philip Sheridan of the regular army. Their armory is in Brown's block, and their captain is Patrick Cullity. The Manchester Veterans, Company I, were organized March 5, 1870, and James M. House is their captain. They have about fifty men and their armory is in Grand Army hall. Section B, First Light Bat-

E. N. Harrington

tery, was organized July 10, 1867, has thirty-five members and two field-pieces, and its armory is situated on Manchester street. Samuel S. Piper is the lieutenant in command. The High School Cadets, a company consisting for the most part of pupils of the high school, was organized June 9, 1873, and Frank H. Challis is captain.

The organization called the Grand Army of the Republic, which arose just after the War of the Rebellion, is represented in Manchester by Louis Bell Post, Number Three. January 20, 1868, the following petitioners for a charter as a "Post" of the Grand Army were enrolled as members by the authorized officers: William R. Patten, Francis W. Parker, Samuel F. Murry, George H. Hubbard, William W. Brown, Charles M. Whitney, Alfred G. Simons, Hilas D. Davis, Edwin P. Richardson and Timothy W. Challis. Large numbers of the soldiers of the late War of the Rebellion soon joined, a constitution and by-laws were afterwards adopted and a hall in Brown's block rented in common with the Manchester Veterans, but subsequently they removed to their present armory in Weeks's block. March 3, 1869, articles of incorporation were adopted and recorded according to the legal form. December 29, 1869, the association formally assumed the name of Louis Bell Post in honor of Brevet Brigadier-General Louis Bell of Farmington, who was killed by the rebels at Fort Fisher, Va., January 15, 1865, while colonel of the Fourth New Hampshire Regiment and commanding a brigade of the Army of the Potomac.

The association was formed for social and for charitable purposes and has kept both ends in view during its existence. By the help of several fairs, which the citizens of Manchester have been glad to assist in making successful, funds for the relief of needy comrades have been supplied, and have been freely bestowed when necessary. Of late the cultivation of social feeling among the members has been promoted by a series of gatherings under the name of "camp-fires," at which the veterans delight to "fight their battles o'er again." This post is the largest in the state, and the members of no organization are united by stronger bonds of friendship and sympathy than those which not only keep Louis Bell Post from dissolution but seem to make it firmer year by year. Under the auspices of this post "Decoration Day," the thirtieth of May, is annually observed in this city with becoming ceremonies.

The commanders of the post and the date of their election follow:

William R. Patten, January 20, 1868.
Reuben Dodge, June 26, 1868.
Timothy W. Challis, December 30, 1868.
James M. House, June 30, 1869.
Reuben Dodge, December 29, 1869.
William H. Vickery, December 28, 1870.
Charles B. Bradley, December 29, 1871.
Silas R. Wallace, December 17, 1872.
George H. Dodge, December 30, 1873.
Samuel S. Piper, December 29, 1874.

MANCHESTER ART ASSOCIATION.

This society was formed in September, 1871, by a few ladies and gentlemen who were interested in art for its own sake or because they gained a livelihood by it, and its origin as well as its subsequent prosperity is due in great measure to Henry W. Herrick, an artist of this city and the president of the association. The primary idea in its formation was to furnish facilities for mutual study and instruction in reference to art matters. It grew to such an extent that during its second year it was established in rooms in the county court-house which had been fitted for its uses. As it was able, it added to its possessions casts, models and books, which were either contributed by citizens or were bought from the proceeds of exhibitions, several of which have been successfully held.

It now rests upon a permanent basis, articles of incorporation having been adopted October 13, 1874. Its library, whose contents have in most cases been chosen with reference to the various trades in which the study of art is of use and which therefore are of a practical educational character, now numbers about a hundred and fifty volumes. The rooms contain a number of charts and diagrams and fifty plaster casts, most of which are the best examples of the antique. It has a present membership of over two hundred and twenty-five persons, some of whom are professional and others amateur artists, others engaged in the different trades and who find the association helpful, and others still who are led to become members solely by æsthetic tastes. Its funds depend upon the annual assessments and upon the proceeds of exhibitions. It has, naturally, as it grew, reached out into a wider field and done much to cultivate a general taste for art, as well as to instruct and assist its members.

OTHER SOCIETIES.

The rest of the societies include associations for various purposes and among them several which are branches of orders which have but recently come into existence.

Granite State Council, Number One, of the United Order of American Mechanics, was chartered March 24, 1873, with the following charter members: Timothy W. Challis, Silas C. Clatur, Levi L. Aldrich, Wesley E. Holt, Nathaniel Southard, B. L. Robinson, B. L. Hartshorn, Emery E. Cobb, James Russell, Joseph L. Stevens, George H. Dodge, Silas R. Wallace, William Dickerman, William H. Vickery, Samuel Clark, A. G. Simons. It was organized for mutual benefit to its members, of whom there are now about fifty, and Silas C. Clatur is its chief officer or Councillor.

Amoskeag Grange, Number Three, Patrons of Husbandry,

was organized in Mirror hall August 23, 1873, as a branch of an order then taking root all over the country and formed especially in the interests of agriculturists. Its charter members are: John B. Clarke, Daniel Farmer, Joseph Cate, Isaac Huse, Jeremiah L. Fogg, John B. Huse, John Hosley, Thomas W. Lane, Mrs. E. C. McQueston, Mrs. H. P. Huse, Mrs. Thomas W. Lane, Miss Emma A. Wilder, Miss Mary E. Smith, Miss Jennie E. Runels, all of Manchester, and Edward C. Shirley of Goffstown. It exists for social and pecuniary benefit and has now about eighty members—residents of this city, Bedford, Goffstown and Candia. John B. Clarke has been its Master and John Hosley its secretary since its organization. There are now over fifty granges in the state and the State Grange was organized in this city December 23, 1873, at the Grand Army hall.

Onward Council, Number Three, Sovereigns of Industry, was formed January 25, 1874, being a branch of a national order which spread among mechanics and artisans very much as the Patrons of Husbandry, a little before, had spread among the farmers. Its charter members were: John J. Dillon, Henry French, Alonzo Durgin, Charles M. Wise, George W. Thayer, Joseph L. Stevens, Bradley B. Aldrich, George R. Simmons, Thomas C. Cheney, B. F. Garland, L. L. Sweatt, Rufus Wilkinson, Charles H. G. Foss, E. L. Carpenter, Atherton W. Quint. It has grown very rapidly, having now over three hundred members, and Charles H. G. Foss is its president. There are now fourteen councils in the state, and the State Council was formed in this city December 22, 1874.

The Irishmen of the city have two societies. St. Patrick's Mutual Benefit and Protective Association was organized March 30, 1868, and its president is C. A. O'Connor. Lodge Number One, Ancient Order of Hibernians, was organized in 1871, has about a hundred members and James Moran is its president. Lodge Number Two was formed in March, 1864, with Daniel F. Healey as its president, and grew up to a membership of sixty persons, but is not now in existence.

There are three societies among the Germans. Granite State Lodge, Number One Hundred and Twelve, Independent Order of Red Men, was formed in 1868 and has now about fifty members. Charles Uhlig is its First Chief. Barbarossa Lodge, Number Three Hundred and Twenty-nine, of the order of Harugari, was organized February 5, 1874, and has about forty members. Hermann Rittner is the chief officer. The Turnverein, a society whose members combine social pleasures and physical exercise, was organized in 1870 and incorporated by the Legislature in 1872. It has about seventy members and owns a hall and grounds in Piscataquog village.

The St. Jean Baptiste Society is the only association among the French residents. It was organized in April, 1871, has nearly two hundred members, and its president is E. L. Gauvreau.

Musical societies are few. The Manchester Choral Union is the most important. It was organized in its present form, mainly through the exertions of E. T. Baldwin, in the spring of 1869, to take part in the "Peace Jubilee" at Boston in the summer of that year. Since then its fortunes and membership have varied, but it is now prosperous. It has about a hundred members, and Daniel C. Gould is its president. There are two among the Germans —the Concordia, with eighteen members, whose director is Martin Netzsch, and the Orpheus, with ten members, whose director is Frederick Scheer.

The Manchester Gymnasium was organized August 11, 1874, to afford its members opportunity for athletic exercise. It has now about fifty members and Frank T. E. Richardson is its president. It has rooms in Wells' block which are supplied with gymnastic apparatus, and it is in a flourishing condition.

The Forrest Dramatic Association was formed in January, 1874, by several persons in the city who are interested in amateur theatricals. It includes some good actors, and has given several exhibitions. Its president is George F. Crosby.

The Manchester Printers' Literary Association, was formed February 4, 1875, by young men employed in the different printing-offices in the city, for literary and social enjoyment. It has about twenty members and its president is Charles F. Coffin.

A number of prominent men of the city organized, December 24, 1874, the Manchester Social Union, a club "for social improvement, amusement and recreation without vice." It has about a hundred and forty members and its rooms are in Merchants' Exchange. Its officers are: president, Daniel Clark; vice-president, John S. Kidder; secretary, Nathan P. Hunt; treasurer, Daniel W. Lane; executive committee, Charles H. Bartlett, George W. Dodge, Charles E. Balch.

Early in February, 1875, about twenty boys of the High school formed an organization under the name of the High School Debating Club, to hold meetings weekly for literary exercises. Frank H. Challis is its president.

FORMER ASSOCIATIONS.

Among associations of various kinds in this city whose day is past the "Manchester District Medical Society," which was organized in June, 1841, and was in existence as late as 1845, is the only society of physicians of which record has been preserved. The "Manchester Mesmeric Institute" was formed in April, 1843, for the advancement of the principles of mesmerism, with the following officers: president, Edward P. Offutt; vice-president, Benjamin Kinsley; secretary, Frederick Smyth; treasurer,

George Marston. It probably had a brief existence. The "Manchester Academy" was an association which was organized, with David A. Bunton as president, for educational purposes. Under its auspices a school was opened, June 12, 1843, in a building on the corner of Elm and Lowell streets, and placed in charge of A. M. Payson. Subsequent principals were John G. Sherburne and Franklin Webster. It was afterwards kept in Harmony hall, farther down Elm street, and was probably discontinued about 1846. This was a few years before Rodney Kendall had opened his "select school" in the old chapel on Central street. He afterwards kept it in a building on the corner of Elm and Hanover streets and in other places, continuing it till about 1860.

In 1844 there was a stir among the working-men of the country, and in many towns and cities they formed "mutual benefit associations" to protect themselves against real or fancied injustice on the part of their employers. One of these was organized in this city, September 7, 1844, by a number of mechanics and laborers, who met at that time at the old Freewill Baptist chapel which was then still situated on Concord street. They chose Alonzo Smith president, Ebenezer Cross vice-president, J. C. Stowell recording secretary, J. M. Barnes corresponding secretary, and William H. Wiggin treasurer. These societies subsided with the feeling which had called them into existence.

The "Manchester Lyceum" was an association of prominent men of the city which was organized to support a course of lectures by speakers from abroad, usually having twelve or fifteen during the winter in the city hall. Single tickets were then sold for ninepence. The association existed the greater part of the time between 1850 and 1860. About 1856 another association was formed to provide lectures upon slavery. The number of lectures and the price of tickets corresponded with those the Manchester Lyceum adopted. It had only a brief existence. The "Manchester Musical Education Society" was organized in December, 1849, had rehearsals in Patten's hall and lived for five or six years. There was an "Antiquarian Sacred Musical Society" in existence in 1858.

The "Excelsior Literary Association," a society of clerks, printers, students, etc., was organized February 4, 1858, and held meetings in a hall in Smyth's block, leasing it and fitting it for use and giving it the name of "Excelsior hall." A few years previously the "Manchester Literary Association" had been formed, and the two held public debates in the city hall. The war terminated the existence of both. The former came to an end in the spring of 1861 and in the fall another association of the same name was formed which survived a year or two longer. About 1856 there were organized several companies for the purpose of loaning money to members upon security, three which existed at that time being termed the "Citizens' Loan Fund Association," the "Manchester Loan and Fund Association," and the "Mechanics' Perpetual Loan Fund Association." Three or four years later another was formed under the name of the "New Perpetual Loan Fund Association," which was in existence as late as 1866. The rest closed their books several years before. A musical society called the "Manchester Chorus and Glee Club" was formed in November, 1873, with William C. Gage as its president, but it lasted only through that winter.

POST-OFFICES, BANKS AND INSURANCE COMPANIES.

THE post-office, in contrast with the banks and insurance companies which have had existence in Manchester, was not an institution called forth by the sudden prosperity which was caused by the building of the mills forty years ago, although there was none in Manchester till 1831, while the villages of Amoskeag and Piscataquog had long since been in possession of them. There are now three: one in the city proper, one at Amoskeag village and one at Goffe's Falls. The banks, again, in distinction from the insurance companies, have flourished uninterruptedly since their organization, and there are now four national banks and five savings banks, while the insurance companies have generally been formed only to perish, there being but one now in existence and that of recent origin.

POST-OFFICES.

On the completion in 1831 of the Mammoth road — the old stage route from Lowell to Concord, passing through what was then the most thickly settled part of Manchester — a post-office was established at the Centre, and Samuel Jackson, the father of Albert and Samuel P. Jackson of this city, was appointed postmaster by the president, Andrew Jackson. Daily, as the stage came by from the north or south, the contents of the mail-bag were examined and the letters for the office were taken out and those to be mailed were forwarded.

When the Amoskeag Manufacturing Company began to lay the foundation of the present city along the river-bank in 1838 and 1839, it was found to be inconvenient for the people, then fast settling, to go to the Centre for their mail, and consequently in February, 1840, a new office was established in Duncklee's block, now occupied by John M. Chandler & Company and Ira Moore, in the part used by Mr. Moore, and Jesse Duncklee was appointed postmaster by Martin Van Buren. The name of the office at the Centre was changed to that of Manchester Centre office, but soon afterwards, at the suggestion of the postmaster, Mr. Jackson, it was deemed inexpedient to keep two offices in operation and thus compel individuals to search both to find their letters, so Mr. Jackson resigned and the office at the Centre was discontinued several months after the new one had been located in what was then known as "Amoskeag new village." Mr. Duncklee had been in feeble health and died in March, 1840, without ever having been able to attend personally to the duties of his office. The vacancy thus caused was filled by the appointment of Paul Cragin, jr., who also received his commission from Van Buren, and who took charge of the office April 23, 1840. Upon the completion of the town hall in 1841 the post-office was removed to that building. When it was burned in 1844, the office was removed to Mr. Cragin's house on Hanover street, the second house east of the First Congregational church, the present residence of Dr. Charles Wells. It remained there but a few weeks and was then kept in a "ten-footer" on Hanover street owned by George A. Barnes, near its present location. Upon the rebuilding in 1845 of the town hall, the present city hall, the office was once more established in it, in the southwest corner.

In 1845 Warren L. Lane, appointed by James K. Polk, succeeded Mr. Cragin as postmaster and held the office till 1849, when Zachary Taylor, a whig president, gave the place to James Hersey. When a Democratic administration again assumed control in 1853 with Franklin Pierce at its head, Col. Thomas P. Pierce was made postmaster, and kept the place two terms, David J. Clark being appointed by Abraham Lincoln in 1861. The office had been removed in the spring of 1854 to its present quarters in a building on Hanover street which was erected by Col. Pierce and Isaac C. Flanders. Mr. Clark held the office one term and was re-appointed, but died in 1865, shortly after his second term began, and Col. Bradbury P. Cilley was appointed by Andrew Johnson. He was succeeded in 1870 by Joseph L. Stevens, appointed by Ulysses S. Grant.

The first clerk was Jason Weston, now in the employ of the Manchester Gas-Light Company, who was employed by Mr. Cragin in 1841 and continued in the office till 1854. Daniel W. Lane, assistant cashier in the City Bank, was for several years head clerk, and John T. Spofford, who now holds that place, began service in 1862. Joel Taylor, who is at the head of the postal delivery force, was appointed July 1, 1849, and advertised about that time in the daily papers that he would, for two cents each, deliver letters immediately upon their arrival, when directed to a particular street and number, and "thus prevent their being taken out and read by others of the same name and perhaps never returned." The free-delivery system was not established till August, 1865. Mr. Taylor continued carrier till 1856, when he resigned his position and was elected city clerk. After a year or more he resumed his old place and remained in it till August, 1861, when he was succeeded by another. He again became carrier in February, 1866, and still holds the position.

It requires some effort of the imagination to see Mr.

Jackson sorting letters in his office at Manchester Centre while the stage waited, forty years ago. The office of which he was the first occupant now employs a postmaster with a salary of twenty-six hundred dollars, three clerks, seven letter-carriers and a mail-messenger; has thirty collection-boxes scattered over the city, none of which is near the Mammoth road; sends and receives thirty-one mail-bags daily, besides newspaper-sacks; and nearly six hundred different papers and periodicals come to it yearly for regular subscribers. Its indefatigable carriers deliver annually a million letters and newspapers and collect a third as many; eighteen hundred letters are registered and twelve hundred registered letters received; forty-nine hundred money-orders are issued, representing ninety thousand dollars, and thirty-eight hundred paid, amounting to eighty thousand dollars; and seven thousand dollars are sent to Great Britain in money-orders.

The postal force at the present time consists of the postmaster — Joseph L. Stevens; clerks — John T. Spofford, James M. House, Charles S. Stevens; letter-carriers — Joel Taylor, Calvin A. Jones, Edwin C. Paul, Henry M. Pillsbury, Harvey L. Currier, William H. Richmond, Henry B. Gillette; mail-messenger — Luther A. Ward.

Though the post-office in Piscataquog village was discontinued eight or ten years before that part of Bedford was annexed to Manchester, yet it has an interest to those who have lived in this city while it was in existence. It was the earliest office established in this immediate vicinity, fifteen years before there was any office in Manchester at all and half as many before one was started at Amoskeag village. In 1816, the time when inland commerce was carried on with the help of the Merrimack river, and the old settlers—among whom were Joseph M. Rowell, Samuel B. Kidder and Samuel Hall—were boatmen, an office was established in Piscataquog village to satisty a growing demand, and James Parker was appointed postmaster. Previous to that time the dwellers in that vicinity obtained their mail from a post-rider, who came through the village on his way from Amherst to Concord. Through such circuitous channels and by such slow conveyances were letters carried that two weeks was required for one from Gilmanton to reach Piscataquog. In 1829 " Squire Parker," as he was generally known, was succeeded by Jonas B. Bowman, and he in 1830 by James McKeen Wilkins. The latter resigned in 1835 and Col. John S. Kidder took his place and remained in it till 1838. He was followed by Leonard Rundlett who occupied the position till the discontinuance of the office in Piscataquog about 1840.

About the time that manufacturing was begun in earnest at Amoskeag village, then a part of Goffstown, the nearest post-office in the town was situated at Goffstown Centre, a place inconvenient on account both of distance and direction. About 1828, therefore, an office was established in Amoskeag village in a building then owned by the manufacturing corporation which preceded the Amoskeag Company and used more recently as a shoe-shop, and Samuel Kimball was the first postmaster, being succeeded in 1830 by Dr. Oliver Dean, the agent of the Company, who was followed in 1835 by Richard Kimball. He held the place till his death in the fall of 1837, when W. H. Kimball was postmaster one year, and then in 1840 the office was removed from the shop to the tavern, and the tavern-keeper, Hugh Moore, became postmaster. It was subsequently moved back to the shop where was a store of which John Ellison and Darwin J. Daniels had become proprietors, and the latter succeeded Mr. Moore in 1845. In 1848 and 1849 A. B. Smith was postmaster. Joseph B. Quimby bought the store and was appointed postmaster in 1850. About 1855 the office was moved to the brick store where it is now kept and which had been built in 1829 for S. K.,

Walter B. and Joseph Jones to occupy. Walter B. Jones was then made postmaster and continued such till 1860, when he was succeeded by his brother Joseph, who held the position till about 1867, when the office returned once more to the shoe-shop and Thomas S. Montgomery was appointed postmaster. When the shop was burned soon after, the office was located in the brick store again, and in 1871 Harris Jesse Poore, the present postmaster, was appointed to succeed Mr. Montgomery.

Through the efforts of some of the dwellers at Goffe's Falls a post-office was established in the passenger-station of the Concord railway at that place in 1872, when the manufacturing industry there had been newly awakened and the office in Manchester was found to be too far for convenience. Isaac W. Darrah was the first postmaster, and, upon his removal from the village about 1865, he was succeeded by the present postmaster — Nathaniel Moore.

BANKS.

The first approach, probably, to a bank in Manchester was the system the Amoskeag Manufacturing Company adopted, not long after its operations had assumed a considerable magnitude, which enabled those in its employ to trust their earnings to its keeping. This plan was begun in 1842 and continued till September, 1856, when the Company refused to receive any more deposits. At that time the sum in its hands was not far from two hundred thousand dollars, and it was gradually paid back as the depositors called for it. About three thousand dollars were left in 1863 and a few hundreds remained five years later, but the money has since been all paid out. The whole system was merely incidental to the Company's business. No especial investments or loans were made on account of the deposits, the paymaster did this business as he did the rest, and the accounts were kept as in other departments of the Company's business.

The Manchester Bank, chartered by the state in December, 1844, was organized in 1845 with the following directors: Samuel D. Bell, Hiram Brown, Jacob G. Cilley, Isaac C. Flanders, Walter French, William C. Clarke and Nathan Parker. At the annual meeting in July, 1845, James U. Parker, Samuel D. Bell, David A. Bunton, Hiram Brown, Jonathan T. P. Hunt, William C. Clarke and Isaac Riddle were chosen directors. James U. Parker was elected president, and Nathan Parker cashier, both continuing in office till the bank ceased to do business.

The bank began operations September 2, 1845, in Patten's building, with a capital of fifty thousand dollars, which was increased in 1847 to seventy-five thousand and in 1848 to one hundred thousand dollars. In 1850 ten thousand dollars were added, and, two years later, fifteen thousand, making a capital in 1852 of one hundred and twenty-five thousand dollars.

In 1848, upon the resignation of Mr. Bell, George W. Pinkerton was elected a director in his place, and in 1849 Daniel Watts of Londonderry was chosen to succeed Mr. Clarke, resigned. Mr. Pinkerton resigned in 1853 and went to Derry, David Gillis being chosen in his place. In 1854 Mr. Brown resigned and went to California and John H. Maynard succeeded him. Patten's building was burned February 5, 1856, and the bank was moved to Merchants' Exchange, being taken across the street in the fall to the rooms on the corner of Elm and Market streets now occupied by the Manchester National Bank.

In 1858, upon the death of Mr. Watts, Gilman H. Kimball was elected a director. In 1860, upon the resignation of Mr. Gillis and his removal to Nashua, Benjamin F. Martin was chosen to succeed him, and in 1864 Phinehas Adams succeeded Mr. Riddle. In 1865, upon the decease of

Mr. Hunt, Charles Chase was elected in his stead and the officers were as follows: James U. Parker, president; Nathan Parker, cashier; James U. Parker, David A. Bunton, John H. Maynard, Phinehas Adams, Benjamin F. Martin, Charles Chase, directors. In 1866 the bank ceased doing business, and in that year and the spring of 1867 the stockholders were paid dividends of one hundred and forty dollars per share, and there is still a small balance of profits to be divided among them. The semi-annual dividends were about four per cent. on an average.

The Manchester National Bank, which succeeded to the business and location of the old Manchester Bank, was organized in April, 1865, under an act of Congress, by the choice of the following officers: Nathan Parker, president; Charles E. Balch, cashier; Nathan Parker, Benjamin F. Martin, Phinehas Adams, Gilman H. Kimball, John H. Maynard, David A. Bunton and Horace P. Watts, directors. The only change was made in February, 1874, when Aretas Blood was elected to fill the vacancy caused by the death of Mr. Kimball. The bank began business in 1865 with a capital of one hundred thousand dollars, which was increased, April 2, 1872, to one hundred and fifty thousand. It has paid semi-annual dividends of five per cent. and now has a surplus of fifty-five thousand dollars.

The Manchester Savings Bank, which occupied rooms in common with the Manchester Bank during its existence, and now shares those of the Manchester National Bank, was chartered July 8, 1846, beginning business the same year. It was organized with the following officers: Samuel D. Bell, president; John A. Burnham, Daniel Clark, Herman Foster, Nahum Baldwin, George Porter, David Gillis, William P. Newell, Hiram Brown, trustees. Nathan Parker was chosen treasurer and has held the office ever since.

In 1847, upon the resignation of Mr. Bell as president

John Mosley

and trustee, Hiram Brown was elected in his stead as president, and Nathan Parker as trustee. The same year George W. Pinkerton was chosen to succeed Mr. Burnham, resigned. At the annual meeting in 1848 William P. Newell was elected president, continuing such to the present time, and Daniel Clark, Herman Foster, Nahum Baldwin, George Porter, David Gillis, Oliver W. Bayley, George W. Pinkerton and Nathan Parker, trustees. They were re-elected in 1846, with the exception of Mr. Bayley, who was succeeded by Phinehas Adams. In 1852 Messrs. Porter and Pinkerton were succeeded by William C. Clarke and J. T. P. Hunt. In 1856 Josiah Crosby was chosen in the stead of Mr. Gillis. In 1864 David A. Bunton was elected in place of Mr. Baldwin. In 1865, upon the death of Mr. Hunt, Benjamin F. Martin was elected a trustee, and in 1872 Charles E. Balch was chosen to fill the vacancy caused by the death of Mr. Clarke. By the decease in the early part of 1875 of Messrs. Crosby and Foster two vacancies were caused in the board.

The present officers are: William P. Newell, president; Nathan Parker, treasurer; Charles E. Balch, cashier; Daniel Clark, Phinehas Adams, Nathan Parker, Benjamin F. Martin, David A. Bunton, Charles E. Balch, trustees. The deposits at present are about two million seven hundred and fifty thousand dollars, and the interest paid depositors up to July, 1873, has been equal to six and a half per cent. annually.

The Amoskeag Bank was incorporated by the state June 24, 1848, and began business in October of that year with a capital of one hundred thousand dollars, which was increased, August 5, 1850, by one-half, and, August 7, 1854, was raised to two hundred thousand dollars. At the first meeting of the bank, October 2, 1848, Richard H. Ayer, Samuel D. Bell, Mace Moulton, Stephen D. Green, John S. Kidder, Stephen Manahan and Edson Hill were elected directors. Richard H. Ayer was chosen president, and Moody Currier, cashier. In 1849, Mr. Green having left the city, Robert Read was elected a director in his place. In 1850, Mr. Hill having left the city and Mr. Manahan having sold his stock, there were caused two vacancies in the board of directors, which were filled by the election of Isaac C. Flanders and Walter French.

In 1852 Ezekiel A. Straw was elected a director to succeed Mr. Read, who had gone to Nashua. At a directors' meeting, February 14, 1853, Mr. Ayer having deceased, Herman Foster was elected a director in his place, and Walter French was chosen to succeed him as president. Reuben D. Mooers was elected a director to fill the vacancy caused by the resignation of Mr. Bell. At a directors' meeting, May 9, 1853, John S. Kidder was elected president to succeed Mr. French, who was killed by a railway accident at Norwalk, Conn. The latter's place in the board of directors was filled at the annual meeting of 1854 by the election of Amos G. Gale, and James M. Berry was chosen to fill the vacancy caused by the resignation of Mr. Flanders.

In 1855 Adam Chandler was elected a director in place of Mr. Berry, deceased, and in 1861 Henry Putney was elected a director in place of Mr. Gale, deceased. In 1862, Mr. Mooers having left town, Edson Hill was chosen a director to succeed him. March 1, 1866, a new bank having been organized under United States control, the stock of the old bank was reduced to one hundred thousand dollars; July 1, to twenty thousand dollars; and, October 1, the balance was paid to the stockholders. In 1868, Messrs. Moulton and Putney having died and Mr. Chandler having resigned, Daniel F. Straw, Lucien B. Clough and George B. Chandler were elected directors in their stead. The affairs of the bank were closed that year.

It had already been practically succeeded by the Amoskeag National Bank, which was organized November 1,

1864, with a capital of one hundred thousand dollars, which was increased, June 12, 1865, to two hundred thousand dollars. At the time of organization Moody Currier was elected president and George B. Chandler cashier, both of whom still hold their respective offices. The directors elected at that time were: Moody Currier, John S. Kidder, Stephen D. Green, Edson Hill, Henry Putney, Adam Chandler, Daniel Clark, Darwin J. Daniels and Horace Johnson. January 9, 1866, Mr. Daniels having died, Stevens James was chosen in his stead. January 8, 1867, Otis Barton and John S. Elliot were elected to fill the places of Messrs. Clark and Putney. In place of Adam Chandler and Mr. Johnson, Reed P. Silver and Henry Chandler were chosen, January 14, 1868. January 10, 1871, Herman Foster was elected to fill the vacancy caused by the death of Mr. James. January 13, 1874, David B. Varney was elected in the stead of Mr. Barton. At a meeting of the directors, March 1, 1875, John B. Varick was chosen to fill the vacancy caused by the death of Mr. Foster.

From its start in 1848 till June, 1870, the bank had occupied the rooms in the second story of Union building on Market street now used by the Manchester Gas-Light Company, but then it exchanged them for its present quarters in Merchants' Exchange. The present officers are: Moody Currier, president; George B. Chandler, cashier; Moody Currier, John S. Kidder, Stephen D. Green, Edson Hill, John S. Elliot, Reed P. Silver, Henry Chandler, David B. Varney, John B. Varick, directors.

The Amoskeag Savings Bank, which has occupied rooms with the state and national bank of the same name, was chartered June 19, 1852, and held its first meeting four days later, when Walter French was elected president; Isaac C. Flanders, William Richardson, Frederick Smyth, Samuel H. Ayer, Jacob G. Cilley, John S. Kidder, Timothy W. Little and Stephen Manahan, trustees. At the first meeting of the trustees, June 24, Moody Currier was appointed treasurer. At the first annual meeting, June 30, 1853, Mr. Ayer declined a re-election and Oliver W. Bayley was chosen in his stead, and Mace Moulton was elected president in place of Mr. French, deceased. June 28, 1855, Joseph Knowlton was elected in place of Mr. Smyth. July 2, 1857, Stephen D. Green, Stevens James and Warren L. Lane were chosen to succeed Messrs. Flanders, Kidder and Bayley. Stevens James was succeeded, June 24, 1858, by Jacob F. James.

June 30, 1859, Moody Currier and Justus D. Watson were chosen to fill the vacancies caused by the death of Messrs. Manahan and Lane. June 27, 1861, William Whittle was elected to fill the vacancy caused by the death of Mr. Richardson. June 26, 1862, Darwin J. Daniels was chosen in the stead of Mr. Currier. June 25, 1863, Messrs. Daniels and Little having died, Moody Currier and Benjamin F. Martin were elected in their stead. June 30, 1864, Stevens James was chosen in place of Mr. Watson, deceased. June 29, 1865, Mace Moulton and Henry C. Merrill were elected, one in place of Mr. Knowlton, deceased, and the other in place of Mr. Martin. At a special meeting, March 13, 1867, Mr. Moulton having died, Moody Currier was elected in his stead as president, and George B. Chandler as trustee. June 25, 1868, Joseph E. Bennett was chosen to succeed Stevens James. June 24, 1869, Lucien B. Clough was elected in the stead of Mr. Whittle. June 30, 1870, James A. Weston was chosen to succeed Mr. Chandler. June 29, 1871, George W. Riddle was elected to fill the vacancy caused by the death of Mr. Cilley.

The present officers are: president and treasurer, Moody Currier; trustees, Moody Currier, Stephen D. Green, Jacob F. James, Henry C. Merrill, Joseph E. Bennett, Lucien B. Clough, James A. Weston, George W. Riddle. The amount of deposits is about three million dollars.

The City Bank was chartered by the state July 2, 1853, and was organized that year with the following officers: Isaac C. Flanders, president; Edward W. Harrington, cashier; Isaac C. Flanders, Samuel W. Parsons, Joseph Kidder, William C. Clarke, Oliver Bayley, William H. Hill, Andrew G. Tucker, directors. In 1859 Joseph A. Haines was elected a director to succeed Mr. Bayley, who went to Boston. In 1863 Clinton W. Stanley took the place of Mr. Clarke and David R. Leach succeeded Mr. Hill.

The bank commenced business in 1853 with a capital of one hundred thousand dollars, which was increased to one hundred and fifty thousand the next year. It paid annual dividends of eight per cent. while it remained a state bank. In August, 1865, it was converted into the City National Bank, at which time Isaac C. Flanders, who had been its president from the organization, presented his resignation as president and director. He was succeeded in the former capacity by Clinton W. Stanley and in the latter by Alpheus Gay. In 1868 Mr. Tucker was succeeded by Thomas Morgan. Daniel W. Lane, who had been connected with the bank since 1855, became in 1865 assistant cashier. The bank at first occupied rooms in the block on the southern corner of Elm and Hanover streets, built by P. B. Putney and George A. Barnes, but a few months later it was moved into the building now occupied by the post-office and which was built by Col. Thomas P. Pierce, then postmaster, and Isaac C. Flanders, president of the bank. In December, 1870, it was moved to its present location in the south-east corner of Merchants' Exchange. The present officers are: Clinton W. Stanley, president; Edward W. Harrington, cashier; Daniel W. Lane, assistant cashier; Clinton W. Stanley, David R. Leach, Samuel W. Parsons, Joseph Kidder, Thomas Morgan, Joseph A. Haines, Alpheus Gay, directors. The bank has paid eight annual dividends of eight per cent. since it started, and now has a surplus of seven thousand dollars.

The City Savings Bank, which has occupied the same rooms as the City Bank and its successor, was chartered June 25, 1859, and was organized in August with the following officers: Joseph Kidder, president; Edward W. Harrington, treasurer; Samuel W. Parsons, James Hersey, John D. Bean, R. N. Batchelder, James S. Cheney, Andrew G. Tucker, J. C. Ricker, Bradbury P. Cilley, James S. Cogswell, John F. Duncklee, trustees. In 1861 John C. Young was elected to succeed Mr. Duncklee, who removed to Boston. In 1863, upon the death of Mr. Cogswell, Lewis W. Clark was chosen in his stead. In 1864 William H. Boyd was elected to succeed Mr. Hersey, deceased. In 1867 Mr. Batchelder was succeeded by William B. Johnson, and Mr. Tucker by Henry Chandler, both of the retiring trustees removing from the city. In 1870 Hilas Dickey was elected to succeed Mr. Clark, and the latter was chosen in 1872 to fill the vacancy caused by the death of Mr. Cheney.

The present officers are: Joseph Kidder, president; Edward W. Harrington, treasurer; Samuel W. Parsons, William H. Boyd, Jedediah C. Ricker, Lewis W. Clark, John D. Bean, John C. Young, Bradbury P. Cilley, Hilas Dickey, William B. Johnson, Daniel W. Lane, trustees. The total amount of deposits is about half a million dollars, and the bank has paid an average of six per cent. annually on deposits.

The Merrimack River Bank was chartered by the state July 14, 1855, with a capital of one hundred and fifty thousand dollars, and its first officers were: William G. Means, president; Frederick Smyth, cashier; David Cross, Waterman Smith, John H. Moor, William Whittle, William P. Newell, Benjamin F. Martin, William G. Means, directors. In 1857 Phinehas Adams was elected to succeed Mr. Whittle. In 1859 Benjamin F. Martin was elected president and Joseph B. Clark, director, both in place of Mr. Means.

The next year Messrs. Martin, Newell, Moor and Adams were succeeded as directors by Aretas Blood, William W. Brown, Natt Head and R. N. Batchelder, Waterman Smith being elected president. The annual dividends averaged about ten per cent.

In 1865 the name of the bank was changed to that of the First National Bank of Manchester, and it was put under United States jurisdiction, becoming a government depository and disbursing agent of the United States. Thomas Wheat succeeded Mr. Blood as a director in 1868 and in 1870 Frederick Smyth was elected to take Mr. Batchelder's place. Dr. Brown died in 1874. The present officers are: Waterman Smith, president; Frederick Smyth, cashier; David Cross, Waterman Smith, Joseph B. Clark, Natt Head, Thomas Wheat, Frederick Smyth, directors. The bank has always occupied rooms in Smyth's block. Its dividends have averaged ten per cent., and it has a surplus of seventy-five thousand dollars.

The Manchester Five Cents Savings Institution was chartered June 26, 1858, and organized with the following board of officers: Waterman Smith, president; David Gillis, George Porter, vice-presidents; Frederick Smyth, treasurer; Benjamin F. Martin, Joseph B. Clark, Isaac Smith, William B. Webster, Frank A. Brown, George Thompson, John B. Clarke, Peter S. Brown, Frederick Smyth, Josiah S. Shannon, John L. Kelly, James M. Varnum, Alonzo Smith, Thomas Wheat, Warren Page, Albe C. Heath, Warren S. Peabody, Joseph A. Haines, trustees. The president and vice-presidents were *ex-officiis* members of the board of trustees.

In 1859 William G. Perry was elected a trustee in place of Frank A. Brown, deceased. In 1860 Benjamin F. Martin and William G. Perry became vice-presidents in place of Messrs. Gillis and Porter, C. W. Johnson and David Cross succeeding Messrs. Martin and Perry as trustees.

The same year Stephen Palmer was elected a trustee to succeed Isaac Smith. In 1861 George Thompson succeeded Mr. Martin as vice-president, and the former's place on the board of trustees was filled by Natt Head. In 1863 Stephen Palmer was chosen vice-president to take Mr. Thompson's place, Ebenezer Ferren was elected trustee to succeed Mr. Palmer, and Mr. Thompson was again made a trustee, to succeed Peter S. Brown, deceased. In 1865 Charles H. Bartlett was elected to fill the vacancy in the board of trustees caused by the death of Alonzo Smith. In accordance with an act of the legislature, June 30, 1865, the bank assumed the name of the Merrimack River Savings Bank.

In 1866 Joseph F. Kennard, John Brugger and Joseph L. Stevens were elected trustees in place of Messrs. Thompson, Haines, and Peabody. In 1867 Martin V. B. Edgerly was chosen a trustee to fill the vacancy caused by the death of Mr. Johnson. In 1868 Charles Williams was elected a trustee to succeed Mr. Webster. In 1869 Freeman Higgins was chosen to fill the vacancy in the board caused by the death of Mr. Page, and A. O. Dillingham was elected a trustee in that year. In 1871 Joseph L. Stevens became vice-president, succeeding Mr. Perry, and Francis B. Eaton became a trustee, taking Mr. Ferren's place. In 1873 William W. Brown was elected a trustee in place of Mr. Williams, and upon his death in the next year was succeeded by William Crane of Candia. Francis B. Eaton then became vice-president, succeeding Mr. Stevens, and his place as a trustee is yet unfilled.

In the present board of officers the president is Waterman Smith; vice-presidents, Stephen Palmer, Francis B. Eaton; treasurer, Frederick Smyth; trustees, Frederick Smyth, Natt Head, Joseph B. Clark, John B. Clarke, Josiah S. Shannon, John L. Kelly, James M. Varnum, Thomas Wheat, A. O. Dillingham, David Cross, Albe C. Heath,

J. T. James.

Martin V. B. Edgerly, Charles H. Bartlett, Joseph F. Kennard, John Brugger, Freeman Higgins, William Crane, the president and vice-president, *ex-officiis*. The amount of its deposits is about one million two hundred thousand dollars, and its dividends have averaged about seven per cent. The bank occupies rooms in common with the First National Bank.

The People's Savings Bank was organized in August, 1875, and began business on the first of October, with the following officers: president, Person C. Cheney; cashier, George B. Chandler; trustees, Person C. Cheney, Elijah M. Topliff, Atherton W. Quint, Henry M. Putney, Moody Currier, Charles H. Bartlett, Abraham P. Olzendam, Edson Hill, George W. Riddle, George B. Chandler. It was formed on the guarantee principle, and a fund of fifty thousand dollars, as security for depositors, was subscribed before it began business. Its deposits, March 1, 1875, were a little over a hundred thousand dollars. It occupies rooms with the Amoskeag National Bank.

INSURANCE COMPANIES.

Ever since the town was fairly started in life there have been attempts made to form insurance companies, but few of those have been successful. The first endeavor, however, was an exception to the rule, and it resulted in the establishment of the Amoskeag Mutual Fire Insurance Company, which was organized December 24, 1840, and continued in existence some four or five years. Samuel D. Bell was its president during that time and David A. Bunton was at first secretary and treasurer but was afterwards succeeded by David Hill. It was revived in 1860, when Isaac Riddle was chosen president and Elihu T. Stevens secretary and treasurer. They remained the officers during the half dozen years the company did business. The Manchester Mutual Fire Insurance Company was organized and began business in July, 1858, and was dissolved in a year or two afterwards. John S. Elliot was its president and Jeremiah D. Lyford secretary and treasurer.

In 1869 the New Hampshire Fire Insurance Company, the first and only stock insurance company in the state, was chartered and organized. Its president was Ezekiel A. Straw; its vice-president, James A. Weston; its secretary, Isaac W. Smith; its treasurer, George B. Chandler; its general agent, John C. French: and these have since continued in office with the exception of Mr. Smith, who was succeeded in September, 1870, by John C. French. In 1873 George W. Eastman was chosen assistant secretary. It began business April 6, 1870, with a capital of one hundred thousand dollars, which has since been increased to two hundred and fifty thousand dollars. Its cash assets are four hundred thousand dollars.

A number of companies have been incorporated at different times, but none of them have done any business and scarcely one has been organized. In 1851 the Manchester Insurance Company was chartered; in 1855 the Manchester City Fire and Marine Insurance Company, from whose name the word "City" was dropped in 1862; in 1867 the City Fire Insurance Company; and in 1869 the State Fire Insurance Company.

MANUFACTURES.

THE record of the real Manchester is little more, for a time at least, than the record of its manufacturing. The first cotton-mill at the Falls was started only a year before the name of Derryfield was thrown aside, so that Manchester and its manufacturing industries are almost one in years as they are one in fact. The first ventures in cotton-spinning seem small at this day, and there was little accomplished till Massachusetts capitalists had computed the power of the waterfall at Amoskeag and the Amoskeag Company sprung from their foresight and enterprise. A clear statement of the origin and growth of Manchester's manufactures necessarily involves a slight repetition of what has already been referred to as an element of its life.

Cotton goods were first made upon the Merrimack in 1809 at Amoskeag Falls in what was then Goffstown. The first cotton-mill in the state, however, was built in New Ipswich in 1803. It was there that Benjamin Prichard's fingers learned the trade, and he, coming over to this part of the county, located himself in Bedford and spun cotton at the old "Goffe place." This was too small a field for Mr. Prichard's operations, and so he joined himself with Ephraim, David and Robert Stevens, and they built a small mill on the west side of the falls at Amoskeag village in 1809. The enterprise assumed still larger proportions the next year by the formation of a stock company, first called the "Amoskeag Cotton and Wool Factory" and incorporated in June as the "Amoskeag Cotton and Woolen Manufacturing Company." At the first meeting of the directors, James Parker, Samuel P. Kidder, John Stark, jr., David McQueston and Benjamin Prichard were present. James Parker was chosen president and Jotham Gillis, clerk. The latter became, also, the first agent, Dr. William Wallace of Bedford, who was appointed, declining to serve. Mr. Gillis was followed by Philemon Walcott, John G. Moor and Frederick G. Stark. The latter's salary was one hundred and eighty dollars a year. There was thus at that time in Manchester one corporation which owned one mill without pickers or looms. The cotton was picked and the yarn woven in the neighborhood, a "smart weaver" earning thirty-six cents a day.

The company's dividends were not so many and so large as hope had declared them, and after 1815 little was done till 1822, when Olney Robinson bought the property of the company and resumed business. He is said to have been "inclined to outside speculation rather than to his legitimate business," and he was soon succeeded by Larned Pitcher and Samuel Slater of Providence, R. I. He had bought machinery and borrowed money of them and gave them a mortgage of his mill.

But in 1825 Willard Sayles and Lyman Tiffany—who, as well as Slater, were members of the firm from which has descended the one which sells for the Amoskeag Company its goods to-day — Oliver Dean and Ira Gay were admitted to partnership, and from this point onward the story is one of continued prosperity. Dean, Sayles and Tiffany had all been engaged in manufacturing in Norfolk county, Massachusetts, whose streams afford a number of small water-powers, and brought with them to Manchester a practical acquaintance with the business and abundant means. Dr. Dean became agent of the firm and moved to Amoskeag village in 1826. The business then received a fresh impulse. In that year the old mill was enlarged, a new one, known as the "bell mill" because the bell which called the operatives hung upon it, and another upon an island in the river, were built, and the manufacture of sheetings, shirtings and tickings begun. The latter acquired an unrivalled reputation under the name of "A. C. A" tickings, "A. C." standing for Amoskeag Company," and the second "A" marking the class of goods. The mill upon the island where these tickings were made was burned in 1839, and the old and bell mills in 1848. Thus in fifteen years only two new mills had been built, and the business, which a few years later required a capital of a million dollars, was still carried on as a private enterprise.

THE AMOSKEAG MANUFACTURING COMPANY.

Thus far we have had to do with the operations of a firm, the failure of a company, the building of two or three mills, but at seven o'clock in the evening of the thirteenth of July, 1831, five men sat in the counting-room of the company which then owned the mills and accepted an act passed by the state legislature twelve days before, which allowed them to form the Amoskeag Manufacturing Company with a possible capital of a million dollars. The men were Ira Gay, Willard Sayles, Oliver Dean, Larned Pitcher and Lyman Tiffany, who also acted as attorney for Samuel Slater. Dr. Dean presided at the meeting and Ira Gay was chosen its clerk. At a meeting the next day by-laws were adopted, the annual meeting was appointed in July and the organization perfected. Lyman Tiffany was chosen president; Lyman Tiffany, Ira Gay and Willard Sayles, directors; Ira Gay, clerk; Oliver Dean, agent and treasurer.

The property of the old firm was exchanged for stock in the new company, and the latter acquired by purchase a title to land on both sides of the river, mostly, however, on the east side, where engineers had decided were the best sites for mills and the best tracks for canals. In 1835 the new organization bought the property and interest of the Bow Canal Company, the Isle of Hooksett Canal Company, the Amoskeag Locks and Canal Company and the Union Locks and Canal, all of which, as their names imply, had built canals at different points on the river. The Hooksett Manufacturing Company was merged with the Amoskeag in 1836 and the Concord Manufacturing Company shared the same fate the next year. The Amoskeag Company thus had obtained a full title to all the water-power on the river from Manchester to Concord and all the land in Manchester on the Merrimack available for mill-sites. It was also in possession of large tracts of land adjacent to the river and extending for some distance from it.

Having thus cleared the way, they soon began operations in earnest. In 1836 the wooden dam which had hitherto checked the river's flow at Amoskeag Falls was thoroughly repaired in order to answer the purposes of a coffer-dam, and the next year was begun the construction of a wing-dam of stone with guard-locks on the east side, which was completed in 1840. At the same time the farther from the river of the two present canals was built by Lobdell and Russell. In 1838 a contract was made with Russell, Barr & Company, of which firm Isaac C. Flanders, afterwards president of the City Bank, was a member, to construct the "lower canal," and the contract was fulfilled. The first building put up on the east side of the river was what was then the Stark Mills counting-room, at the foot of Stark street, part of which was temporarily used for a counting-room by the land and water-power department of the Amoskeag Company. The next was the one designated as "number one, Stark block," where the agents and clerks of the mills boarded with S. S. Moulton till November, 1839, when the Manchester House was finished and William Shepherd, its present proprietor, took charge of it. The first mills built on the east side were what were then number one and number two mills of the Stark corporation, which were erected for that company in 1838 and 1839.

At that time a number of men who have since been well known in Manchester were in the pay of the Amoskeag Company. Hiram Brown, afterwards mayor of the city, was employed to oversee the stone-work; Phinehas Stevens, the father of A. G. and G. W. Stevens, now civil engineers of the Manchester and Amoskeag corporations respectively, was its mill-wright and wheel-wright; John D. Kimball was an overseer of carpenter-work; T. J. Carter was the resident engineer; Henry S. Whitney was an overseer of general out-door work; Warren Paige had charge of the lumber-yard; Nahum Baldwin, Daniel L. Stevens and Charles Hutchinson were employed in the planing-mill; George F. Judkins managed the saw-mill and Samuel Boice was employed in it; Samuel B. Kidder has had charge of the locks and canals from then till now; Andrew Bunton, the father of the Manchester agent of the United States and Canada Express, and Levi Sargent were contractors for stone; John H. Maynard was the head carpenter; Jonathan T. P. Hunt, the father of Nathan P. Hunt, and Joseph E. Bennett, the present city clerk, were employed as masons in the building of the mills.

The company laid out the site of a town with a main street running north and south, parallel with the river, with other streets running parallel with this and across it, reserving land for public squares, and in 1838, having divided part of its land into lots suitable for stores and dwellings, sold it, bringing into the market by this and subsequent sales a large part of the land on which the city of to-day stands. In 1838 they sold a site and privileges for mills to a new company which had been incorporated as the Stark Mills, and built for them, in this and subsequent years, the factories they now occupy. After the burning of their old mills at Amoskeag they finished in 1841 two new ones just below the Stark mills for their own use, and added to them in subsequent years as their needs required. In 1845 they sold land and built mills and a printery for a new corporation which had been organized as the Manchester Mills. To meet a demand for machinery for their own mills and those they erected for others, they built in 1840 a machine-shop, in 1842 a foundry and in 1848 replaced both these by new and larger ones, beginning at that time the manufacture of locomotives, building new shops for mechanical purposes when needed. In 1859 was begun the manufacture of the famous Amoskeag steam fire-engines. Some time after they had finished mills for the larger corporations already mentioned they built for the convenience of individual enterprises a building known as "Mechanics' Row" at the northern end of the canals, and also sold land and erected shops for small corporations which were subsequently organized. They carried out meanwhile their original idea of a city, building boarding-houses and tenements for their own operatives and those of the other corporations, giving away land for churches and public buildings, selling it to manufacturers and business men, and continuing a liberal policy to the present time. The company has now a capital of three million dollars, divided into shares of a thousand dollars each, which are quoted at seventeen hundred and fifty dollars.

The first directors of the company, as has already been said, were Lyman Tiffany, Ira Gay and Willard Sayles, elected in 1831. In 1834 Ira Gay was succeeded by Oliver Dean. In April, 1836, it was voted not to restrict the number of directors to three, and to those already chosen were added P. T. Jackson, William Appleton, George Bond, Samuel Frothingham, Daniel D. Brodhead and George Howe.

AMOSKEAG MANUF'G CO.

COUNTING HOUSE AND BUILDINGS ON UPPER CANAL.

These were re-elected at the annual meeting of that year, but in 1837 the board was so changed as to consist of Oliver Dean, Willard Sayles, George Howe, Samuel Frothingham, Francis C. Lowell, John A. Lowell, Daniel D. Brodhead, Samuel Hubbard and William Appleton. In 1838 Samuel Frothingham, John A. Lowell and Daniel D. Brodhead were succeeded by George W. Lyman, Nathan Appleton and James K. Mills.

The annual meetings had hitherto been held at the old counting-room in Amoskeag village, but in 1840 the stockholders met there at noon and adjourned to assemble in fifteen minutes at the counting-room in Manchester. At that time David Sears and Samuel Frothingham took the places of Messrs. Hubbard and Mills. In 1852 Joseph Tilden succeeded Francis C. Lowell and the directors were authorized to appoint a place for the annual meetings, which were thereafter held at Manchester. From that time changes in the board of directors were few. In 1847 William Amory took the place of Mr. Sayles and was himself succeeded in 1841 by Robert Read. In 1853 Gardner Brewer was chosen to succeed Mr. Tilden, and in 1856 Jonathan T. P. Hunt to succeed Robert Read.

In 1857, at the annual meeting in July, it was voted to adjourn till October and the meetings have since been held in the latter month. In that year David Sears resigned his directorship and his place was left unfilled. In 1861 the number of directors was reduced to six and Oliver Dean, George Howe, George W. Lyman, William Appleton, Gardner Brewer and Jonathan T. P. Hunt were chosen. These, with the exception of William Appleton, were reelected the next year, when it was voted to have but five directors. In 1865 Daniel Clark succeeded Mr. Hunt. In 1866 the number of directors was increased by the addition of T. Jefferson Coolidge and Thomas Wigglesworth. In 1871 Oliver Dean and George W. Lyman declined farther service, and George Howe, having ceased to be a stockholder, was ineligible, and William Amory, John L. Gardner and William P. Mason were elected to fill the vacancies. In 1874 Charles Amory was elected to take Mr. Brewer's place, made vacant by his death.

After the organization of the corporation Lyman Tiffany was elected president and held the office till succeeded by Joseph Tilden. Upon the latter's death Dr. Dean was chosen president in 1853 and continued as such till 1871, when he resigned. He remained a director till his death. In 1871 Gardner Brewer was made president and continued such till his death in 1874, when Daniel Clark was chosen to fill the vacancy. Dr. Dean was treasurer from the first till 1836. Then Francis C. Lowell held the office one year and in 1837 William Amory, the present treasurer, was elected. The first proprietors' clerk was Ira Gay, who was followed in 1833 by George Daniels, and he in 1836 by Hiram A. Daniels. Robert Read was chosen in 1837 and the next year he was succeeded by William G. Means, who remained clerk till the election of the present one, E. A. Straw, in 1853.

Dr. Dean, who had been the agent and treasurer of the private company which built the mills at Amoskeag, was the first agent of the Amoskeag Company and continued such till 1834, when he moved to Framingham, Mass., and was succeeded in 1835 by Harvey Hartshorn, who remained till 1837 when he was succeeded by William P. Newell. When the Hooksett mills were bought by the Amoskeag Company, a new department was thus created, which was under the charge successively of Hiram A. Daniels, Joshua and Stephen Ballard, William L. Killey and T. W. Wattles. These were sold in 1865 to a new corporation. When the company began its operations on the east side of the river, the "Land and Water-Power Company" came into existence, and when the company put up for its own use on the east side, first mills and then a machine-shop, two more divisions were made with separate books and officers, known as the " Amoskeag New Mills " and the " Machine-Shop." William P. Newell continued the agent at the old mills at Amoskeag from 1837 to 1846, when he was succeeded by Phinehas Adams, who remained one year. His place was taken by C. W. Blanchard, who staid till the mills were burned in 1848. Hartford Ide was paymaster at the old mills for a time and was succeeded by George Daniels, who remained a number of years. He was followed, in turn, by Hiram A. Daniels, George W. Kimball and Hiram Forsaith.

The first agent of the land and water-power department was Robert Read, who was succeeded in January, 1852, by Ezekiel A. Straw, who had been in the employ of the Company as a civil engineer. The first paymaster was William G. Means, now of Andover, Mass., and then Joseph Knowlton. When the " new mills " were built, David Gillis, now of Nashua, was chosen agent and was succeeded by Mr. Straw in 1856. The first paymaster was Charles Richardson, who held the place till succeeded by his nephew, Charles L. Richardson, in 1854. The first agent of the machine-shop, after it was finished in 1840, was William A. Burke, now of Lowell. He continued such till 1847 when he resigned and his place was taken by Oliver W. Bayley. He resigned in 1855 to become agent of the Manchester Locomotive Works and was succeeded by Cyrus W. Baldwin, and not long afterwards Mr. Straw assumed charge of this department also. The first paymaster at the machine-shop was Joseph Knowlton, who was followed, in turn, by William G. Means, Edward Kendall, Justus D. Watson and Horace M. Gillis.

In July, 1856, the land and water-power department and the mills were united and placed in Mr. Straw's care, and in July, 1858, these two and the machine-shop were put under one head, Mr. Straw, the present agent, then assuming exclusive control of the Company's operations in Manchester, subject only to the directors. The selling agents are Gardner Brewer & Company of Boston. The present superintendent of the mills is William G. Perry, the assistant superintendent Herman F. Straw and the superintendent of the machine-shop Nehemiah S. Bean. The engineer is Edwin H. Hobbs, and the paymaster Charles L. Richardson, who has been in the Company's employ thirty years.

The Company once owned fifteen hundred acres of land on the east side of the river, about two-thirds of which are still retained in their possession, much of it being unimproved. They own land on the west side, also, and are now engaged in making a new channel for the river and straightening its course so as to obtain more room in their mill-yard. The latter's front extends along Canal street from Central to Stark, and its rear along the river from the yard of the Manchester Mills past the buildings of the Stark corporation. Its length on the upper canal is one thousand and eighty feet, and about nineteen hundred and sixty feet on the lower. Its boarding-houses and overseers' houses occupy the space bounded by Stark street on the north, Merrimack street on the south, including a block on the latter's southerly side, Canal street on the west and Elm back street on the east, except where the Franklin-street church and the public library stand. Their tenements occupy, besides, the land bounded by Canal street on the west, Elm back street on the east, Mechanic street on the south and Spring street on the north, except a piece whose eastern limit is Elm back street and which runs westerly on Spring and Water streets one hundred and fifty feet. The Company owns tenement-houses, also, north of Bridge street between Elm and Canal streets. All these houses, like those of the other corporations, are rented at a low rate to those who are in the employ of the corporation, or leased on favorable terms to boarding-house keepers on condition of their boarding operatives at a fixed rate. After the Company began its operations on this side of the river, the house on the north side of Water street, now occupied by Dr. E. M. Tubbs, was built as a residence for the agent of the machine-shop. Mr. Burke lived in it during his agency, and then Mr. Bayley, till he built the house on the corner of Myrtle and Elm streets, now owned by Col. Franklin Tenney, and went there to live. The Company then exchanged it for the house on the corner of Pine and Hanover streets, then owned by the Stark Mills and occupied by their agent, Mr. Adams, and now in the hands of the Roman Catholics and used by them for an orphan asylum. The next which was built of the "agents' houses," so called, was the one on the north side of Market street, just below the city hall, which was intended for the agent of the Amoskeag new mills and occupied by the first agent, Mr. Gillis. After he left it, it was vacant for a time and acquired the reputation of a haunted house. It has since been remodeled and made into tenements for overseers. The next one in date was the double house whose north front is on Water street and its south front on Mechanic street. The latter half was occupied by Mr. Straw, when he was the engineer of the land and water-power company. When he left it, Cyrus W. Baldwin, the agent of the machine-shop at that time, occupied it, and he was succeeded as a tenant by Chester A. Dresser, who was then superintendent of the Amoskeag Company's upper mills. He was followed by William G. Perry, the present occupant, who is now superintendent of both the upper and the lower mills. The northern half was first occupied by William G. Means, clerk of the land and water-power department. Upon his departure, he was succeeded by Aldus M. Chapin, a civil engineer in the company's employ, and he by Mr. Perry, who was at that time superintendent of the Amoskeag Company's upper mills. Then Oliver H. Moulton lived in it, when he took Mr. Dresser's place, and afterwards the present occupant, Israel Dow, took possession. The house on the corner of Franklin and Merrimack streets was built for the residence of the agent of the land and water-power company, and Mr. Read, the first agent, came over from the other side of the river where he had been living, and took possession of it. When he was succeeded as agent by Mr. Straw, the latter went into it and lived there till 1874, when he moved to a house of his own.

The present dam at Amoskeag Falls was built in 1871 by the Company, after Mr. Straw's plans and under his personal supervision. Its predecessor had lasted thirty-four years, had become leaky and unsafe, was built low and in the wrong place. The old one ran straight across, but the one which took its place curved around so as to give a wider entrance from the river, was built two feet higher and farther down the stream. It is in two parts, the main dam, from the west side to the bridge, being four hundred and twenty feet long, and the canal wing, from the bridge to the gate-house, being two hundred and thirty feet long, making a total length of six hundred and fifty feet. It is eight feet wide at the top, averages twelve feet in height, and cost, all things included, about sixty thousand dollars. The upper canal extends from the basin at the dam to the weir at the foot of Central street where it empties into the lower, and is five thousand four hundred and eighty feet long. The lower begins at about the same place and extends to the weir below the Namaske Mills where it empties into the river. It is six thousand nine hundred feet long and runs a part of the way over the track of the old Blodget canal. Till 1855 the canal was connected with the Merrimack, near the old McGregor bridge, by a set of locks, the Company having been under obligation to keep the canal open to the public as when it was owned by the

Amoskeag Locks and Canal Company, but the legislature of 1855 gave permission to discontinue the locks. The openings of the canals at the guard gates are five hundred and ten feet square. The canals' width at their head is seventy-three feet, and at the weirs fifty feet, with an average depth of ten feet. The fall from the upper to the lower canal is twenty feet, and from the lower canal to the river, thirty-four feet.

When one crosses the canal-bridge at the foot of Stark street he finds a long building on his left, reaching down the canal. It is really two buildings, the counting-house and the cloth-room. The former is three stories high, one hundred feet in length by thirty-six in width. The upper story contains the hall, which is used only for stockholders' meetings. The second story is occupied by the counting-room and agent's rooms, while in the lowest story are found the engineer's and superintendents' rooms. The cloth-room is a three-story building, three hundred and sixty feet long and thirty wide. Here are employed forty males and twenty-five females in packing two hundred thousand pounds of cloth a week. The canal front is finished by a three-story building, five hundred and four feet long and thirty wide, used as a spinning-mill, with one story devoted to carding.

Directly back of these and still on the "upper level," taking their power from the upper canal, are number one, number two, number three and number six mills, finding their limit at the water-way which flows from the upper to the lower canal.

Number one and number two mills are northern-most and are exact duplicates of each other. They were the first mills upon the Amoskeag corporation, were built separately, one hundred and fifty-seven feet long by forty-eight wide, and six stories high, in 1841, but in 1859 and 1860 were united by what is called number six mill, eighty-eight feet long by sixty wide. There is a picker-house, fifty-nine feet in length and thirty-two feet in width, at each end of the buildings, which form now one large mill. It contains five hundred looms for weaving tickings and other heavy goods, machinery for making yarns for seven hundred and fifty gingham looms located in another mill, two hundred and eighty-eight cards and thirty-three thousand spindles. In this mill are employed four hundred operatives, three females to one male. The machinery is driven by four turbine water-wheels from seven to nine feet in diameter, aggregating eight hundred horse-powers. The mill produces daily six thousand pounds of tickings, etc., and three thousand pounds of fine yarns for ginghams.

Number three mill, directly to the south of this triple combination, was built in 1834 and thoroughly re-built in 1870. It is five stories in height and four hundred and forty feet long, while its width varies from sixty-five to seventy-two feet. At its south end is a three-story picker-house, one hundred and thirty-five feet long by sixty wide. The mill contains eight hundred looms, two hundred and sixty-four cards, four thousand mule-spindles and twenty-five thousand throstle-spindles, weaving chiefly denims and cotton flannels, sixty thousand pounds a week. There are employed three hundred and fifty males and one hundred and fifty females. The machinery is driven by three turbine wheels from seven to nine feet in diameter, aggregating seven hundred and fifty horse-powers. There is also a Corliss engine of eight hundred horse-powers in this mill, to be used in case of a scarcity of water.

At the upper end of the mills on the lower level is a low building, four hundred and seventy-two feet long and thirty wide, used as a bag-mill, which has forty bag-looms, employs twenty-five males and sixty females, and turns out nine thousand sixteen-ounce bags a week. To the south for five hundred feet along the canal extends another low building, thirty feet wide, used as a store-house.

AMOSKEAG MANUF'G CO.'S MILLS.

UPPER YARD

Behind the latter is number four mill, which was built in 1846 and enlarged in 1872. The original building was seven stories high, two hundred and sixty feet in length by sixty in width. In the fall of 1872 an extension was built in the rear, one hundred feet long and sixty feet wide In the rear, also, are two picker-houses, three stories high, fifty-six feet in length by thirty-seven in width. The mill contains seven hundred and thirty-two looms, three hundred and twenty cards and twenty-five thousand spindles, and produces about fifty-five thousand pounds a week of drillings, denims and tickings. It gives employment to three hundred and fifty females and one hundred and twenty-five males, and its machinery is driven by four turbine wheels, with an aggregate of one thousand horse-powers.

Number five mill is just north of the one last mentioned. It is two hundred and fifty-eight feet long by sixty wide, and has a picker-house, sixty-two feet in length by forty-four in width, in the rear. It contains five hundred and seventy-six looms, one hundred and seventy-six cards, fifteen thousand throstle spindles and twelve thousand mule-spindles. Here are woven twenty thousand pounds a week of sheetings from thirty-six to one hundred inches in width. The mill employs eighty males and two hundred and fifty females, and its machinery is driven by two turbine wheels, which have an aggregate of five hundred horse-powers.

The building at the north of number five mill, occupied as a dye-house and gingham mill, consists of a centre-piece and two wings. The south wing is the dye-house, and is two hundred and three feet long, sixty-seven feet wide, and three stories high. In it are employed seventy-five males and seventy-five females. It has a capacity for dyeing sixty thousand pounds of yarn a week, and all the colored yarn used in the mills is dyed here. The middle part is one hundred and twenty feet long, sixty-seven feet wide, three stories high, and is occupied by dressing machinery for ginghams. The north wing is of the same length and breadth as the dye-house, but four stories high. It has seven hundred and fifty looms which make one hundred thousand yards of gingham a week. The operatives who are employed in the centre and the north wing number four hundred females and one hundred and twenty males.

A new mill was built in 1874, just at the north of these buildings and parallel with them. It is two hundred and sixty feet long, sixty-eight feet wide, four stories high, and will contain twelve hundred looms for weaving ginghams.

The bleachery and napping-house, for bleaching and napping flannels, are in a small building, one hundred and ten feet in length and thirty-six in width, in the rear of the old gingham-mill and near the river. They employ from fifteen to twenty operatives. There is also a drying-house of two stories in height, sixty feet long and thirty-six wide. A bridge, four hundred feet in length and sixteen in width, has been thrown across the Merrimack, just here, to the Company's land on the west side, where its coal-sheds are located, to which a branch track runs from the North Weare railway below Granite street. Near the coal-sheds is a store-house for cotton with a capacity of from fifteen thousand to twenty thousand bales, equal to a year's stock.

The machinery is all driven by water, but for heating and other purposes there are fourteen upright boilers, of one hundred and fifty horse-powers each, located in four boiler-houses. All the buildings are furnished with fire-escapes and hydrants with hose attached into which water from the Company's reservoir on the hill may be let at any moment. The basements of the mills are provided with supply-pumps for furnishing water.

The total number of operatives in the mills is twenty-five hundred, of whom eighteen hundred are females. Seventy-five men are engaged in taking care of the yard.

The corporations all employ night-watchmen to patrol their grounds. The Amoskeag Company has nine mills, containing one hundred and twenty-five thousand spindles and thirty-five hundred looms, making six hundred thousand yards a week of different goods, of which three hundred and fifty thousand yards are colored. There are fourteen water-wheels, seven on each level, which have an aggregate of thirty-five hundred horse-powers. The mills use two hundred and twenty-five thousand pounds of cotton a week. They consume annually six thousand tons of coal, a thousand cords of wood, two hundred and fifty tons of starch, twelve thousand gallons of oil, three hundred thousand dollars' worth of dyestuffs. The colored goods consist of tickings, denims, fancy shirtings and ginghams; the white goods, of drillings, flannels, sheetings and bags. During the late war the mills made enormous quantities of army goods. The pay-roll is about eighty thousand dollars a month.

There are spun in the mills every year one hundred and thirty million skeins of yarn, each eight hundred and forty yards long, which make a total length of sixty million miles, enough to go around the world twenty-four hundred times. Woven into a belt of cloth twenty inches wide, like ordinary ticking, they would just about put a girdle about the earth. The daily production of cloth is one hundred thousand yards, nearly fifty-seven miles, or two and a quarter yards each second of working time, one yard for every second in the year.

The machine-shops, though their products have done as much of late years as the cotton goods to spread the reputation of the Amoskeag Company, are rather low, unremarkable buildings, a complete contrast to the tall mills, and are situated on the right as one enters the yard, on the the lower level and in the rear of the Stark mills. There are two machine-shops, distinctively such, though the other buildings in their vicinity are connected with their department. One is three hundred and eighty-one feet long and thirty-six wide; the other, three hundred and twenty feet long by forty wide: both three stories in height. The former was built in 1840, when the building of new mills called for machinery. The second was built in 1848, to accommodate an increasing business. A foundry was built in 1842 and a new one in 1848. The present foundry is one hundred and fifty-four feet in length by eighty in breadth. There is also a building on the edge of the lower canal, five hundred and fifty feet long and thirty feet wide, used for miscellaneous purposes; and a row of sheds, two hundred feet in length and thirty in width.

At the southern end of the "lower shop" the first part of the lower story is the "setting-up" room, where the steamers are put together. Beyond is a room where castings are cleaned and which contains the heavy tools and lathes, among the latter being one which swings twenty-four feet and is said to be the largest lathe in New England. In the second story looms are made, and in the third machinery is put together. Beyond this building is one which was used during the late war as a gun-barrel rolling-mill, but which is now a paint-shop and drying-house. Next is the "pickling-room," where the castings are dipped in acid to clean them from the sand which adheres to them when they come from the foundry. In the latter, which is the next building and forms the northern end of this row, are made such castings as the company does not buy.

The lower floor of the "upper shop" is used as a place in which to make frames and cylinders for steam fire engines, and one end is occupied as a repair-shop. The next story is used as a belt-shop, wood-shop and tin-shop, and in it are made gears and rolls. In the third story is a wood-room, and screws, cotton-machinery and steamer-work are also made in it. In the attic tools are ground and polished and cotton-machinery put together. Beyond is the blacksmith-shop, where the deafening trip-hammers are at work, and, still farther beyond, a stone building in which the process of softening iron is carried on.

At the southern end of the eastern row of buildings are several store-rooms, which were used as counting-rooms for the Machine-Shop and the Land and Water-Power Company, when those departments had individual existence. Next is a spindle-room, and then successively, a boiler-shop, a store-house, and a pattern-house in which are locked up the patterns for machinery and which completes the row.

The shops were originally built to make machinery for the mills, but gradually the business was enlarged, and there were made, besides, locomotive and stationary engines, boilers, heavy tools, turbine wheels, etc. The first locomotive was built for the Northern railway in 1849, and sixty were turned out yearly, some hundreds having been made before their manufacture was given up. During the late war the shops made forty thousand stands of arms for the United States government, and some turret-work for the "monitors" was manufactured here.

The shops still make what new machinery the Amoskeag Company needs and repair the old, but their main business is the manufacture of steam fire engines, which was begun in 1859. There are annually turned out fifty steamers besides hose-carriages. Five hundred have already been built and the quality is improved each year. The catalogue includes first-class and second-class engines, engines with double and single pumps, and "self-propellers," so called, whose steam takes the place of horses as a motive power. The hose-carriages are made to be drawn by horses or men, are made single or double, with two wheels or with four. Of the steamers, the United States government has bought thirty-three; New York city, forty-five; Boston, twenty; Brooklyn, nineteen; New Orleans, eighteen; Pittsburgh, fourteen; San Francisco, thirteen; Philadelphia, twelve;

Detroit, nine; Albany, eight; Cambridge, five; Manchester, four. They are scattered all over the United States from Maine to Oregon, and are found generally at the national soldiers' asylums, navy-yards and arsenals. There are ninety-nine owned in New York State, ninety-one in Massachusetts, sixty-three in Pennsylvania, twenty-seven in New Jersey, twenty-two in California, nineteen in Maine, eighteen in Louisiana, eighteen in Illinois, seventeen in New Hampshire and twelve in Connecticut, these ten States owning nearly four-fifths of all which have been made. But they represent Manchester's industry far beyond the limits of this country, twenty-two having been sent to foreign lands. There are a large number in the Canadas, New Brunswick and Nova Scotia; there are two in London, England, named in honor of Queen Victoria and the Princess Alexandra; and one in Amoor (Russia), Shanghai (China), Sydney (New South Wales), Lima (Peru), and Copiapo (Chili).

The machine-shops employ four hundred and fifty men and have a monthly pay-roll of twenty thousand dollars. They consume annually five hundred tons of coal, four hundred cords of wood, six hundred gallons of oil, one hundred and fifty thousand feet of lumber, twelve hundred tons of cast iron, wrought iron and steel, fifty thousand pounds of wrought brass and brass castings.

The Company occupies a carpenter-shop in Mechanics' Row, which gives employment to a dozen men who make large beams and columns for the mills and put in mill-wheels. In a neat brick building, at the upper end of the Row, are located the pumps which raise the water of the Merrimack to the Company's reservoir in the square bounded by Blodget, Harrison, Oak and Russell streets, and from which it flows to the corporation to be used in the tenements and to be available in case of fire. The pumps are double and of the kind termed "bucket and plunger," with a thirty-three inch stroke up and down, make thirty strokes a minute and are driven by a wheel of sixty horse-powers. They deliver forty-five thousand gallons of water an hour, or over one million gallons in twenty-four hours, into the reservoir. The latter is four hundred feet long, one hundred and fifty wide and eighteen deep, has a capacity of eleven million gallons and is one hundred and ten feet above the level of Elm street at the city hall. The square in which it is located contains about six acres and a half. The Amoskeag Company supplies the other corporations with water from it at the price of one-tenth of one per cent. upon their capital stock. A ledge upon the "Company's hill," so called, in the eastern part of the city, belongs to the Amoskeag corporation and supplies all the stone used in the mills, employing fifty quarrymen and a large number of laborers.

The Amoskeag Company thus has a total force of nearly four thousand employees and a total pay-roll averaging nearly one hundred and fifty thousand dollars a month, and consumes yearly over eight thousand tons of coal, twenty-five thousand bales of cotton, fourteen hundred cords of wood and sixteen million two hundred and fifty thousand cubic feet of gas. The Company pays taxes in Manchester, Bedford, Merrimack, Hooksett, Pembroke, Bow, Concord, Goshen and Washington, this state, and in Newark, Vt. Its tax for 1874 was about sixty-three thousand dollars.

In addition, the Company owns and operates what was formerly known as the Namaske Mills, having bought the property in February, 1875.

THE STARK MILLS.

This corporation was chartered in 1838, and began operations the next year. Its first officers were chosen September 26, 1838, Nathan Appleton being the first president, continuing such till June 26, 1871, and being then succeeded by Israel Whitney, who remained till October 2, 1872. Charles Amory then took his place, and he was succeeded, October 9, 1873, by T. Jefferson Coolidge.

Nathan Appleton, George W. Lyman, Willard Sayles, Francis C. Lowell, William Appleton, William Amory and Samuel Henshaw were chosen in 1838 as the first directors. William Amory was succeeded the next year by David Sears, but was re-elected in 1841 in place of Mr. Lowell. The latter was elected the next year to succeed Mr. Henshaw and was himself suceeded in 1846 by Joseph Tilden. In 1848 Franklin H. Story was elected to fill the vacancy caused by the resignation of Mr. Sayles, and in 1854 Mr. Tilden was succeeded by Samuel Frothingham. In 1857 Mr. Sears resigned, but it was not till the next year that his place was filled, William Amory and Samuel Frothingham then resigning and the three vacancies being filled by the election of Israel Whitney, J. Ingersoll Bowditch and John C. Lee. In 1861 Nathan Appleton, and in 1862 William Appleton, resigned, and thereafter there were but five directors. In 1871 Messrs. Lyman and Story were succeeded by Gardner Brewer and Charles Amory. In 1872 T. Jefferson Coolidge was elected to fill the vacancy caused by the resignation of Mr. Whitney. In 1873 J. Lewis Stackpole was chosen to succeed Mr. Lee. Upon Mr. Brewer's death in 1874 Lewis Downing was elected to fill the vacancy.

The first treasurer was William Amory, who was elected October 24, 1839, and was succeeded, January 1, 1848, by Charles Amory, but was re-elected June 29, 1852, and is the present treasurer. George W. Kimball was clerk of the proprietors from September 26, 1838, to June 29, 1840, being then succeeded by John A. Burnham, who had been agent since September 26, 1838. He was succeeded as clerk and agent, November 6, 1847, by Phinehas Adams. George W. Tilden was paymaster from February, 1839, to

THE STARK MILLS, MANCHESTER, N. H.

August, 1852, when he was succeeded by William B. Webster, who remained till 1864, when the present paymaster, Daniel C. Gould, jr., was appointed. The first selling agents were J. W. Paige & Company, who were followed in 1864 by Gardner Brewer & Company. The original capital was five hundred thousand dollars, which was increased in January, 1845, to seven hundred and fifty thousand; in June, 1846, to one million; in June, 1847, to the present sum, one million two hundred and fifty thousand dollars. The par value of the shares is one thousand dollars each. They were worth six or seven hundred dollars apiece when Mr. Adams was chosen agent, rose to fourteen or fifteen hundred dollars during the war and are now quoted at eleven hundred.

The Stark Mills own fourteen acres of land, one third of which is occupied by the mill-yard, situated just above the Amoskeag yard and lying wholly on the upper canal with a front of ten hundred and twenty-two feet from Stark to Bridge streets. The rest of the land is in four pieces and part of it is occupied by overseers' and boarding-house blocks and the agent's house. One piece is bounded by Mechanic street on the north, Elm back street on the east, Stark street on the south and Canal street on the west. The square just above, included between Elm back street, Water, Canal and Spring streets, is owned by the Amoskeag Company, excepting a section bounded on the east by Elm back street and running westerly one hundred and fifty feet on Spring and Water streets, which belongs to the Stark Mills. The latter own also a piece bounded on the north by Bridge street, on the east by Elm back street produced, on the south by Spring street and on the west by Canal street, except the lot on which the North grammar-school house stands. Six acres of this, whose northern, southern and eastern boundaries are Bridge and Charles streets and Elm back street produced, are unoccupied.

The mills own still another lot, one hundred and twenty-five feet long and one hundred feet wide, on the corner of Vine and Concord streets, which is occupied by tenement-houses. The first house which was used as the agent's was built for Mr. Burnham, the first agent, on the north-east corner of Pine and Hanover streets, and was occupied by him and his successor, Mr. Adams. This was exchanged with the Amoskeag Company for the house on Water street which they had built as a residence for the agent of the machine-shop. Mr. Adams occupied this till he moved to a house of his own, and it is now rented.

Number one and number two mills, the first cotton-mills in operation on this side of the Merrimack river in this city, were built, one in 1838 and the other in 1839, and are exact counterparts of each other. They are situated on the western side of the yard at its lower end and their wheels are driven by water from the upper canal. They are both one hundred and fifty feet long by fifty wide, with a picker-house at the north, one hundred and twelve feet in length and one at the south, thirty feet in length. They are united by an addition erected in 1844, eighty feet long and fifty-eight wide, thus becoming one building, five hundred and twenty feet long including the picker-houses, and six stories high. It has twenty-two thousand spindles and six hundred and sixty looms, which are driven by one large and four smaller turbine wheels, with an aggregate of eleven hundred horse-powers. There are employed in it four hundred females and a hundred males, and its daily production is twenty-six thousand five hundred yards of cotton goods.

Number three mill, built in 1846, stands upon the western side of the yard at its upper end. It is, including a picker-house at each end, three hundred and eighty feet long, sixty feet wide and seven stories high. Its machinery, driven by one large and three smaller turbine wheels, which have a total of nine hundred horse-powers and are fed by water from the upper canal, includes twenty-two thousand spindles and six hundred and sixty looms. It employs one hundred males and four hundred females, and makes daily twenty-six thousand five hundred yards of sheetings, shirtings and drillings, thus being, in respect to machinery, operatives and product, similar to the combination of the first two mills.

A building where linen goods are bleached is situated in the northwest corner of the yard. It is seventy-five feet long, forty feet wide, three stories high, and it has a capacity for bleaching seven thousand yards a day. Back of the northern picker-house of the lower mill is a building, forty-five feet in length, thirty-five in width and three stories in height, the lower story of which is used for drying yarns and the two upper for card-rooms. Just at the north of this is a building, sixty-eight feet long, twenty feet wide and two stories high, one-half of which, up and down, is used for bleaching yarns, and the other half for sizing.

The continuous line of buildings, three stories in height, which fronts on Canal street, is begun at the southern end by the linen-mill, one hundred and seventy feet long and thirty feet wide. It has fifteen hundred spindles and one hundred looms, driven by power from number one mill, employs fifty operatives, nearly all females, and makes six thousand yards of crash and towelings a day. The next division is seventy-eight feet long, and is occupied, in the lower story as a shearing-room, in the second as a belt-room, and in the third as a card-room. Next comes the counting-room, thirty feet long and ten feet wider than the rest of the line, with a store-house over it. The cloth-room is next in order and occupies all three stories for one hundred and eight feet. The repair-shops extend northward from this point one hundred and ninety feet and are divided into a waste-house, store-room for iron, paint-shop, blacksmith-shop, wood-shop, and repair-shop for iron and steel work. The rest of the building, four hundred and forty-six feet in length, is occupied by five store-houses for cotton and linen. There are two boiler-houses, which supply heat for the mills and for some mechanical processes.

The mills have forty-four thousand cotton-spindles and thirteen hundred and twenty cotton-looms, fifteen hundred linen-spindles and one hundred linen-looms. They employ nine hundred and fifty females and two hundred and fifty males, with a pay-roll of forty thousand dollars a month. The corporation leases of the Amoskeag Company twenty mill-powers. The mills are provided with the necessary apparatus for extinguishing fires and the hydrants are supplied with water from the Amoskeag Company's reservoir. The mills consume no coal, but use yearly thirty-six hundred cords of wood, sixty tons of starch, six thousand gallons of oil, three hundred tons of flax, fifteen thousand bales of cotton and one million seven hundred and fifty thousand cubic feet of gas.

The mills make crash and towelings in linen goods, sheetings, drillings, cotton duck and bags in cotton goods. At first only sheetings and drillings were made, but, after the fire of 1850 which destroyed the upper story of number two mill, this was fitted with looms for the manufacture of bags, invented and patented by Cyrus W. Baldwin. There were at first ten looms which made four hundred bags a day. When the late war produced a scarcity of cotton, it was resolved to make bags from linen instead, and Mr. Adams was sent to Europe in 1863 by the corporation to get an idea of the linen-machinery used abroad. He had machinery built in England at a cost of forty thousand dollars and brought it across the ocean, and the making of linen bags was then begun. After the war, when cotton was cheaper, it took the place of linen in the bags, and the linen-looms have since been used for the manufacture of crash and towelings. The bags are known as the "seamless bags," being woven in one piece, and have acquired an excellent reputation. They are made of all sizes, from a capacity of three pints to that of four bushels, and are used for holding specie, ore, grain and bread, and for sugar-straining. The mills make goods which measure from one yard to four yards and a half per pound. Their yarns are coarser and their goods heavier to the yard than any others made in the city, and they use more cotton in proportion than any other mills here. Their sheetings are from thirty-six to sixty-one inches wide, drillings from thirty to fifty-one inches, cotton duck from twenty-eight to fifty-six inches. They make from twenty-four hundred to ten thousand bags a day; eighteen million yards of all kinds of goods a year or sixty thousand yards a day, fifty-four thousand of cotton goods and six thousand of linen goods.

THE MANCHESTER MILLS.

The Amoskeag Company had early begun in their mill at Hooksett, which had some six or eight thousand spindles, the manufacture of delaines, a business then unknown in this country. The fabric was made without trouble, but the manufacturers had neither sufficient knowledge nor machinery to compete successfully with others in printing the cloth after it was made, and it was sold from the loom to a firm in Taunton, Mass., who printed it on their own account. But it was determined to go into the business on a larger scale, and in 1839 the Manchester Mills, composed for the most part of stockholders in the corporations already in existence, was incorporated with a capital of a million dollars. Mr. Straw was sent to Europe in 1844 to acquire a knowledge of the structures and machinery used there for printing delaines, and brought back from the manufactories into which he gained access on one pretext and another a knowledge which was made use of in the erection of the works of this company, whose first mill was built in 1845 and which got under way the next year.

In 1847 this corporation sold its property to one which had been chartered the previous year, with a capital of fifteen hundred thousand dollars, under the name of the Merrimack Mills. In July, 1849, its name was changed to that of the Manchester Print-Works, and in 1852 its capital was increased to eighteen hundred thousand dollars. Its average dividends during its existence were nine per cent. and during the late war it paid five semi-annual dividends in succession of ten per cent. each, but its prosperity subsequently declined. In 1873 it was authorized by the legislature to reduce its capital to five hundred and forty thousand dollars, and its property was sold at auction, March 26, 1874, the old stockholders having the privilege of subscribing for stock in a new corporation in proportion to the amount they held in the old. The property was bought by a corporation, chartered in 1873 under the name of the Manchester Print-Works and Mills, with a capital of two million dollars. Its name was changed in 1874 to that of the Manchester Mills.

David Sears was president of the first corporation till July, 1846, and was then succeeded by Oliver Dean, who continued in office till October, 1871, when William Mixter was chosen in his stead and remained president of the Manchester Print-Works corporation which has not quite gone out of existence.

The first directors of the Merrimack Mills were Jabez C. Howe, Oliver Dean, Nathan Appleton, George Howe and William Amory. In 1848 David Sears succeeded Oliver Dean. The next year the corporation assumed the name of the Manchester Print-Works. In 1855 Samuel R. Payson was added. In 1857 in place of David Sears and Jabez C. Howe, Sidney Homer and James Ellison were elected. In 1858 Sidney Homer was succeeded by David Sears, jr. In 1862 Samuel W. Swett was elected in place of Nathan Appleton. In 1867 Charles W. Freeland was chosen to succeed James Ellison. In 1869 Samuel W. Swett and George Howe gave place to T. Jefferson Coolidge and Samuel Johnson. In 1871 Nathan Parker and David B. Jewett were elected in place of William Amory and David Sears, jr. In 1873 C. W. Freeland, S. R. Payson, Samuel Johnson and D. B. Jewett were succeeded by Walter Hastings, A. E. Hildreth, Caleb W. Loring and Samuel Fay, and in 1874 Samuel R. Payson, Caleb W. Loring, T. Jefferson Coolidge, Nathan Parker, Joseph C. Hovey and Gilbert R. Payson were chosen directors.

The first treasurer was Isaac Livermore, who remained till 1852, when he was succeeded by Charles Amory, who remained till 1871, when William H. Thompson took his place. Upon the latter's retirement in 1873, Charles H. Dalton was elected and is the present treasurer of the Manchester Print-Works. George B. Upton was clerk of the proprietors till 1846, when he was succeeded by F. A. Hussey, who remained such till 1849, when Oliver Macy took his place. The latter was succeeded in 1859 by Josiah S. Shannon, the present clerk of the Manchester Print-Works.

The manufacturing and the printing departments have sometimes been under the direct management of one man, sometimes under the management of separate agents responsible only to the directors, and sometimes there has been a manager of the printing department subordinate to the agent of the whole. The first agent of the manufacturing department was George B. Upton, who remained till November, 1845, and was succeeded by William P. Newell, who left March 1, 1853, when his place was taken by Waterman Smith. The latter continued agent till June, 1871, and was then succeeded by A. M. Wade, who remained only till December. Then H. M. Thompson took his place, remaining till February, 1874, when Joseph Stone succeeded him. The first superintendent of the printing department was James Peacock, who remained till 1848, when William P. Newell, the agent of the mills, assumed the whole control, and kept it till his withdrawal from the agency. In December, 1852, John P. Lord took charge of the printery and remained its manager a year, when Charles H. Dalton succeeded him. The latter held the control till 1864, though Samuel Webber became manager under him in 1858 and remained till Mr. Dalton's departure, when John M. Ordway was made superintendent. He continued till 1866, when the whole establishment passed into the management of Waterman Smith, agent of the mills. Archibald M. Graham came in May, 1865, and was manager under Mr. Ordway and Mr. Smith till about 1869. James Dean was appointed superintendent and took the entire control of the printery in 1870, and since then there has been no change. The first paymaster at the mills was F. A. Hussey, who was succeeded in 1848 by Oliver Macy. He remained till 1854, when Josiah S. Shannon took his place and has continued to occupy it. John P. Lord was paymaster at the print-works till 1851, when Andrew N. Baker succeeded him and has remained paymaster since.

The Manchester Print-Works and Mills, which had been chartered in 1873 and had bought the property of the Manchester Print-Works in 1874, was organized May 13, 1874, by the choice of Lyman Nichols as president; Lyman Nichols, Samuel Fay, William H. Hill, Moody Currier, Benjamin P. Cheney, Samuel R. Payson and William O. Grover as directors; Asa Fowler as clerk. These were re-elected at the annual meeting in October. At the June session of 1874 the legislature allowed the corporation to assume the name of the Manchester Mills. It has a capital of two million dollars in shares of one hundred dollars

Warren L. Lane

each. The treasurer for a few months was Charles H. Dalton, who was succeeded by John C. Palfrey. The agent of the manufacturing department is Joseph Stone; the superintendent of the printing department, James Dean. The selling agents are White, Payson & Company, Boston and New York. The paymaster at the mills is Josiah S. Shannon; at the print-works, Andrew N. Baker.

The Manchester Mills own about forty-three acres of land in all. An acre and three-quarters, which takes up the space (except a lot on the south side of Merrimack street which belongs to the Amoskeag Company) bounded on the north by Merrimack street, on the east by Franklin street, on the south by Pleasant street and on the west by Canal street, is occupied by boarding-house and overseers' blocks. A house, also, which was built for the agent of the mills, stands on the corner of Pleasant and Franklin streets. It has been occupied by Messrs. Newell, Smith and Thompson, and now is tenanted by Mr. Dean, the superintendent of the print works.

Five acres, bounded on the north by the waste-way through which the water flows from the upper into the lower canal, on the east by Bedford street, on the south by Granite street and on the west by State street, are occupied by overseers' and boarding-house blocks. There are four acres in Piscataquog village which are occupied in the same way, including two lots on Granite street on which dwelling-houses stand, one of which has been used as a residence for the superintendent of the print-works. Mr. Peacock, the first superintendent, lived in the house now occupied by William Whittle, on the corner of Granite and Main streets. There are eight acres of unoccupied land in Piscataquog which belong to the Manchester Mills. The mill-yard contains a little over thirteen acres, included between the Amoskeag Company's yard and Granite street and extending eleven hundred feet on the lower canal and thirteen hundred and ten feet on the river. There are ten acres on the south of Granite street, extending eight hundred and thirty feet on the canal and seven hundred and eighty-five on the river, to the yard of the Namaske Mills.

The Manchester Mills lease forty mill-powers of the Amoskeag Company. They have hydrants and fire-escapes connected with the buildings, and also a steam fire-engine with an organized company. They use the water of the canal for general purposes, and their tenements are supplied from the city's reservoir. The corporation is divided into two distinct and yet connected departments, for manufacturing and for printing. The former occupies all of the mill-yard but three and two-fifths acres.

Number one mill is situated at the upper end of the yard and was built in 1845. It is four hundred and thirty-seven feet long, sixty feet wide and six stories high. The southern half was burned in 1855 and re-built. At its upper end is a wheel-house, thirty-five feet long and thirty wide; in its rear a boiler-house, containing six boilers with an aggregate of four hundred horse-powers; and back of the lower end is a three-story picker-house, fifty-two feet wide and sixty feet long. The mill contains forty-five thousand spindles and eleven hundred looms, which are driven by two turbine wheels, each with a diameter of eight feet and of five hundred horse-powers. There are employed in the mill one hundred and twenty-five males and two hundred and seventy-five females, and its weekly production is two hundred thousand yards of print-cloths.

Just south of this is number two mill, built in 1850, three hundred and twenty-four feet long, sixty feet wide and six and a half stories high. In the rear, at its northern end, is a picker-house, forty-eight feet in length by twenty-seven in width, four stories high. There is, also, behind the mill, a boiler-house, fifty feet long and forty-six feet wide, whose upper story is used for wool-drying and which contains six boilers of four hundred horse-powers. The mill has a thousand looms, ten thousand worsted-spindles and twenty thousand cotton-spindles, driven by a turbine wheel with a diameter of eight feet and of five hundred horse-powers. The mill employs one hundred and sixty-five males and seven hundred females and makes two hundred thousand yards of worsted goods a week.

Number three mill is situated in the northwest corner of the yard upon the river-bank. It is five hundred and eighty-seven feet long, forty-two feet wide for one half of the way and thirty-six feet wide for the other half. It is three stories high and is used for storage. At the lower end, between this mill and number one mill, is a waste-house and wool-picker, one hundred and twelve feet long, fifty feet wide and one story high for the most part.

Number four mill is a part of the canal building now devoted to other purposes, and number five mill is the west wing of the printery, not to be used in future for manufacturing. Number six mill is situated on the river a little below number three mill. It is one hundred and fifty-three feet long, sixty feet wide on an average, and five stories high. The lower story is used by the printing department as a place in which to cleanse worsted goods. It contains six hundred of the looms mentioned as in number two mill, they being operated in connection with each other. There is a boiler-house east of it, eighty feet in length and thirty in width, three stories high the greater part of the way, which contains a Corliss nest boiler of three hundred and twenty-five horse-powers.

Between the boiler-house and the picker-house of number two mill are a store-room for oils and paints, thirty feet long, fifteen feet wide and one story high, and a store-room and room for washing wools, one hundred and thirty feet long, forty-six feet wide and one story high. Between number three and number six mills is an irregular one-story building, of an average length of one hundred and forty feet and an average width of forty-three, used as a dye-house for cottons and wools. In front of this is a one-story building, two hundred and twenty-seven feet long and seventy-two feet wide, used as a dye-house, where the "fancy-colored" goods are dyed. On the south side of Granite street and east of the canal is a store-house, one hundred and sixty feet long and one hundred and ninety-two feet wide, which for a width of one hundred and ten feet is occupied by the manufacturing department for storage. The canal building is eleven hundred and twenty-seven feet long and thirty wide, being occupied for eight hundred and fifty-five feet of its length by the offices, store-rooms, cloth-rooms, harness-rooms and repair-shops of the manufacturing department.

There are four mills in operation, which have ten thousand worsted-spindles and sixty-five thousand cotton-spindles and twenty-one hundred looms, driven by three water-wheels with an aggregate of fifteen hundred horse-powers. They give employment to four hundred and seventy-five males and ten hundred and twenty-five females, make four hundred thousand yards a week, or seventy thousand yards a day, of print-cloths and worsted dress-goods, and have a pay-roll of forty-five thousand dollars. There are consumed annually in the mills three million pounds of cotton, two million pounds of wool, three thousand tons of coal, forty tons of starch, ten thousand gallons of oil and seven million cubic feet of gas.

The printing department occupies three and two-fifths acres of the mill-yard and some of its buildings stand on the land south of Granite street. The first printery was built in 1845, but was burned in 1853, when another took its place. The present printery is composed of a centre and east and west wings. The centre is one hundred and fifty-nine feet long by sixty-five feet wide, three stories in height, fire-proof, with iron beams and masonry floors. The first floor is a large printing-room in which the fifteen printing-machines are located. The second floor is used for finishing and packing prints and the third floor for steaming. The east wing is two hundred and twenty-eight feet in length by fifty-three in width and four stories in height. In a part of the first story is located a turbine wheel and the remaining space is used for storage. In the second story is the engraving-room and rooms for pressing and packing worsted goods. The third and fourth stories are used for "aging" prints or keeping them till the colors become "fast." The west wing is two hundred and eighty feet in length, one hundred and six feet wide at the northern end, sixty-six feet wide at the southern end, and three stories high. In the first story prints are washed and dried; the second is a cloth-room; and the third is used for aging prints.

The color-shop, in which are made the colors for printing, is a one-story building next to Granite street, one hundred and thirty-five feet in length, forty-two feet wide at the east end and sixty-four feet wide at the west end. The madder dye-house, where print-cloths are dyed, is on the river-bank just north of the west wing of the printery. It is a one-story building, one hundred and thirty-nine feet long, eighty-eight feet wide for about one-half of the way and sixty feet wide for the rest. The bleachery, for bleaching print-cloths, is one hundred feet long, eighty-nine feet wide and one story high. The fancy dyeing-house, where worsted goods are dyed, is ninety-two feet long, fifty-four feet wide and one story high. The boiler-house is an iron-roofed, one-story building, one hundred and twenty feet in length by fifty-four feet in width. It contains twenty-two tubular boilers and three upright Corliss boilers. Two hundred and seventy-five feet in length of the canal building at its lower end are occupied by offices, repair-shops and store-rooms for the print-works. On the south side of Granite street are the laboratory buildings in which are made the chemicals for use in the various departments of the works. The print-works occupy eighty-two feet in width of the store-house on the south side of Granite street and east of the canal.

The printing department employs six hundred operatives and has a monthly pay-roll of twenty-five thousand dollars. It prints seven hundred and twenty thousand yards of print-cloth a week and dyes two hundred thousand yards of worsted goods. About one-third of the cloth is made in the mills; the rest is bought outside. It consumes annually ten thousand tons of coal, twelve hundred cords of wood and three million cubic feet of gas, and uses ten thousand dollars' worth of drugs a week.

THE LANGDON MILLS.

A company by the name of the Langdon Mills was incorporated in 1846 and again in 1853, but the last charter was granted June 27, 1857, in which Daniel Clark, John S. Kidder, Jacob G. Cilley and Adam Chandler were named as grantees, and the capital stock was fixed at two hundred thousand dollars. It was not, however, till 1860 that the corporation was organized, and the first meeting was held in April of that year, when Charles L. Richardson was chosen proprietors' clerk. At the next meeting Gardner Brewer was chosen president; Gardner Brewer, William Amory, John R. Brewer, Henry B. Rogers and John A. Burnham, directors; William Amory, jr., treasurer; William L. Killey, clerk. Mr. Killey was appointed agent, and his son, William E. Killey, paymaster. The latter was succeeded in April, 1866, by another son, Walter S. Killey, the present paymaster. The selling agents are Gardner Brewer & Company of Boston. There was no change in the officers till the death of Mr. Brewer in 1874, when E. A. Straw succeeded him as director, and William Amory, who had been president during Mr. Brewer's absence in Europe, was elected to that position. The capital was increased in 1861 to two hundred and twenty-five thousand dollars, and in 1868 to five hundred thousand. The shares have a par value of a thousand dollars each and are rarely sold, the last that were disposed of bringing fourteen hundred and fifty-two dollars.

The corporation's land includes a lot six hundred and fifty feet long and two hundred and twenty feet wide, bounded by Elm, Langdon, Canal and Brook streets, upon which stand the agent's house, on the corner of Elm and Langdon streets, one overseers' block and two boarding-house blocks. The Langdon buildings form the northern limit of the cotton-mills on the upper canal. The mill-yard has a length of six hundred and eighty-three feet upon the canal and is two hundred feet deep. The building farthest north is used as a store-house, is one story in height, two hundred and ninety feet in length and thirty feet in width. The counting-room building, on the left to one entering the yard, is fifty-six feet long, thirty wide, two stories high and is occupied by offices. Adjoining it on the south is the cloth-room building, one hundred and thirty-six feet long, thirty feet wide, and a story and a half high. Number one mill is two hundred and twenty feet long, fifty feet wide and five stories high, with a picker-house, sixty-four feet in length by thirty in width and three stories high, at its south end. This mill was built and owned by the Blodget Paper Company, which was chartered in 1853 for the manufacture of wall-paper. The mill and part of the present store-house were standing, when, upon the suspension of the paper company, the property was sold at auction and passed into the possession, successively, of Gardner Brewer & Company, the Amoskeag Manufacturing Company and the

Langdon Mills. In this mill sixty males and one hundred and fifty females find employment, and its fifteen thousand spindles and three hundred looms, driven by a turbine wheel of two hundred horse-powers, make forty-five thousand yards a week of fine sheetings, shirtings and silesias.

Number two mill, situated at the south of number one, was built in 1868, two hundred and eighty-four feet long, sixty-six feet wide, and four stories high, with a three-story picker-house at its northern end, sixty-three feet in length by fifty in width, two stories of which are used for a store-room and repair-shop. In it are employed seventy males and one hundred and eighty females. It contains eighteen thousand and forty-eight spindles and four hundred looms, which are driven by a turbine wheel of three hundred horse-powers, and which make fifty thousand yards a week of the well-known "Langdon G. B." sheetings.

The mills are heated from a boiler-house in their rear, sixty feet long and twenty-five wide, which contains two boilers of a hundred horse-powers each, and part of which is used for a blacksmith-shop. The buildings are well provided with sprinklers, hose, hydrants and fire-escapes. The mills contain thirty-three thousand and fifty-six spindles and seven hundred and four looms, which produce daily sixteen thousand yards of sheetings, shirtings and silesias. They employ five hundred operatives, with a monthly pay-roll of fifteen thousand dollars; lease eight mill-powers of the Amoskeag Company; and use annually three thousand bales of cotton, a thousand cords of wood, two thousand gallons of oil, fifty thousand pounds of starch, and seven hundred and fifty thousand cubic feet of gas.

THE NAMASKE MILLS.

This corporation was organized in 1856 as the Amoskeag Duck and Bag Mills, but ten years later its name

AMOSKEAG MANUF'G CO.,

MACHINE SHOPS AND LOWER MILL YARD.

was changed by act of the legislature to that of Namaske Mills. It had a capital of sixty-eight thousand dollars. When it was organized, Nathaniel Webster was the president and agent; E. A. Straw, treasurer; and William B. Webster, clerk. In 1864 Mr. Straw became both president and treasurer, and William B. Webster both agent and clerk. The stock then passed wholly into the hands of Mr. Straw. It owned five acres of land and one mill built in 1856 and set in operation the next year, situated at the southern extremity of the lower canal. The property, with the exception of the woolen machinery, was sold in February, 1875, to the Amoskeag Company.

The mill was built with the intention of making bags and duck cloth, but since the war it has produced a different class of goods, making annually one million five hundred thousand yards of ginghams and one-third as many yards of shirting flannels. It uses two mill-powers, has one hundred and eighty-eight looms, six thousand and thirty-six cotton-spindles, sixteen hundred woolen-spindles and five sets of woolen-cards, makes six thousand yards of cloth a day, employs one hundred and sixty operatives and has a pay-roll of six thousand dollars a month. It uses annually six hundred tons of coal, two hundred thousand pounds of wool, three hundred and fifteen thousand pounds of cotton, a thousand gallons of oil, twenty-four thousand pounds of starch, ten thousand dollars' worth of coloring matter and six hundred thousand cubic feet of gas.

THE DERRY MILLS.

This corporation was organized in 1865, with a capital of one hundred thousand dollars. Waterman Smith was chosen president; Waterman Smith, Samuel R. Payson and Gilbert R. Payson, directors; Josiah S. Shannon, treasurer and proprietors' clerk. Mr. Smith was succeeded as president in 1870 by S. R. Payson, and in 1871 as director by George Mixter. The pay-master is Harrison Spooner. The first agent was W. B. Underhill, who was succeeded, in 1870, by George Mixter, and he in 1874 by the present agent, George F. Lincoln.

The mills, which have now passed into the hands of S. R. Payson, are three in number, and are situated upon Cohas brook at Goffe's Falls. There are three dams, with a fall of fifteen, thirteen and nine feet respectively, amounting to one hundred and fifteen horse-powers in all. The mills contain about thirty-five hundred spindles and a few looms, and gave employment in 1873 to one hundred and sixty operatives. The average weekly production is fifteen thousand yards of cassimere, two hundred dozen stockings and four thousand pounds of shoddy, with a daily consumption of five hundred pounds of wool.

THE MANCHESTER LOCOMOTIVE WORKS.

These works were started in 1853 as a private enterprise by several individuals under the name of Bayley, Blood and Company and were called the Vulcan Works. In 1854 the company obtained a charter and became a corporation, called the Manchester Locomotive Works, which has a present capital of one hundred and fifty thousand dollars. The manufacture of locomotive engines was begun in the fall of 1854, shops of brick having been erected in the spring and summer of that year, with a capacity of turning out twenty locomotives annually. But the business steadily increased and at the present time the works are capable of making fourteen locomotives a month, and, when in full operation, give employment to seven hundred men and have a monthly pay-roll of thirty thousand dollars.

The shops are situated on Canal street between Hollis and Dean streets and occupy five acres, besides an iron-foundry and an acre of land at the lower end of Elm street, which were acquired by purchase of the Manchester Iron Company in 1865 when that passed out of existence. The machine-shop is a substantial building, parallel with Canal street, two stories in height, four hundred feet in length and eighty-four in width. The wood-shop is also a two-story building, one hundred feet long and forty feet wide; the blacksmith-shop is three hundred and thirty feet long and fifty feet wide; the boiler-shop, two hundred and five feet long and fifty-two feet wide. A new building has been erected the past year which is used for making locomotive-tanks. This, like all the others, is made of brick, and is two hundred and thirty feet in length by thirty-six in width.

All the iron castings, of which three million five hundred thousand pounds were used in 1873, are made at the company's iron-foundry at the foot of Elm street. One million eight hundred thousand pounds of boiler-plates are used yearly, forty-five hundred tons of coal and a thousand cords of wood; and there are made two hundred thousand pounds of brass castings and two million five hundred thousand pounds of forgings, yearly. The company manufactures all the heavy forgings, frames, axles, etc., which it uses; and, indeed, every part of a locomotive but the boiler and tank iron and a few minor parts is made at the works. Two furnaces are constantly in operation, making the best of iron from scrap, most of which accumulates at the works. The company has turned out seven hundred and eighty-six engines, which have been sent to all parts of the United States, to South America and the Dominion of Canada. John A. Burnham, of Boston, is president of the company; William G. Means, of Andover, is treasurer. The first agent was Oliver W. Bayley, who was succeeded in 1857 by the present agent, Aretas Blood, who resides in Manchester and has the personal superintendence and immediate management of the business.

AMOSKEAG AXE COMPANY.

The Blodget Edge Tool Manufacturing Company was incorporated in 1853, began the erection of buildings at the northern end of the upper canal in 1854 and was regularly organized January 7, 1855, by the election of E. A. Straw as president; E. A. Straw, Moody Currier, David J. Clark, Cyrus W. Baldwin and Phinehas Adams, directors; Jacob G. Cilley, clerk and treasurer. In 1857 the latter was succeeded by James A. Weston. In 1858 E. A. Straw, Amos G. Gale, T. W. Little, Joseph A. Haines and Cyrus W. Baldwin were chosen directors. In 1859 Moody Currier succeeded Mr. Baldwin as a director and T. W. Little became clerk and treasurer in Mr. Weston's place. In 1861 George B. Chandler succeeded Mr. Gale as a director.

In 1862 a new corporation was chartered, called the Amoskeag Axe Company, which bought the property of the former company and was organized August 14, 1862. Moody Currier was chosen president; E. A. Straw, Moody Currier, Thomas P. Shaddick, T. W. Little, Henry C. Reynolds, directors; T. W. Little, clerk and treasurer. These were all re-elected in 1863, but upon the death of Mr. Little in that year, Moody Currier was chosen treasurer in his stead and Henry C. Reynolds clerk. The latter was also made agent, the offices of clerk, treasurer and agent having hitherto been combined in one. The only changes since have been the election in 1866 of George B. Chandler as a director to succeed Mr. Shaddick, and the retirement of Mr. Haines. The capital stock is seventy thousand dollars, owned by the officers of the company. The company employs sixty men and makes yearly one hundred and forty-four thousand tools—axes, hatchets and picks—of the best imported steel, which bring about a hundred and forty thousand dollars.

THE MANCHESTER GAS-LIGHT COMPANY.

A corporation by the name of the Manchester Gas-Light Company was originally chartered in 1846 with a capital of three hundred thousand dollars, but the company was not formed till after the granting of another charter, July 10, 1850, fixing the maximum capital at one hundred and twenty-five thousand dollars. The first meeting of the grantees was held at the Manchester House, February 10, 1851, when there were present David A. Bunton, Jonathan T. P. Hunt, Ezekiel A. Straw, William G. Means, David Gillis, Samuel P. Greeley, Herman Foster, Robert Read and John S. Kidder. Robert Read was chairman of the meeting, and William G. Means, clerk. The capital stock was fixed at sixty thousand dollars in shares of one hundred dollars each.

At the next meeting, February 22, Robert Read, E. A. Straw, David Gillis, William P. Newell and John S. Kidder were chosen directors, and at a directors' meeting Robert Read was chosen president, and Herman Foster clerk. The next year the capital was increased to seventy-five thousand dollars, and in April Herman Foster was chosen treasurer, and Jonathan T. P. Hunt agent. In 1853 all the officers were re-elected and the capital was increased to one hundred thousand dollars, remaining unaltered till the present. There was no change in the officers till 1856, when E. A. Straw was chosen president to succeed Robert Read, and the next year in place of the latter William Amory was elected director. He, however, declined to serve, and the next year William Amory, jr., was chosen in his stead.

In 1861 Benjamin F. Martin was elected a director in place of David Gillis, and in 1862 Moody Currier in place of John S. Kidder. In 1865 William Amory, jr., was succeeded by Nathan Parker. J. T. P. Hunt, the agent, died,

February 23, 1865, and Charles F. Warren, the present agent, was appointed in April of that year. In 1869 Waterman Smith was elected a director in place of William P. Newell, and was himself succeeded in 1873 by Phinehas Adams. Mr. Foster was clerk and treasurer till his death in the spring of 1875. Charles E. Balch was elected, February 24, 1875, as treasurer, and Lucien B. Clough was chosen clerk *pro tem.*

The works are situated in the southern part of the city, on the western side of Elm street, near the Manchester and Lawrence railway, on a lot of land four hundred feet square. The first building was begun in 1852. The company has laid twenty-three miles of pipe, from two to fourteen inches in diameter, which interlace the compact part of the city, extending to Piscataquog village, to the northern end of Elm street, to Bakersville and on the east to Wilson hill. The company can furnish now three hundred and fifty thousand cubic feet of gas in twenty-four hours, and will be able, when contemplated improvements are made, to increase this amount to seven or eight hundred thousand cubic feet. It uses annually over six thousand tons of coal and makes over fifty million cubic feet of gas, of which the mills use about three-fifths and individuals the rest, though the city in its corporate capacity consumes, for ordinary use and for its two hundred and fifty street-lamps, one million six hundred thousand cubic feet, at a cost of one cent an hour for every burner. The cost of the gas to individuals is two dollars and seventy cents a thousand feet; to those who consume ten thousand feet a month, two dollars and a half. The corporations obtain it for two dollars and twenty cents a thousand feet, by contract. The average price is thus about two dollars and forty-one cents.

SUMMARY.

The corporations in the city employ about nine thousand persons and have a monthly pay-roll of about three hundred and eleven thousand dollars. They use every year twenty-six thousand one hundred tons of coal, eight thousand cords of wood and about thirty million feet of gas. The mills have about three hundred thousand spindles and eight thousand looms, and make one hundred and forty-three miles of cloth a day. The Manchester Locomotive Works can turn out fourteen locomotives a month and the Amoskeag Manufacturing Company fifty steam fire-engines a year.

MISCELLANEOUS MANUFACTURERS.

There have been given thus far sketches of the incorporated manufacturing companies in Manchester. The manufacturing of the city, however, is not entirely included in these, but quite a large fraction is contributed to the whole sum by individuals and firms in different parts of the city, generally situated on either the northern or the southern edge of its compact portion. Besides selling mill-sites and leasing mill-powers to other corporations, the Amoskeag Company erected near the northern limit of the lower canal a long building called "Mechanics' Row," and leased it in sections to manufacturers of miscellaneous goods, furnishing them with water-power. Though very few of the original tenants hold their leases, the different kinds of business now carried on there are not much unlike those which were started twenty-five years ago. Of late the southern part of the city, near the railway station, where some of the heavier manufacturing was begun about the time when Mechanics' Row was settled, has proved more attractive to manufacturers on account of the larger space it affords and its proximity to the railways. Steam-power is used exclusively there.

The pioneer of Mechanics' Row is Benjamin S. Stokes, who started the Granite File Works there in 1851. He employs fourteen men and uses ten tons of steel in making three thousand dozen files a year.

John A. V. Smith succeeded in 1870 to the control of a business which was begun when the Row was peopled. He employs twelve men and uses four thousand dollars' worth of stock in making six thousand fliers a year.

Yeaton & Company (Elizabeth Yeaton, Albinus Philbrick) have been a long time in business in the Row and make fifteen thousand dollars' worth yearly of power-loom harness, employing fourteen men.

John Cleworth began business in the Row in 1852. He keeps six hands at work and makes fifteen thousand reeds a year, or twelve thousand dollars' worth, using a pound of steel to a reed.

Benjamin H. Chase settled in the Row in 1858, succeeding to a business already established. He uses from eight to ten thousand dollars' worth of stock a year, and makes annually fifteen thousand power-loom pickers and fifteen thousand running feet of leather belting.

Hiram Forsaith came to the Row in 1866. He employs ten men in making from ten to twelve thousand dollars' worth annually of machinery.

The Manchester Machine-Card Factory, whose proprietors are Bisco & Denny (Dwight Bisco, Joseph A. Denny, George Bisco, Charles A. Denny), was started in the Row in 1857. They keep twenty-one machines in operation and use annually nineteen thousand square feet of leather and as many pounds of wire in the manufacture of machine-card clothing.

James Baldwin & Company, who came to the Row in 1859, employ fifty men and use from three hundred to five hundred thousand feet of lumber a year. They turn out fifty thousand bobbins a week, besides shuttles and wooden wares, or fifty thousand dollars' worth a year.

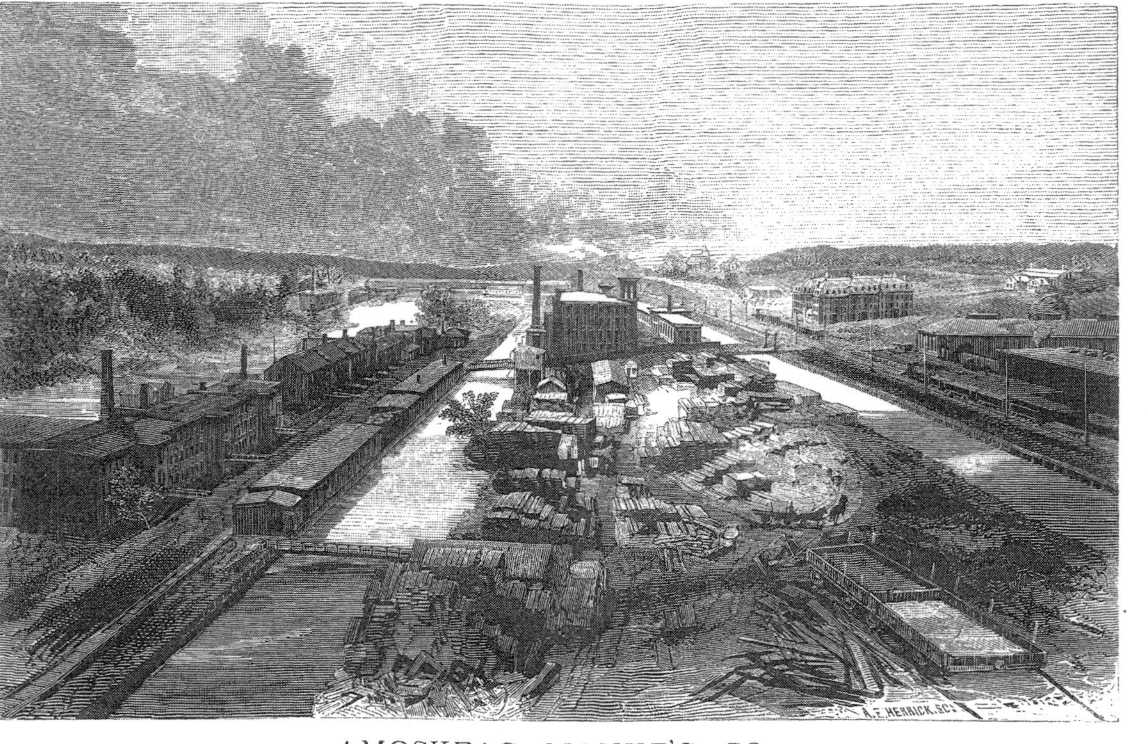

AMOSKEAG MANUF'G CO.

MECHANICS' ROW AND LUMBER YARD.

William W. Hubbard came to the Row in 1860. He employs thirty men and uses five hundred thousand feet of lumber in the manufacture of forty thousand dollars' worth annually of doors, sashes, blinds, moldings, etc.

Piper & Reynolds (Benjamin H. Piper, Henry C. Reynolds) began business in the Row in 1867. They employ nine men and use yearly two hundred cords of walnut and oak in the manufacture of thirty-five thousand spokes, forty thousand axe-handles, and thirty-five thousand hatchet- and hammer-handles.

Charles B. Bradley succeeded in 1870 to a business which was started in 1859 and left him by his father. He employs five hands and uses from eighty to a hundred dozen calf-skins, from four hundred to five hundred dozen lamb-skins and from a thousand to fourteen hundred yards of cloth of all kinds, in covering from one hundred and fifty to one hundred and seventy-five thousand rolls a year.

John Brugger & Son (Sebastian Christophe) employ from one hundred and twenty-five to one hundred and fifty persons in their hosiery-mill at Mechanics' Row, besides a large number of others who do their work by hand and at their homes in the city and vicinity. The annual production is eighty thousand dozen pairs of stockings. The firm have recently bought a mill and water-privilege at Goffstown, but have not yet occupied the place.

A. P. Olzendam occupies a hosiery-mill at Mechanics' Row, one hundred feet long and thirty wide, three stories high, and the Amoskeag Company built for him the past year an addition, one hundred feet long, forty-two feet wide and three stories high with a basement. He employs about one hundred and twenty operatives in the mills and several thousand seamers and knitters outside. He has recently added fifty fancy hand-looms to his machinery, and, when it is all in operation, will make eighty thousand dozen pairs of stockings a year, using six or seven hundred pounds of wool a week. He makes also all the paper boxes used in packing his goods.

Horace and Holmes R. Pettee occupy a grist-mill in Mechanics' Row and grind annually seventy-five thousand bushels of corn for their wholesale trade and twenty thousand bushels of various grains for customers.

John B. McCrillis & Son (John A. McCrillis), who have a shop in Mechanics' Row in addition to their manufactory in Janesville, are the proprietors of a business which has been twenty-five years established. They employ forty men and make annually two hundred and fifty carriages and twenty-five sleighs. They have repositories in northern New York and in Michigan.

These include all the tenants of Mechanics' Row. In the upper part of the city, however, is located the carriage manufactory of Alden W. Sanborn, who employs twenty-five hands and makes a hundred carriages yearly, some of which are sent to California and Australia. He has been in business in Manchester twenty-five years, seven of them in his present location.

Orrin E. Kimball, also located in the northern part of the city but owning a tannery in Bakersville, employs twenty-five men in making skins for roll-covering, nearly three hundred thousand dollars' worth a year. He tans fifty thousand sheep-skins and ten thousand calf-skins yearly, besides finishing over a hundred thousand skins which are sent from other tanneries and pulling two hundred thousand pounds of wool.

The Amoskeag Paper-Mill was first started in 1853 as the Manchester Paper-Works, Benjamin F. Martin & Company (George W. Goddard) being proprietors, but the latter soon retired, leaving Mr. Martin the sole owner. He sold it in 1865 to Hudson Keeney, and he in turn disposed of it to S. D. Warren, of whom Col. Martin bought it in 1869. The latter sold it in 1874 to John Hoyt & Company

(W. J. Hoyt, J. C. Sawyer). It is located on the upper canal just above the Langdon Mills, and makes daily two tons of print and book paper, using four tons of stock and employing fifty-five persons.

The Uncanoonuc Paper-Mill, P. C. Cheney & Company (Person C. Cheney, Elijah M. Tubbs) proprietors, situated on the site of the old cotton-mills at Amoskeag village, gives employment to thirty-five persons in the mill proper and fifteen in the waste-works. The proprietors make two tons of manilla paper a day and handle one hundred and twenty-five tons of waste a month.

Samuel C. Forsaith & Company (William E. Drew) employ at their machine-shop near the foot of Franklin street from fifty to sixty men, using annually from one hundred to one hundred and twenty-five thousand dollars' worth of stock, including two hundred tons of cast iron, seventy-five tons of wrought iron and steel and thirty-five thousand feet of lumber. They make bolt-forging machines, newspaper-folding machines, power spring-hammers, etc.

Albion H. Lowell, in the same locality, employs fifty men in the manufacture of seventy-five thousand dollars' worth yearly of iron fences, ornamental iron work and castings, using from a ton and a half to two tons a day of cast iron.

Joseph L. Smith, near by, employs a dozen men and uses half a million feet of lumber a year, turning three-fourths of it into boxes and the rest into matched and planed boards, etc.

The Manchester Shoe and Leather Company, whose shop is located in the same part of the city, was organized in July, 1872. Andrew C. Wallace is its president; Daniel W. Lane, treasurer; and S. A. Felton, agent. It uses five thousand feet in all. It employs from fifty to sixty persons and manufactures annually sixty thousand dollars' worth of shoes or fifty thousand pairs. The company also manufactures a water-proof dressing for boots and shoes.

William Corey and Company (J. P. Martin), near the corner of Franklin and Auburn streets, employ twenty persons in the manufacture of knitting-needles and knitting-machines. They make three thousand needles a day and use a pound of cast steel for every five hundred needles.

Josselyn & Marston (L. H. Josselyn, C. L. Marston), in the same neighborhood, make annually thirty thousand factory brushes and fifty thousand boot and shoe brushes.

J. S. Holt & Company (W. S. Holt, H. C. Holt), soap manufacturers on Amherst street in Towlesville, carry on a business established by the senior partner in 1852. They manufacture by steam, employ five men and make yearly twenty-six hundred barrels of soft soap and about twenty-five thousand pounds of hard soap. They also render tallow and deal in soap stock of all kinds.

David B. Varney's brass-foundry is situated on Manchester street, between Pine and Union, on the site of the steam-mill of Baldwin, Gould & Company, which was burned in 1852. The business was begun in 1850 by Hartshorn & Darling; in 1857 the firm became Darling & Varney: and since the death of the senior partner in 1868, Mr. Varney has managed the works alone. The most important part of the work done is the manufacture of ornamental brass and copper mountings for locomotives and steam fire engines, between seven and eight thousand pounds of composition castings being used monthly in this branch of the work alone. Among his customers are the Amoskeag Company, who buy from him the brass work on their famous steam fire engines, and the Manchester Locomotive Works, besides railroad corporations. Bells for engines are also made at the establishment and a large amount of general jobbing is done. Some parts of the business are carried on in few places in the country. Mr. Varney manufactures one hundred thousand dollars' worth of goods a year, employs twenty-five men, melts from ten to twelve thousand pounds of metal each month, and consumes annually from seventy-five to one hundred tons of hard coal and twenty thousand bushels of charcoal.

John B. Chase & Company, leather-dressers at the lower end of Elm street, employ three men in finishing thirty thousand skins, or twenty thousand dollars' worth, a year.

Jeremiah Hodge, who was located for some years in Mechanics' Row but has recently removed to the foot of Elm street where he has built a large block, uses half a million feet of lumber yearly in the manufacture of doors, window-frames, moldings, etc.

Arthur Dinsmore & Company, located in Hodge's building, employ thirty men and use two million feet of lumber a year, turning about half into boxes and the rest into matched and planed boards and building lumber of all kinds. They make from the log at their saw-mill near Massabesic lake six hundred and fifty thousand feet of lumber yearly, and cut half a million feet at their steam-mill in Newbury, N. H.

Andrew C. Wallace employs thirty-five men in a planing-mill, saw-mill and box-shop, in a building at the foot of Elm street on Cemetery brook, which he bought in 1875 of Thomas R. Hubbard. He makes yearly one million five hundred thousand feet of lumber into packing-boxes and sells nearly a million feet of lumber besides.

Thomas R. Hubbard, in A. C. Wallace's building, employs forty men in the manufacture of machinery and knitting-needles, and operates a grist-mill, with a capacity of two hundred bushels a day, and a cider-mill, with a capacity of fifty barrels a day, both using steam-power.

Ira Cross, in the same building, employs half a dozen

men, making twelve thousand bobbin-winders and a hundred thousand patent thumb-screws yearly.

Austin, Johnson & Company (Thomas Johnson, Jeremiah Austin, C. A. Flint) began business in this city in 1874 in the southern part of the city, near the Portsmouth railway. They employ fifty men, use one million five hundred thousand feet of lumber a year, and make annually fifty thousand window-sashes, twenty-five thousand blinds, seventy-five hundred doors and as many door-frames, and one million five hundred thousand feet of molding of different widths.

The Amoskeag Brewery in Piscataquog village, of which Andrew C. Wallace is the proprietor, employs six men and brews yearly six thousand barrels of ale, using fourteen thousand bushels of barley and fifteen thousand pounds of hops.

John S. Kidder & Company (Charles H. Hill) grind at their steam-mill on Granite street seventy thousand bushels of corn annually and ten thousand bushels of all kinds of grain for custom-work.

Watts & Holmes (Horace P. Watts, William F. Holmes) grind at their mill on Piscataquog river seventy-five thousand bushels of corn and about the same amount of wheat.

George H. Hubbard makes half a million cigars yearly; James B. Scott makes one hundred thousand yearly.

Thomas F. Glancy makes annually one hundred and thirty thousand bottles of beer and fifty thousand bottles of soda; Vickery & Company, one hundred and eighty thousand bottles of beer; F. L. Gray, one hundred and fifty thousand bottles of beer and soda.

Lincoln & Porter (George F. Lincoln, Alfred Porter) employ half a dozen men in a mill with eight looms at Goffe's Falls, in making four hundred yards a day of crash toweling.

FORMER MANUFACTURERS.

There have been started, since the cotton-mills were built on the river, quite a number of manufacturing enterprises, of different kinds and of more or less importance, which have come to an untimely end, the source of considerable loss to their originators. Several manufacturing companies have also been incorporated, but were never organized.

Of these latter were the Manchester Bleachery, chartered in 1853, with men prominent in connection with the Amoskeag Company named as grantees; and the Manchester Bleachery, chartered again in 1856, neither of which began operations. In 1857 the Merrimack Water Power Company was incorporated, with power to buy the property of the Amoskeag Company, if two-thirds of the stockholders of the latter would vote to sell, but there was nothing done about it. The Merrimack Steam and Gas Pipe Company was chartered in 1853, but never did business.

Of the failures in manufacturing, perhaps the most noteworthy was that of the Blodget Paper Company, which was chartered in January, 1853, with an authorized capital of one hundred thousand dollars, which was increased to three times that sum by an act of the June session of the legislature of that year. The company was formed for the manufacture of paper-hangings, occupied a mill on the upper canal now owned by the Laugdon Mills, and at one time employed one hundred and forty hands, used fourteen tons and a half of paper a week and made eight thousand rolls of paper-hangings a day. William M. Shaw was its agent, and John S. Kidder its clerk and treasurer. It ceased operations after several years.

The Manchester Iron Company, chartered in 1853, began operations in October of that year with a capital of twenty thousand dollars, occupying a foundry, machine-shop, pattern-house and engine-house at the lower end of Elm street, the buildings now owned by the Manchester Locomotive Works and used for the manufacture of castings. The Iron Company made castings of all sorts and at one time employed sixty men and used a thousand tons of coal annually. John B. Fish was then its president; J. T. P. Hunt, its treasurer; Henry C. Merrill, its clerk.

The Manchester Machine Company, chartered in 1853, began in 1855 the manufacture of scales in part of one of the Iron Company's buildings. Isaac Riddle was president of the company; Nathan Parker, treasurer; J. C. Tasker, clerk; George W. Pinkerton, agent.

These two companies were subsequently united under the name of the Manchester Iron Company, Amos G. Gale becoming president, succeeded later by David A. Bunton, and Darwin J. Daniels treasurer and clerk. The company lost money and the buildings and land were sold, December 9, 1865, to the Manchester Locomotive Works, for eight thousand dollars.

The Manchester Car and Machine Works was incorporated in 1854, with a capital of fifty thousand dollars. It occupied a building in the southern part of the city on the line of the Concord railway, now used as a brewery, and at one time employed forty-five men. Hiram Brown was then its president; J. E. Earle, its clerk; Samuel Shepherd, its treasurer and agent. It afterwards assumed the name of the Fulton Works, Samuel C. Crombie becoming its agent, and engaged in the manufacture of doors, sashes and blinds. The company dissolved after a time and the property was bought by Col. Waterman Smith, who moved the building to Goffe's Falls and made it into a mill and afterwards disposed of the land to the Hon. E. A. Straw, who sold it to Tucker & Mathes. They built upon it a brewery and operated it for some time. The property was mortgaged to the Manchester Savings Bank and finally fell

B. F. Martin

into its hands and was sold, near the close of 1874, to Dunn, Harris & Company, who have begun the business of brewing in the building.

The Manchester Oil-Cloth Carpet Factory was incorporated in 1854, with an authorized capital of sixty thousand dollars, but its operations were not very extensive.

The Belmont Print-Works were situated on Cemetery brook, near Hallsville. The mill was built by the Hon. Frederick G. Stark for wheelwright purposes but was bought by Charles Barnes in 1850 and used for a paper-hanging manufactory. In 1855 it passed into the hands of John P. Lord, who had been manager at the Manchester Print-Works, and he fitted it for the printing of delaines and calicoes. The works were owned at one time by Mr. Lord and Henry Buckley and printed seven thousand yards daily or over two million in a year. The old mill was unused for some time after their business ceased, but near the close of 1873 F. F. & C. M. Downs began in it the manufacture of shoes and continued the business a few months.

The Eagle Paper Company was never incorporated but began in 1857 the manufacture of wrapping paper from resinous bark, making from eight hundred to a thousand pounds a day, but shortly came to an end.

The New England Excelsior Company began, about the same time, the manufacture of "excelsior" filling for mattresses, occupying one end of the building owned by the Fulton Works. G. G. Fenner was then agent. About 1860 its name was changed to that of the American Excelsior Company and it began the manufacture of the same article in Mechanics' Row and afterwards removed to Amoskeag village, where it remained till about 1872 and then moved to another part of the state. When it went to Amoskeag village William Blanchard became the agent of the company and afterwards proprietor of the business. The late John L. Davis was the foreman of the company nearly all the time it was located here.

NEWSPAPERS.

THE newspapers of Manchester have been numerous, many of them of an ephemeral character, many devoted to special ends, and but few of them now survive under the names with which they were started. Of a number of them, issued for advertising purposes merely and for gratuitous distribution, and of several amateur papers published in 1872 and 1873, this chapter makes no mention. It makes brief record, with as much accuracy as possible, of those sheets which professed to be newspapers or literary journals and which were bought and sold as such.

The Amoskeag Representative, the first newspaper printed in Manchester, was established by John Caldwell and its first number issued Friday, October 18, 1839, its publication being continued weekly thereafter. Its name was changed to that of Manchester Representative January 22, 1841. It was about the size of the Mirror & American of the present time. It advocated the principles of the Democratic party and at the time when the second paper, the Amoskeag Memorial, was started, had quite a circulation, which subsequently decreased and the paper was sold, December 7, 1842, to Kimball & Currier, and merged with the Manchester Democrat, another venture in the journalistic field.

The second paper was the Amoskeag Memorial, whose publication was begun Wednesday, January 1, 1840, by Joseph C. Emerson, who was born in Weare, learned the printer's trade at Concord and now resides at Cleveland, Ohio. It was started as a neutral paper and remained such till the appearance of the Manchester Democrat in 1842, when it began the advocacy of the principles of the Whig party. At the commencement of the second volume, January 6, 1841, its name was changed to that of Manchester Memorial. Joseph Kidder became its editor February 17, 1841, at which time he sold to Mr. Emerson the People's Herald, which he had published at Pembroke for two months previous, having issued four numbers. The Memorial then assumed the double title of Manchester Memorial & People's Herald and kept it till June 5, 1842, when the latter half was dropped. It was enlarged, June 9, 1841, to the size of the Mirror & American. May 26, 1841, Mr. Emerson associated with himself as publisher O. D. Murray, now of Nashua, and in the succeeding January, when Mr. Kidder resigned the editorship, the publishers announced themselves as editors. The establishment was bought, September 2, 1842, by Samuel F. Wetmore and A. A. Wallace, who continued its publishers till August 21, 1844, when Mr. Wallace retired and left the paper in the hands of Mr. Wetmore, the senior partner. Its name was changed, September 6, 1844, to that of Manchester American. In September, 1845, Mr. Wetmore started the Semi-Weekly American, of which John H. Warland was editor. April 17, 1846, the establishment passed into the hands of James O. Adams, who at once discontinued the semi-weekly issue. He remained the publisher and editor of the American till May, 1852, when, having another weekly paper upon his hands, he sold the American to Gen. Joseph C. Abbott, now United States Senator from North Carolina, and Edward A. Jenks, now connected with the Concord Monitor. A few weeks later they bought the Saturday Messenger, Henry A. Gage, one of the owners of the latter, being admitted to partnership, and they published the American & Messenger under the name of Abbott, Jenks & Company, Mr. Abbott being the editor. A daily had been issued during the campaign of 1848 and again in 1850 during the progress of the Parker murder trial, but the first regular issue of the Manchester Daily American occurred September 4, 1854. Charles G. Warren subsequently bought the interest of the two junior partners and the publication was continued by Abbott & Warren. Both the daily and weekly were sold in 1857 to John H. Goodale of the Manchester Democrat and united with that paper.

Upon the appearance of the Memorial, in January, 1840, John Caldwell of the Representative began the publication of a neutral and literary paper of the size of the new sheet, with the title of the Manchester Magazine, whose matter was selected from what had once appeared in his own paper. This was continued but three months.

July 4, 1840, Joseph C. Emerson of the Memorial began the publication of the Manchester Workman. It was a campaign paper, advocated the claims of Gen. Harrison for President of the United States and was discontinued after his election.

The first number of the Star of Bethlehem, a religious paper which advocated the doctrines of the Universalists, was issued in this city, January 2, 1841. It was published by a company with the title of the Fraternal Association, of which A. C. Bagley was agent, and the editors were Abel C. Thomas and Thomas B. Thayer. It was continued here about a year and was then removed entirely to Lowell, it having been for some time published simultaneously in that city and in Manchester. It is a curious fact that the type for its first number was once all "set" for printing, but some pecuniary difficulty arose and it was "distributed" without having been used.

Soon after the mills were started a large number of papers sprang into a brief existence, some of them being hardly worth dragging from obscurity. Among them were the Manchester Engine, an illustrated journal of fun, which was continued for six weeks, and the Owl, a scurrilous paper which appeared by night, at odd times, for nearly a year. The names of the publishers were not given.

The Literary Souvenir was a weekly paper which was begun in Lowell in 1838 by A. B. F. Hildreth, but in its fourth year was removed to Concord, and four months later to this city. Emerson & Murray of the Memorial were its publishers, and S. H. Napoleon Bonaparte Everette was its editor. He was an eccentric man who styled himself "Rag Emperor" and his name was printed in the paper with that title. The Iris & Literary Record was a monthly magazine which had been published at Hanover by E. A. Allen, but in the summer of 1842 was bought by Emerson & Murray and removed to Manchester. Mr. Everette was the editor of both this and the Souvenir. These two were united the first of September and published under the name of the Iris & Souvenir. Mr. Murray soon afterwards retired and left Mr. Emerson in sole possession of the business. The latter in December, 1842, began the Semi-Weekly Advertiser, which was edited by Col. Isaac Kinsman of Pembroke, and was continued but four or five weeks. In January, 1843, Mr. Emerson sold all his newspaper property to Willard N. Haradon, who bought at the same time the interest of the senior partner in the Manchester Allodium, whose first number was issued January 14, 1843, by James Bursiel and a man of the name of Hamlet, the second number bearing the names of Hamlet & Haradon. The Allodium was a neutral and literary paper ornamented with cheap engravings on wood. This firm continued its publication till April 8, 1843, when E. D. Boylston, now the senior editor of the Farmers' Cabinet at Amherst, purchased it of them and also bought the Iris & Souvenir of Mr. Haradon, continuing both papers under different names and in a different fashion. The Allodium became the Manchester Transcript, which was removed a few months later to Great Falls and there deceased, and instead of the Iris & Souvenir he established in August, 1845, a religious and temperance journal under the name of the New Hampshire Magazine, which was published for a year and was then discontinued.

April 26, 1842, W. H. Kimball and Joseph Kidder, who were associated under the name of Kimball & Kidder, issued the first number of the Manchester Democrat, a weekly paper which advocated the principles of the Democratic party, and which must not be confounded with the Union Democrat which was started in 1851. After a few months George W. Morrison and Moody Currier, then partners in the practice of law, bought Mr. Kidder's half of the paper. Then Mr. Morrison sold his interest to Mr. Currier, who was the editor during his connection with it and for a while afterwards but who retired from its ownership in October, 1843, his share being bought by E. D. Davis. In the early part of 1845 Mr. Kimball sold his interest to Chandler E. Potter, then a practising attorney-at-law, and in September of that year Mr. Potter assumed the whole management. In August, 1846, he associated with him as publisher Edward Hutchins, continuing as editor himself, and resuming entire control the next year. In the fall of 1848 he sold the paper to John H. Goodale, now of Nashua, and W. H. Gilmore, now connected with the Concord People. In January, 1851, Mr. Gilmore retired to start a new paper, called the Union Democrat, and Mr. Goodale continued the sole editor and proprietor. In 1857 the latter bought the Daily American and American & Messenger, continued the publication of the former and united the latter with the Democrat under the name of the Democrat & American. Soon afterwards Simeon D. Farnsworth, then a school-teacher of Concord, came to this city and entered into partnership with Goodale and the firm became Goodale & Farnsworth. In the fall of 1861 the latter bought out his partner and continued the sole proprietor till April, 1863, when, having become a paymaster in the army, he leased the daily and weekly to Gage, Moore & Company (Henry A. Gage, Orren C. Moore, James O. Adams), and the name Democrat was dropped from the title. In August, 1863, O. C. Moore sold his interest to Sylvester C. Gould. In December, 1863, Mr. Farnsworth bought back the lease and sold both papers to John B. Clarke, who united them with the Mirror. The last issue of the Daily American was dated December 26, 1863.

The Gleaner, to which the general testimony ascribes a low and scurrilous character, was first issued Saturday, November 12, 1842, its publisher being William A. Hall and its editor John Caldwell, who was then publishing the Representative. It was suspended in the latter part of 1845. There was an effort made at one time to call Elm street Broadway, and the Gleaner, according to its heading, was printed at "Exchange Building, No. 88 Broadway, opposite Methodist church."

The Manchester Palladium, another of Mr. Caldwell's enterprises, was begun May 21, 1846, and continued about six months.

The White Mountain Torrent was a temperance paper, started at Concord in April, 1843, and edited by the late Moses A. Cartland of Weare. In September of that year it was bought by Willard N. Haradon, J. C. Stowell, George S. Wilson and Samuel Young and moved to Manchester. It was published here till November, being still edited by Mr. Cartland, and then returned to Concord.

The Manchester Operative was begun Saturday, December 30, 1843, by Willard N. Haradon and was published ostensibly, as its name would hint, in the interests of manual laborers. It is said to have gained a good circulation, but its last number was issued November 16, 1844, and it

J. P. Newell

Eng'd by F. O'Brien, N. York.

was then removed to Lowell and united with the Operatives' Magazine & Lowell Offering. It was at first owned and edited by Mr. Haradon alone; February 24, 1844, its columns stated that it was published by Mr. Haradon and conducted by John G. Sherburne and E. R. Wilkins; March 30, Mr. Haradon again appeared as the sole manager; April 20, Haradon & Wilkins were the publishers and proprietors; August 31, Mr. Haradon again appeared, for a single number, alone; September 7, it was published by an "association of practical printers," consisting of W. N. Haradon, George S. Wilson, J. C. Stowell and Samuel E. Young, under the name of Haradon, Stowell & Company, Mr. Stowell being the editor. October 12, the name of the firm was changed to J. C. Stowell & Company and by them it was published till its decease.

The Independent Democrat was begun in this city May 1, 1845, by Robert C. Wetmore, a brother of S. F. Wetmore of the firm of Wetmore & Wallace of the Memorial. It was removed after a few weeks to Concord, where it became a strong paper under the editorship of the Hon. George G. Fogg and was subsequently united with another paper to form the present Independent Statesman.

July 3, 1845, was issued the first number of the Manchester Mercantile Advertiser, published by Charles H. Chase, now a jeweler of this city. It was suspended after an existence of nearly five months and then Mr. Chase began the publication of the Manchester Saturday Messenger, whose first number was issued November 29, 1845. The Messenger appeared, March 28, 1846, with J. E. Davis, jr., and Israel P. Chase as publishers. E. D. Davis took Mr. Chase's place in the firm on the fifteenth of August of the same year. They continued its publication till March 20, 1847, when they disposed of the establishment to William H. Gilmore and Israel P. Chase. Joseph Kidder, who had been its editor from the start, resigned his charge at the

21

close of the second volume, November 20, 1847. Mr. Chase was thereafter the principal editor till he retired from the paper, June 24, 1848. Subsequently Henry A. Gage bought Mr. Gilmore's interest, and, May 26, 1849, associated with him Francis F. Forsaith, who then became the editor. He withdrew January 25, 1851, and was succeeded by Benjamin F. Wallace, who had been for several years the principal of Piscataquog Village Academy. The Messenger had been started to occupy a place which was supposed to be left vacant by the Democrat and the American, the only two other papers then published in Manchester and both political. The Messenger was intended to be entirely free from political matter and to have an especial local value. When Mr. Wallace assumed the editorship, however, the Messenger threw off neutrality and assumed the position of a Whig journal. In 1852 it was sold to Abbott, Jenks & Company (Joseph C. Abbott, Edward A. Jenks, and Henry A. Gage), the owners of the American, and united with that paper.

The New Hampshire Temperance Banner, established in 1847 as the organ of the New Hampshire State Temperance Society, was issued monthly under the supervision of the executive board and published at the office of the Manchester Democrat. The late Moses A. Cartland of Weare was a part of the time its editor and a part of the time it was edited by members of the board. After three or four years it was removed to Concord and united with some other journal.

The Old Hero was a campaign paper issued in 1848 from the office of the Manchester American, in advocacy of the claims of Gen. Zachary Taylor for the presidency of the United States, in honor of whose military reputation it was named. It was continued but a few months.

September 9, 1848, the first number of the Manchester Telescope was issued by Haradon & Kieley (Willard N.

Haradon, John Kieley). It was devoted to news and amusement, was cheaply illustrated and had a limited circulation. After an existence of about two years its name was changed by Mr. Haradon, who had become its sole proprietor February 19, 1849, to that of Haradon's Weekly Spy. A subsequent change made it the Manchester Spy and under this title it was published till the beginning of 1852, when it was sold to the publishers of the Farmers' Monthly Visitor and incorporated with that paper.

The Merchants' Own Journal, in the main for advertising purposes merely, was begun in November, 1848, by Haradon & Storer (W. N. Haradon, F. D. Storer) and was issued for a short time.

About 1849 the late Dr. Thomas R. Crosby, then a practicing physician in Manchester, conceived the idea of publishing an agricultural paper in the city, and at length, having associated with himself James O. Adams as publisher, issued the first number of the Granite Farmer February 26, 1850. It was a weekly of eight pages, and, according to the announcement on its first page, was "published under the patronage of the New Hampshire State Agricultural Society." At the beginning of the fourth volume, in January, 1853, the Rev. A. G. Comings of Mason became associate editor, but he removed from the state about March, 1853, and the twelfth number was the last which bore his name. The paper was sold October 5, 1853, to the Hon. Chandler E. Potter and was united not long afterwards with the Farmers' Monthly Visitor.

The Manchester Daily Mirror was started as a morning paper Monday, October 28, 1850, by Joseph C. Emerson. With the seventh number appeared the name of F. A. Moore as that of the editor. He was succeeded as editor, December 16, 1850, by Edward N. Fuller. Monday, June 23, 1851, it was changed from a morning to an evening paper. Mr. Emerson began Saturday, February 22, 1851, under the name of the Dollar Weekly Mirror, a weekly paper, made up from the columns of the daily, of which also Mr. Fuller was the editor. In February, 1852, he retired from the editorship and his place was filled by John B. Clarke. He held the position till September 1, when Mr. Emerson, who had been engaged in the manufacture of fireworks, lost heavily by fire and became financially embarrassed. He struggled along till October 20, when he sold at auction the daily and weekly, which were bought by John B. Clarke, who has owned and edited them ever since. He bought in 1863 of S. D. Farnsworth the Daily and Weekly American, in which the Manchester Democrat had been swallowed up, and united the latter with the Dollar Weekly Mirror, and the former with the Daily Mirror, which has since been known as the Daily Mirror & American. In 1863 he bought of Francis B. Eaton the New Hampshire Journal of Agriculture, which had already absorbed the Granite Farmer and the Farmers' Monthly Visitor, and united it with the weekly under the name of the Dollar Weekly Mirror & New Hampshire Journal of Agriculture. July 8, 1865, its name was changed to that of Mirror & Farmer and under this it has since been published. The office of publication was in Patten's block on Elm street till the fire of February, 1856, then in Riddle's building on the corner of Hanover and Elm streets till October 1, 1863, and since then in its present location in Merchants' Exchange on the corner of Manchester and Elm streets.

January 24, 1851, the first number of the Union Democrat, a weekly paper in the interest of the Democratic party, was issued by William H. Gilmore & Company. June 18, 1851, the firm became Campbell & Gilmore (James M. Campbell, William H. Gilmore) and Mr. Campbell became the editor. August 15, 1855, Mr. Gilmore left and Mr. Campbell became the sole proprietor. May 28,

1861, Walter Harriman, afterwards governor of the state, was associated with Mr. Campbell and the paper was published as the Weekly Union by Campbell & Harriman till March 31, 1863, when Col. Thomas P. Pierce took Harriman's place, and the name of Union Democrat was again adopted. The Manchester Daily Union had been issued in 1856 as a campaign paper, but its first regular issue was dated Tuesday, March 31, 1863. January 1, 1864, the firm became James M. Campbell & Company, Charles Lamson being the junior partner. August 1, 1864, Alpheus A. Hanscom, who had been the editor and proprietor of the Maine Democrat at Saco, Me., from March 1, 1843, till May 15, 1864, bought Mr. Lamson's interest and the firm became Campbell & Hanscom, under which name it has ever since continued. September 1, 1872, George A. Hanscom, a brother of the junior partner and who had learned the printer's trade in his brother's office at Saco but had followed the sea for many years, and James L. Campbell, a son of the senior partner, were admitted as members of the firm. The Democrat was published in Patten's block on Elm street till the fire of February, 1856 and then in Riddle's building on the corner of Hanover and Elm streets and in Merchants' Exchange, corner of Manchester and Elm streets, till February, 1874, when it was issued from the building which the proprietors had then just completed on Manchester street.

The Farmers' Monthly Visitor, which had been published at Concord by Gov. Isaac Hill since 1838, was suspended in 1849 but revived in this city in 1852, when Rowell, Prescott & Company (Joseph M. Rowell, George P. Prescott, Chandler E. Potter) became its proprietors and Judge Potter its editor. It was published as an octavo of thirty-two pages and its first number was issued in Manchester, as the first number of its twelfth volume, in January, 1852. Judge Potter bought the Granite Farmer of Mr. Adams

October 5, 1853, and Dr. Crosby retired from the editorship two weeks later. In 1854 the latter was united with the Visitor and published in folio form under the name of the Granite Farmer & Visitor. Judge Potter, having bought out his partners, was then the sole proprietor and editor. About a year later Lewis H. Hildreth of Westford, Mass., a writer upon agriculture, came to Manchester and entered into negotiations in reference to a paper. As a result he and James O. Adams each bought a third of the Farmer & Visitor, Judge Potter retaining a third and Mr. Adams' name appearing as that of the editor. Hildreth, however, remained but a few months and about April, 1857, the paper was sold at auction to John C. Merriam & Company (Henry C. Adams), and it was issued, July 18, 1857, as a new paper under the name of the Granite State Farmer. Subsequently Merriam retired and Henry C. Adams owned it for a while and then sold it to S. A. Hurlburt, who was the sole proprietor and editor—James O. Adams then leaving the editor's chair—till the latter part of 1859, when Gilmore & Martin (William H. Gilmore, Warren Martin) bought the paper and issued it in folio form as the New Hampshire Journal of Agriculture. Zephaniah Breed and Moses A. Cartland, both of Weare, became the editors. In 1861 the paper was sold to Francis B. Eaton, who published it till January, 1863, when he sold it to John B. Clarke, who united it with the Dollar Weekly Mirror, of which he was then the owner, under the name of the Dollar Weekly Mirror & New Hampshire Journal of Agriculture.

The Crusader, a temperance paper published under the auspices of the New Hampshire State Temperance Society, was begun in Concord about 1850. In December, 1851, it was published simultaneously in Concord and Manchester and in February, 1852, was published altogether in this city. It was not long afterwards moved to Concord, united with the Phœnix of that city and afterwards absorbed by the New Hampshire Gazette at Portsmouth.

In 1853 Benjamin F. Stanton and William B. Burnham issued for a short time a small sheet devoted to phonography called the Junto Organ.

A paper called the Ladies' Enterprise was begun January 1, 1854, and published weekly for a time.

The "Know-Nothing" movement, which began in 1854, created a demand for an especial political organ, and in September of that year the Stars and Stripes was established as the medium of communication for that party and was published weekly. Marquis D. L. Stevens was its publisher and Jonathan Tenney, then principal of the high school and now deputy state superintendent of public instruction for New York, was its editor. At the end of a year Edwin Bartholomew became its editor and proprietor and Benjamin F. Wallace, principal of the Piscataquog academy, had some connection with it. It was removed not long afterwards to Laconia and absorbed in the Winnipesaukee Gazette.

The New Hampshire Journal of Medicine, a monthly octavo of thirty-two pages, was first issued at Concord in August, 1850, with E. H. Parker, M. D., as editor. In October, 1852, Dr. George H. Hubbard of this city was associated with Dr. Parker, and in October, 1853, became the sole editor. It was removed to Manchester in July, 1856, and continued till December, 1859, when it was suspended, at the close of the eighth volume.

The New Hampshire Journal of Education was a monthly publication, established in January, 1857, as the organ of the New Hampshire State Teachers' Association. Edwin Bartholomew was the publisher and the Rev. William L. Gage, now settled in Hartford, Conn., the chief editor. Among the associate editors were Jonathan Tenney, Benjamin F. Wallace and Simeon D. Farnsworth of this city.

At the close of its first volume it was removed to Concord and there continued till the end of the year 1862, when it was suspended. While it was published there the Rev. Henry E. Sawyer, now of Middletown, Conn., and a brother of Joseph B. Sawyer of this city, was the chief editor and John P. Newell and John W. Ray of this city were among his associates in the work.

The Literary Visitor, a monthly paper, was begun January 1, 1859, as the organ of the Excelsior Literary Association by George W. Batchelder and Martin A. Haynes, the latter of whom is now editor and proprietor of the Lake Village Times. It had a small circulation and only eight numbers appeared.

The True Republican was a weekly paper which was started February 4, 1859, by Benjamin F. Stanton, now the editor and proprietor of the Bradford, Vt., Opinion. With him were afterwards associated Hector Canfield, now a clergyman of North Attleboro', Mass., and Orren C. Moore, now one of the editors and proprietors of the Nashua Telegraph. The paper was continued about a year under the titles of True Republican, City Messenger & Republican and Manchester Republican.

Moore's Musical Record, a "magazine of musical art, science, literature and news," John W. Moore, editor, was begun in January, 1857, and published monthly by John W. Moore & Company for two years. In January, 1869, he, Samuel C. Merrill, Charles Clough and Sylvester C. Gould began the publication of the Manchester Daily News, but his partners retired one by one and he was left alone the first of April. He continued the News till May 6 and then suspended it till September, when he published nineteen numbers and then discontinued it finally. He had resumed in June the publication of the Musical Record but suspended it in January, 1870.

La Voix du Peuple, a weekly paper issued in the inter-

A. P. Olzendam

ests of the French population in Manchester, was begun February 25, 1869, and was continued through seventeen numbers. A. L. Tremblay & Company were its proprietors and editors.

The Labor Journal was started March 24, 1870, by Daniel S. Holt, now of Washington N. H., professedly in the interests of the laboring classes. It was suspended after thirteen numbers.

The Public Forum was a weekly paper which was started September 30, 1871, as a Democratic journal by George J. Foster & Company, Joshua L. Foster being its editor. After the publication of thirteen numbers it was removed to Dover, its name changed to that of Foster's Democrat and a new volume begun. It is still published there.

The New Hampshire Journal of Music was begun January 1, 1872, by Imri S. Whitney, and is published monthly. John W. Moore was its editor till the close of 1874.

The Saturday Night Dispatch was begun Saturday, January 24, 1874, by Merritt S. Hunt, who had been connected with papers in Pittsburgh and Titusville, Pa., and has been published weekly since. James O. Adams was associated with Mr. Hunt as editor and proprietor from September 1 to December 1, 1874, since when the paper has been owned and edited by Hunt & Everett, Henry H. Everett being the junior partner.

The New Hampshire Sunday Globe was issued for the first time Sunday morning, February 7, 1875, by Rollins & Kingdon (Ai Rollins, S. S. Kingdon) and has been published weekly since. It is the only Sunday paper in the state.

MANCHESTER IN THE REBELLION.

THE War of the Rebellion is so fresh in the minds of the people of to-day that they do not need to be reminded that it was begun by the attack on Fort Sumter April 12, 1861. Abraham Lincoln, then President of the United States, issued on the fifteenth of that month a call for seventy-five thousand volunteers to enlist for three months, and on the next day Ichabod Goodwin, then governor of the state, issued a proclamation to Joseph C. Abbott, the adjutant-general, ordering him to enlist from the enrolled militia one regiment of volunteers to fill the quota of the state, which was seven hundred and eighty men. The news of the bombardment of Sumter was announced in Manchester early in the morning of the thirteenth and intense excitement was at once aroused. When the call for troops came, John L. Kelly was among the first to offer his services as a recruiting officer and he was appointed and assigned to Manchester and vicinity and opened an office in the city hall April 18. It was at once thronged with men anxious to enlist, and, as fast as the papers could be made out, they were enrolled.

In the meantime the Manchester Mechanics' Phalanx, the Abbott Guard and the Union Guards all local military organizations, held enthusiastic meetings and voted to tender their services to the government. The "military exempts," or men too old to be required by law for military duty, also held several meetings and pledged their aid, and the young men of the city organized for drill and held themselves ready for future calls. The physicians offered their services free to the families of all who would enlist, the banks volunteered loans to the state and many employers gave furloughs to those who left them for the field, promising to care for their families while they were gone and to give them work when they returned. In fact, words convey but a faint idea of the feeling which prevailed. The volunteer was the hero of the hour and nothing was too much to do for him. The papers were full of presentations to the departing troops and the women joined in furnishing them with all the comforts they could carry. After the first battles had occurred and the need of aid for the wounded had thus arisen, the women of the city associated to send supplies and continued this work all through the war.

Fifty-six men were enlisted by Captain Kelly the first day and in seven days the roll contained the names of one hundred and thirty-one recruits. His men went to Concord April 27 and joined the First regiment, which was encamped there. April 22 the Abbott Guard, seventy-seven men, were enlisted in a body by the Hon. Frederick Smyth, who had been appointed a recruiting officer, and two days later they went to Concord and were afterwards mustered into the Second regiment. April 25 the Mechanics' Phalanx was enlisted by Capt. John N. Bruce and went into camp at Portsmouth May 7. Before they left Manchester the members were presented with revolvers by Mayor D. A. Bunton, in accordance with a vote of the city government. Thus, in seven days after the first recruiting office was opened in this city, Manchester had four companies ready for the field, Capt. Kelly's men having been divided into two companies.

The first public meeting had already been held, April 17, by the military exempts. Speeches were made by Retyre Mitchell, who presided, Dustin Marshall, Isaac Riddle, the Hon. Theodore T. Abbot, Justin Spear and the Hon. Hiram Brown. The next day the young men held a large and enthusiastic meeting at which Thomas P. Pierce, then postmaster, presided. At this meeting George C. Gilmore, Edwin P. Richardson, Stephen G. Clarke, the Hon. Edward W. Harrington, Thomas Baxter, R. N. Batchelder, Andrew C. Wallace and James M. Varney were appointed a committee to form military companies to be ready in case of need.

The women of the city had been from the first active in providing the volunteers with articles which were not furnished by the government, and nearly every regiment went into camp carrying with them substantial tokens of the interest the citizens had in their welfare. April 29 the ladies of the several religious societies held a union levee for the benefit of the volunteers. Samuel Webber presided and patriotic speeches were made by the Hon. Daniel Clark, the Hon. George W. Morrison and others. It was voted at this meeting to request the President to continue in office Thomas P. Pierce, the postmaster of the city, who at the first call for troops had offered his services to the governor of Massachusetts and had joined the Fourth regiment of that state, of which he was lieutenant-colonel.

The first official action of the city government respecting the war was taken April 17, when a resolution was passed which instructed the mayor to cause flags to be put upon the city hall and on the liberty-pole on Merrimack square, "to be kept there until they were recognized as the national emblem all over the country." May 21 the "relief committee" of the city government voted a dollar and a half a week to the wife of each volunteer and a dollar a week to each child.

Baldwin's Cornet Band went into camp as the band of the First regiment May 15. Its members were supplied with money to buy revolvers and blankets by the city government. The Rifle Rangers, a company enlisted by James W. Carr, went into camp at Portsmouth May 27.

August 2 the mayor called a meeting of all persons who were in favor of sustaining the government and putting down the rebellion, and a large assembly answered the summons. Speeches were made by the Hon. Walter Harriman, the Hon. William C. Clarke, Simeon D. Farnsworth, the Hon. Frederick Smyth, the Hon. Samuel Upton, Michael T. Donohoe and others, and resolutions were adopted which pledged Manchester's last man and last dollar to the cause.

The First regiment, composed of three months' men, returned from the field August 5, and five days later its members who belonged in this city were given a grand welcome home.

August 8, the Irish volunteers recruited by Capt. Donohoe went into camp at Concord as a part of the Third regiment; August 13, the second company of the Abbott Guard, enlisted by Capt. Rufus F. Clark, left this city to form a part of the same regiment; and August 20, the Amoskeag Rifles, under Capt. Robert C. Dow, also went to Concord to join the Third.

The Fourth regiment went into camp on the trotting-park at the upper end of Elm street, naming their camp "Camp Sullivan." The Stark Guards, under Capt. J. R. Bagley, went first to Concord, but, as the Third regiment was already full, they were recalled to Manchester August 27 and joined the Fourth at Camp Sullivan. The regiment started for the field September 27. Its band was composed for the most part of Manchester men and its leader was Walter Dignam.

It had been announced by the middle of August that a battery would be accepted and one was recruited by Capt. Samuel Webber, then manager at the Print-Works, Lieutenant Frederick M. Edgell and Lieutenant Edwin H. Hobbs. It contained one hundred and fifty-four men, mostly from this city, who were mustered in September 26, under Capt. George A. Gerrish. They left for the seat of war October 29, marching to Nashua and there taking the cars.

The Seventh regiment was raised by Gen. Joseph C. Abbott, was encamped at Camp Hale upon the trotting-park and left for the war January 14, 1862. The Eighth regiment, under Col. Hawkes Fearing, jr., was mustered in December 23, 1861, and encamped on the trotting-park, naming its camp "Camp Currier" in honor of the Hon. Moody Currier of Manchester, then a member of Gov. Berry's council. The Eighth went from here to Fort Independence in Boston Harbor January 25, 1862, sailing from there in two detachments February 16. A company of cavalry was raised in Manchester in the fall of 1861 by Dr. David B. Nelson.

In June, 1862, during an adjustment of the sums due from the state to the different cities and towns for aid furnished to the families of volunteers, it was ascertained that up to that time Manchester had furnished for the war over seventeen hundred men or more than one-fifth of all who had gone from the state.

The recruiting offices were now closed and their furniture sold, but in July, 1862, an imperative call for more men re-opened them and the city contributed some men to the Ninth regiment, then already in process of formation. They were mustered in at Concord and left that city for the field August 25, 1862.

The efforts of the citizens under the new call were, however, mainly directed towards filling the Tenth or Irish regiment, which was considered peculiarly a Manchester regiment. A mass meeting in its aid was held on the evening of July 11 at Smyth's Hall, when eloquent addresses were made by Joseph Kidder, who presided, the Hon. George W. Morrison, the Hon. David Cross, the Hon. William C. Clarke, Col. Bradbury P. Cilley, Col. John B. Clarke, Michael Lyons, Lieut-Col. John Coughlin and Major Jesse F. Angell. The city government passed a resolution July 18, offering a bounty of fifty dollars to each volunteer and the city furnished the greater part of six companies for the Tenth. Its camp was on the trotting-park and was called " Camp Pillsbury " in honor of the Hon. Oliver Pillsbury of Concord, a member of Gov. Berry's council. The regiment was mustered in September 5 and left for the field September 22. It was put under command of Col. Michael T. Donohoe, then a captain in the Third regiment which was stationed in South Carolina.

An immense fair which continued three days was held May 14, 15 and 16, 1863, in aid of the Sanitary Commission, which was employed in the relief of the soldiers at the front, and a little over four thousand dollars was raised.

The quota of Manchester under the call of August 4, 1862, for three hundred thousand men was four hundred and twenty. One hundred and fifty beyond its previous quota were already in the field and thus only two hundred and seventy were left to be raised. In this state of affairs the wards formed organizations and raised funds to procure substitutes, prominent citizens who were exempt from duty hired men to fill the quota and at length the city government voted, October 4, 1863, to pay every man who was drafted three hundred, dollars which he might use to procure a substitute or retain as a bounty if he was willing to enlist. So that when the draft took place, October 6, 1863, very few of the drafted went to the field.

March 29, 1864, the city offered a bounty of one hundred and fifty dollars to all veterans who re-enlisted, and many then in the field re-entered the service when their terms expired. The Manchester National Guards, under

Nathan Parker.

Capt. James O. Chandler, were mustered into service May 9, 1864, for a period of sixty days and ordered to service at Fort Constitution in Portsmouth harbor. They were mustered out July 27. The Martin Guards, under Capt. George C. Houghton, were mustered into service July 25, 1864, for ninety days and sent to Fort Constitution. When their term of service expired, they re-enlisted and became the tenth company of the First regiment of heavy artillery. In August, 1864, a company of heavy artillery was raised here by Capt. James O. Chandler. Manchester was also represented in all the military organizations which formed part of New Hampshire's quota, with the exception of the Thirteenth and Seventeenth regiments.

Among the inevitable results of the war was great suffering among the sick and wounded near the front, and in the last years of the struggle the states established hospitals of their own and brought to them the sick and wounded who belonged to their regiments. In accordance with this plan one was established in Manchester in the fall of 1864. It was called the Webster United States General Hospital, and Dr. Alexander T. Watson of New York was the surgeon in charge. Among his assistants were Dr. Richard J. P. Goodwin and the late Dr. William W. Brown, both of Manchester, and Dr. William A. Webster, formerly of this city. Mrs. Eliza P. Stone and Mrs. M. Jennie Buncher, both of this city, were appointed to have charge of the cooking and diet, receiving commissions from the United States October 25, 1864, and taking up their residence at the hospital. They were assisted by the late Mrs. Hannah G. Moore, of this city, Miss Elizabeth J. Dudley, now of Jamaica Plain, Mass., Miss Mary J. Knowles, now of Nashua. Hospital buildings were built upon the trotting-park, some of which still remain, which would accommodate six hunded patients and they were generally full. The Hon. Alpheus Gay, now mayor of the city, and John C. Young built them on contract for thirty-nine thousand five hundred dollars. They were opened for the reception of patients November 16, 1864, and closed in September, 1865. During that time there were about fifteen hundred patients in all, of whom thirteen died at the hospital. Religious services were held there Sundays and it was frequently visited by the citizens, who took a great deal of interest in it.

The war came to an end in 1865 and the regiments gradually came back from the field. The Tenth, Twelfth and Thirteenth were received together June 27 at Manchester. They were escorted in procession through the streets and a collation was furnished them in a grove in the rear of the city hall. Speeches of congratulation were made by Col. Thomas J. Whipple, the Hon. Daniel Clark, Gen. Michael T. Donohoe, Gen. Aaron F. Stevens and others. The Fourth did not come home till August 30, when it met a most enthusiastic reception at Smyth's hall, being welcomed in behalf of the city by the Hon. Frederick Smyth, then governor of the state, the Hon. Daniel Clark and others.

After the war there was a commission appointed by the state to compile a roll of all the men who enlisted in New Hampshire and to credit them to the cities and towns which could prove that they enlisted as part of their quota. The list which follows, derived from that source and from others, gives the names of all who could be proved to have enlisted from Manchester, and of a few others taken from the original muster-rolls. It is followed by a list of those who were field, staff or line officers when they were mustered out.

THE MANCHESTER SOLDIERS.

FIRST REGIMENT.

Richard N. Batchelder, Quartermaster; Francis H. Pike, Fife-Major.

COMPANY C.

John L. Kelly, Martin V. B. Richardson, Charles O. Jennison, Michael O'Flynn, William Mayne, Robert Loyd, Patrick Bohan, Charles J. Andrews, Charles H. Allen, James W. Atherton, Abraham Brown, Frank Burr, Jerome Blaisdell, William H. H. Black, Henry Bourrell, Charles A. Cressey, Haskell P. Coffin, Francis Cahill, Charles Conner, Thomas F. Cary, Francis H. Conner, John W. Clark, George H. Champlin, Augustus B. Caswell, Charles H. Demerrett, Edward O. Dodge, John M. Evans, Page Gould, John Gardner, John Goff, Daniel Gile, Marshall Hutchins, Frank B. Hackett, William W. Haselton, Joseph Haselton, Sumner A. Hodgkins, Dennis Hynes, Daniel Kidder, Frank L. Kendall, John L. Lear, William Major, Charles Mace, jr., Alden E. Metcalf, Charles H. Morrison, Frederick G. Manning, Michael Marden, William F. Ordway, Samuel W. Pierce, Robert Richards, Albert E. Rogers, George F. Rennett, James Rooney, George W. Ringlar, David W. Rollins, Edmund T. Reynolds, Noble Squares, Charles H. Sanborn, Addison W. Tobie, George Weaver, George W. Wells, Thomas Welch, Robert McAnalsey, Peter O'Brien, Edwin F. Baldwin.

COMPANY H.

William H. D. Cochrane, Christian Spicer, Ernest Weinhold.

COMPANY K.

Hollis O. Dudley.

SECOND REGIMENT.

Thomas P. Pierce, Colonel; Samuel G. Langley, Adjutant; Sylvanus Bunton, Surgeon.

COMPANY A.

Charles D. Tuttle, John C. Benarchad, Albert Lovett, Patrick McGrath, Alexander Bellic, John W. Riley, Julius A. Alexander, Thomas Adams, John Coleman.

COMPANY B.

George Nelson, Thomas Kenney, Charles Donnolly, George Coyle, Albert Kaison, George Bullen, John Cammel, Michael Colligan.

COMPANY C.

Michael Mullins, John Smith, David Brown, James H. Platt, Richard A. Lawrence, Benj. F. Chase, Alvin L. Wiggin, Frank O. Robinson, Alfred W. Berham, Lemuel M. Cox, Abner H. Clement, David W. Colburn, Frederick R. Allen, John A. Barker, Charles W. Brown, William Calef, Henry F. Carey, John H. Cole, Harvey M. Colby, Andrew M. Connel, George W. Craig, Hazen Davis, jr., John Davis, Frederick W. Dearborn, Thurlow A. Emerson, Henry H. Everett, Bernard J. Farley, William Fitzgerald, Barnett E. Fowler, Charles L. French, George R. Hanson, Cornelius Hastings, William M. Holmes, John Adams, William Brown, Daniel Duffee, George Dexter, James Griffin, George Gilbert, James Howard, Thomas Jones, William Jones, William Kelley, Thomas Lockhart, Peter Lawson, Lewis Severence, Daniel Murry, John Newton, James Peaks, William Davis, Lewis Fistte, Charles A. McLauflin, Harvey Hill, William Hudson, James J. Lord, John A. Mason, Elijah Morse, Charles McGlaughlin, George F. Perry, George Pickup, Timothy H. Pike, Jonathan C. Quimby, John E. Richards, George H. Sargent, Alfred J. Sanborn, William Smith, John M. Stearns, Alvin R. Smith, Horatio N. Stevens, Laroy D. Sherburne, Charles L. Tabor, William H. Tilton, George B. Tuttle, Franklin R. Tucker, Franklin F. Wetherbee.

COMPANY D.

James Dalton, William Flynn, George Schultz, Thomas Smith, John Thompson, Arthur McGinniss, Earnest Waltham, Samuel Woods, John McDonald, John Gibson, James Johnson, William Conner, John Lane.

COMPANY E.

John Gartley, James Tracey, John Miller, Thomas Riley, Terrence Riley, Henry Schwenke, Edward Smith, John Costelle.

COMPANY F.

Joseph Lemmons, John Jarchan, Henry Benton, Henry Brank, James Cunningham, John Donnolly, George McCormick, Charles Mason.

COMPANY G.

Andrew Quinn, William Brown, William S. Bennett, Andrew Christensen, Michael Corcoran, Charles Elliott, William H. French, Custer Jackson, John Peters, William Steele, Charles Smith, John Travis.

COMPANY H.

Thomas Beatry, George P. Williams, Frank A. Eastman, Abial A. Hannaford, Lucius Farmer, Henry J. Flanders, Nathaniel F. Swett, Joseph Tallen.

COMPANY I.

David M. Perkins, Rodney A. Manning, Thorndike P. Heath, William H. Griffin, Hazen B. Martin, Edward L. Bailey, Joseph A. Hubbard, Oscar A. Moar, Albion Simonds, Albert E. Sholes, Arthur E. Buckminster, Perkins C. Lane, Charles Vickery, Charles H. Smiley, Stephen J. Smiley, Samuel T. Newell, Daniel W. Newell, William H. Appleton, Lyman M. Aldrich, James G. Burns, Frank M. Boutelle, Nicholas M. Biglin, James R. Carr, John S. Calley, Leonard B. Corliss, Jesse E. Dewey, George B. Damon, Lyman A. Dickey, Moses L. Eastman, Orrin S. Gardner, Joseph H. Gleason, Norman E. Gunnison, Eugene G. Hazewell, Martin A. Haynes, Charles T. Hardy, Luther P. Hubbard, James M. House, Moses A. Hunkins, Edgar D. Kenaston, George F. Lawrence, John E. Ogden, Samuel H. Oliver, Charles F. Parrott, Henry M. Pillsbury, Solon F. Porter, Albert B. Robinson, Levi H. Sleeper, jr., Josiah S. Swain, William W. Wood, Charles B. Wright.

COMPANY K.

Benjamin F. Ashton, Charles G. Sargent, James Curley.

COMPANY UNKNOWN.

Samuel Kaskie, Charles Wing, John Williams, William G. Stark, James Donnolly.

THIRD REGIMENT.

Alvin H. Libby, Adjutant; Henry Hill, Chaplain; Harrison B. Wing, Principal Musician.

COMPANY A.

Rufus F. Clark, John R. Hynes, Ruthven W. Houghton, Frank L. Morrill, Charles A. White, Roger W. Woodbury, Thomas Johnson, John N. Chase, Amos D. Baker, Thomas T. Moore, George E. Johnson, Richard T. Holland, Samuel George, John W. Evans, John M. Evans, William Hammet, James Sullivan, George J. Woodman, Albert G. Dane, George H. Webster, Eli E. Bowman, Samuel D. Brelsfords, David Bryant, James G. Fernald, Charles O. Ferson, Edward Shehan, John F. Stokes, William E. Hamnett, William L. Bennett, Ira J. Adams, Haskell W. Banfill, Charles N. Buckman, George W. Bridgeham, William O. D. Brown, Harrison S. Cass, Robert A. Challis, Albert N. Clough, Daniel F. Colby, Harrison J. Copp, Gideon Coty, H. J. Cummings, Charles O. R. Davis, Joseph Dupray, Charles O. Emery, Charles O. Ferson, W. W. Flanders, John Flood, George T. Fogg, Thomas F. Gay, Albert George, Charles O. Gibson, Charles Gilbert, Walter A. Green, Cyrus Gorman, John W. Goodwin, Thomas Hanson, Henry T. Hatch, John Houseman, William S. Hodgman, Andrew J. Holmes, William H. Huntress, William M. Karney, George H. Lawrence, Luke Leaf, George W. Lee, Samuel H. Little, Nathaniel Marshall, James McEwen, David H. Newton, Stephen W. Niles, Austin E. Perry,

James D. Proudman, William H. Ramsey, John H. Sanders, George H. Webster, Hiram C. Squires, Collins P. Tebbetts, Leander White, John R. Whitten, William H. Carter, George S. Thomas, Edward Reynolds, Alpheus Chickering.

COMPANY C.

John Kerwin, Michael J. Connelly, Thomas Casey, Hugh Duffey, Matthew Byrns, John Casey, John McClemens, John Crosbie, Eugene Cadorath, John Eagan, Timothy Healey, Robert O'Connell, Michael E. A. Galvin, Thomas McEnry, Michael T. Donohoe, Robert H. Allen, Walter Cody, Joseph J. Donohoe, James Wilson, John Curran, Byron Costello, Patrick Larkin, John McIntire, Daniel Mahoney, David Moore, Peter Pelkey, James Quinlan, James Smith, Lewis Potter, Charles Hall, Stephen Welsh, Dustin Marshall, William Allen, Peter Smith, Joseph Potter, Edwin O'Brien, Francis Sheridan, William Sprague, Edmund Hackett, George Allen, William Baker, John Barrett, John Booth, George H. Briggs, David Bryant, Bernard Farry, James Henderson, Robert P. Murry, George A. Woodburn, Samuel Whittaker, James Welch.

COMPANY D.

William H. Maxwell.

COMPANY F.

George Stearns, James B. F. Towns.

COMPANY G.

Charles Gilbert.

COMPANY H.

Charles F. French, Henry B. Eastman, Henry C. Page, Charles Harvey, Jacob Boutells, Albert Blood, Charles F. Burnham, John S. Cole, Edward Cotter, John B. Davis, William H. Foster, Frank Ferren, William Gracy, David Gracy, Levi Gardner, Charles E. Harris, William H. Hill, Franklin Halladay, William E. Handy, Isaac H. Kingsbury, Robert C. Dow, Henry F. Hopkins, Morris Hennessy, Robert Vincent, Walter J. Richards, Eben R. Adams, David A. Page, Julius Griggs, Lanson Blake, Daniel N. Atwood, Americus Briggs, Albert H. Lockwood, James O'Neil, Albert H. Stevens, Donald Smith, William Todd, James Walsh, George Bailey, John Crowson, Peter Quigley, William H. Knox, William H. Knowlton, Daniel Luce, Alexander Le Mudge, Alden E. Metcalf, Daniel S. Morrison, Charles Morgan, Jerome B. McQueston, George Murdough, Timothy Parker, Walter J. Richard, James C. Roach, Albert H. Stevens, Volney F. Simmons, Joseph H. Wallace, Anson T. Williams, Patrick Woods, Patrick Welch.

COMPANY I.

William Johnson, David Earles, William G. Nichols.

COMPANY K.

Edwin Brackett, James H. A. A. Stead, John Whitney, Francis Boynton, Thomas Robinson, Andrew McNeil, Thomas Thomason, Varnum H. Hill, Corwin G. Parker.

FOURTH REGIMENT.

John L. Kelly, Quartermaster; Benjamin F. Fogg, Commissary Sergeant.

BAND.

Walter Dignam, Francis H. Pike, Henry Murphy, Lemuel H. James, John O'Brien, Alonzo Buntin, Frederick T. Page, Samuel A. Porter, John Harrington, William Dignam, Eugene K. Foss, H. Augustus Simonds, Eliphalet Dustin, John Googin, Orrin N. B. Stokes, Henry Lewis, James A. Farnham, Reinhold T. Trumblum.

COMPANY A.

Patrick McGee, Augustus Steuger.

COMPANY B.

Martin J. Staunton, Martin V. B. Richardson.

COMPANY C.

Jackson Dustin, Joseph L. C. Miller, Perley B. Rand, George D. Stiles, George S. Tuck, William O. Woodbridge, George M. Kidder, Cornelius E. Parker, Robert A. Seaver, Daniel W. Rollins, Eben H. Nutting, Alanson W. Barney, William G. Burke, Daniel W. Knox, John Lovett, Byron Putnam, William E. Robinson, Chauncey Smith.

COMPANY D.

Charles O. Jennison.

COMPANY E.

Frank B. Hutchinson, Cyrus H. Hubbard, Charles H. Reed, Stephen Kendrick, Charles Whiting, Edward O. Hill, Thomas L. Newell, Francis W. Parker, Andrew J. Edgerly, John H. Baker, Alvard E. Wilson, Charles M. Whiting, Robert Hume, Edwin Weathersfield, Lyman Wyman, Charles Brackett, John Malone, John L. Mack, James M. Dickey, John Lynch, Anson E. Hall, Frank A. Allen, Edson Wyman, Horace G. Heath, Woodbury Wyman, John G. Hutchinson, Horatio N. Bickford, George F. Davis, Charles H. Williams, George W. Williams, Frank Matthews, Oscar Perkins, Orrin Corrigan, William H. Webster, Charles A. Newton, Hermann Greager, Thomas S. Burns, Emory Wyman, Michael Curdy, Carleton C. Richardson, William K. Cobb, Henry C. Osgood, John P. Smith, Charles A. Newton, John G. Hutchinson,

Charles H. Allen, William H. H. Allen, Francis A. Allen, Rufus Bailey, William Bonner, James M. Cummings, Patrick Castless, Isaac K. Colby, Charles A. Cressey, Owen Corigen, Joseph P. Cressey, Amos Cressey, George E. Dunell, James M. Dickey, jr., Daniel Emery, John Fallon, Alpheus D. Flag, William Gunneil, James F. Griffin, George H. Harris, William Hagerty, John Hobert, John Hackett, William B. Hart, Charles H. Lee, John Lynch, Charles C. Livingston, Lewis S. Merrill, James Mockler, Harlan E. Page, Levi Putnam, Thomas P. Philbrook, Benjamin F. Quimby, Daniel S. Russell, Henry K. Richardson, George W. Robinson, Larkin Sargent, John Stewart, Joseph T. Snow, Benjamin Spaulding.

COMPANY F.

William Haskell, Charles L. Brown, James Murphy.

COMPANY G.

Peter O'Brien, Lyford Hunt, Michael Shaunnessey, Dennis Hines, William H. Brooks, James M. Fogg, John Gardner, John E. Gerry, Charles C. Marsh, John Mullen, Michael Madden, Dana Runels, Dennis Walsh, William Beede, Edward Fields, Thomas J. Galvin, Patrick Conway, Amos W. Brown, Morris Foley, Dennis Gile, Zebina Annis, John Smith, Stephen C. Chapman, Frank Buss, Elbridge Geary, Patrick Dowd, Richard Smith, Charles P. Gleason, Peter O'Brien, Jerome Blaisdell, Francis Cahill, George A. Runnels, James M. Allen, Michael Brosnahan, William H. Brooks, James Merrow, Frederick D. Wood, Jeremiah Spelan, George H. Stewart, Charles T. Marden, Patrick Broderick, Terrence Trawley, William Gunston, Jeremiah Kelleher, John Pickett, Daniel Sullivan, William Sullivan, Cornelius Sullivan, Owen Tully, Lawrence Hern, Michael McHugh, John Smith, Richard Smith, John Frank, Peter Williamson, William H. Thompson, Patrick Broderick, Almos Cushing, Patrick Donnelly, James Donovan, Benjamin F. Fogg, Edward Field, James Ferry, Thomas Follen, Hiram B. Frost, Louis J. Gillis, James Garman, Dennis Hoynes, John Howard, Cornelius Kennedy, Dennis Keefe, James Larkin, John O. Mason, Charles C. Marsh, Patrick McDonald, James Melasky, Charles Marden, Frank Quinn, John Quinn, James Quinn, Patrick Quinn, William H. Reynolds, Michael Reardon, Timothy Reardon, Martin J. Staunton, Ashel Stoddard, Abraham S. Sanborn, John Shea, Dennis Tehan, Francis B. Willey, Dennis Walch, Clark E. Wilson, John Walch, John Murphy, Owen Tulley.

COMPANY H.

William Bonner, Orren Bush, Daniel H. May, Charles H. Bartlett, Samuel D. Marckrey, Bartholomew Maloney, Curtis R. Hartly.

COMPANY I.

George W. Stevens, Ephraim F. Brigham, Jonathan P. Nichols, John H. Powers, Herman Nichols, Benjamin K. Quimby, Benjamin H. Smith, Benjamin W. Smith, Enoch C. Stevens.

C. E. Potter

COMPANY K.

Job R. Giles, Harvey M. Weed, Charles L. Batchelder, Charles M. Currier, George W. Hackett, Israel N. Gale, Samuel B. Mace, James Wyman, Albert G. Ormsby, Clinton Farley, John F. Davis, George E. Fitch, John Barry, Benjamin Welch, Robert Clayton, George W. Stevens, Morris C. Wiggin, Samuel M. Dole, William H. Sanborn, Monroe Stevens, Joseph Wallace, Fernando C. Spaulding, Benjamin Hartshorn, William S. Barker, Joseph W. Bailey, Albert Cass, Edward Dolton, James Fern, Frank A. Garland, Charles A. Hackett, Frederick W. Lougee, Patrick O'Connell, Nelson J. Pierce, William H. Perkins, Horace J. Parker, William Shever Horatio H. Stevens, Henry D. Tompkins, George Wyman, Joshua B. Webster.

COMPANY UNKNOWN.

James H. German, William Hall, William A. Viltman.

FIFTH REGIMENT.

Samuel G. Langley, Lieutenant-Colonel.

COMPANY A.

Thomas Brown, John Evans, Charles Taylor, Alfred Brown.

COMPANY B.

George Stanton, Frank Howard, Thomas Knight, James O'Connell, Alex. Ross, William Hickman, John Myers.

COMPANY E.

Walter Summerfield, George E. Houghton, Oscar E. Carter, Cornelius H. Stone.

COMPANY F.

George B. Jenness.

COMPANY G.

Thomas Smith.

COMPANY H.

Warren Clark, Samuel T. Smith, James Stetson, George Bradley, Abram Cameron, Edward Choppenger.

COMPANY I.

George Nichols.

COMPANY UNKNOWN.

Walter Barnes, Hila Davis, Thomas Burns, Thomas B. Langley.

SIXTH REGIMENT.

COMPANY A.

Charles White, Charles B. Seavey.

COMPANY B.

Charles J. Gardner, Edward R. Barnett, Charles L. Davenport, Allison Towns.

COMPANY D.

John Fitch.

COMPANY K.

Ti Tison, Owen Kelley.

COMPANY UNKNOWN.

Lafayette Pettingill.

SEVENTH REGIMENT.

Joseph C. Abbott, Lieutenant-Colonel; William W. Brown, Surgeon; Henry Boynton, Assistant Surgeon.

COMPANY A.

Nicholas Gill, Granville P. Mason, Edward May, Virgil H. Cate, William C. Knowlton, James Williams, Oliver P. Hanscom, James Appleton, Benjamin F. Clark, John S. Merrill, Granville L. Fuller, Henry Burke, John Hobin, Charles H. Hall, William R. Thompson, Henry S. Benton.

COMPANY B.

Charles H. Dwinnels, Alfred B. Shemenway, Henry G. Lowell.

COMPANY C.

Robert Rochester, Charles F. G. Ames, Patrick Crosby.

COMPANY D.

Frank Moore, James Collins, John Allen.

COMPANY E.

Henry F. W. Little, George F. Robie, Michael Dean, Charles G. Pyee, Henry C. Dickey, Joseph Blanchett, Lewis Ash, George W. Putnam, Louis Seymour, Erlan V. Villingham, Charles H. Abbott.

COMPANY F.

Francis M. Kennison, Thomas Gilmore, John Harking.

COMPANY G.

Walter McDonald, Patrick O. Day, James Doherty.

COMPANY I.

James McCarty, Joseph Freschl, William Smith, Charles Caine, John O. Silver, Avery Bixby, John G. Markham, Wesley Glidden, Edwin B. Hodgeman, Silas L. Darrah, Charles A. Rowell, John Hatch, Calvin Brown, Adam Going, William A. Clifford, Frederick G. Merrill, Elwin Sturtevant, John Hennessey, Newell R. Bixby, Benjamin F. Clark.

COMPANY K.

Henry Osborn, James A. Hills, Henry T. Robbins.

COMPANY UNKNOWN.

Warren E. F. Brown, James Spinnington, William Hall.

EIGHTH REGIMENT.

Hawkes Fearing, jr., Colonel; Charles A. Putney, Quartermaster.

COMPANY A.

Robert Jones, James Murry, James S. Monroe.

COMPANY B.

Robert Keefe, Thomas Harrison, Frederick Lunt, Joseph S. Abbott, Charles Mills, James Wilson, John Lawton, Alonzo W. Flanders, William Waugh.

COMPANY C.

John Bradley, Joseph Collins, George Darling, William H. Ingraham, William Moore, Thomas Rhodes, John Shairbartt, Henry J. Warren, Daniel McCarty, John Collins, Edward M. Cobb, Gustavus Olson, Thomas Connelly, Cornelius Healy, jr., William J. Gannon, William Jones, Lawrence Foley, Edward Boyle, Michael Healey, Dennis O'Brien, Thomas Gannon, Jeremiah Driscoll, Thomas Fitzgerald, John Harrington, Daniel Haggerty, Patrick Kelley, John Smith, Thomas J. Fitzgerald, John Milan, Howard Judkins, Timothy Breen, Thomas Blake, Patrick Bohen, James H. Ballou, James Flynn, Francis Kelley, John Mullin, James T. Martin, Peter A. Shedd, Cornelius Crowley, John Collins, Michael Carney, Patrick Conner, John Delaney, Peter Doherty, James Daley, John Dowd, Patrick Driscoll, John Fowler, John Flemming, Morrice Fitzgerald, Thomas Flaherty, Thomas Flynn, Michael Fox, John Gibbons, Patrick Gleason, John Gallagher, Bernard Gallagher, Peter Gaffrey, Michael Griffin, John Hartnett, Patrick Harrington, John Howe, Patrick Henlihen, James McNally, Timothy McCarthy, Hugh McDermott, John McCarthy, Dennis Murphy, William McIntire, Daniel McIntire, Michael Murry, James Martin, Patrick Crosby, Daniel McMillen, John Murphy, James H. McDonald, Edward McCabe, Timothy Mahoney, Michael Martin, Hugh McIntire, Daniel McNally, William O'Donnell, Michael O'Neil, Timothy O'Conner, Felix O'Neil, James Palmer, Patrick Reagan, William Shea, Michael Savage, Martin Shea, Michael Sullivan, Michael Shea, Patrick Sullivan, jr., Patrick Sullivan, Joseph St. John, Matthew Taft, John Walsh, Stephen Tobin.

COMPANY D.

James Miles, Joseph J. Ladd, Thomas M. Leavitt, William E. Hubbard, Hiram D. Kidder, John H. Austin, Theodore L. Page, John C. Aldrich, Francis Gilbert, John R. Knox, Israel J. Langmaid, Barnabas B. Russell, Daniel Stevens, Josiah Limbury, Carl Miller, Charles Meger, Francis Davenport, Richard J. Holmes, Patrick Sullivan, Watson D. Bean, Charles Conway, John Gora, Rodolph Helfreich, Peter Miller, Daniel Wyman, William McCann, James Miles, Curtis Smith, Jacob F. Chandler, John B. Willard, John H. Austin, John C. Aldrich, George Hope, Joseph A. Spear, Samuel Weston, Thomas M. Leavitt.

COMPANY E.

James Higgins, Benjamin Schuyler, James Bruther, Charles J. Mace, Charles F. Smith, Walter Veasey, Benjamin F. Philbrick, Thomas H. Rogers, James F. W. Fletcher, William E. Brown, Nathan H. Pierce, Sylvester Clogston, John Dickey, Charles Kershann, George S. McIntire, Thomas A. Plummer, John H. Robinson.

COMPANY F.

Augustus C. Annis, Cyrus S. Burpee, Charles E. Rowe, George F. Dunbar, John F. P. Robie, George W. Allen, George G. Blake, Jerry W. Blye, Elisha T. Quimby, Charles P. Stevens, Edwin R. Stevens, Ralph Stone, Daniel Kirby, John Fogg, Enos Shehan, James Linery, John Smith, Augustus C. Ames, Henry H. Dunbar, John F. P. Raley, James Senter, John Burns.

COMPANY G.

Charles Cook, Joseph Crawford, Charles Davis, Edward B. Leonard, John Milan, Thomas G. Fitzgerald, Henry Thompson, Jehiel Thompson, Marcus M. Currier, Marcus M. Tuttle, Robert N. Colley, Albert A. M. L. Young.

COMPANY H.

George Dunham, Charles Meyers, F. H. Conner, James Sullivan, James Hazzard, Dennis Lane, John Winahan, Patrick Manning, John O'Brien, Michael Sullivan, James Lane, Charles Meier, John Willett, John Williams, Daniel Nyhan, Isaac Allen, Augustus Brull, John H. Campbell, Joseph Campbell, Thomas P. Crowley, John Crowley, Manuel Floris, Joseph Hamner, James Kelley, Patrick McLaughlin, William Palmer, Philip Ray, William Strong, William Towle, Solomon Vradenburgh, Tobias C. Brummer, John Connell, Frederick Gaitna, Paul Gray, Samuel Jones, Peter Miller, Harris Stanley, John White, John Williams, George M. Gilman.

COMPANY K.

Dennis F. G. Lyons, Cornelius Moriarty, Francis H. Conner, Timothy Rourke, John Kelleher, Robert Swiney, Michael O'Grady, Patrick Dowd, Jonathan Hartshorn, Bartholomew Moriarty, James Hazard, Ezra S. Bartlett, Patrick Brosnahan, Patrick Burke, Michael Broderick, Thomas Brennan, John Casey, Patrick Cuddy, Daniel Curran, Michael Corcoran, Maurice Devine, Thomas Doherty, Patrick Desmond, Samuel E. Emery, Thomas Fox, Michael Farmington, Michael Finncan, Charles H. Gorman, John Griffin, James Hennesey, John Harriman, Alfred J. Harriman, Sylvester Harriman, John Harwood, John Holland, Patrick Kearin, William Keafe, Thomas Kane, Michael Kenney, Timothy Kearin, John Lattimer, Joseph Leafe, James Edwards, George Husted, George Martin, Thomas Robinson, Rowell T. Libby, Charles Williams, William Gushe, James Hill, James McCormick, John Mullen, Patrick Looney, James Meagher, Thomas Murphy, Edward Mettimus, Michael Mahoney, Michael Mullen, Dennis McCarty, Patrick Manning, Eugene Moriarty, Patrick McKean, Cornelius Moriarty, Dennis McCarty, William D. O'Conner, Dennis O'Sullivan, John O'Brien, Charles O'Conner, Richard Phelan, John F. Pettingall, Patrick Regan, William Rourke, Elbridge Reed, William Smyth, James Sullivan, John Sullivan, Michael Sullivan, John Shea, 1st, John Shea, 2d, Patrick Shea, Philip Shugree, John Thornton.

COMPANY UNKNOWN.

George M. Gilman.

NINTH REGIMENT.

William A. Webster, Surgeon.

COMPANY A.

Ira S. Abbott, James Murry, Lewis Meyers, Joseph T. Morrill, Henry F. Jefts, William A. McGarnet, Lewis T. Mitchell, Nathaniel Webster, Drew A. Sanborn, George W. Randall.

COMPANY B.

Warren H. Edmunds, Joseph H. Wallace, Joseph E. Hartshorn, Jeremiah Carroll, Lorenzo B. Gould, Henry N. Howe, Arthur W. Caswell, James T. Prescott, Mathew P. Tennant, Henry N. Willey, Frento T. Eastman, James H. Shanley, William N. Harnden.

COMPANY C.

William Welpley.

COMPANY D.

John E. Mason, George G. Armstrong.

COMPANY E.

Henry O. Sargent, Cyrus B. Norris, Asa Brown, Amos S. Bean, William C. Flanders, John B. Hoit, F. B. Hackett, Joseph E. Provencher, Enoch O. Shepherd.

COMPANY F.

Charles P. Welsh, James Robston, James M. Lathe, William A. Canfield, Hiram S. Lathe, Oliver Buckminster, Charles A. Cummings, Charles A. Carlton, Freeman L. Lathe, Sylvester J. Hill, William P. Mason, Augustine M. Westcott.

COMPANY G.

John Antles, Henry Edwards, John Smith.

COMPANY H.

Mans L. Chase.

COMPANY I.

Jacob Krusa.

COMPANY K.

James Gordon.

COMPANY UNKNOWN.

Alonzo L. Day.

TENTH REGIMENT.

Michael T. Donohoe, Colonel; John Coughlin, Lieutenant-Colonel; Jesse F. Angell, Major.

COMPANY A.

Ichabod S. Bartlett, Andrew W. Doe, John B. Sargent, Hiram S. Barnes, Alfred G. Simons, William H. Allen, Orrin A. Clough, James B. T. Baker, Warren A. Burrell, Frazer A. Wasley, Charles B. Chapman, Isaac Quint, Daniel Atwood, Charles W. Atwood, Miles Aldrich, Joseph W. Batchelder, Warren Batchelder, Joseph Bailey, Henry A. Bailey, Daniel S. Butler, Hiram H. Currier, Hiram O. Chase, John C. Crowley, Alfred A. Clough, John A. Cochrane, George W. Conner, George A. Clark, Ira P. Emery, Nelson C. Fish, Daniel S. Gilman, Elbridge G. Gammon, Justin Hutchinson, James H. Harris, George H. Hall, Dexter L. Huntoon, Horace Holcomb, James S. Hutchinson, Henry Hartley, Ebenezer A. Johnson, Edwin R. Jones, Morseley W. Kendricks, Charles L. Morrison, George W. Newell, John Pondon, Zara Sawyer, Septimus Starks, Daniel F. Stark, Henry M. Sanborn, Andrew J. Wentworth, Alfred Wheeler, John C. Worster, Charles C. Webster, Benjamin F. Knowlton, Tristram Cilley, Royal Cheeley, Charles W. Smith, Michael Honberry, William K. Stevens, Albrum P. Colby, Charles C. Balch, Charles Bonnor, Wilson A. Bartlett, Stillman P. Cannon, George Carlton, John Crosby, Jeremiah Connor, Israel W. Chase, Joseph Demarse, Jeremiah C. Allen, Frank Hutchinson, Thomas Trumbull, William A. Barrett.

COMPANY C.

Michael Doran, John W. Davis, Charles E. Strain, William Doran, Orrin F. Emerson, Henry Esmerie, Patrick F. Fox, George W. Graves, William W. Hazelton, William W. Hersey, William Hulm, Samuel L. Mitchell, William O. Heath, David Kisby, George B. Lewis, Charles H. Mayhew, Joseph O. Melie, Delano Prescott, Joseph Perkins, David A. Quimby, David L. Ridley, Edwin O. Smith, Patrick Shegree, Charles E. Sargent, Owen Sullivan, Martin Toole, Barnard Untret, William W. White, Henry Walley, Henry O. Merrill, Albert F. Nelson, Hanson Tippett, William F. Ordway, John Murphy, Marshall Hutchins, Stillman B. Hazelton, Joseph R. Hazelton, Charles Johnson, Jr., Charles H. Leonard, Cornelius W. Strain.

COMPANY D.

A. O. Ambody, Daniel B. Abbott, Andrew Dunn, Michael Dalton, Francis Dubin, Charles W. Foss, Rufus B. Hall, Edward Loverly, John A. Mason, George W. Madden, Joseph C. Osgood, Joseph Peno, Zelotus L. Place, Henry L. Quimby, Moses E. Quimby, Thomas B. Quimby, M. E. Raymond, George H. Wyman, George N. Wheeler, James J. Baldwin, Isaac Mitchell, James Robinson, John Murphy, Alex. Campbell, Charles H. Gardner, Michael F. Corcoran, John M. Caswell.

COMPANY E.

John Martin.

COMPANY F.

John Bary, Eldad Butler, Oliver Burns, James Boyle, Patrick Curran, Wiggin Connolly, Jeremiah Cochran, Joseph Clayton, Michael Cochran, Edmund Duggan, Michael Donovan, James N. Drew, Michael Early, Michael P. Flynn, James Flemmings, Thomas Gogin, Patrick Gurry, John Horngan, Michael Handley, Timothy Hedily, James R. Jenkins, Lawrence Larkin, John Sanders, Hugh McManus, Thomas Murphy, Michael Mara, Patrick Navin, John O'Flynn, David O'Brien, John O'Brien, William W. Pinkham, John Parker, John Quinn, John Ryerden, John Sullivan, Charles H. Thompson, Russell Town, Bernard White, William Wall, John Ward, Joshua Powers, Michael L. G. O'Brien, John L. O'Brien.

COMPANY G.

William Higgins, Charles W. Willey, Argus McGinniss, William Johnson.

COMPANY H.

George W. Chapman, Uriah H. Foss, Charles H. Hall, Charles W. Drew, Washington I. Baker, Henry C. Dickey, David H. Dickey, Charles J. Esty, James P. Gould, David M. Glover, Clinton C. Hill, George T. Hastings, Benjamin F. Harrington, Albert Q. Perry, John Ray, Charles W. Wiley, George H. Hubbard, Foster Kimball, John Ryan, William P. Williams, Stephen M. Baker.

COMPANY I.

William Ryan, Thomas Taylor, Charles Ward.

COMPANY K.

John Ahern, David Allen, John Bryson, Fred Conway, Cornelius Cary, John Cole, James Crombie, Patrick Devine, William Devan, John Doherty, Patrick Fowler, Richard Gallagher, John Garvey, Timothy Harrington, Daniel D. Healey, James Healey, Henry Hayes, Michael Mahoney John Martin, Patrick O'Brien, Patrick Paine, William H. Percival, Charles Plunkett, Jeremiah D. Sheehan, Thomas Solon, 2d, Dennis Sullivan, Michael Sullivan, Timothy Tehan, James Thompson, Patrick Welsh, Roger Sheady, William Hastings, Jeremiah Deedy, James Duffee, Patrick Early, Dennis Fenton, Thomas Jones, Thomas Kelley, James Kennington, Patrick Lavan, Peter H. Lee, Daniel Loftis, Patrick McCarty, William Miller, William Mulligan, Thomas Murry, Hugh Murphy, Charles H. Hodgdon, James Anderson, Francis Madden, John Driggs, John Kelley, Patrick Doyle, James Madden.

COMPANY UNKNOWN.

William F. McPherson, Sullivan B. Abbott, David Reed, John Connor, James Burns.

ELEVENTH REGIMENT.

COMPANY C.

Jeremiah D. Lyford, Andrew J. Frye, John F. Clarke, Edward C. Emerson, Charles F. Johnson, Ezra B. Glines, Enoch T. Farnham, Albert F. Sargent, George E. Dudley, Loammi Searles, Lucien S. Buckland, Charles W. Baker, William W. Fish, True O. Furnald, Lyman W. Griffin, Humphrey M. Glines, Alexander Hutchinson, Israel Henno, James W. Resslar, Levi B. Lewis, John B. Marsh, Charles Millen, John L. F. Phelps, G. A. W.

Respectfully
William P. Riddle

Barker, Moses Richardson, Benjamin Stevens, Luther M. Smith, Luther G. V. Smith, Gilman M. Smith, Daniel R. Woodbury, Ira Gardner Wilkins, Frank W. Page, Ira E. Wright, Edward Adams, Joseph B. Clark, Hollis O. Dudley, Oliver Williams.

COMPANY D.

John White, John Smith.

COMPANY E.

Caleb J. Kimball, William O. Stevens, Daniel Whitney, Charles H. Tufts, Joseph Cross, William Dickerman, Amos B. Shattuck.

COMPANY UNKNOWN.

Charles LeGranger, William Barton, Joseph Martin, James Arnold, John White, Joseph Kerr, Michael Quinn, Westley Chester, Peter Robinson.

TWELFTH REGIMENT.

COMPANY A.

Martin Davis, Joseph Sharp, Charles Bowers, Jacob McCormick, John McGraw, Alex Conchard.

COMPANY B.

Henry J. Lindner, John Smith, Henry Thomas, Albert Mumford.

COMPANY C.

James H. Gordon, Nathan E. Hopkins, Philip Levi, Raphel Reimaun.

COMPANY D.

William Weldon, Robert Hill, Charles Mardinan, Henrick Fisher, James Agnew, Ira Taylor, Charles A. Heath, John McConnell, George Alland, Hans Anderson, Solomon Sweeney.

COMPANY F.

Robert Barnard, John Howard, Hibbard Nolan, Lorenzo D. Watson.

COMPANY G.

Philip Warren, Andrew Floyd, William J. Wallace, Thomas Dalton, Edward Brown.

COMPANY I.

Charles Lawrence, Henry Killan, Frank Wilson, Joseph Martin, Martin Oswald, Patrick Mc Carty, Thomas Hornsby, Charles Williams.

COMPANY K.

Henry Carr.

COMPANY UNKNOWN.

James Cooper, William Sutton, George Forrest, Julius Lyford, James C. Dempey, George Parker, James Lane, Victor Bauman, Hiram C. Hohler.

FOURTEENTH REGIMENT.

COMPANY C.

John R. Green.

COMPANY D.

John N. Bruce, Silas R. Wallace, Stephen M. Wilson.

COMPANY UNKNOWN.

Patrick Clark, Alex Danvers, Lewis Norrop, Michael O'Brien, John Shibin, William Warren, James A. Bumford.

FIFTEENTH REGIMENT.

COMPANY E.

Henry S. Perry, Michael Abbotton, George W. Brown, Joseph K. Hazelton, Charles H. Martin, Ervin D. Tobie.

SIXTEENTH REGIMENT.

COMPANY G.

S. F. McQuestion.

EIGHTEENTH REGIMENT.

COMPANY F.

Solomon Towns, Gustavus B. Wells, Charles Way, Peter Bully, Benjamin Chandler, Mathew Burns, John Duffy, James Davis, Henry Morton, William Ferguson, John Garrett, Joseph Jenno, Joseph Granther, Timothy Jacobs, Patrick Keller, John Johnson, Francis W. Kennison, Joseph Lesherville, Arvil Lemarche, Scott McGuire, John McCarty, Thomas Reynolds, Patrick Lowery, James Lewis, William Masterson, Alden Oliver.

COMPANY H.

Jackson C. Bickford, John J. Ryan, Adilon E. Port, Edwin Mulligan, Michael P. Mulligan, Peter Locke.

COMPANY I.

M. Thomas H. McGuire, David Magoon, Edward W. Cowan, Nathaniel A. Tuttle, Albert T. Bowers, Charles W. Bills, Augustus B. Corey, Benjamin C. Cook, George B. Jackson, Thomas S. Knowles, Robert J. McFarland, Charles H. Lee, Owen Evans, Barney Flynn, George H. Howe, John McFee, Patrick Mack, James Smith, William H. Plummer, John F. Rounds, Zachariah B. Stewart, Amasa J. Pervier, Patrick Sullivan, Charles Wilson, George T. White.

COMPANY K.

Horace Pickard, Miles J. Colby, Peter Robinson, John A. Lindsay, Walter A. Green, Patrick Prescott, Edward N. Tuttle, Edward K. White, John Copp, Jeremiah Sheehan, George C. Moore.

NEW ENGLAND CAVALRY.

David B. Nelson, Major; George T. Cram, Adjutant; Arnold Wyman, First Lieutenant.

TROOP K.

Joseph Austin, John A. Jones, Henry G. Ayer, Thomas Bouguge, Jonathan B. Chapman, Jason N. Childs, John G. Chubbs, George E. Clark, Matthew N. Colby, Charles R. Dunham, Emerson A. Dunham, James D. Gage, George Hanchett, William H. Hart, William Holton, James W. Jenness, Philip Jones, Charles S. Kidder, Richard A. Lawrence, Hugh Mills, Henry E. Newton, Charles L. Prescott, John G. Page, William H. Palmer, Francis H. Phillips, Moody Quimby, Hiram Stearns, Lewis E. Taplin, Charles H. Wilson, David F. Wilson.

TROOP M.

George W. Berry, Eugene Bowman, John Francis Colby, Minor Hawks, Henry P. Hubbard, Nathan P. Kidder, Cyrus Litchfield, William C. Powers, Arthur W. Russell, Albert P. Tasker, Ebenezer Wilson.

FIRST NEW HAMPSHIRE CAVALRY.

TROOP A.

David A. Connor.

TROOP B.

Benjamin F. Philbrick.

TROOP C.

John Farrell.

TROOP D.

Joshua Voce.

TROOP E.

Andrew J. Roberts.

TROOP F.

William H. Griffin, James H. Robinson, John C. Colburn, Charles F. Elliott.

TROOP G.

Edward F. Brown, John Baird, Emerson A. Dunham, Henry H. Aldrich, James N. Bean, Charles A. Brown.

TROOP H.

William A. Piper, William A. Kelley, Edwin R. Packard, Jewett W. Perry.

TROOP I.

William H. Palmer.

TROOP K.

James D. Gage, John G. Page, Charles L Prescott, Hugh Mills, Charles M. Jason, James H. French, Jonathan B. Chapman, Warren Forsaith, William H. Hart, Jason N. Childs, Moody Quimby, D. F. Wilson.

TROOP M.

Henry B. Hubbard, Enoch Lovell, Charles S. Kidder, John F. Colby, James H. Parks, Gustavus H. Best, William C. Powers.

TROOP UNKNOWN.

Andrew Hill, Thomas Daley, Daniel Lannigan, John O'Hara, Joseph Randolph, George E. Spaulding, Thomas A. Collins, Hugh R. Richardson, Allen W. Bonney, Henry F. Hopkins, Abbott N. Clough, Henry J. Webster, Daniel Doyle, Joseph Jackson, Richard Tobine, Louis Rumann, George Atkins.

HEAVY ARTILLERY.

COMPANY A.

Jonah S. Kennison, Henry Porquet, Albert P. Young.

COMPANY B.

James Collins, jr., Edward A. Young.

COMPANY C.

Charles W. Wingate, George J. Hunt, Heber C. Griffin, Willard Buckminster, Charles P. Green, Levi H. Sleeper, jr., William A. Gilmore, Albert F. Quimby, Alonzo Day, James M. Quimby, William S. Parsons, Edson Sullivan, John S. Allen, Elbridge G. Baker, James A. Baker, Andrew M. Backer, James O'Brien, Charles D. Buntin, George B. Boutelle, William E. Boutelle, Francis Brown, Marston L. Brown, Willard S. Baker, Charles

Bean, George W. Brown, George Conet, Charles H. Cole, Stanford H. Chase, John J. Crockett, David B. Dickey, James M. Dickey, Warren H. Day, John H. Day, Reuben Dodge, William E. Denney, John G. Durant, Charles F. Dockum, Henry T. Foss, William R. Forsaith, Warren Green, John S. Gamble, Elbridge Gerry, Madison Gerry, Edwin G. Howe, Sullivan D. Hill, George Howard, William Hurlin, Michael Harris, Charles H. Hodgeman, Lowell S. Hartshorn, Newton Hollis, Ezekiel Hall, Westley E. Holt, Joshua R. Hastings, Manley W. Jenkins, Joseph Kelley, George W. Knight, Ormond D. Kimball, Oscar E. Leonis, Charles H. Martin, Nathaniel H. Metcalf, George E. Mayhew, William F. Moore, Bradley Merrill, Henry C. Morris, George W. Nichols, Hezekiah H. Morse, Benjamin K. Barker, Christopher Barker, Orrin F. Pillsbury, Henry M. Pillsbury, Chester L. Page, Frederick Payne, Moses O. Pearson, Albert B. Robinson, Horace L. Richardson, Edwin J. Ross, Dennis W. Reardeau, Noah W. Randall, Everett Stevens, William W. Sweatt, David A. Wilson, George W. Sawyer, Robert Stewart, Andrew W. Stoton, George W. Taylor, Edward W. Tillotson, Joseph E. Walker, James M. Wallace, Sullivan B. Wallace, Nahum A. Webster, Charles F. Whittemore, Nathan B. White, Daniel A. Wells, John W. Willey, William Q. Young, Francis York, James O. Chandler, James R. Carr, James G. Burns.

COMPANY F.

James P. Gallison.

COMPANY K.

David P. Stevens, George C. Houghton, Alfred Howard, George H. Ames, Franklin A. Brackett, Herbert W. Churchill, William Fisk, Albert F. Goodhue, Frank L. Gilman, Charles E. Green, John Grammo, Leander E. Hall, Charles A. Hall, Charles H. Haddock, George A. Palmer, Lewis J. Smith, George E. Swain, Sylvester S. Walsh, Charles L. Bailey, Edward J. Wing, John E. Johnson.

COMPANY L.

Walter Smith, Sedley A. Loud, Peter Burns, Pierre Michoa, Oliver Jepson, James Maloney, Henry W. Twombly, Horace G. Kimball.

COMPANY M.

John W. Dickey, George K. Dakin, Ezra D. Cilley, Elijah E. French, John R. Bean, Ephraim Fisk, John L. Sargent, Charles W. Boyd, George T. Bean, Philander Hopkins, Alfred R. Crosby, William G. Cutler, Clark S. George, Albert T. Hamblett, James W. Learned, George A. Shepard, Gustavus Soule, Nathan B. Tilton, Ira P. Twitchell, Thomas Welch, Charles E. Young, Henry W. Clark, Horace H. Bundy, Charles Clark, Charles M. Dinsmore, Washington L. Gray, Henry R. Noyes, Orrin S. Silloway, Charles L. Taylor, Asa P. Wright, Henry Bennett, Frank L. Edmunds,

Edward M. Dakin, George Applebee, Joseph Comfort, Alfred Comfort, John McCauley, Orlando Proctor, Ezra N. Norris, James Richards, John Kating, Daniel Davis, Henry Blair, George A. Martin, Benj. B. Bunker.

VETERAN RESERVE CORPS.

Albert Blood, James Byles, Jeremiah Connor, James N. Cummings, Patrick Dowell, Jerome C. Davis, F. E. Demeritt, Henry B. Eastman, Davis Emery, Harvey Hill, William H. Knowlton, Andrew Currier, Michael Powers, John L. Collins, John Brown, William W. Eastman, Stephen O. Gould, Thomas G. Gould, Patrick Haullihan, Joseph R. Marble, William Murry, Henry C. Faye, William E. Robinson, William Smith, John Smith, Enoch E. Stevens, Charles Stewart, George W. Varnum, J. A. Sargent, Franklin R. Tucker, Patrick Welsh, Cyrus S. Burpee, Hiram G. Gove.

MARTIN GUARDS.

Edward Wing, Edward P. Kimball, John C. Pennock, Sydney F. Sanborn, Wiggin T. Abbott, Howard P. Smith, Joseph P. Frye, Charles P. Gilbert, Lewis J. Smith, George W. Davis, Charles H. Bradford, Dennis A. Burbank, Frank A. Brackett, Charles W. Dimick, Henry Eaton, William Fisher, Austin G. French, George W. Farnham, Alfred T. Goodhue, Charles J. Goodwin, Frank L. Gilman, Horace P Page, Charles W. Gardner, Charles E. Green, Alfred Howard, Charles Hadlock, Charles Hall, L. A. Hyatt, Leander Hall, Martin A. Hoff, Clinton Jones, Frank C. Jewett, Marshall Keith, John Leighton, Charles H. Moulton, Matthew Morrow, Charles E. Morse, Ira S. Osgood, John H. Prescott, George A. Palmer, David P. Stevens, Myrick E. Smith, George E. Swain, Benj. T. Sherburn, Sylvester S. Walsh, Charles Weeman, Elbridge Wasson.

NATIONAL GUARDS.

Edwas A. Hasman, John C. Hardy, George E. Kennison, William O. Ladd, William H. Lord, Albert B. Morrison, Henry C. Norris, Charles Putnam, John E. Ricker, Frank H. Redfield, George H. Ray, Charles A. Smith, Charles H. Stevens, George W. Swinborne, Nathaniel A. Tuttle, Alonzo F. Warren, Charles F. Whittemore, Frank M. Boutelle, Aldano Neal, Edward M. Tillotson, William E. Boutelle, Charles C. Hilton, George F. Kelley, George J. Hunt, William Buckminster, Charles P. Green, Orrin N. B. Stokes, Madison Gerry, George Canfield, Emery W. Alexander, Andrew Armstrong, Leroy S. Batchelder, Elihu B. Baker, George W. Ballou, James Buckminster, Charles B. Bradley, Andrew M. Bowker, George Boutelle, Albert F. Barr, John S. Corliss, Marcus M. Currier, Stanford H. Chase, Charles J. Chase, Alex. Cooper, Benj. Keally, John Carney, William E. Dunbar,

Levi W. Dodge, Edward W. Dakin, Frank L. Edwards, Frank W. Favour, Heber C. Griffin, George A. Gordon, Daniel W. Gould, Charles George, Henry T. Goodhue, Newton Hollis, Rhodes Hanson.

FIRST LIGHT BATTERY.

George A. Gerrish, John Wadleigh, Henry F. Condict, Lyman W. Bean, Robert Burns, David Morgan, Joseph T. Durgin, Ira P. Fellows, Howard M. Farrar, John L. Fish, George E. Fairbanks, Jerry E. Gladden, John H. Goodwin, William H. Goodwin, George W. Griswold, Clark S. Gordon, Eben Gove, Adams Gowing, Simon B. Hill, John D. Hall, Albert T. Hamlett, Wesley E. Holt, Cleaves W. Hopkins, Greely W. Hastings, James A. Johnston, William B. Kenney, Daniel P. Ladd, Dudley P. Ladd, LeRoy McQuesten, Thomas W. Morrill, Horace P. Marshall, Charles W. Offutt, Christopher C. Perry, Henry C. Parker, Charles Peoples, George W. Parrott, William D. Perkins, Henry C. Patrick, Daniel M. Peavey, Thomas Randlett, Henry S. Rowell, Francis Reeves, Charles H. Shephard, Alexander Simpson, Henry A. Sloan, Gustavus Soule, John L. Sargent, Albert C. Stearns, Leander G. Sylvester, Frank Senter, Edwin R. Sias, Nathan B. Tilton, Frank W. Taber, William B. Underhill, Samuel J. Whittier, George K. Dakin, Edwin H. Hobbs, Ephraim Fisk, Gilman Stearns, Ezra D. Cilley, John K. Piper, Orrin Taber, William W. Roberts, Alonzo M. Caswell, Samuel S. Piper, William N. Chamberlin, Henry A. Campbell, Samuel Cooper, Irving S. Palmer, Frank E. Demeritt, Ambrose Ingham, Alexander A. Brown, Daniel Kelley, Charles E. French, John Carling, George W. Varnum, Hilliard L. Eaton, Philander Hopkins, George E. Glines, William L. Babbett, Marcus H. Bundy, Elisha H. Burrill, Charles W. Boyd, LeRoy T. Bean, Edwin N. Baker, James M. Buswell, William H. Blackburn, Henry E. Bond, Henry Baker, Robert Crowther, James Carr, William Carr, William G. Cutler, Henry W. Clarke, Kittridge J. Collins, Homer Canfield, Thomas C. Cheney, Charles P. Cox, James P. Carpenter, Frederick J. Croning, Durrill S. Crockett, Chauncy C. Dickey, John W. Dickey, John Drown, Charles A. Doe, Martin V. B. Day, Thomas Welch, Luther E. Wallace, Thomas J. Whittle, Frederick S. Worthen, Morrill N. Young, Charles E. Young, D. Washington Grey, Albert R. Holbrook, Charles Pearson, Charles J. Rand, Isaac L. Roberts, Orrin S. Silloway, Charles L. Taber, Sylvester F. Webster, Charles Wenz, James F. Sargent, William G. Custer, Walter Cutler, Alfred R. Crosby.

FIRST REGIMENT U. S. SHARP-SHOOTERS.

COMPANY E.

Levi H. Leet.

SECOND REGIMENT U. S. SHARP-SHOOTERS.

COMPANY G.

Abner D. Colby, Henry A. Colby, Elijah Hanson, Jonathan S. Johnson, Charles W. Stevens.

NAVY.

James Hayes, George E. Ashton, John M. Custalow, Peter Dowd, Walter Lee, James Smith.

MARINES.

Michael Kane.

BATTERY B UNITED STATES ARMY.

Charles J. Anderson.

FIRST ARMY CORPS.

Dennis F. G. Lyons.

THIRTEENTH NEW YORK ARTILLERY.

Henry Boyd.

FIRST REGIMENT UNITED STATES ARMY.

Joseph H. Knowlton.

REGIMENT UNKNOWN.

Albert Miller, John Reilley, Daniel Thornton, Alexander Frazier, John Jefferman, Joseph Hart, John Riley, John Thompson, Amos R. Witham, Emile Keller, James Brown, Timothy Hallisey, James Anderson, Albert Burns, William R. Clement, George Carpenter, William H. Goodwin, John McPherson, Thomas Smith, Thomas Whelston, Alfred Mixsan, Charles Brockway, Jesse F. Williams, James White, Henry Wood, William Romer, William H. Jackson, James Lynch, Thomas Powell, John Pender, Samuel Siegel, James Sullivan, James Smith, James S. Williams, John Murphy, James McCanney, William E. Stearns, James A. H. Grant, James M. Mayhew, John Kerin, John Smith, John Milano, John Richards, Jerome Yates, Solomon Leaks, Joseph Bess, George H. Judson, Charles Dorsey, John H. Johnson, Isaac Williams, Samuel Urbine, Thomas Meade, William H. Daggs, Pruy Gilveatt, Frank Thompson, James Casley, James Sullivan, James W. Brown, James Boyles, George Branson, Pasqual Canard, John Brown, David Dudley, James Gordon, Frank L. Gilman, Charles C. Webster, Charles L. Davenport.

FIELD, STAFF AND LINE OFFICERS.

BRIGADIER-GENERALS.

Joseph C. Abbott, Michael T. Donohoe.

COLONELS.

Thomas P. Pierce, Edward L. Bailey, James W. Carr, Hawkes Fearing, jr., John Coughlin.

LIEUTENANT-COLONELS.

Samuel G. Langley, Francis W. Parker.

MAJORS.

Thomas Connolly, Jesse F. Angell, David B. Nelson.

ADJUTANTS.

Alvah H. Libby, Joseph J. Donohoe.

CHAPLAINS.

Henry Hill, Silas F. Dean.

SURGEONS.

William W. Brown, Sylvanus Bunton, William A. Webster, John Ferguson.

ASSISTANT SURGEONS.

George W. Manter, William G. Stark, James P. Walker.

QUARTERMASTERS.

Richard N. Batchelder, John R. Hynes, Charles A. Putney, Foster Kimball.

CAPTAINS.

John L. Kelly, Hollis O. Dudley, Varnum H. Hill, Rufus F. Clark, Ruthven W. Houghton, John Kirwin, Robert H. Allen, Roger W. Woodbury, William H. Maxwell, Charles A. White, Robert C. Dow, James A. Hubbard, James H. Platt, George W. Huckins, Thompson S. Newell, William W. Mayne, Granville P. Mason, William C. Knowlton, George F. McCabe, Charles Cain, Frank Robie, Joseph Freschl, Warren E. F. Brown, William J. Gunnon, Cornelius Healey, Joseph J. Ladd, Nathan H. Pierce, James Kelliher, Asa T. Hutchinson, John E. Mason, John M. Carswell, Laurence F. Larkin, Thomas C. Trumbull, Michael F. Corcoran, John B. Sargent, Cornelius W. Strain, John L. O'Brien,

George H. Hubbard, Patrick Doyle, James Madden, Joseph B. Clark, Amos B. Shattuck, Ira G. Wilkins, John N. Bruce, William E. Stearns, George T. Cram, George A. Gerrish, George K. Dakin, James O. Chandler, George C. Houghton, John E. Johnson, Abner D. Colby.

FIRST LIEUTENANTS.

Martin V. B. Richardson, Dustin Marshall, Michael J. Connolly, Walter Colby, William E. Hamnett, Walter J. Richards, Frank L. Morrill, Frank C. Wasley, David M. Perkins, Charles A. McGlaughlin, Alvah S. Wiggin, Oscar A. Moar, Patrick K. Dowd, Charles O. Jennison, Andrew J. Edgerly, Benjamin F. Fogg, Daniel Gile, Charles M. Currier, Virgil H. Cate, Clement F. S. Ames, Lawrence Foley, William E. Hubbard, Henry G. Cushing, James Miles, Robert Swiney, Michael O'Grady, Willard N. Haradon, Andrew W. Doe, Michael T. H. Maguire, Charles Johnson, Charles H. Gardner, Alfred G. Simons, Jeremiah D. Lyford, Ira G. Wilkins, Edwin H. Hobbs, Ezra D. Cilley, James R. Carr, James G. Burns, Charles L. Bailey, Ephraim Fisk, William N. Chamberlin.

SECOND LIEUTENANTS.

Charles Vickery, Charles L. Brown, Robert A. Seavey, Frank B. Hutchinson, William Jones, James F. W. Fletcher, Cyrus S. Burpee, Charles E. Rowe, Henry O. Sargent, Cornelius Donohoe, Alonzo L. Day, Ichabod S. Bartlett, Thorndike P. Heath, Edward K. White, John K. Piper, Orrin Taber, John R. Bean, Moses O. Pearson, Reuben Dodge, H. A. Lawrence, Edward J. Wing, Thomas J. Whittle.

RESIDENCE OF EX-GOV. FRED'K SMYTH.

RESIDENCES.

AMONG these pages will be found engravings of some of the finest dwellings in the city and the following descriptions not improperly accompany them.

THE RESIDENCE OF THE HON. FREDERICK SMYTH.

Ex-Governor Smyth's house is finely situated on rising ground just east of Amoskeag Falls, on the spot where the Pennacooks lived when the Merrimack swarmed with fish and the Indians came to the Falls to catch them. The grounds contain about ten acres and include the site of a former Indian village, where many interesting relics of the aboriginal dwellers have been exhumed. On the eastern side runs Elm street and on the western the River road, while North street and Salmon street form, respectively, the northern and southern boundaries.

The house, which is built of brick with granite trimmings, two stories high with a French roof surmounted by a tower, was begun in 1867 and finished in 1873. It was designed by Gov. Smyth and his wife and built from plans by Bryant & Rogers of Boston. It is a spacious and convenient dwelling, with walnut wainscotings and marble thresholds. The rooms in the second story are finished each with a different kind of native wood and the ceilings are frescoed to correspond. The windows command a view of the Merrimack for a mile up and down, the mills, the falls, the bridge and islands, and from them can be seen the whole city, the towns across the river, Joe English hill, the Uncanoonucs and the Francestown range of mountains.

THE RESIDENCE OF COL. WATERMAN SMITH.

Col. Smith's house was built in 1873 and is situated in a most conspicuous and healthful location on the summit of Wilson hill, which rises to the east of the city proper. The first floor is one hundred and eighty-six feet above the level of Elm street, about the height of the tallest church steeples. It was built of wood from plans by W. H. Myers of this city and painted in two shades to represent the colors of dressed and undressed granite. The house is modeled after an Italian villa, is three stories high, overtopped by a tower, and is made with large rooms, wide halls and stairways. The prospect from its windows is fine, including a view of the towns to the east and south, the city spread out at the foot of the hill with the river on its farther edge and the hills beyond in Goffstown and Francestown. The grounds contain twelve acres and are gradually taking on an appearance of much beauty.

THE RESIDENCE OF COL. B. F. MARTIN.

Col. Martin's house, on the northeast corner of Elm and Brook streets, standing in grounds which contain an acre and are kept in admirable order, was substantially rebuilt in 1865 in accordance with designs by George Harding of Boston. It is a wooden house, two stories high, French-roofed, handsomely slated and surmounted by a tower. The inside is beautiful and convenient, arranged with much taste. It is situated on the main avenue of travel and yet removed from the noise and bustle of that section of it where business is carried on. It is in the midst of some of the finest houses in the city and suffers little by comparison with them.

REPRESENTATIVE MEN.

THE following classes of persons, as representatives of Manchester's industry and life, were invited to place their portraits within these pages: the members of congress, attorney-generals of the state, mayors, clerks and treasurers of the city, judges of courts, presidents and cashiers of banks, agents of the large corporations, prominent manufacturers, commanders of the Amoskeag Veterans; and, in addition, two members of the medical, one of the ministerial and one of the legal profession, whose prominence in the city's history entitled them to such recognition. Brief sketches follow of those who are represented by their portraits.

COL. PHINEHAS ADAMS.

Phinehas Adams was born in Medway, Mass., June 20, 1814, and is thus about sixty-one years old. He is the son of Phinehas and Sarah W. (Barber) Adams. He was one of a family of eleven, four sons and seven daughters, of whom but three besides himself survive—Sarah A., the wife of Dr. E. B. Hammond of Nashua, Mary J., the widow of the late James Buncher, and Eliza P., the widow of the late Ira Stone, both of Manchester. His father was a manufacturer and started the first power-loom in this country at Waltham, Mass., in the year of Mr. Adams's birth. His father moved to Waltham, when he was but a few years old, then to Cambridge, Mass., and subsequently to Nashua,

N. H., where he kept hotels, and at length to Walpole, Mass., where he became the agent of a mill of which Dr. Oliver Dean and others, as well as himself, were owners. Mr. Adams learned manufacturing with his father in his early years and then went to the academy at Wrentham, Mass. While he was there his father became financially embarrassed and in 1829, when he was a little over fifteen years old, he was obliged to leave school and go to work in the Merrimack Manufacturing Company's mills at Lowell, Mass., and soon rose to be overseer. In December, 1833, he went to Hooksett, N. H., to be an overseer in the Hooksett Manufacturing Company's mills of which his father was then agent. Not long afterwards he became an overseer in mills of the Pittsfield Manufacturing Company at Pittsfield, N. H., and then returned to his former place at Lowell. In five years from the time he first went there he was promoted to be a clerk in the counting-room and left Lowell finally in December, 1846, and succeeded William P. Newell as agent of the old mills of the Amoskeag Manufacturing Company on the west side of the river at Amoskeag Falls. In November, 1847, he was appointed agent of the Stark Mills, which position he has ever since held.

Mr. Adams was a director in the Merrimack River Bank from 1857 to 1860, a director in the Manchester Bank from 1864 till it ceased to do business; and has been a trustee in the Manchester Savings Bank from 1846 till the present time and a director in the Manchester National Bank since it began business in 1865. He has been a director of the New England Cotton Manufacturers' Association, and was one of the Presidential electors from New Hampshire in 1872. He acquired the title of colonel by service as the chief of Gov. Straw's staff in 1872 and 1873.

Col. Adams married, September 24, 1839, Miss Elizabeth P. Simpson of Deerfield, N. H., by whom he has had two children, who are now living — Elizabeth, wife of Daniel C. Gould of this city, paymaster at the Stark mills, and Phinehas, jr., in partnership with E. C. Bigelow of Boston in the cotton business.

Mr. Adams is a man whose life is based upon the highest ideas of right and wrong. Extremely conscientious, of the strictest integrity, he has a character beyond all question. Kindly and affable, of remarkable generosity, he is highly respected by all his fellow-citizens and his personal popularity would have ensured his election to any office in their gift, if he could have been induced to accept it.

CHARLES E. BALCH.

Charles Edward Balch was born March 17, 1834, at Francestown, N. H., and is the son of Mason and Hannah (Holt) Balch. There were, besides himself, a half-brother and half-sister, of whom the former, Mason H. Balch, survives and is living upon the homestead. His father was a farmer and his education was acquired at the district school and at Francestown Academy. In the spring of 1852 he entered the dry goods store of Otis Barton & Company of Manchester as book-keeper, in which position he remained two years when he became clerk in the Manchester Bank and Manchester Savings Bank. When the former was succeeded by the Manchester National Bank in 1865, Mr. Balch was elected its cashier, which position he now fills. He is a trustee of the Manchester Savings Bank, having been elected in 1862, and a member of its investing committee. He is also a director and one of the finance committee of the New Hampshire Fire Insurance Company and treasurer of the Gas-Light Company. Mr. Balch married, July 30, 1867, Miss Emeline R. Brooks, of Bath, Me., daughter of the Rev. N. Brooks, now of this city.

Mr. Balch is a cautious, prudent man, an excellent financier, with a mind naturally capable and sharpened by experience and trained to view things from a financial standpoint. He has always shrunk from public life and refused political honors, but enjoys to a very high degree the confidence of the public in the responsible position which he holds. He combines the attributes of a courteous gentleman with a punctilious regard for the proprieties of life.

THE HON. CHARLES H. BARTLETT.

Charles Henry Bartlett was born in Sunapee, N. H., October 15, 1833, and is thus between forty-one and forty-two years of age. He is the son of John and Sarah J. (Sanborn) Bartlett. He had four brothers and three sisters, of whom all but one sister survive. Joseph S. resides in Claremont; Solomon, John Z., George H., Mrs. John Felch, Mrs. Thomas P. Smith, in Sunapee. He was educated at the academies in Washington and New London, this state, and then began the study of law with Gov. Metcalf at Newport. He studied subsequently with George & Foster at Concord and Morrison & Stanley at Manchester, being admitted from the office of the latter to the bar of Hillsborough county in 1858. In that year he began the practice of his profession at Wentworth, N. H., and in 1863 came to this city, where he has since practiced, from 1866 till 1868 in company with the late James U. Parker and the remaining time alone.

He was clerk of the New Hampshire senate from 1861 to 1865, Gov. Smyth's private secretary in 1865 and 1866, treasurer of the state reform school in 1866 and 1867. In June, 1867, he was appointed clerk of the United States district court in New Hampshire, which position he now holds. In the same year he was unanimously elected city solicitor but declined a re-election and in 1872 was elected, as the nominee of the Republican party, mayor of the city,

Waterman Smith

and served till February 18, 1873, when he resigned in accordance with the policy of the national government at that time which forbade United States officials from holding offices in the gift of states or towns. His last official act as mayor was to order the city treasurer to pay the amount due him for salary to the Firemen's Relief Association. Mr. Bartlett has been a trustee of the Merrimack River Savings Bank from 1865 to the present time and a trustee of the People's Savings Bank from its begining in 1874. He was the Master of Washington Lodge of Free Masons from April, 1872, to April, 1874, and now holds the position of United States commissioner, to which he was appointed in May, 1872.

Mr. Bartlett married, December 8, 1858, at Sunapee, Miss Hannah M. Eastman of Croydon, N. H., by whom he has one daughter — Carrie B. Bartlett.

Mr. Bartlett has a keen, well balanced mind, whose faculties are always at his command. He thinks readily, but acts cautiously and seldom makes a mistake. Hence he has been financially successful in almost everything he has undertaken. He is one of the most practical lawyers in the state and was for several years in charge of the law department of the Mirror, giving general satisfaction, and his withdrawal, when his business compelled it, was a source of much regret to the readers of that paper.

JOSEPH E. BENNETT.

Joseph Everett Bennett was born in New Boston, N. H., August 9, 1817. He is the son of Stephen and Hannah Bennett, and is the third child in a family of seven sons and four daughters. Of these, Stephen M., John J., and Salome, the widow of the late Joseph Battles, reside in Manchester, and Jacob, Andrew J., and Hannah, the widow of the late Joel Wilkins, live in New Boston. His father was a builder, and he began, when eleven years old, to learn the mason's trade, and afterwards worked as a journeyman in Peterborough, Lowell and other places.

He spent two terms at Francestown Academy under the instruction of the late Benjamin F. Wallace, afterwards principal of the Piscataquog Village Academy in this city, and taught a district-school in the same town one winter. At the age of eighteen years he became a pupil at New Hampton Institution, in this state, and, graduating there in 1838, entered Waterville College, now Colby University, at Waterville, Me., the same year. He continued there through Freshman and Sophomore years, spent the next twelve months in teaching, at Searsmont, Me., and then entered Yale College as a Junior, graduating there in the class of 1843.

The succeeding fall and winter he taught at Searsmont, was elected school committee during his residence there, and came to Manchester in the spring of 1844 to work for J. T. P. Hunt, with whom he had become acquainted while at work in Lowell and who was then building mills for the Amoskeag Company. He worked for Mr. Hunt till 1847 and then became foreman for J. F. Andrews of Nashua, continuing in his employ the greater part of the time till 1860. During this time he assisted in the rebuilding of the state-house at Montpelier, Vt., and in the construction of the passenger-station and freight-house at Manchester, mills at Manchester, Southbridge, Mass., and other places, and the Church of the Immaculate Conception at Boston. During this time he retained his residence in Manchester, and he spent his winters in teaching in Maine, and at New Boston and Manchester, in this state, having been master of the schools at Piscataquog village, Hallsville and Webster's mills, and the North and South grammar schools.

In 1860, leaving the employ of Mr. Andrews, he returned to Manchester and went to work for himself, being in company one year with his brother, John J. Bennett, and two years with Lyman Fellows of Concord. In 1865 he was elected city clerk and has occupied that position ever since. He has been selectman and ward-clerk of old ward five, has been either assessor or clerk of the board of assessors seventeen years at different times, was elected by the Democrats alderman from ward five in 1849, and, as a Free-soiler, was chosen representative to the general court in 1851 and 1852. He represented ward five in the school committee in 1852 and 1857. He is a trustee of the Amoskeag Savings Bank, having been elected in 1868. Mr. Bennett is a prominent Free Mason, was Master of Lafayette Lodge in 1865 and 1866, High Priest of Mount Horeb Royal Arch Chapter in 1870 and 1871 and has been for a long time Recorder of Trinity Commandry. He has been always prominent in connection with the First Baptist church and society and did his part in the building of their new house of worship. In March, 1845, he married Miss Susan Dyer of Searsmont, Me., by whom he had three children, none of whom survive.

The long time during which Mr. Bennett has held the responsible position of city clerk is a proof of the confidence the public reposes in him. Many efforts have been made to regulate this office by the rule of rotation while he has held it, but they have all failed, chiefly because no incoming mayor who was new to the office felt as if he could do without his valuable services and those who had already been mayor appreciated them too highly to be willing to be without them. He sees things clearly and from a practical point of view and his honesty is unquestioned. He is a man of independent notions and from his position exerts a good deal of influence upon the city government.

ARETAS BLOOD.

Aretas Blood was born October 8, 1816, at Weathersfield, Vt. He is the son of Nathaniel and Roxcellana (Proctor) Blood, and one of a family of five sons and two daughters, of whom but two sons besides himself survive — Benjamin Franklin and Sewell, resident in Waltham, Mass. When three years of age, he moved with his father to Windsor, Vt. There, going to school two months in the year till he was seventeen years old, he was apprenticed to the blacksmith's trade, worked at it two years and a half and then became a machinist. He left Windsor in the fall of 1840 and went to Evansville, Ind., where he worked at his trade a year, till June 17, 1841. Then he started eastward, stopping at all the cities on the way in search of employment, but finding none till he came to the town of North Chelmsford, Mass.

Remaining there about a year, he went home to Windsor in July, 1842, and staid there till October. Then he went to Lowell, Mass., and worked seven years in the machine-shop, and thence to Lawrence, where he began the manufacture of machinists' tools for the large machine-shop then in process of erection there. Two years later he removed to the shop itself and made by contract machinery of all kinds, tools, turbine wheels, locomotive and stationary engines, etc. September 7, 1853, he came to this city to establish works for the building of locomotives and became a partner in the firm of Bayley, Blood & Company, who were first located in Mechanics' Row and made there their first stationary engine, which they have still in use. The concern was first called the Vulcan Works, but new buildings were built in the spring of 1854 upon the present location of the works, the manufacture of locomotive engines was begun in the fall and the firm was incorporated that year under the name of the Manchester

Locomotive Works. Oliver W. Bayley then became the company's agent, but was succeeded in 1857 by Mr. Blood, who has ever since resided in Manchester and given his personal attention to the business.

Mr. Blood was a director of the Merrimack River Bank from 1860 till its name was changed in 1865 to that of the First National Bank and from that time till 1868 a director of the latter. He has been since 1874 a director of the Manchester National Bank.

He married in Lowell, September 4, 1845, Miss L. K. Kendall, by whom he has two children—Nora, the wife of Frank P. Carpenter of this city, and Emma, who resides at home.

Mr. Blood has proved one of the most successful builders of locomotive engines in the country, and his success has been no accident. Bred a machinist, he understands a locomotive thoroughly and knows how it should be made in every part. Sharp and keen in business, he never takes undue risks. Like Gen. Grant, whom he is said to resemble in looks, he is able to manage large numbers of men with ease. Hence the pecuniary success of the establishment he represents. A self-made, self-relying man, he sees clearly from the begining the result at which he aims and has the mental power and executive ability to attain it. A very high-minded man, unexceptionable in private life, his word is as good as his bond and the latter is as good as that of any man in the state.

DR. WILLIAM W. BROWN.

William Whittier Brown was born in Vershire, Vt., August 28, 1805, the son of Ebenezer and Mary (Whittier) Brown. He was the third of nine children, of whom one brother—Jonathan, of Eden, Vt.,—and two sisters—one the widow of the late Alvah Avery of Corinth, Vt., and the other the widow of the late Rev. Nathaniel L. Chase of this city — survive. He acquired his education at the academies in Bradford and Randolph, Vt., and in Hudson, N. Y., and began in 1828 the study of medicine with Dr. John Poole at Bradford. He attended lectures at Hanover, N. H., and graduated from the New Hampshire Medical Institution of that place in 1830. He at once began practice at Poplin, now Fremont, this state, and remained there till 1835, when he removed to Chester where he acquired an extensive business during his ten years' practice. At one time he practiced in Boscawen, N. H.

In 1846 he removed to this city, where he kept his residence till his death. He spent one year, including parts of 1849 and 1850, in California, where he acquired some propeity. He was appointed, October 19, 1861, surgeon of the Seventh New Hampshire regiment and served till the autumn of 1864, when want of health compelled his resignation. He was appointed pension-surgeon but resigned on account of the small fees allowed. He died in this city January 6, 1874, of pneumonia. He was five times married and had seven children but was only survived by his last wife.

Dr. Brown received from Dartmouth College the honorary degree of Master of Arts, was elected a fellow of the New Hampshire Medical Society in 1836 and was its president in 1869, while at the time of his death there were but two members who had been longer connected with the society. He was a director of the Merrimack River Bank from 1869 till it was succeeded in 1865 by the First National Bank and was a director of the latter from that time and a trustee of the Merrimack River Savings Bank from 1873 till his decease. He was a member of the Franklin-street Congregational church, was frequently chosen one of the officers of the society connected with it and was elected its president in 1855, 1867 and 1868.

Dr. Brown was a man of clear and practical mind and combined a strong love for the profession he followed with an intense application to it. In fact, he was never idle, was never seen at places where time could be lost, but was always to be found at his home or office, attending his patients or at some religious meeting or literary entertainment. He was remarkably fond of reading, and, besides making himself familiar with all that was fresh in the science of medicine, he kept pace with all the news of the day, and books and papers were his constant companions. Excelled by few, if any, practitioners in the state, he had a very large business and always commanded the respect of the public wherever he was.

THE HON. DAVID A. BUNTON.

David Augustus Bunton was born, October 18, 1805, at Goffstown Centre, N. H. He is the son of Andrew and Lavinia (Holden) Bunton, and the third in a family of five sons and two daughters. Of these survive Lavinia, the widow of Robert Richards, of Bristol, P. Q., Sarah Jane, the widow of John Gilchrist of Goffstown, Jesse, of Milton, Mass., Dr. Sylvanus, formerly of this city and now of Mont Vernon, and William, now residing in Boston. He comes of an old New Hampshire family, his grandfather having been carried captive from Allenstown to Quebec by the Indians in 1746. When the Revolutionary War broke out, he enlisted among the first, was at the battle of Bunker Hill, and was killed at White Plains in 1776. Mr. Bunton acquired a common-school education in Goffstown, taught two winters at the "east village" in the same place, and was employed by his father in tanning and currying hides till he was twenty-one years of age.

Then he went to Massachusetts and was employed in several places in quarrying and cutting stone, working two years upon the Bunker Hill monument and also upon the United States arsenal at Augusta, Me. Returning to Goffstown in 1831, he built a saw-mill and grist-mill upon the Piscataquog river at Goffstown Centre, where P. C. Cheney & Company's paper-mill now stands. He operated these mills and also kept a store for a time.

Mr. Bunton had already been employed by Dr. Oliver Dean, one of the capitalists who conceived the idea of building the city of Manchester upon the Merrimack, to do some stone-work for him, and in the fall of 1836 Dr. Dean confided to him the plans of the Amoskeag Company in regard to the acquisition of territory and the erection of mills and engaged him to work for the Company. He agreed, and in January, 1837, moved to Manchester, his being nearly the first family in town. From that time till 1846 or 1847 he remained in the Company's employ and built for it by contract, among other things, the first stone dam at Amoskeag Falls, the dam at Hooksett, the extension of the canals, the foundation of the first mills for the Manchester corporation, boarding-houses, etc.

He left the Company's employ when it ceased to do work by contract, and in 1849 was appointed superintendent of the Manchester & Lawrence Railroad, then just beginning business, having been employed before and after in negotiations with landholders upon the route. He resigned the office of superintendent after a few months and was elected a director, a place he had vacated to become superintendent, and continued in that position till about 1860. For about five years after he left the Company he was en-engaged in the grocery business with George W. Adams, now of the firm of Adams & Lamprey. For some time afterwards he was busied in selling wild lands in Coos county, where he had an interest in thousands of acres. About 1858 he became interested in the Manchester Iron Company which was engaged in the manufacture of scales

F T Stuart, Boston

Frederick Smyth

GOVERNOR OF NEW HAMPSHIRE 1865-66.

in the lower part of the city. This failed some years afterwards and he was employed in settling its affairs. In company with the late Gilman H. Kimball of this city, he was engaged two years in cutting wood and lumber in Goffstown. In 1864 he was sent out to Fredericksburg by Gov. Gilmore to administer to the needs of the soldiers who had been wounded in Grant's campaign before Richmond. In 1865 he went to live in Cambridge, Mass., while his sons went through Harvard College. He spent six years there and then returned to Manchester and has since been engaged in stone-work.

In 1842 Mr. Bunton was elected as the first Whig representative to the general court from Manchester and was re-elected in 1843. He was elected alderman in 1847 and served as mayor in 1861 and 1862, being elected by the Republican party. He has been a director of the Manchester Bank and Manchester National Bank and a trustee of the Manchester Savings Bank ever since their organization.

Mr. Bunton married in 1831 Eliza Jane Adams, daughter of John Adams of Sutton, N. H., by whom he had seven children, of whom the two youngest — William A. and George W. — are living.

It will be noticed that Mr. Bunton played a very importtánt part in the city of Manchester in its early years and enjoyed to a great degree the confidence of the corporations and finally that of the city, having been twice elected to its highest office. This confidence has never been misplaced. Honest, liberal, trusting almost to a fault, his heart is always in every good word and work. To the young men of the city he has been of especial service, aiding them by his word, by the use of his name and by personal commendation.

THE HON. G. BYRON CHANDLER.

George Byron Chandler was born November 18, 1832, in Bedford, N. H. He is the son of Adam and Sally (McAllister) Chandler and one of a family of four children, three sons and one daughter, of whom two besides himself survive—Henry, of the firm of Plumer, Chandler & Company, and John M., of the firm of John M. Chandler & Company, both of this city. He acquired an education at the academies in Piscataquog village, Gilmanton, Hopkinton and Reed's Ferry, taught school two seasons in Bedford, one in Amoskeag village and one in Nashua and assisted his father on the farm till he was twenty-one years of age. At the age of seventeen he spent one year, however, as a civil engineer in the employ of the Boston, Concord & Montreal Railroad.

In March, 1854, he came to this city and became a bookkeeper for Kidder & Duncklee. In one year from that time, March, 1855, he was appointed teller of the Amoskeag Bank and held the position till the organization of the Amoskeag National Bank in 1864, when he was chosen its cashier and now holds that position. He has been a long while cashier of the Amoskeag Savings Bank and in 1874, upon the organization of the People's Savings Bank, he was appointed its treasurer. He was a director of the old Amoskeag Bank in the last year of its existence and a trustee of the Amoskeag Savings Bank from 1867 to 1870. He was a director of the Blodget Edge Tool Manufacturing Company in 1861 and since 1866 has been a director of the Amoskeag Axe Company, which succeeded it. In 1867 he was elected a director of the Manchester and Lawrence Railroad, but resigned in 1872 to become its treasurer. He was elected, as the nominee of the Democratic party, state senator in 1874.

Mr. Chandler married, in 1862, Miss Flora A.,—daughter of the late Hon. Darwin J. Daniels, once mayor of the city,—who died in May, 1868, and by whom he had one daughter who survived her mother but a short time. For his second wife he married, in 1870, Miss Fannie R., daughter of Col. B. F. Martin of this city, by whom he has one child—Benjamin Martin.

Mr. Chandler comes of a fine family and was reared, under the best of home influences, to habits of honesty and accuracy. His father and mother were estimable people, of strong minds and straightforward, upright lives. The lofty ideas that were instilled into him in youth he has never forgotten and his integrity has never been questioned. He has had the handling of vast sums of money and the different corporations he represents have entire confidence in his honesty, capacity and financial shrewdness. He is a liberal man and good citizen and but once has he turned aside from the life of a banker to enter into that of politics, and then only for a short time, positively refusing a second nomination from his party for the position he had once held.

THE HON. P. C. CHENEY.

Person Colby Cheney was born in Holderness, N. H., now Ashland, February 25, 1828. He is the son of Moses and Abigail (Morrison) Cheney and was one of a family of eleven, five sons and six daughters. Of his three surviving brothers, one, Dr. O. B. Cheney, is the president of Bates College at Lewiston, Me.; another, E. H. Cheney, is the editor and proprietor of the Granite State Free Press at Lebanon, N. H.; and the third, Moses Cheney, jr., was a manufacturer of paper at Henniker, but has retired from business. The five sisters now living are Sarah B., wife of the Rev. S. D. Abbott of Needham, Mass.; Abby M., wife of George Washburn of Ashland, N. H.; Ruth E., wife of Joseph W. Lord of Wollaston, Mass.; Marcia A., wife of J.

P. F. Smith of Meredith; Hattie O., wife of Dr. C. F. Bonney of Manchester. When he was seven years of age, his father, a manufacturer of paper at Holderness, moved with his family to Peterborough and established himself anew. His youth, except what time he occupied in acquiring an education in the academies at Peterborough and Hancock in this state and at Parsonsfield, Maine, was spent in the paper-mill, and when his father sold his business in Peterborough to A. P. Morrison and returned to Holderness, he remained as manager of the mill.

In partnership with others he built a paper-mill and established himself in business in Peterborough in 1853, and, soon buying the interest of his associates, continued the business in his own name. In August, 1862, he went from Peterborough to take part in the War of the Rebellion, having been appointed quartermaster of the Thirteenth regiment. Exposure and overwork in the campaign before Fredericksburg brought on a sickness which sent him home and forbade his return to service, and he was discharged in August, 1863. In 1866 he removed to Manchester and associated himself with Thomas L. Thorpe as a dealer in paper stock and also as a manufacturer of paper at Goffstown. In 1868 E. M. Tubbs & Company, of which firm Mr. Cheney had become a member three years before, bought out Mr. Thorpe's interest and the business was continued under the name of P. C. Cheney & Company. After the burning of their mill at Goffstown in 1871, they rebuilt the old mill at Amoskeag village and resumed business there, having since built a new mill at Goffstown. The firm has also, till recently, had an interest in paper-mills at Henniker and West Henniker, this state.

Mr. Cheney was elected a representative from Peterborough in 1853 and 1854, was chosen railroad commissioner in 1864, and mayor of Manchester in 1871. He would have been re-elected mayor the next year had he not positively refused a re-nomination. He was a director of the Peterborough Bank when he came to Manchester and has been president of the People's Savings Bank since its organization in 1874. He married May 22, 1850, Miss S. Anna Moore, who died January 8, 1858, leaving no children. He married June 29, 1859, Mrs. Sarah W. Keith, daughter of Jonathan White, formerly of Lowell, Mass., by whom he has one daughter, Agnes Annie Cheney. He was nominated by the Republican party for governor in 1875 and wherever he was known obtained more than the usual party vote, but there was no choice by the people. He will undoubtedly be elected governor in June by the legislature.

Mr. Cheney is a man of clear and vigorous insight, of an earnest and strongly sympathetic nature, generous, patriotic and high-minded. Possessing great administrative capacity, he has been a very successful man of business. Untiring in his efforts for the good of others, he cares more for his friends than himself, and in consequence when an opportunity is afforded them to do him a favor, he meets with the most cordial support. Interested in all movements for the public good, he is very popular in whatever capacity he appears before the people.

THE HON. JOSEPH B. CLARK.

Joseph Bond Clark was born at Gilford, N. H., June 21, 1823. He is the son of Samuel and Betsey (Clement) Clark, and had four brothers and four sisters. One brother — Samuel C., a lawyer at Lake Village, N. H.,— and a sister — Hannah B., wife of William G. Hoyt of Moultonborough, N. H., — survive. He lived at Gilford till he was seventeen years of age and then went to New Hampton

Institution and spent three years in acquiring an education. He entered Brown University at Providence, R. I., in 1844 and was graduated there in 1848. He then spent six years in teaching in Massachusetts and New Hampshire. Meanwhile he was studying law, part of the time with the Hon. Asa Fowler of Concord, and later with Stephen C. Lyford of Laconia from whose office he was admitted in 1853 to the Belknap county bar. He was then principal of the academy at Wolfeborough and continued in that position till he came to Manchester in January, 1855, and began the practice of his profession. In September, 1862, he received a commission as lieutenant in the Eleventh regiment and left his business to take part in the War of the Rebellion. In March, 1863, he was promoted to be captain, was wounded May 6, 1864, in the battle of the Wilderness and was discharged June 4, 1865.

Mr. Clark was city solicitor in 1858 and 1859, representative in the state legislature from ward one in 1859 and 1860, and mayor of the city in 1867. He was appointed solicitor for Hillsborough county in 1861 and re-appointed in 1866, holding the office for ten years in all. He was a director of the Merrimack River Bank from its beginning in 1858 till it was succeeded by the First National Bank and has been a director of the latter since it was organized in 1865. He has been a trustee of the Merrimack River Savings Bank from its beginning in 1858 and a director of the Nashua, Acton & Boston Railroad since its organization in 1872.

Mr. Clark married September 12, 1862, Mrs. Mary Jane (Peabody) Smith, daughter of James H. and Roxanna Peabody of this city, who died August 15, 1873, leaving two children — Mary P. and Joseph M.

It will be seen that Mr. Clark has led an active, stirring life since he came into the practice of his profession. He has taken part in whatever might be prominent in society at any time, interesting himself in politics, military affairs, banking, railways, etc., and his election to the mayoralty of the city testifies to the confidence with which he has been regarded as a public man. Cautious, prudent and thoughtful, a hard worker and a true friend, he has made a good name in the city and is favorably known throughout the state. He is a good citizen and was one of the foremost men and most liberal givers in the construction of the First Baptist church.

THE HON. LEWIS W. CLARK.

Lewis Whitehouse Clark was born August 19, 1828, at Barnstead, N. H. He is the son of Jeremiah and Hannah (Whitehouse) Clark, and has one sister — Sarah M., wife of Samuel E. Batchelder of Illini, Ill. He acquired his preliminary education in the common schools at Barnstead and in the academies at Pittsfield and Atkinson and then entered Dartmouth College where he was graduated in 1850. From August, 1850, to December, 1852, he was principal of the academy at Pittsfield. Meanwhile he studied law, at first with the Hon. Moses Norris and then with A. F. L. Norris, at Pittsfield, and was admitted to the Belknap county bar from the office of the latter, September 3, 1852. He then began the practice of his profession at Pittsfield and continued there till April 2, 1860, when he came to Manchester and formed a partnership with the Hon. George W. Morrison and the Hon. Clinton W. Stanley. He dissolved his connection with them in November, 1866, practiced alone for a year or two and then associated himself with Henry H. Huse, continuing this partnership till May 24, 1872, when he was appointed attorney-general of New Hampshire to fill the vacancy caused by the death of the Hon. William C. Clarke, which position he has since retained. He was one of the representatives from Pittsfield to the state legislature in 1856 and 1857, and in 1865 was the nominee of the Democratic party for member of congress from the second congressional district.

Mr. Clark married December 29, 1852, Miss Helen M., daughter of the late Capt. William Knowlton of Pittsfield, by whom he has one daughter and one son, Mary Helen and John Lew.

Few men in New Hampshire have so many warm personal friends as the subject of this sketch. A very liberal man, of patriotic and high-toned impulses, he is widely known and widely liked. He has no superior in the state as a ready off-hand speaker, felicitous in language, eloquent in thought and generous in every impulse. He is an admirable advocate before a jury, and whenever he appears as a public speaker, whether in the performance of his professional duties as the attorney-general of the state, as a political orator or in any other capacity, he acquits himself with signal ability.

JOHN B. CLARKE.

John Badger Clarke was born January 30, 1820, at Atkinson, N. H., the son of Greenleaf and Julia (Cogswell) Clarke. His mother was the daughter of Dr. William Cogswell of Atkinson and Judith Badger of Gilmanton and was one of a family of nine, of whom two still survive — Francis Cogswell of Andover, Mass., formerly president of the Boston and Maine Railroad, and George Cogswell, a physician of Bradford, Mass. Mr. Clarke had one sister — Sarah the wife of Col. Samuel Carleton of Haverhill, Mass., who still survives, and four brothers. Of the latter, Francis, a physician at Andover, Mass., died July 10, 1852; Moses, a physician at Cambridge, Mass., died March 27, 1864; William C., attorney-general of New Hampshire, died April 25, 1872; and the Hon. Greenleaf Clarke, the

Clinton W. Stanley

only surviving brother, resides upon the homestead in Atkinson.

Mr. Clarke obtained his preliminary education at Atkinson Academy, entered Dartmouth College in 1839 and graduated in 1843, and was offered the Latin oration, which he declined. In his senior year he was elected president of the Social Friends Society. After graduation he became principal of the academy at Meredith Bridge, now Laconia, N. H., and taught there from August, 1843, to August, 1846, studying law meanwhile with Stephen C. Lyford. He then removed to Manchester and continued his studies with his brother, William C., till the fall of 1848, when he was admitted to the bar of Hillsborough county. The next year he went to California, sailing from Boston February 2, 1849, and spent two years there and in New Mexico, Central America and New Grenada, eleven months of the time in the mining regions, part of the time with pick-axe and shovel and part in the practice of his profession. Returning east in the spring of 1851, he staid eight weeks in Salem, Mass., with a view of entering into practice there, but returned in the following May to Manchester, opened an office and soon had a living business. February 14, 1852, he took charge of the editorial department of the Manchester Daily Mirror, then published by Joseph C. Emerson, agreeing to devote half of his time to it. He continued its editor from that time till the first of September, when, it having become apparent to him that Mr. Emerson, who had met with a heavy pecuniary loss in the summer, must sell or fail, he gave up his position and devoted himself exclusively to his profession. The Mirror establishment, the daily and weekly papers and the job-printing department connected with them, were sold at auction October 20, 1852, and Mr. Clarke became the owner and editor, retired from his profession and devoted himself entirely to journalism. Since then he has added to the Mirror the Daily

American, the Weekly American, in which the Messenger and the Democrat had already been merged, and the New Hampshire Journal of Agriculture which included the Granite Farmer and the Farmers' Monthly Visitor. The circulation of the Weekly Mirror is now more than twenty-one times as large as when he bought the establishment and the circulation of the Daily Mirror more than three times as large.

Mr. Clarke was chosen in 1864 one of the delegates from New Hampshire to the national Republican convention which re-nominated Abraham Lincoln for president of the United States, and at that time was elected for four years a member of the national committee of one from each state and by that committee was appointed one of the executive committee of seven, which consisted of Ex-Gov. Claflin of Massachusetts, Ex-Gov. Ward of New Jersey, the Hon. Henry J. Raymond of the New York Times and three others beside himself. He was bitterly opposed to the Know-Nothing movement of 1854 and 1855, believing in the largest religious toleration and in carrying out the ideas of the Puritans, who came to this country "to worship God according to their own conscience." Since 1852 he has refused to be a candidate for any office resulting from the direct suffrages of the people, believing that it would interfere with his position and power as an independent journalist, and for similar reasons has declined office in the various agricultural societies of New England.

He was elected president of the Tri Kappa Society of Dartmouth College in 1863. In 1866 he was appointed by Gov. Smyth one of the trustees of the New Hampshire College of Agriculture and the Mechanic Arts, and in 1867, 1868 and 1869 was elected state printer. He was for two years lieutenant-colonel of the Amoskeag Veterans and was elected its commander at two different times but declined the honor. Since the organization of the Merrimack River

Savings Bank in 1858 he has been one of its trustees. In 1872 he spent the summer in Europe, traveling through England, Ireland, Scotland, France, Germany and Switzerland.

Mr. Clarke married, July 29, 1852, Miss Susan Greeley Moulton of Gilmanton, N. H., by whom he has two sons—Arthur Eastman, born May 13, 1854, and William Cogswell, born March 17, 1856. They graduated from the high school in Manchester, spent a year at Phillips Academy in Andover, Mass., and then entered a special course in the Chandler Scientific School at Hanover, N. H., from which the former graduates in 1875 and the latter in 1876.

THE HON. WILLIAM C. CLARKE.

The late William Cogswell Clarke, a brother of the preceding, was born at Atkinson, N. H., December 10, 1810, the eldest son of Greenleaf and Julia (Cogswell) Clarke. He obtained his early education at the academy in Atkinson and entered Dartmouth College in 1828, graduating there with high honors in 1832. He was then for a year principal of the academy at Gilmanton, while beginning the study of law, which he subsequently pursued at the law school of Harvard University and in the office of Stephen C. Lyford at Meredith Bridge, now Laconia. When admitted to the bar in 1836, he began practice at Meredith Bridge and four years later, upon the creation of Belknap county, he was appointed county solicitor. He held this office till the spring of 1844, when he removed to Manchester and engaged in practice. In 1846, at the first city election, he was nominated for mayor, but withdrew his name after the first ballot. In 1849 he was elected city solicitor and held the office two years. In 1850 he was a delegate from Manchester to the state constitutional convention and in 1851 received the appointment of judge of probate for Hillsborough county, which office he filled with great acceptance until 1856, when his removal was among the political changes of the period. In 1855 he was offered, but declined, a position on the bench of the supreme court. In 1863 he was appointed attorney-general of the state, succeeding the Hon. John Sullivan, then recently deceased. He was re-appointed in 1868 and held the office until his death in 1872.

Judge Clarke was a director of the Manchester Bank from its organization in 1845 till 1849 and of the City Bank for ten years subsequent to its organization in 1853, and was also a trustee of the Manchester Savings Bank from 1852 till his death. He was for many years a trustee of the Manchester Atheneum, the germ of the present city library, and when the latter succeeded it in 1854, he was elected a member and clerk of the board of trustees, holding both positions till his death. He was the first treasurer of the Manchester & Lawrence Railroad, holding that position from July 31, 1847, till his resignation took effect, February 8, 1849, and was its clerk from February 28, 1854, till his death, being also its attorney when in the general practice of his profession. In 1854 he was appointed and served as a member of the national board of visitors to the West Point Military Academy.

Although always shunning purely political office, Judge Clarke was prominent and influential in the Democratic party until the outbreak of the War of the Rebellion, when he became a conspicuous leader of those Democrats who favored the most vigorous measures for its suppression. After these ceased to have an independent organization he acted with the Republican party.

In 1834, while yet a student of law, he married Miss Anna Maria, only daughter of Stephen L. Greeley of Gilmanton, N. H. His wife, now resident in Lake Village, N. H., two sons and two daughters, survive him. Stephen

G. is a member of the firm of Stanley, Brown & Clarke, lawyers of New York city; Greenleaf is connected with the New York Evening Post; Anna N. is the wife of Robert M. Appleton, a manufacturer at Lake Village; and Julia C. is a teacher in the state normal school at Framingham, Mass. Judge Clarke died suddenly at his residence in this city April 25, 1872. His final illness was very brief and he was able to attend to his official duties until within a few days of his death.

Judge Clarke was one of the earliest members of the Second Congregational or Franklin-street church, and one of the original officers of the society, both of which he helped largely to upbuild. In person he was well proportioned and a very fine looking man. The esteem and affection in which he was held was indicated by the large attendance at his funeral not alone of his fellow townsmen, but of distinguished men from all parts of the state. The pall-bearers were the Hon. Ira Perley of Concord, formerly chief justice of the supreme court, the Hon. Asa Fowler of Concord, formerly judge of the supreme court, the Hon. Daniel Clark, formerly United States senator and now judge of the United States district court, the Hon. E. A. Straw, then just elected governor of the state, the Hon. David Gillis of Nashua, the Hon. Nathan Parker, the Hon. Moody Currier and Col. Phinehas Adams.

His character was well portrayed in the resolutions which were drawn up by the Hon. Isaac W. Smith, now justice of the superior court of judicature, and adopted by the bar of Hillsborough county at the term of the supreme court held the next month after his death. In these he is said to have been "a public officer faithful and upright, discharging his official duties with signal ability; a lawyer of large experience in his profession, of well balanced judgment and discretion, well read in the principles of the law and faithful alike to the court and his client; a citizen patriotic and public-spirited; in his private relations a gentleman of unblemished reputation, distinguished for his high-toned character, affable manners and uniform courtesy; and illustrating in his public and private life the character of a Christian gentleman governed by the principles which he was not ashamed to profess."

DR. JOSIAH CROSBY.

Josiah Crosby was born in Sandwich, N. H., February 1, 1794, and was the son of Dr. Asa and Betsy (Hoit) Crosby, she being the daughter of Col. Nathan Hoit of Moultonborough, for many years judge of the court of common pleas. They had ten children. John, the eldest, died in Sandwich in 1872; Asa, a merchant of New York, died in Hayti, W. I., in 1826; Betsy, widow of the late Samuel Beedy, died at Edinboro', Pa.; Josiah, the subject of this sketch, was the next in order of birth; Sarah, the widow of the late Dr. Gilman M. Burleigh, formerly of Sandwich, resides at Dexter, Me.; Mary, the widow of the late Daniel Stevens, lives in Edinboro', Pa.; Nathan has been judge of the police court at Lowell, Mass., for the past thirty years; Dixi, who was many years professor in the medical school at Dartmouth College, died in 1873; Grace Reed married the late Dr. Enos Hoyt, formerly of Northfield, N. H., but subsequently of Framingham, Mass., where she now resides; one child died in infancy. Dr. Asa subsequently married Miss Abigail Russell, daughter of Thomas Russell of Conway, by whom he had seven children, of whom five died young. Alpheus, first professor of Greek and Latin and then of Greek alone at Dartmouth College from 1833 to 1849, and subsequently principal of the state normal school at Salem, Mass., died at Salem in 1874; Thomas Russell, who once practiced medicine in this city and was afterwards professor at Norwich University at Norwich, Vt., and in the scientific school at Dartmouth College, died in 1874.

The subject of this sketch received his preliminary education at Fryeburg, Me., and at Amherst, N. H., studied medicine with his father and at Hanover with Dr. Nathan Smith, and graduated in 1816 from the medical school at Hanover, succeeding that year to his father's practice in Sandwich. Thence he removed to Deerfield, then to Epsom as a more central location, and then to Concord as a still larger place. He was afterwards induced to go to Lowell, Mass., by the influence of a prominent manufacturer of that town who was in search of a trustworthy physician. He soon acquired a large practice there, but was called by the death of his father-in-law to Meredith Bridge, now Laconia, where he took charge of the estate. Among the property were some mills at Meredith Bridge and he formed a company under the name of the Belknap Mills, becoming its agent and remaining such till its failure in 1837. When his brother Dixi, then a physician in the same town, forsook his practice to become a professor in the medical school at Hanover, he succeeded to his business and practiced there till March, 1844, when he came to this city, where he pursued his profession till his death, which occurred January 7, 1875, from the effects of a paralytic shock.

Dr. Crosby married, in 1829, Miss Olive L. Avery, who survives him, together with two sons — Stephen L., a civil engineer and now resident in Manchester, and George A., who has become heir to his father's practice.

Dr. Crosby was a representative from Manchester to the state legislature for two years, was a member of the state constitutional convention of 1850 and was one of the school committee of this city in 1849, 1850 and 1851. He was a trustee of the Manchester Savings Bank from 1856 till his death. He became a member of the New Hampshire Medical Society in 1818, and in 1850 was its president. In 1857 he was elected one of the vice-presidents of the

American Medical Association and was an honorary member of the Massachusetts Medical Society. Upon his coming to Manchester he at once took the lead of the profession in the city, acquired a very large practice and became widely known in the state and beyond it as a contributor to medical journals. He gained a high reputation by introducing into medical practice the application of adhesive plaster in making extensions of fractured limbs, a method highly commended at the time and now in use all over the world. He was also the inventor of an invalid-bed for the use of patients with fractured limbs, which proved its utility by its general adoption.

Dr. Crosby was a man of the highest rank in his profession, studious, careful and thorough; of perfect honor, purity and integrity. He was a gentleman of the old school, gentle-mannered and kindly, of fine personal appearance and held in the highest esteem by the residents of a city in which he scarcely had an enemy. He was the instructor of many young men in the course of his practice and was their friend and counsellor as well. He was a man of very regular and methodical habits which prolonged his life to a hale old age.

THE HON. MOODY CURRIER.

Moody Currier was born April 22, 1806, at Boscawen, N. H. He afterwards lived in Dunbarton and Bow, working on a farm in the summer, going to school in the fall and teaching in the winter. District schools were then kept but six weeks in the year and Mr. Currier acquired all the English studies at home, studying evenings by the light of pitch knots and tallow candles. He fitted for college at Hopkinton Academy and then entered Dartmouth College, graduating, together with the Hon. Daniel Clark of this city, in the class of 1834.

Yours very truly

E. A. Straw

The succeeding fall he taught school in Concord, and, in company with the Hon. Asa Fowler of that city, edited the New Hampshire Literary Gazette. Then he went to Hopkinton and was principal of the academy there for a year, and in 1836 went to Lowell, Mass., to take charge of the high school there, continuing its master till the spring of 1841, when he removed to Manchester. During his stay at Hopkinton and Lowell he had studied law, and, upon coming to this city, he was admitted to the bar and formed a partnership with the Hon. George W. Morrison for the practice of his profession. The Manchester Democrat, a weekly newspaper, was started in 1842 by Kimball & Kidder, and soon afterwards the latter's interest was bought by Morrison & Currier. The latter gave part of his time to editorial labor, and later bought Mr. Morrison's fourth of the paper, disposing of his own interest in it not long afterward. His partnership in legal practice with Mr. Morrison was dissolved in 1843, and he pursued his profession independently till 1848, when he became cashier of the old Amoskeag Bank then just organized, and has continued in the banking business ever since.

When the Amoskeag Savings Bank was organized in 1852, he was appointed its treasurer and still holds the office. He has been president of the Amoskeag National Bank since its organization in 1864,. director of the People's Savings Bank from its formation in 1874, director of the Blodget Edge Tool Company during its existence and president and treasurer of the Amoskeag Axe Company since it succeeded the former in 1862, director of the Manchester Gas-Light Company since 1862, director of the Manchester Mills since its organization in 1874, treasurer of the Concord & Portsmouth Railroad since 1856, treasurer of the Concord Railroad in 1871 and 1872, and is the treasurer of the New England Loan Company.

He was clerk of the New Hampshire Senate in 1843 and

1844; was elected a member of that body by the Republicans of the third district in 1856 and 1857, being its president in the latter year, and was elected a councilor by the Republicans in 1860 and 1861. He was the chairman of the war committee of the governor and council for the first fifteen months of the war and did the chief business of that body, showing great executive ability in raising and equipping troops and starting into life a new military organization. Manchester in particular has reason to be grateful to him for what he did.

Mr. Currier has three times married; first, Miss Lucretia C. Dustin, December 8, 1836; second, Miss Mary W. Kidder, September 5, 1847; third, Miss Hannah A. Slade, November 16, 1869. He has had three children, of whom one survives—Charles M., teller of the Amoskeag National Bank in this city.

Mr. Currier is a marked man. He does his own thinking and has carved out his own success. He has built up and now manages the largest banking institutions in the state, and his great reputation with the outside world is justly that of a financier. But his ability in that line is equaled, if not excelled, by his remarkable scholarship. Educated for a profession and once a teacher, lawyer and editor, he has found time, in the midst of the busy life he has since led, to preserve and strengthen the tastes of a lover of art and literature. Well versed in the exact sciences, keeping pace with modern thought in art, science and religion, perfectly at home among the Latin and Greek authors, he has educated himself to read French at sight, is familiar with German, Italian and Spanish, and has written enough fugitive pieces of poetry for his own recreation to fill a volume. It is remarkable to find literary tastes and financial capacity united, both in such high degree, and we know of no other business man in the state who is so fine a scholar.

COL. M. V. B. EDGERLY.

Martin Van Buren Edgerly was born in Barnstead, N. H., September 26, 1833. He is the son of Samuel J. and Eliza (Bickford) Edgerly and was one of a family of nine children, five sons and four daughters, of whom five besides himself survive. Andrew J. of North Haverhill, N. H., is adjutant-general of the state; Joseph G., Clarence M. and Araminta C. are all resident in this city, the first having been for the past eight years its superintendent of public instruction, the second an insurance agent and the last a teacher in the public schools; Hannah A. is the wife of Ambrose Pearson, a civil engineer of Wilton, N. H.

The subject of this sketch came to this city with his parents when twelve years old, went to school for a time and then worked in the mills and machine-shop of the Amoskeag Manufacturing Company, where he remained till October, 1856, when he opened a drug-store in company with Lewis H. Parker. In a little less than a year he removed to Pittsfield, N. H., and in 1859 he entered into the insurance business, becoming an agent of several companies, among which was the Massachusetts Mutual Life Insurance Company of Springfield, Mass. In 1860 he was appointed by that company its general agent for New Hampshire and opened an office in Manchester, whither he removed in November, 1863, having become the general agent also for Vermont and northern New York. In 1868 he was appointed superintendent of all the company's agencies and spent two years in establishing agencies in the west, while retaining his own at home. In 1870 he resigned his place as superintendent but continued in charge of the northern New York, Vermont and New Hampshire agencies and in September, 1874, accepted in addition the Boston agency, the oldest in the company.

Mr. Edgerly acquired the rank of colonel by service as the chief of Gov. Weston's staff in 1871, was a delegate in 1872 to the national Democratic convention at Baltimore which nominated Horace Greeley for President, was the treasurer of the Democratic state committee in 1871 and 1872, and is now a member from New Hampshire of the Democratic national executive committee. He served as alderman of this city from ward four in 1874. He has been a trustee of the Merrimack River Savings Bank since 1864, a director of the New Hampshire Fire Insurance Company since its organization in 1869, a director of the Suncook Valley Railroad since 1871 and was commander of the Amoskeag Veterans in 1873 and 1874. In December, 1874, he was appointed by President Grant an alternate commissioner to represent the state of New Hampshire at the centennial celebration of the nation in 1876 at Philadelphia, Pa.

Col. Edgerly married, March 7, 1854, Miss Alvina Barney of Danbury, by whom he has had three children of whom two are living—Clinton Johnson and Mabel Clayton.

Mr. Edgerly is a man of excellent business habits and remarkable executive ability. He has a strong, clear mind, determines what is to be done and then does it at once. This combination of discernment and energy have given him his great success in the insurance business, greater than that of any other man in New Hampshire. He is a man of fine personal appearance, of gentlemanly bearing and a liberal disposition, which with his social nature have enabled him to gather about himself a host of personal friends. He is perfectly honorable in his dealings, is a good citizen and has been often talked of as the Democratic candidate for mayor of the city and for other and higher political offices, but has steadily and sensibly declined, with rare exception, to allow the use of his name.

THE HON. MOSES FELLOWS.

Moses Fellows was born at Brentwood, N. H., November 7, 1803. He is the son of Simon and Dorothy (Bartlett) Fellows, and one of a family of three sons and four daughters, of whom all but one — Hannah, wife of John Calef of this city — survive. George, Stephen and Ploome, the wife of John Gordon, reside in Brentwood ; Dorothy, widow of the late Samuel Hanson, and Sally, widow of the late Richard Bartlett, reside in Kingston.

Mr. Fellows spent the early part of his life in Brentwood upon his father's farm and in his store, acquiring an education in the district school, and in 1826 went into business for himself, continuing in Brentwood till May, 1833, when he removed to Manchester, taking up his abode in that part of it known as Moore's village or Goffe's Falls, where he has ever since resided. For nineteen years he continued in business there, nearly all of the time a wholesale manufacturer of shoes, but he met with reverses and retired from business in 1852 and has since occupied himself in the cultivation of his farm. Mr. Fellows, while in Brentwood, was a member of the state militia, being commissioned captain, but resigned in 1827. After his coming to Manchester, he was chairman of the board of selectmen in 1842, 1843 and 1846, and also in the latter year a member of the first board of aldermen the city chose. In 1847 and 1848 he was sent as a representative to the legislature and was mayor of the city in 1850 and 1851. Capt. Fellows married, July 5, 1829, Mrs. Nancy Bartlette, by whom he had one daughter, who died in 1853.

In the early days of the city, Mr. Fellows, a manufacturer of shoes upon a large scale and with many men in his employ, was a prominent citizen and had a large influence. He is a very genial man, courteous and affable, entertaining in conversation and so very companionable, and has had many warm friends who were ready to make sacrifices for him. Since he retired from business, however, he has mixed little in public life and has had no opportunity to develop his stronger characteristics.

THE HON. HERMAN FOSTER.

Herman Foster was born at Andover, Mass., October 31, 1800, and was the son of John and Mary (Danforth) Foster. His mother died two years after his birth, survived by one daughter, Sabra, who married Dr. Isaac Tewksbury of Hampstead and since deceased. His father subsequently married Miss Lucy Hastings of Bolton, Mass., by whom he had six children, of whom Charles, the eldest, died at Charlestown, Mass., in 1850 ; two others died at an early age ; and there are now living Emily, the wife of Ebenezer S. Badger of Warner, John, a wealthy retired merchant of Boston and formerly the head of the firm of Foster & Taylor, and George, late state senator from this district and resident in Bedford.

Mr. Foster's father was a merchant and moved, when the former was ten years old, to Nottingham West, now Hudson, this state, subsequently removing to Warner. Mr. Foster acquired his education at the common schools and at the academy in Derry, intending to pursue a collegiate course. This design he was compelled to relinquish by the partial failure of his eyesight. Dartmouth College, however, conferred upon him in 1861 the honorary degree of Master of Arts. He taught school for a time in several places in Massachusetts and then established himself in a mercantile business in Boston. After following this pursuit for some years he went to Warner, where his father then resided, and began the study of law in the office of the Hon. Henry B. Chase of that town and was admitted to the bar in 1839. In November of the next year he came to

Manchester and began the practice of his profession, continuing here from that time till his death and building up a large office business. In 1851 he formed a partnership with the Hon. Isaac W. Smith and subsequently with the Hon. B. F. Ayer, now of Chicago, Ill., dissolving his connection with the latter in the early part of 1857, since when he has practiced independently. He died February 17, 1875, at his residence in this city, of a chronic difficulty of the lungs. He married November 8, 1826, Miss Harriet Mary Ann Whittemore, daughter of Amos Whittemore, of West Cambridge, now Arlington, Mass., by whom he had two children, who died in infancy, Mrs. Foster being thus the only surviving member of the family.

Mr. Foster was treasurer of the town of Manchester in 1842 and 1843 and solicitor of the city in 1857. He was sent to represent the city in the house of representatives of the state in 1845 and 1846, and again in 1868 and 1869. He was state senator in 1860 and 1861, being president of the senate in the latter year. In August, 1862, he was appointed by President Lincoln assessor of internal revenue for the second district of New Hampshire, resigning in February of the next year. He was the treasurer and clerk of the Manchester Gas-Light Company from its organization in 1850 till his death. He was a director of the Amoskeag Bank from 1853 till its books were closed in 1868, a director of the Amoskeag National Bank from 1871 till his death, and was a trustee and one of the committee of investment of the Manchester Savings Bank from its organization in 1846. He was one of the founders of the First Unitarian Society and was its president in 1863 and 1864.

Mr. Foster was a marked man, of positive traits of character. Coming here when the town had just begun a new life, he grew up with it in the confidence and respect of its inhabitants. His perception was accurate, his judgment sound and trustworthy, his intelligence wide and clear. He was a strong, decided, independent man. He had a remarkable memory for dates and places, persons and things. In business he was very methodical, cautious, painstaking, slow to make up his mind but sure of it when he expressed it. He was a safe counsellor, an upright and honest man and a good citizen.

THE HON. E. W. HARRINGTON.

Edward Wetherbee Harrington was born June 21, 1816, at Acton, Mass. He is the son of Edward and Polly (Wetherbee) Harrington, and has one sister, Mary H., the widow of the late Eliab Grimes of Acton, Mass., and one brother, Phinehas, who left this city for California in 1850. He worked on a farm in the summer and went to the district school in the winter till he was eighteen years old, when he went to Boston to work in a grocery store, remaining there till 1838, when he returned to his home in Acton.

At that time his brother was engaged in brick-laying on some of the mills then in process of construction in Manchester, and his prophecy of the speedy growth of a large city induced Mr. Harrington to come to this place on the first of January, 1839. March 26, 1839, he opened a restaurant in a building on Elm street near Lowell, now occupied as a market by R. M. Miller, and which was the first house completed on the eastern side of Elm street. There were then no hotels and no other restaurant, but there were a large number of people at work upon the mills, and this gave him a large business. In the fall of 1841 he removed to the basement of Union building now occupied by H. D. Corliss, which was the first building finished on the western side of Elm street. Mr. Harrington continued to occupy the restaurant till October, 1853, when the

D. B. Varney

City Bank was organized and he became its cashier, continuing such till its dissolution and becoming cashier of the City National Bank which succeeded it.

Mr. Harrington was foreman of the first hook-and-ladder company in the city, whose house occupied the lot on the corner of Market and Franklin streets where the Franklin-street church now stands, and was assistant-engineer of the fire department in 1856, 1858 and 1862. He acquired the rank of captain from his long service as commander of the "Stark Guards," a military company organized in 1840. He was elected mayor by the Democratic party for the year 1859 and re-elected for the succeeding year. In 1864 and 1865 he was the Democratic candidate for governor of the state and in 1867 and 1869 for representative to congress. He was a member of the national Democratic convention at Charleston in 1860 which nominated Stephen A. Douglas for president and of the succeeding convention in 1864 which nominated George B. McClellan. He was also a delegate to the "national union convention" which was organized by Reverdy Johnson and which met at Philadelphia in 1866. Mr. Harrington is a very prominent Free Mason, having taken the thirty-third degree. He was Master of Washington Lodge in 1857, the first year of its existence under a charter, Commander of Trinity Commandry in 1865 and 1866, High Priest of Mount Horeb Royal Arch Chapter in 1857 and 1858, and at one time Grand High Priest of the Grand Chapter of the state.

Mr. Harrington married in May, 1843, Miss Frances M. Dearborn, who died in November, 1844, leaving one daughter, Frances M., the wife of John P. Bartlett, city solicitor of Manchester. In May, 1849, he married Miss Margaret A. Bond, by whom he has had four children, of whom two — Edward W., jr., and Delana B. — are still living and reside at home in this city.

Mr. Harrington has been a leading man in the history of

this city. Self-made, relying upon his own judgment, he dares do what he thinks is best. He is a man with what Lord Bacon calls "good roundabout common sense." His mind is well balanced, his conclusions are better than his reasons, and his instinctive ideas in reference to the values of property or what is best for the city are generally worth more upon their first expression than the judgments of others after long reasoning. He made a good mayor, was the first to pave the streets and the first who had the courage to introduce steam fire engines in the face of large organizations which favored the old hand-engines. Liberal in his ideas and liberal with his purse, he has done a great deal to help those who could not help themselves, particularly young men. Few men are better versed in the ways of the world or understand better the motives which actuate mankind.

GEN. NATT HEAD.

Natt Head was born at Hooksett, N. H., May 20, 1828, and is the son of Col. John and Anna (Brown) Head. He was one of a family of five children — Hannah A., wife of Col. Josiah Stevens of this city; the late Sally B., wife of Hall B. Emery of Pembroke, N. H.; Natt, the subject of this sketch; William F., of Hooksett; John A., who resides in Iowa. His father, who died in 1836, was a farmer and largely engaged in lumbering. He, in company with his brother William F., succeeded to his father's business and they are extensive farmers, lumber-dealers and manufacturers of brick in Hooksett, and, in company with Frank Dowst, contractors and builders in Manchester. They have furnished a large part of the brick used in this city for the past fifteen years.

Mr. Head, as the contractor, built several miles of the old Portsmouth railway, which ran from Suncook to Candia, built the new railway and bridges from Suncook to Hooksett and the Suncook Valley railway from Suncook to Pittsfield. When the soldiers' military asylum near Augusta, Me., was burned, he was sent to assume the charge of the institution during the illness of the deputy governor and afterwards rebuilt the asylum. He has filled various town offices, was appointed in 1857 deputy sheriff, and was a representative from Hooksett in the state legislature in 1861 and 1862. In 1863 and 1864 he was the chief of Gov. Gilmore's staff and in 1864 was chosen adjutant-, inspector- and quartermaster-general of the state, which office he held till 1870. He was the Republican candidate for state senator from the Second district, in 1875, but there was no election by the people.

Gen. Head was for a long time a director of the New Hampshire Agricultural Society and has been its president for ten or a dozen years, and for the past four or five years has been a director of the New England Agricultural Society. In 1869 he was appointed by Gov. Stearns a trustee of the New Hampshire College of Agriculture and the Mechanic Arts. From his father, who was for many years an officer in the state militia, and from his grandfather, Capt. Nathaniel Head, who served as an officer through the Revolutionary War, Gen. Head inherits military taste and spirit. In 1847 he was appointed fife-major in the Eleventh regiment of the state militia and served four years, and in later times he was the chief bugler of the Governor's Horse Guards. He was the commander of the Amoskeag Veterans of Manchester in 1869, 1870, 1871 and 1872, is an honorary member of the Boston Lancers and is the first sergeant in command of the first company of infantry in the Ancient and Honorable Artillery Company of Boston.

Gen. Head is a prominent Free Mason, being a member of Washington Lodge, Mount Horeb Royal Arch Chapter,

Adoniram Council and Trinity Commandry of Manchester. He is also a member of the Supreme Council, having taken all the degrees of the Ancient and Accepted Scottish Rite, including the thirty-third, and all the degrees in the Rite of Memphis to the ninety-fourth. He is also a member of Howard Lodge and Hildreth Encampment of Odd Fellows, at Suncook, and a member of Oriental Lodge of the Knights of Pythias of the same place.

Gen. Head has been a director of the Suncook Valley Railroad since it was organized, and the president of the China Savings Bank at Suncook since it was started. He was a director of the Merrimack River Bank from 1860 till it was merged in the First National Bank and has been a director of the latter since it was formed in 1865.

Gen. Head married, November 18, 1863, Miss Abbie M. Sanford of Lowell, Mass., by whom he has had three children — Annie Sanford, Lewis Fisher and Alice Perley. The son died March 4, 1873.

Gen. Head stands conspicuous for social, genial qualities, for good nature and strong, sound sense. He is always practical, his opinions are good on all topics to which he has given any attention and he never ventures opinions on subjects with which he is not familiar. He is a successful business man and won a lasting popularity among soldiers and citizens during the late war by his earnest and liberal efforts in his position as adjutant-general of the state. Few men have so wide a circle of strong personal friends. He has been talked of for some of the highest offices in the gift of the people of the state and for some years past has had votes at all the nominating conventions of his party for governor.

THE HON. JOHN HOSLEY.

John Hosley was born May 12, 1826, in Hancock, N. H., of Revolutionary stock, his grandfather having been a captain in the war of 1775. He is the son of Samuel and Sophia (Wilson) Hosley and was one of a family of nine, of whom also survive Martha E., wife of George G. Wadsworth of Franklin, N. H., and Lucretia J., wife of Oliver Dearborn of Manchester. He was brought up on his father's farm and gained what education the common schools of Hancock afforded till he was twenty years old. In 1846 he came to Manchester and entered the employ of Moses Fellows at Goffe's Falls as a shoe-cutter and continued with him three years. Then he entered one of the weaving-rooms in the Amoskeag Company's mills.

He continued in the Company's employ till 1851 when he went to California and was gone about two years. Upon his return in 1853 he went into the grocery business in company with Jacob Nichols. After a year, however, he became an overseer in the Amoskeag mills and continued in that position till he was elected mayor in 1865 by the city councils to fill the vacancy caused by the death of the Hon. Darwin J. Daniels. In the fall of that year he was elected by the people, being nominated as a citizens' candidate, and served through 1866. Since that time he has been engaged in farming till 1874, when he was elected collector of taxes by a Democratic board of mayor and aldermen, which office he now holds.

Mr. Hosley represented ward one in the common council in 1856 and 1857, in the board of education in 1861 and 1862, in the board of mayor and aldermen in 1863 and 1864, and was elected a member of the latter board from ward six in 1871. He was a member of the "national union convention" which met at Philadelphia in 1865. He is a Free Mason and has been chosen master of Lafayette

Lodge but declined the position, and has held the highest office in Hillsborough Lodge of Odd Fellows. Mr. Hosley married, in 1854, Miss Dorothy H. Jones of Weare, by whom he has had one child, Marion J., who is living.

At a glance one sees that Mr. Hosley is a man of no common abilities. He has grown up with Manchester as town and city and has done his part in moulding its policy in governmental affairs. He is a man who has had heretofore and always will have a large following of men who believe in his wisdom, his capacity and especially his strict integrity. His record as a mayor showed well financially and his administration was one of the most economical ones in the history of the city. He is a genial gentleman, well versed in the courtesies of life, and a very close and accurate observer of human nature.

THE HON. JACOB F. JAMES.

Jacob F. James was born in Deerfield, N. H., July 9, 1817, and is the son of Moses and Martha (Young) James. He had six brothers and one sister, of whom there survive Joseph Y., of Warren, Penn., Josiah S., of Raymond, N. H., and Mary F., the wife of Loring Pickering, of Brooklyn, N. Y. His father, a farmer, removed to Candia shortly after the birth of his son, and the latter spent his boyhood in farming. At the age of fourteen he went to Lowell and became an operative in one of the carding-rooms in a mill owned by the Lowell Manufacturing Company.

After spending four years in Lowell, he left the mills and entered the old Baptist seminary at New Hampton, N. H., since removed to Fairfax, Vt., where he spent two years, Dr. Charles Wells and Joseph E. Bennett of this city being pupils of the institution at the same time. In April, 1837, he returned to Lowell to take charge of the carding-room in which he had worked, and, three years later, he left that mill to superintend a carding-room for the Massachusetts corporation in the same place.

In February, 1842, he accepted an invitation to come to Manchester and take charge of the two carding-rooms in number one mill belonging to the Stark Mills, and in less than two years was made overseer of all the carding-rooms in the yard, keeping this position till September, 1845, since when he has devoted himself to making surveys and conveyances, a business of which he had acquired a knowledge at school.

In 1845 Mr. James was elected, by the Whig party, representative to the general court from Manchester, and was re-elected the next year. In the spring of 1847 he was elected mayor and served through 1847 and 1848 and till October, 1849, when he was displaced by the election of Warren L. Lane. He was the nominee of the Republican party in the fall of 1856 and was elected by a large majority, serving through 1857. He was the chief engineer of the fire department in 1851 and 1855. In 1862 he was the second member of the committee which had charge of building the new high-school house and devoted considerable time to the superintendence of the work. He was six years one of the county commissioners for Hillsborough county, being elected in 1864 and re-elected in 1867. Since 1867, as a member of the committee which has the public cemeteries of the city in charge, he has given much attention to their care and decoration. He has been a trustee of the Amoskeag Savings Bank since its organization.

Mr. James married, in 1840, Harriet, the daughter of Charles Priest of Lancaster, Mass., who is still living. They have had three children, all of whom are dead.

Mr. James has borne a very conspicuous part in Manchester since it became a city. He has enjoyed to a remarkable degree the confidence of the people, a confidence he has never forfeited. Honest and trustworthy in whatever position he holds, whether as the highest official of the city, as the executor or administrator of the numerous estates with the settlement of which he has been entrusted, or as a guardian of children, he always discharges his duties conscientiously and with high notions of right and wrong. Careful, prudent and circumspect, he is highly esteemed by those who have been obliged to look to others for advice in business or other relations.

THE HON. WARREN L. LANE.

Warren Lovejoy Lane was born at Sanbornton, N. H., August 31, 1805, and was the son of Daniel and Lydia (Lovejoy) Lane. He was the eldest of a family of two sons and three daughters, of whom he was the last survivor. His grandfather on his mother's side enlisted as a minute-man in the Revolutionary War and was wounded at the battle of Bunker Hill. He died March 4, 1861, over fifty-five years old.

His father died when he was quite young, leaving him the responsibility which falls upon the eldest son. He removed to Hampstead, N. H., when he was about fourteen years of age and was apprenticed to a manufacturer and tanner and then was a clerk in a country store. While there he married, September 23, 1827, Miss Sally C., daughter of Dr. Joshua Sawyer of Hampstead, by whom he had three sons and one daughter, of whom only Daniel W. Lane, assistant cashier of the City National Bank, survives. He early took an interest in political matters, was often elected to the town offices and in 1841 and 1842 represented Hampstead in the popular branch of the state legislature. While a resident of that town he held a military commission from Gov. Morrill, Gov. Harvey and Gov. Harper. In 1832 he received from President Van Buren the appointment of deputy United States marshal and took the census of thirteen towns in Rockingham county.

RESIDENCE OF B. F. MARTIN, ESQ.

In 1842 he removed to Manchester and engaged in the West India goods trade, but in 1845 he was appointed postmaster by President Polk and served four years. He had been in 1844 chairman of the board of selectmen and in 1849 was elected mayor of the city by the Democratic party. In 1850 he was the chief engineer of the fire department and the same year was appointed special justice of the police court. In 1851 he was appointed insurance commissioner by Gov. Dinsmoor, and in 1853 he was made deputy-sheriff for Hillsborough, Rockingham and Merrimack counties, holding that position till the overthrow of the Democratic party in 1855.

In the early days of Manchester Mr. Lane was one of the active, stirring and prominent men. Before he was appointed special justice of the police court his reputation was such that he was made, by consent of the parties interested, what would now be called a referee or final arbitrator, in numerous cases. He possessed a sound, strong mind and a clear head and was disposed to do what was fair and right between man and man. His social nature was largely developed and he drew around himself a large circle of admiring friends who delighted to honor him with some position. He always filled with great acceptance the offices he held and from their number can be deduced his popularity.

COL. B. F. MARTIN.

Benjamin Franklin Martin was born July 21, 1813, at Peacham, Vt. He is the son of Truman and Mary (Noyes) Martin and one of a family of five sons and four daughters, of whom but two besides himself survive, Truman and Hannah N., who live on the homestead at Peacham. He assisted his father in farming, acquiring meanwhile an education in the common schools and at Peacham Academy, till he was eighteen years of age, when he went to Meredith Bridge (now Laconia) to learn the trade of a paper-maker in his brother's mill. He spent one year there and then went to Millbury, Mass., and worked a year as a journeyman in a paper-mill. At the end of that time he went into business with his brother-in-law, the late Thomas Rice, at Newton Lower Falls, Mass., where he manufactured paper till 1844, when the partnership was dissolved and he bought a mill at Middleton, Mass., and remained there nine years.

In 1853 he had perfected arrangements to remove to Lawrence, Mass., but in consequence of some inducements which were offered him, he came to Manchester instead and built the Amoskeag paper-mill upon the upper canal just above what are now the Langdon mills. He sold it in 1865 to Hudson Keeney but bought it again four years later and continued in business as a manufacturer of paper till 1874, when he retired, selling his mill to John Hoyt & Company.

Mr. Martin was elected by the Republicans of ward three a member of the common council in 1857 and 1858, alderman in 1860, and representative to the state legislature in 1863 and 1864. He acquired the rank of colonel by service upon Gov. Gilmore's staff in 1863 and 1864, and was a delegate to the national Republican convention at Chicago which nominated Abraham Lincoln for President in 1860. In 1859 he was an assistant engineer of the fire department. He was elected a director of the Merrimack River Bank upon its organization in 1845, became its president in 1859, and dissolved his connection with it the next year. Upon the organization of the Merrimack River Five Cents Savings Institution in 1858, he became one of its trustees and was elected a vice-president in 1860, resigning soon after. In 1860 he was chosen to succeed David Gillis as a director in the Manchester Bank, and, upon the formation of the Manchester National Bank, was elected a director. In 1865 he was chosen a trustee of the Manchester Savings Bank and now holds both of these positions. He has been a director of the Manchester and Lawrence Railroad for the last ten years and a director of the Concord and Portsmouth Railroad since its name was changed from that of the Portsmouth and Concord Railroad.

Col. Martin married, January 3, 1836, Mary Ann Rice, a sister of the Hon. Alexander H. and Willard Rice, of Boston, by whom he has had three daughters, of whom Fanny R., the wife of the Hon. George B. Chandler of Manchester, is living.

Col. Martin is a man with a strong mind, clear and quick to see, practical, well balanced, and his strong constitution and active temperament have enabled him to do a large business during his life and to do it with great success. He is a very generous man, gives liberally to all benevolent enterprises and is one of the chief supporters of Grace church. He makes a good citizen and has been repeatedly spoken of for state senator and mayor. A man of a courteous, gentlemanly, dignified bearing, of a strong social nature, he has many warm personal friends.

THE HON. JOHN P. NEWELL.

John Plumer Newell was born July 29, 1823, at Barnstead, N. H. He is the son of William H. and Olive (Dennett) Newell, who are now living, and was one of thirteen children, of whom all but one survive. They are as follows, in the order of birth: Moses D. of Elo, Wis.; Betsey H., the wife of David Clark of Farmington; Mary F., the wife of John Hanscom of Northwood; Charles D. of Concord; John P., the subject of this sketch; Harriet, the wife of Charles S. Emerson of Pittsfield; Samuel A. of Cato Falls, Wis.; William J. of Lawrence, Mass.; Olive, the wife of N. E.

Cate of Northwood; Albert M. of Gilmanton; Lafayette V. of Portsmouth; Arthur C. of Farmington.

Mr. Newell spent his early life upon his father's farm, acquiring an education in the high school at Barnstead and fitting for college at the academies in Rochester, Pittsfield and Gilmanton. He entered Dartmouth College in 1845 and graduated in 1849 at the head of his class. After graduating he taught the academy at Pittsfield, studying law meanwhile with A. F. L. Norris, till March, 1851, when he came to Manchester to take charge of the high school, which he taught till the summer term of 1853. He then resumed the study of law in the office of S. H. & B. F. Ayer of this city and was admitted in August to the bar of Hillsborough county. Early in the winter of 1853 he opened an office in Manchester and continued in the practice of his profession till the spring of 1855, when he resumed charge of the high school, continuing its principal till the fall of 1862. In May, 1863, he became principal of Pinkerton Academy at Derry, N. H., and held the position till the summer of 1865, when he returned to Manchester, where he has since made his home, being engaged in general business.

Mr. Newell was elected by the city councils in February, 1873, mayor of Manchester and was one of its representatives in the legislature in 1872 and 1874. He was elected in 1856 president of the first Young Men's Christian Association in this city and served one year and since 1869 has been the president of the present Association. He has been since 1872 a deacon of the Hanover-street church, since 1868 president of the society connected with it and for ten years was superintendent of its Sunday-school.

Mr. Newell married, August 14, 1855, Mary W., daughter of the late Chief Justice Samuel D. Bell, by whom he had one child, who died in infancy. His first wife died August 28, 1858, and he married, January 15, 1863, Elizabeth

M., daughter of the Hon. T. T. Abbot, formerly mayor of the city, by whom he has one child, Mary Bell, now living.

Mr. Newell is a fine scholar, a Christian gentleman and a pleasant, agreeable man. He has always, whether mayor of the city, teacher of the high school or president of the Young Men's Christian Association, of which he has been so earnest a supporter, exerted an elevating influence upon those with whom he has come in contact. He is an able and popular speaker and while in the legislature was a member of commanding influence. He is painstaking, methodical, conscientious, in whatever position he is. If his nature was as aggressive as his convictions are just and his principles strong, he could easily become one of the most popular and influential men in the city.

A. P. OLZENDAM.

Abraham Peter Olzendam was born, October 10, 1821, in Barmen, Prussia. He is the son of Abraham P. and Johanna (Rittershaus) Olzendam, and one of a family of two sons and five daughters of whom he is the sole survivor. His early life was spent in the acquirement of a common-school education and in learning the arts of manufacturing, dyeing and coloring. In 1848 he left his native country and came to America, landing at New York. For ten years he lived in Massachusetts, putting in practice in different mills the knowledge of his trade which he had gained at home, and then, in 1858, came to Manchester that he might better his fortunes.

Here he was employed at dyeing and color-mixing in the Amoskeag and Manchester mills till 1862, when he began an independent business, starting a hosiery-mill and continuing to operate it ever since. Mr. Olzendam was sent by the Republicans of ward three as a representative to the state legislature in 1873 and 1874. He has been a trustee of the People's Savings Bank since its organization in August, 1874. He married, October 1, 1851, Therese Lohrer of Dresden, Saxony, by whom he had eight children, of whom five, Clementine, Alexander H., Gustavus, Sidonia and Lewis survive and are living at home. After the death of his first wife, Mr. Olzendam married, May 8, 1872, Mrs. Susie J. Carling.

Mr. Olzendam has risen to a very honorable position in this city, primarily by closely attending to his business as a manufacturer and since then in addition by showing himself an excellent citizen, liberal, high-minded, disposed to do what he can to aid every benevolent object and to further the growth and prosperity of the city. Manchester is better for his coming and his staying. A genial gentleman, he enjoys the acquaintance and confidence of a large number of warm personal friends. Many men, as fortune favors them, withdraw more and more from society and give out less and less towards it, but society feels his prosperity and enjoys with him his success.

THE HON. NATHAN PARKER.

Nathan Parker was born in Litchfield, N. H., November 21, 1808, and is the son of Deacon Matthew Parker and Sarah Underwood, daughter of Judge James Underwood of Litchfield. He was the youngest of six children and is the only survivor. He lived in Litchfield till he was sixteen or seventeen years of age, acquiring his education at the academies in that town and in Henniker, and then went into business in Merrimack, whence he removed in April, 1840, to Manchester, continuing in trade and soon making for himself a large and profitable business. The town was then just rising and Mr. Parker sold large quantities of goods to the corporations and others who were building factories or houses.

Upon the organization of the Manchester Bank in 1845 he became its cashier and continued to hold the office till the Bank was dissolved. He has been the treasurer of the Manchester Savings Bank since it was organized in 1846 and a director and president of the Manchester National Bank since it was formed in 1865. From 1867 to 1871 he was a director and the treasurer of the Concord Railroad, and again, since 1873, its treasurer; he was once treasurer and for the past two or three years has been a director of the Manchester & Lawrence Railroad and for the past three or four years a director of the Concord & Portsmouth Railroad. In 1855 and 1856 he was a member of the state senate and would have been its president if he had been disposed to accept the office. He was a member of the New Hampshire house of representatives in 1863 and 1864.

Mr. Parker married in September, 1837, Miss Charlotte M. Riddle of Merrimack, a grand-daughter of Capt. Isaac Riddle, a wealthy farmer, mill-owner and contractor of Bedford, who built the first canal-boat which was floated on the Merrimack river. She died in October, 1859, leaving one son, Walter M., who is employed in the Manchester Savings Bank.

Mr. Parker belongs to a family of able, clear-headed, keen-minded men, who never act without a reason and who are circumspect and generally wise in all their actions. He is best known to our people as a financier and there is no man in New Hampshire who enjoys the confidence of the public in a greater degree in this respect than does the subject of this sketch. He could have succeeded in any profession in life, whether that of a merchant, lawyer, railway manager or manufacturer. He finally chose the business of banking and has always looked upon the money placed in his keeping through the different banks he manages as funds in trust for him to care for according to the best of his ability. As a result, he has always kept the investments on the safe side, running no risks and meeting with no losses to speak of. All the institutions with which he has been connected have been very successful, managed with a conscientious scrupulousness and with a due regard for the acts of incorporation. He is a pattern banker and his name has become a synonym with honesty.

THE HON. C. E. POTTER.

Chandler Eastman Potter was born March 7, 1807, at Concord, N. H., and was the youngest of the four sons of Joseph and Anna (Drake) Potter, of whom none now survive. His childhood and youth were spent at home upon his father's farm and in attending the district school till he was eighteen years of age, when he went to the academy at Pembroke, N. H., and was there fitted for college under Master John Vose. He entered Dartmouth College in 1827 and graduated in 1831. He taught in 1832, 1833 and 1834 select or high schools, in Concord one year and in Portsmouth, N. H., two, and in 1835 was sent from the latter town a representative to the state legislature. He again taught in the high school in Portsmouth from 1835 to 1838, reading law while there with the Hon. Ichabod Bartlett and afterwards, from 1841 to 1843, with Pierce & Fowler at Concord.

He then began practice at East Concord and in March, 1844, came to Manchester and became the editor and proprietor of the Manchester Democrat, which position he continued to hold till the fall of 1848 when he sold the paper. He had already, in June, 1848, been appointed justice of the police court of Manchester and retained that office till July, 1855. In 1852 and 1853 he edited the Farmers' Monthly Visitor and in 1854 and 1855 the Granite Farmer & Visitor.

Truly yours
C. W. Wallace

Judge Potter married, November 1, 1832, Miss Clara A., daughter of John Underwood of Portsmouth. She died at Manchester March 19, 1854. To them were born four children, of whom Joseph H., of Hillsborough, N. H., and Treat of this city survive. His second marriage, November 11, 1856, was with Miss Frances Maria, daughter of Gen. John McNeil of Hillsborough, a soldier of 1812. After this marriage Judge Potter took up his residence in Hillsborough upon the Gov. Pierce farm, in the cultivation of which he found employment. He died suddenly, August 3, 1868, at Flint, Mich., whither he had gone in the previous July to look after some property.

Judge Potter was an antiquarian in taste, was elected a member of the New Hampshire Historical Society in 1841, one of its vice-presidents in 1852 and its president in 1855, 1856 and 1857. He was elected in 1851 a corresponding member of the New England Historic-Genealogical Society, and in 1856 a corresponding member of the Maryland Historical Society. He was the author of a history of Manchester, which was published in 1856, and of the military history of New Hampshire from 1623 to the War of the Rebellion in 1861, partially revised Belknap's History of New Hampshire and was a voluminous writer otherwise.

Judge Potter had much natural ability, but he was so constituted that he did not bring out the great powers of his mind except on compulsion. He needed the stimulus of friends or the inspiration of a great occasion to do himself full justice, and always put off the labor of preparation till the last minute. He had a vast store of information upon historical subjects and a great fund of personal anecdotes with which he was wont to amuse and interest his friends. He was well informed upon all the topics of the day, political, educational and moral, talked ably and was remarkably entertaining in conversation, but disliked the task of writing out his thoughts. With a short-hand reporter to take down his thoughts as he uttered them, he could have furnished daily enough matter for the leading articles in a good-sized newspaper.

GEN. WILLIAM P. RIDDLE.

William Pickle Riddle was born in Bedford, N. H., April 6, 1789, being named for a well-known clergyman of that town, and died in Piscataquog village in Manchester of neuralgia May 18, 1875, being then over eighty-six years of age. He was the eldest of the five sons of Isaac and Ann (Aiken) Riddle, of whom Isaac, of this city, is now living. There were three children by a subsequent marriage, of whom one, Margaret Ann, wife of Gen. Joseph C. Stevens of Lancaster, Mass., survives. Mr. Riddle was the grandson of Gawn Riddle, who came over with his brothers from the north of Ireland, being of Scotch extraction, and settled in Londonderry about 1737, whence they removed to Bedford about 1758.

Mr. Riddle was educated at the academy in Atkinson, N. H., and, when twenty-two years old, engaged in trade in Piscataquog village. With his father and two brothers he formed the firm of Isaac Riddle & Sons, which was largely engaged in mercantile and manufacturing business, and as one of the firm he took an active part in the construction of the Union Locks and Canals by which the Merrimack was made navigable from Concord to Lowell and in the establishment of a line of daily canal-boats from Concord and Boston. Upon the death of his father in 1830, the firm was dissolved and he carried on the business, both at Bedford and Merrimack, in his own name, managing saw-mills, grist-mills and stores, operating in woodlands and continuing the boating and rafting business till the Concord railway was built in 1842. The old yellow store in Piscataquog village was the scene of most of his operations and his business was very extensive. He furnished building lumber for Lowell, Boston and Newburyport, spars and ship-timber for the United States navy-yard at Charlestown, Mass., and material for the railways then being built in Massachusetts. He dealt largely in hops, buying them all over this state, Vermont and Canada, marketing them in Boston, New York and Philadelphia and sometimes exporting them. In 1846, having been for a number of years deputy-inspector of hops, he was made inspector-general for the state and held the office as long as it was in existence. The Piscataquog steam-mills were built by him in 1848. About 1860 he retired from active business. He was always much engaged in agriculture, owning several farms, and was a patron of the state and county fairs.

He had from his youth a taste for military affairs. When but twenty-five years of age he organized a company known as the "Bedford Grenadiers" and was its first captain. Five years later he was promoted to be major of the old Ninth regiment of state militia and rose through the ranks of lieutenant-colonel, colonel and brigadier-general to that of major-general, which position he held till his resignation in 1835. He also assisted in the formation of the Amoskeag Veterans in 1854 and was their first commander.

Gen. Riddle was a prominent man in civil affairs, frequently moderator of the town-meetings, representative to the legislature, county road-commissioner, etc. He was a member of the association which built the old Piscataquog meeting-house in 1820 and was one of the building committee. He superintended the construction of many of the bridges across the Piscataquog river and was the president of the Granite Bridge Company which built the toll-bridge across the Merrimack at Merrill's Falls where Granite Bridge now is.

Gen. Riddle became a Mason in 1823 and in the succeeding year was active in the formation of Lafayette Lodge, which was started in Bedford but removed to this city. He was one of its charter members, allowed it the use of his hall for twenty-five years without compensation and was the last survivor but one, if not the last, of its projectors. He was also a member of Mt. Horeb Royal Arch Chapter and of Trinity Commandry of Knights Templars.

In politics Gen. Riddle was first a Whig and afterwards a Republican and an ardent supporter of the government during the late War of the Rebellion. In religion he was a Unitarian and was one of the founders of the First Unitarian church in this city.

He married in 1824 Miss Sarah, daughter of Capt. John Ferguson of Dunbarton, N. H., by whom he had seven children, of whom three survive — George W. of this city, William Q. of New York city and Daniel W. of Waterloo, N. Y. This sketch of his life shows him to have been one of the most prominent men of his day in this section of the state of New Hampshire. His mind was of a very practical turn, keen and active, and executive ability was one of his most conspicuous characteristics. He belonged to the old school of gentlemen, liberal, genial and hospitable, and filled with credit the various places of responsibility to which he was called.

COL. WATERMAN SMITH.

Waterman Smith was born, July 16, 1816, in Smithfield, R. I., which had been originally granted to his ancestors, for whom it was named. He is the son of Waterman and Sally (Cory) Smith and is descended from Quaker ancestry on both sides. He had five brothers and three sisters, of whom there survive Elisha A. and Martin H., living in Cranston, R. I., and Ann Eliza and Sarah A., living in Providence, R. I.

He was brought up on his father's farm and was educated

from the time he was seven till he was fourteen in Greenville Academy in his native town. Then he was sent to Bolton Seminary, a Quaker institution in Bolton, Mass., and remained there four years, returning to Smithfield to learn the machinist's trade in his father's shop. He spent two years there and then three more in learning manufacturing in his brother's cotton-mill in Cumberland, R. I. At the end of that time he went to Thompson, Conn., to superintend the Slater Mills.

When the property was sold in 1842 he went to Scituate, R. I., to fit up a carding-room for Brown & Huse, and continued in their employ about two years. Then he went to Philadelphia, where he spent five or six years as the superintendent of the John L. Hughes Mills. Returning to Smithfield, he remained there about three years, in charge of the Georgia Mills. In 1851 he went to Cohoes, N. Y., to re-fit for J. C. Howe & Company, of Boston, the Ogden Mills there. In March, 1853, he came to Manchester and became the agent of the Manchester Print-Works, of which J. C. Howe & Company were the selling agents. He remained in this position till July, 1871, when he resigned and went to California, spending a year in traveling over that state, several of the western territories and part of the British dominions. Since his return in 1872 he has been chiefly occupied in the care of his property. During the thirty-one years from 1840 to 1871 there were but three months when he was not engaged in manufacturing.

Col. Smith, politically, has been a Whig and a Republican and now calls himself a Liberal Republican. He acquired the rank of colonel by service on Gov. Smyth's staff in 1865. He was chairman of the board of education in this city from 1860 to 1867, and has taken a personal interest in the construction of school-houses. During the existence of the Merrimack River Bank he was one of its directors and after 1860 its president, and he has been president of the First National Bank and the Merrimack River Savings Bank from their beginning.

Col. Smith married in 1840 at Thompson, Conn., Anna C., eldest daughter of Shadrach Randall of North Providence, R. I., by whom he has had four sons and five daughters, of whom the latter only survive. Sally W., is the wife of John H. Andrews of this city; Nattie B., is the wife of Capt. J. C. Currier of San Francisco, Cal.; Harriet Newell is the wife of Harry H. Hale of Boston, Mass.; and Augusta G., and Nellie are living at home in this city.

Col. Smith is a man of fine personal appearance, tall, strong and of great muscular activity. Being so constituted and possessing a strong mental endowment besides, he naturally attracts the public attention in all his movements. He can do nothing on a small scale. All his plans are for large enterprises with great combinations of forces, whether as a manufacturer, builder, operator in real estate or farmer. He is continually uneasy at not doing a larger business, his mind is never at rest, and if he had nothing to do, he would be miserable. He is always seeking new fields of thought and adventure. Yet he is cautious and prudent, and has amassed a very handsome property. While he was the agent of the Manchester Print-Works, he worked hard early and late for the prosperity of that corporation, and, as a rule, seems to have made it a point to do all he undertakes to do thoroughly.

THE HON. FREDERICK SMYTH.

Frederick Smyth was born in Candia, N. H., March 9, 1819. He is the son of Stephen and Dolly (Rowe) Smyth — she being a daughter of Isaiah Rowe, a soldier of the Revolution — and was one of a family of five children, three sons and two daughters, of whom three besides himself survive, — Gilman C., of this city, Abraham C., who

RESIDENCE OF WATERMAN SMITH, ESQ.

resides in Missouri, and Sarah, the widow of the late Jacob S. York of this city. He spent his early life in working upon his father's farm and in acquiring an education at the district-school and, for a short time, under Dr. Coleman at Andover, Mass., and then went into trade in Candia in partnership with Thomas Wheat. In 1838 they abandoned the business and came to Manchester, where Dr. Wheat is now a physician. Mr. Smyth, then nineteen years of age, became a clerk in a large dry-goods and grocery store, and subsequently went into business for himself. In 1844 he married Emily, daughter of John Lane of Candia, but has had no children.

In 1849, 1850 and 1851 he was city clerk. In 1852, 1853 and 1854 he was elected mayor, each time by increased majorities, and again in 1864, when there was hardly any opposition. He has been conspicuous in connection with many improvements, among which may be mentioned the planting of many of the trees which shade the city's streets, the establishment of the free public library and the annexation of Amoskeag and Piscataquog villages. In 1855 he was appointed by Gov. Metcalf chairman of a board of commissioners to locate and build a house of reformation for juvenile offenders, which they accomplished in the face of much opposition. In 1857 and 1858 he was a member from Manchester of the popular branch of the state legislature.

In 1861 he was appointed by the United States government a commissioner to the International Exhibition at London, England, and acted as one of the jurors at the distribution of the awards. At that time he made an extended tour upon the continent of Europe as a commissioner of the United States Agricultural Society. In 1865 he was elected governor of the state and re-elected in 1866. In 1865 he received from Dartmouth College the honorary degree of Master of Arts. In 1866 he was chosen by Congress, for six years, one of the managers of the national asylums for disabled soldiers, and was re-elected in 1872 for another term of six years.

Gov. Smyth was elected in 1851 treasurer of the New Hampshire Agricultural Society, and served for some ten years, when he was chosen president, holding the office several years. He is a trustee of the New Hampshire College of Agriculture and the Mechanic Arts, a vice-president of the New England Agricultural Society and the United States Pomological Society and one of the directors of the United States Agricultural Society. He was cashier of the Merrimack River Bank from its formation in 1856 till it gave place in 1865 to the First National Bank, of which he has been the cashier since its organization and a director since 1870. He has also been a trustee and the treasurer of the Merrimack River Savings Bank since its organization in 1858.

Gov. Smyth has made a name not only in this city and state but in the nation. He is self-made in the strongest sense of that term, and, with no money but what his own hands earned and with no education except that which he picked up at the school and academy, he has risen from the humblest sphere in life to the highest offices in the city or in the gift of the people of New Hampshire. With the principles he learned at home of love for the Bible, the church and the school-house, with a sharp, keen, well-balanced mind, with an activity and persistency that never tire, he has been able to accomplish such great results as are indicated in the preceding sketch. Of a generous and obliging nature, with an instinctive disposition to help all who came to him for advice, for money or for position, though they came from the lowest walks of life, he has always possessed the elements of great popularity, and, as mayor of the city for several terms and as governor of the state, he has been excelled by no one in this respect.

During the war he was a great worker for the soldiers at home and in the camp, doing all he could for their personal comfort. He has many warm personal friends and stands by them to the last. As a financier, he has been remarkably successful, but, possessed, as he is, of great executive ability, would have succeeded as well in other callings in life. He stands preëminent as a citizen, ever ready to do his part for education, morality, religion or for whatever pertains to the general adornment of the city.

THE HON. C. W. STANLEY.

Clinton Warrington Stanley was born December 5, 1830, at Hopkinton, N. H. He is the son of Horace C., and Mary Ann (Kimball) Stanley and had two brothers and one sister. The brothers are now living — Benton M. P., at New London, N. H., and Edward W., on the homestead at Hopkinton. He acquired his preliminary education at the district-school and academy in Hopkinton and entered Dartmouth College in 1845 at the age of fourteen, being the youngest man in his class. He graduated in 1849 and began the study of law, pursuing it at first in Hopkinton with the Hon. Hamilton E. Perkins, now of Concord, from July, 1849, till April, 1851, and then with the Hon. George W. Morrison of this city.

August 9, 1852, he was admitted to the bar of Hillsborough county from Mr. Morrison's office and then went to Hopkinton, where he remained till April, 1853, when he returned to Manchester and began practice in company with Mr. Morrison. The partnership has since existed in various forms, John L. Fitch, now deceased, Lewis W. Clark and Frank Hiland being at times partners, till September 11, 1874, when Mr. Stanley accepted the appointment of associate justice of the circuit court of this state, which position he now holds. He has held the office of United

States commissioner from 1857 to the present time and has been president of the City National Bank since its organization in 1865. He married, December 24, 1857, Miss Lydia A. Woodbury of Weare, N. H. He has no children.

Judge Stanley's intellect places him in the foremost rank of able men in the state. With remarkable natural capacity, a quick and vigorous thinker, he has the art of putting his thoughts without difficulty into practical forms. He excels in whatever he turns his attention to, whether law, finance or politics. He grapples very readily with any new subject that arises and should he occupy the bench many years would be eminent as a judge. His mind is very active, he keeps himself familiar with all the questions of the day and has his own opinions on all of them. A man of quick comprehension and large energy, he has been able to do a great deal of mental labor. He has been very successful as a lawyer, attending to the finances and practical work of an office which has done a large business for many years.

THE HON. E. A. STRAW.

Ezekiel Albert Straw was born in Salisbury, N. H., December 30, 1819. He is the eldest son of James B. and Mehitable (Fisk) Straw and one of a family of seven children, five sons and two daughters, of whom three besides himself survive — Miranda, wife of Benjamin F. Manning, Abigail and James B., all resident in Manchester. His father, after a few years' residence in this state, removed to Lowell, Mass., where he entered into the service of the Appleton Manufacturing Company. Mr. Straw acquired his education in the schools of Lowell and in the English department of Phillips Academy at Andover, Mass., where he gave especial attention to practical mathematics.

Upon leaving this institution, he was, in the spring of

1838, employed as assistant civil engineer upon the Nashua and Lowell railway, then in process of construction. In July, 1838, he was sent for by Mr. Boyden, the consulting engineer of the Amoskeag Manufacturing Company, to take the place of T. J. Carter, the regular engineer, who was kept from work by sickness. He came to this city July 4, 1838, expecting to remain but a few days, and has ever since made it his home. This was before a mill had been built upon the eastern side of the river and before the Company's first public sale of land. Among his first duties were the laying out of the lots and streets in what is now the compact part of the city and assisting in the construction of the dam and canals. In November, 1844, he was sent by the Amoskeag Company to England and Scotland to obtain the information and machinery necessary for making and printing muslin delaines, and the success of the Manchester Print-Works, which first introduced this manufacture into the United States, was due to the knowledge and skill he then acquired. He continued in the employ of the Amoskeag Company as civil engineer until July, 1851, when he was appointed the agent of the land and water-power department of the Company, that, the mills and the machine-shops then being managed separately under different agents. In July, 1856, the first two were united and put in charge of Mr. Straw, and in July, 1858, all three were combined under one management and Mr. Straw assumed the entire control at Manchester of the Company's operations.

Mr. Straw was prominent in the early years of the town's prosperity in connection with all its material improvements and has always retained his interest in the city. He was a member of the committee to provide plans and specifications for the rebuilding of the town-house in 1844 and one of the first committee appointed to devise plans for the introduction of water into the town. He has been connected with all the subsequent plans for the same purpose and when the board of water commissioners, who have had charge of the construction of the present water-works, was appointed, in 1871, he was made its president and has held the office ever since. He was chosen in 1854 a member of the first board of trustees of the public library and has held the office ever since, the present library building, erected in 1871, owing much to his interest and care.

Mr. Straw was elected in 1859 representative from Manchester to the state legislature, was re-elected in 1860, 1861, 1862 and 1863, and during the last three years was chairman of the committee on finance. In 1864 he was elected to the state senate and was re-elected in 1865, being chosen its president in the latter year. He was also chosen on the part of the senate one of the commissioners to superintend the rebuilding of the state-house. In 1869 he was appointed by Gov. Stearns a member of his staff. In 1872 he was elected by the Republicans of New Hampshire governor of the state and re-elected in 1873. In 1870 he was appointed by President Grant the member from New Hampshire of the commission to arrange for the centennial celebration of the independence of the United States at Philadelphia, Pa., in 1876, and is one of the executive board of that commission.

Gov. Straw was the treasurer and principal owner of the Namaske Mills from its organization in 1856 till its dissolution, and after 1864 its sole proprietor. In 1874 he was chosen a director of the Langdon Mills. He was the president and one of the directors of the Blodget Edge Tool Manufacturing Company from its organization in 1855 till its dissolution in 1862, and since that time has been a director of the Amoskeag Axe Company which succeeded it. He was one of the first directors of the Manchester Gas-Light Company when it was organized in 1851 and has been its president since 1856. Since the organization of the New England Cotton Manufacturers' Association he has been its president and president of the New Hampshire Fire Insurance Company since it was organized in 1869. He has received the honorary degree of master of arts from Dartmouth College. Gov. Straw was one of the founders of the First Unitarian society in 1842, its clerk and treasurer from that time till 1844, its president from 1853 to 1857, and was the chairman of the committee which built its present house of worship.

Gov. Straw married, April 6, 1842, at Amesbury, Mass., Miss Charlotte Smith Webster, who died in Manchester, March 15, 1852. To them were born four children—Albert, who died in infancy; Charlotte Webster, the wife of William H. Howard of Somerville, Mass.; Herman Foster, assistant superintendent of the Amoskeag Company's mills in Manchester; Ellen, the wife of Henry M. Thompson, formerly agent of the Manchester Print-Works and now agent of the Lowell Felting Company at Lowell, Mass.

Gov. Straw, in our judgment, is the ablest man in New Hampshire. In a room full of people, the judges of our courts, the managers of our railways, the professors of our colleges, he would take the lead of all. He is conversant with more subjects than any man we know of, whether art or science, manufactures or financial themes. He is a great reader and his tenacious memory makes all he reads his own. Not long after he came to this city, the Amoskeag Company began to look upon him as competent to manage its whole business and it gradually fell into his hands. In time the other corporations, the city and the state looked to him for advice, and for many years he has been the foremost man in Manchester and for the past few years the leading man in shaping the policy of the state. Of great mental capacities, he is able to turn off a vast amount of work with the greatest ease. He never seems in a hurry, though probably surrounded by more business than any other man in the state. He never looks to others for his opinions, and, though willing to fall into line with his friends and his party in non-essential things, he cannot be swerved from his ideas of what is right by political considerations or fear of unpopularity. He enjoys truth and takes pleasure in doing what his judgment dictates. A very generous man, liberal in his gifts to the poor and to all charitable institutions, to him more than to any other man is Manchester indebted for its great prosperity.

D. B. VARNEY.

David Blake Varney was born in Tuftonborough, N. H., August 27, 1822. He is the son of Luther and Lydia (Blake) Varney, and was one of four children, two sons and two daughters, of whom, besides himself, one brother survives—Edward, who resides in Boston. When four years of age he moved with his parents to Dover, N. H., where he remained till he was sixteen years of age, helping his father upon the farm and acquiring an education in the Dover schools. In 1838 he went to Portsmouth to learn the trade of a machinist, where he spent three years. Then returning to Dover he worked two years there and in March, 1843, came to this city and worked at his trade in the Amoskeag Company's machine-shop. In 1854 he was appointed superintendent of the locomotive department and remained in the shop till 1857.

He then entered into partnership with H. I. Darling, for the manufacture of brass and copper work, and the firm, under the name of Darling & Varney, began business in the foundry on Manchester street. Mr. Darling died in 1868 and left him proprietor of an extensive business, which he has since managed alone. Mr. Varney was a member from ward three in this city of the popular branch of the state legislature in 1871 and 1872 and has been a director of the Amoskeag National Bank since January, 1874. He married in 1848 Harriet B. Kimball of this city, by whom he has had three daughters, of whom two are now living—Emma L. and Annie M.

Mr. Varney has been a very popular man with all who knew him ever since he came to this city. His mental qualities are all good and practical and always at his command. Indebted to his own skill and forethought for his pecuniary success, liberal and genial, he has always been a highly respected citizen. He is a man who could obtain the suffrages of the people whenever he would allow his name to be used, but he has never been ambitious to hold a conspicuous place in public affairs.

THE REV. C. W. WALLACE.

Cyrus Washington Wallace was born in Bedford, March 8, 1805. He is the son of Thomas and Mercy (Frye) Wallace, and was one of a family of five brothers and two sisters, of whom two besides himself are living—Alfred, resident in Washington, D. C., and Mrs. Hannah Pollard of Woburn, Mass. His early life was spent in agricultural and mechanical pursuits and he acquired an education in the district-school of his native town and at Oberlin Seminary, Oberlin, O. He was fitted for the ministry under the instruction of the Rev. Heman Rood and the Rev. Aaron Warner at the theological seminary at Gilmanton, and, having been licensed to preach by the Londonderry Presbytery in April, 1838, came to Manchester in May, 1839, to supply the pulpit of the First Congregational church, then situated at Amoskeag village. After its removal to its present house of worship, he was ordained and installed as its pastor January 8, 1840. He resigned the pastoral charge in August, 1873, but continued to preach in his old pulpit till the December following, since when he has supplied the pulpit of the First Congregational church in Rockland, Mass., though retaining his residence in Manchester. He was the first minister to hold regular Sunday services in the new village on the east side of the river and his pastorate was longer than that of any other Manchester clergyman. He was sent to the state legislature in 1867 and 1868 by the Republicans of ward four, and in the latter year received the degree of Doctor of Divinity from Dartmouth College. He married, May 19, 1840, Miss Susan A. Webster, who died May 15, 1873. He afterwards married, September 30, 1874, Miss Elizabeth H. Allison. He has had no children.

No man is more strongly identified with the early history of the city than the Rev. Dr. Wallace. For nearly thirty-five years he bore a part in every intellectual contest and reform in Manchester. He fought without gloves and with a power we have never known equaled by any other clergyman in the state. Thoroughly honest, never double-dealing, he dealt heavy blows upon the abettors of slavery, rum-selling, gambling, Sabbath-breaking, profanity, card-playing, dancing or of whatever else seemed to him wrong. He is puritanical in his notions, very cutting and severe in reproof, but at the same time very kind and tender-hearted, ready to do everything to reform young men and women and to cheer the suffering and the downcast. He is a vigorous, earnest speaker and his extemporaneous efforts upon great occasions have been sometimes very eloquent.

THE HON. JAMES A. WESTON.

James Adams Weston was born upon the "old Weston farm" in Manchester August 27, 1827. He is the son of Amos and Betsey (Wilson) Weston and was the youngest of five children, of whom he alone survives. He traces his

Engd by A.H.Ritchie

Yours truly
James A. Weston.

lineage to the Westons of Buckinghamshire, England, whose descendants, after coming to this country, were prominent in colonial affairs, and the name of one of them has been handed down as that of the founder of the first Baptist church in America. He is of the sixth generation of the descendants of John Weston, who came from England in 1644 and finally settled in Reading, Mass., in 1652. His grandfather, Amos Weston, moved in 1803 to the farm to which his name has since attached and which is situated in the southeastern part of Manchester, then a part of Londonderry. His father, Amos Weston, a man prominent in the affairs of the town, resided on the old farm till 1853, when he moved to Mr. Weston's present residence near the compact part of the city. His mother was a daughter of Col. Robert Wilson and granddaughter of James Wilson, who came from Londonderry, Ireland, about 1728, and settled at the place now known as Wilson's Crossing in Londonderry, N. H.

The subject of this sketch remained at home, assisting his father upon the farm, most of the time till 1846, except when attending or teaching school. He acquired an education at the district school and at the academies in Manchester and Piscataquog village, giving especial attention to mathematics and civil engineering, for which he developed much taste. In the winter of 1844 he taught school at Londonderry and the next winter in Manchester. He had still pursued his studies and in 1846 was appointed assistant civil engineer of the Concord Railroad and began laying its second track. Three years later he removed to Concord and became the chief engineer of the railroad, a position he has ever since held. For several years in connection with that office he performed the duties of road-master and master of transportation of the Concord and Manchester & Lawrence Railroads. As chief engineer he superintended the construction of the branch of the Concord & Portsmouth railway from Manchester to Candia and of the Suncook Valley railway from Hooksett to Pittsfield. In 1856 he moved to this city where he has since resided, devoting himself chiefly to his profession and to the duties of the public offices he has held.

Mr. Weston was the Democratic candidate for mayor of the city in 1861, 1862 and 1868 and was elected in 1867, 1869, 1870 and 1873. He was elected governor of the state in 1871 and 1874. He has been the vice-president of the New Hampshire Fire Insurance Company since it was organized in 1869 and a trustee of the Amoskeag Savings Bank since 1870. In 1871 he was appointed, as the governor of the state, one of a commission to represent the state in matters relating to the centennial celebration of the national independence at Philadelphia, Pa., in 1876, and in 1872 was appointed by congress a member of the centennial board of finance. He married in 1854 Miss Anna S., daughter of Mitchel Gilmore of Concord, N. H., and has three children living—Grace Helen, James Henry, and Edwin Bell.

Gov. Weston has received from the people of this city and state a very large share of public honors and has borne them well. He has never failed to enjoy the confidence of the residents of his native city and to receive votes beyond the strength of his party when a candidate for any office. A very thoughtful, careful, prudent man, patriotic and high-minded in his natural impulses, he has always been earnest to do what he could for the moral and intellectual elevation of the people. He has been through the fiery ordeal of politics and has been pushed by his party far beyond his natural inclinations. He has been successful as an engineer, as a mayor and as a governor, is very practical on all subjects to which he turns his attention, always writes well and sensibly, and appears to good advantage wherever he is placed.

WILLIAM AMORY.

[Through delay in the engraving it became uncertain whether a portrait of Mr. Amory would be done in season for this volume, and consequently the sketch occurs at the end of the series instead of in its natural place, second in the alphabetical order which has been followed.]

William Amory was born in Boston, Mass., June 15, 1804, and is the son of Thomas C. and Hannah R. (Linzee) Amory. He was one of a family of four sons and four daughters, of whom three only, two sons and one daughter, survive. His father, a merchant of Boston, died in 1812, and seven years later his son, then but fifteen years of age, entered Harvard University. He spent four years there and soon after went to Europe to complete his education. He pursued in Germany the study of law and of general literature, for a year and a half at the university in Gottingen and for nine months at the university in Berlin. He occupied the subsequent two years and a half in travel and returned to Boston May 30, 1830, after an absence of five years. There he pursued his legal studies with Franklin Dexter and W. H. Gardiner and in 1831 was admitted to the bar of Suffolk county, without, however, any intention of entering upon legal practice.

In that year he was chosen the treasurer of the Jackson Manufacturing Company at Nashua, N. H., and began business as a manufacturer. Without experience and yet with a mind which study had disciplined and knowledge of the world had made keen, with remarkable energy and enterprise, he was eminently successful and the Jackson Company paid large and sure dividends for the eleven years he continued its treasurer. In 1837 he became the treasurer of the Amoskeag Manufacturing Company, an office which included at that time, when the plan of creating a city upon the Merrimack was just to be carried out, the responsibility and wisdom of a general manager of the Company's interests, as well as the usual financial duties of a treas urer. He has held that office from then till the present time; has been treasurer of the Stark Mills, with the exception of four years and a half, since its organization in 1839; was a director of the Manchester Mills and its successor, the Manchester Print-Works, from the start in 1839 till 1871; and has been a director of the Langdon Mills from its beginning in 1860 and its president since 1874.

Mr. Amory married in January, 1833, Miss Anna P. G. Sears, daughter of David Sears, an eminent merchant of Boston, by whom he has had six children, of whom four survive.

Mr. Amory is a man with whom, more than with almost any one else, Manchester is closely identified and to whose accurate foresight and comprehensive views a very large proportion of its beauty and success is due. To him as the manager of the Company which gave it its first impulses in life and has ever since assisted its growth, it owes in large measure its wide streets, its pleasant squares and its beautiful cemetery. He has pursued a liberal policy and deserves the city's gratitude. As the treasurer of the Company he has met with eminent success. A man of perfect honor and integrity, cautious and prudent, he has looked upon the funds in his possession as his only in trust to be managed with the utmost care. Herein is to be found the secret of his success. Few men stand better than he in the business world of his native city or elsewhere. A gentleman of culture, of the utmost polish, with a very pleasing appearance, he enjoys the affection and respect of many personal friends.

INDEX.

This index aims to be complete so far as it regards the first five chapters and the one which describes Manchester's part in the War of the Rebellion, excluding, however, in these, the lists of town and city officers and of the soldiers in the war. The other chapters are also minutely indexed, with the exception of such names as occur in regular sequence with the subjects under consideration, such as those of the officers of churches, banks, manufacturing corporations and societies of all kinds, of postmasters and schoolmasters, and of the editors and proprietors of newspapers in the chapter upon that theme. In the chapter upon representative men, the name of the subject, only, of each sketch occurs in the index.

Abbot, T. T........................98, 341
Abbott, David........................ 129
Guard...............339, 340, 342
Joseph C.............44, 339, 343
Academy, Manchester.......... 247
Mount St. Mary's 121
Piscataquog Village......... 184
Adams, Phinehas......89, 96, 98, 288, 373
Adjutants........................... 369
Adoniram Council...............212, 219
Advent Church, Second............. 192
Sunday School, Second...... 192
Advertiser, Manchester Mercantile... 329
Semi-Weekly............... 326
Agriculture, New Hampshire Journal of....................332, 334
Aid Society, Manchester Women's... 207
Piscataquog................. 206
Aldermen............................ 45
Ale, made........................... 318
Allodium, Manchester............... 326
American & Messenger..........324, 327
Daily........99, 325, 327, 328, 332
Democrat &................. 327
Excelsior Company........... 321
Manchester...............30, 324
Mirror &.................... 332
Semi-Weekly............... 324
Amherst, shire town................. 17
Amory, William..... 443
Amoskeag, Axe Company... 308
Bank........................ 257
branch of Goffstown church.. 143
branch of Manchester Baptist church..................... 144
Brewery....... 318
bridge.... ....19, 77
brook........................ 69
cemetery in.................. 75
Company's agents' houses... 277
ledge........................ 286
reservoir................97, 286

Amoskeag Cotton and Woolen Manufacturing Company......23, 268
Cotton and Wool Factory...23 267
Duck and Bag Mills.......... 304
Falls..........11, 78, 95, 267, 371
bridge..................28, 78
Grange...................... 243
hall......................... 141
Hotel........................ 79
Insurance Company.......27, 265
Joint Stock Company........ 135
Land & Water Power Co..274, 275
Locks and Canal Co......270, 279
Machine-shop........272, 275, 283
Manufacturing Company..24, 269
Memorial.................... 323
mills........................ 279
fire at..................... 95
production of............... 283
National Bank.............. 258
New Mills................... 275
old mills at................ 275
Paper-Mill.................. 314
Republican.................. 323
Rifles...................... 342
Savings Bank............... 259
steamer company........... 86
steam fire engines....272, 285, 311
Veterans.................... 237
village.....12, 42, 70, 100, 111, 130, 131, 139, 141, 143, 183, 249, 253, 273, 315, 321.
Ancient and Honorable Artillery Company.................. 237, 240
Angell, Jesse F.................. 344
Antiquarian Sacred Musical Society. 248
Aqueduct, City...................... 90
Company, Manchester....... 90
Manchester................. 90
Architecture of churches............ 196
Art Association..................... 242
Arms, made......................... 285
Artillery, Heavy.................345, 364
Thirteenth New York....... 368
Association, Art..................... 242
Excelsior Literary........... 248
Firemen's Relief............ 87
Forrest Dramatic........... 246
Masonic Relief.............. 212
Odd Fellows Building........ 223
Relief..................... 224
of high school alumni........ 119
of Boston Veterans.......... 237
Printers' Literary........... 246
Association, Pythian Relief.......... 231
state teachers'............120, 335
St. Patrick's Mutual Benefit and Protective............ 244
teachers'..................... 119
Union................151, 164, 187
Young Men's Christian..185, 191, 194, 200.
Associations, former................ 246
loan.......................... 248
military...................... 236
working-men's............... 247
Atheneum, Manchester............29, 88
Austin, Jeremiah.................. 318
Ayer, Anna, murder of............. 24
Richard H...............44, 164
Axe-handles, made................ 313
Axes, made........................ 308

Bags, made.....................283, 292
Baker, Andrew N.................. 297
Joseph...................... 70
Bakersville........................ 70
Balch, Charles E.................. 375
Baldwin & Company's steam-mill..96, 99
Baldwin, Cyrus W................. 292
Gould & Company........... 316
James...................... 312
Nahum...................... 271
Baldwin's Cornet Band............ 341
Band, Baldwin's Cornet............ 341
of the Fourth Regiment..... 342
Bands of Hope.................... 235
Bank, Amoskeag.................. 257
National.................. 258
Savings................... 259
City........................ 261
National.................. 261
Savings................... 262
First National.............. 263
Manchester................. 255
National.................. 256
Savings................... 256
Merrimack River............ 262
Savings................... 264
of Amoskeag Company...... 254
People's Savings........... 265
Banks.............................. 254
Baptist church, early.............. 129
Elm-street................ 173
First..27, 101, 143, 147, 170, 199
Merrimack-street.......... 147
Second.................... 171
Society, First.............. 145

Baptist society, Merrimack-street..... 174
Second 189
Sunday-school, First..... 145
Merrimack-street..... 174
Barbarossa Lodge..... 245
Barnes, Charles..... 321
George A.....250, 261
Barrett, James..... 274
Barr, Russell —— & Company..... 270
Bartlett, Charles H.....67, 376
Batchelder, R. N..... 341
Battery, B, U. S. A..... 368
First Light.....240, 367
Bayley, Blood & Company..... 306
Baxter, Thomas..... 341
Bean, N. S..... 276
steamer company..... 86
Bective, Earl..... 220
Beer, made..... 318
Bell, Chief-Justice..... 110
George..... 84
Louis..... 241
Samuel D....31, 32, 41, 84, 89, 134
Samuel N.....67, 89, 91
Belmont Print-Works..... 321
Belting, made..... 312
Benevolent Lodge..... 214
societies..... 206
Bennett, Joseph E.....271, 377
Bennington, battle of..... 18
Betogkom, Simon.....11, 127
Bible Lodge..... 212
Bisco, Dwight..... 312
George..... 312
Black brook..... 69
Blackmar Union..... 233
Blacksmiths' union..... 235
Blanchard, Joseph..... 128
William..... 321
Blazing Star Lodge..... 214
Bleachery, Manchester..... 319
Blinds, made.....313, 318, 320
Blodget Edge Tool Manufacturing Company..... 308
Paper Company.....303, 319
Samuel.....17, 19, 21
Blodget's canal.....20, 278
Blood, Aretas.....91, 307, 380
Bayley, —— & Company..... 306
Board of engineers, first..... 29
of health, first..... 26
Boards, made.....315, 317
Bobbins, made..... 312
Boilers, made..... 285
Bouton, Nathaniel..... 136
Bow Canal Company..... 270
Boxes, made.....315, 317
Bradley, Charles B..... 313
Brass work, made..... 316
Brewer donation..... 89
Gardner.....24, 89
and company.....276,289, 302
Brewery, Amoskeag..... 318
Haines & Wallace's..... 99
Bridge, Amoskeag.....19, 77
at Amoskeag Falls.....28, 78
at Goffe's Falls..... 78
first..... 77
Granite.....27, 77
Manchester & North Weare railway.....78, 101
McGregor's.....19, 77, 278
Bridges..... 77
Brigadier-generals..... 369
Brooks..... 69
Brown, Hiram.....31, 271, 320, 341
Thomas.....31, 232
William W.....345, 381
Bruce, John N..... 340
Brugger, John.....100, 313
Bryant & Rogers..... 371
Buckley, Henry..... 321
Buncher, M. Jennie..... 345
Bunton, Andrew..... 271
David A.....74, 320, 340, 383
Burnham, Henry E..... 84
John A..... 31
pond..... 92

Cabinet, Farmers'..... 326
Cadets, High School,..... 241
of Temperance..... 233
Temperance..... 236
Caldwell, John..... 26
Camp Currier..... 343
Hale..... 343
Pillsbury..... 344
Sullivan..... 342
Canal, Blodget's..... 20, 278
companies..... 270
Canals, present.....79, 270, 278
Captain of the watch..... 85
Captains..... 369
Car & Machine Works, Manchester, 320
Cards, machine, made..... 312
Carey, Henry F..... 229
Carriages, made..... 314
Carter, T. J..... 271

Cassimere, made.................... 306
Castings, made..................307, 320
Cavalry, New England.............. 363
New Hampshire............ 363
Cemetery brook,..............69, 317, 321
Forest..................... 129
Valley..................... 27
Cemeteries........................ 73
Chandler, George B........... 197, 386
James O.................... 345
J. M....................... 211
& Company.............. 250
Peter K.................... 136
Channing, William H............... 162
Chapel, First Freewill Baptist....130, 148, 158, 247.
Chapel hall....................... 155
Chaplains......................... 369
Chapter, Mt. Horeb Royal Arch, 211, 215
Charter, city......................31, 42
surrender of............... 41
Chase, Benjamin H................. 312
John B..................... 317
John N..................... 86
pond....................... 92
Check-lists....................... 43
Cheney, B. H...................... 129
James S.................... 79
P. C................... 315, 387
Choctaw Indian.................... 215
Choral Union, Manchester.......... 245
Christian church, First........... 194
society, First.............. 193
Sunday-school, First......... 194
Christophe, Sebastian............. 313
Church, Baptist................... 129
Elm-street.............. 173
First...27, 101, 143, 147, 170, 199
Merrimack-street......... 174
Second.................. 171
Christian.................. 194
Congregational, First..26, 98, 100, 130, 131, 180, 185, 201.
Franklin-street....168, 185, 201, 203, 205.
Second.................. 167
Episcopal.................. 155
Grace..............28, 157, 196
St. Michael's........28, 156, 196
first....................... 129
free........................ 176
Freewill Baptist, Elm-street 190
First..............117, 186, 189
Merrimack-street......... 191
Church, F. W. Baptist, Pine-street 52, 186
in Piscataquog village........ 204
membership................ 130
Methodist, Elm-street........ 153
First..................130, 137
North Elm-street.......... 153
Second..........28, 152, 175, 221
St. Paul's................. 154
Wesleyan............... 175, 184
Mission...................... 180
Presbyterian............. 130, 185
property..................... 130
Roman Catholic, St. Ann's 120, 194
St. Augustine's............ 195
St. Joseph's........121, 195, 197
Second Advent................ 192
Unitarian........28, 111, 162, 198
Universalist, Elm-street..... 182
First........27, 130, 139, 141, 198
Second.................... 139
Churches, architecture of........... 196
number of.................... 130
Roman Catholic............... 194
Cider, made....................... 317
Cigars, made...................... 318
Cilley, Mrs. J. G................. 208
City.............................. 41
Bank......................... 261
charter...................31, 42
clerks....................... 45
debt......................... 66
Fire Insurance Company..... 266
government................... 83
hall......................29, 82
Hotel........................ 80
marshal...................... 32
Messenger & Republican.... 336
Missionary Society........... 176
National Bank................ 261
officers..................45, 83
property..................... 66
Savings Bank................. 262
solicitors................... 59
treasurers................... 59
Clark, Daniel...30, 31, 67, 89, 204, 341, 346
George T..................... 32
Joseph B..................... 389
Lewis W..................67, 391
Rufus T...................... 342
William C.................... 30
Clarke, John B...........44, 136, 344, 392
Stephen G.................... 341
William C.....31, 89, 143, 342, 344, 395.

Classic hall 173
Clergymen........................ 80
Clerk of police court................ 42
Clerks of city........................ 45
of common council........... 45
of town........................ 39
Cleworth, John........................ 312
Cloth, made........................ 311
Clough, Henry, fell dead............ 132
Lucien B........................ 67
Club, Manchester Chorus and Glee.. 248
Cobb, Sylvanus........................ 211
Cochran, Joseph, jr................32, 84
Cohas brook........................69, 93, 306
locks in........................ 21
settlements on........................ 11
Collector of taxes........................ 42
Colonels........................ 369
Commandry, Trinity....................212, 216
Commissioners of water-works...... 91
Committee, school................112, 122
Concord & Portsmouth railway 75
Manufacturing Company..... 270
railway....................28, 75
square........................44, 72
Concordia........................ 245
Congregational church, First...27, 98, 100, 130, 180, 185, 201.
Franklin-street 28, 168, 185, 201, 203, 205.
Madison-avenue........... 169
Second........................ 167
society, First.........134, 136, 165
Franklin-street 167
Second........................ 165
Sunday-school, First......... 133
Franklin-street............ 170
Congregationalism........................ 183
Constantine, Emperor.............. 220
Constitution, Fort........................ 345
Convent, Roman Catholic............ 195
Converse, George W. F............. 173
Copper work, made.................. 316
Corcoran, Thomas................120, 121
Corey, William........................ 316
Corps, United States Army.......... 368
Veteran Reserve............. 366
Coughlin, John........................ 344
Council, Adoniram................212, 219
common........................ 145
Granite State................... 243
Labarum................212, 220
Onward........................ 244
state........................ 244
Countess d'Ossoli........................ 163
Court, first held in town............. 29
Court-house........................ 82
Courts established........................ 17
Cows, value of........................ 66
Crain, Leland & Moody............. 100
Crash, made........................292, 318
Crombie, Samuel C.................. 320
Crosby, Josiah........................ 398
Cross, David............. 19, 67, 111, 344
Ira........................ 317
Crusader........................ 334
Currier, Camp........................ 343
Moody.................. 343, 400

Dalton, Charles H................. 98
Dam, at Amoskeag Falls..........78, 278
at water-works............92, 93
Daniels, D. J........................ 320
Joel........................ 87
Darling & Varney.................. 316
Hartshorn &..................... 316
Daughters of Temperance........... 233
Davis, John L........................ 321
Moses......................28, 82
Dean, James........................ 297
Oliver,........24, 89, 139, 268, 269
Debating club in high school......... 246
Debt, city........................ 66
Decoration Day..................... 242
Deer Neck........................ 69
Delaines, made........................ 293
Democrat—& American............. 327
Foster's........................ 337
Independent............30, 329
Manchester....26, 28, 324, 325, 327, 332.
Union................80, 327, 332
Denims, made........................283
Denny, Charles A..................... 312
Joseph A..................... 312
Department, fire..................... 85
police........................ 84
Derryfield, chartered................ 13
classed, by itself............. 24
with Litchfield............. 19
history of.................... 15
name of, changed to Manchester........................ 21
Derry Mills........................ 305
DeWitt Clinton Encampment........ 217
Dexter, Henry M..................... 136
Dickey, George E...............198, 200
Dignam, Walter........................ 342

Dinsmore, Arthur.................... 317
Dispatch, Saturday Night.........80, 337
Districts, highway.................. 21
school..........19, 25, 27, 109, 112
Division, Excelsior.................. 233
Manchester, No. 3.......... 232
No. 19.................... 233
Niagara.................... 233
Doctors............................ 80
Dollar Weekly Mirror............... 332
and New Hampshire Journal of Agriculture....... 334
Domestic Benevolent Society......... 174
Donohoe, Michael T... .....342, 344, 346
Door-frames, made.................. 318
Doors, made.................313, 317, 320
Dorr pond.......................... 92
Dow, Robert C...................... 342
Downs, C. M..................... ... 321
F. F....................... 321
Drew, William E................... 315
Drillings, made..................283, 292
Duck, made......................... 292
Dudley, Elizabeth J................ 345
Dunn, Harris & Company........ ... 321

Eagle Paper Company............... 321
Earl Bective....................... 220
Earle, J. E........................ 320
Eastburn, Manton............ 159
Eastman, Ira A..................... 30
Eaton, Francis B................... 89
Hosea....................... 80
Edgell, Frederick M................ 343
Edgerly, Martin V. B............... 403
Education, N. H. Journal of......... 335
Election, city, day of changed......42, 60
first 31
Eliot, John......................11, 127
Elliott, Lon........................ 77
Ellison, John...................... 253
Elm street............ ....44, 67
Emerson, J. C...................27, 95
Encampment, DeWitt Clinton....... 217
Mount Horeb,.............. 217
Mount Washington.......... 228
Trinity...................216, 217
Wonolanset........ 225
Engineers of fire department......86, 105
Engine, fire 26, 44
at Piscataquog village......26, 86
at Stark Mills................ 26
companies.................. 86
Manchester................. 326
Engine-house......................... 86
first.......................... 26
Engines, Amoskeag steam fire....272, 285, 311.
Enterprise, Ladies'.................. 335
Episcopal church.................28, 155
parsonage.................... 159
Sunday-school............... 159
Excelsior Company, American....... 321
New England............. 321
Division.................... 233
hook and ladder company.... 86
Literary Association......... 248
made........................ 321
Exchange, Merchants', fire at........ 98
Expresses........................... 79

Factories, value of.................. 66
Fairbanks, Alfred G............ 82
Fair in aid of soldiers.............. 344
Falls, Amoskeag.......11, 78, 95, 267, 371
Goffe's...11, 249, 254, 306, 318, 320
Merrill's.................... 77
school-house................ 111
Fanning, J. T....................... 92
Farley, Luther...................... 31
Farmer, Daniel D................... 24
Granite..............331, 332, 333
& Visitor...... 334
Mirror &.................. 332
Farmers' Cabinet................... 326
Monthly Visitor......331, 332, 333
Farnsworth, Simeon D............... 342
Fearing, Hawkes, jr................. 343
Fellows, Joseph W................84, 85
Moses...................31, 405
Felton, S. A........................ 315
Fenn, William H................... 136
Fenner, G. G....................... 321
Field Officers...................... 369
File Works, Granite................. 312
Files, made............ 312
Fire alarm telegraph................ 87
Fire at Amoskeag Company's mills..95, 96
Amoskeag village......95, 96, 100
Baldwin & Company's steam mill....................96, 99
bridge of North Weare railway,..................... 101
First Baptist church......147, 199
Janesville 99
John Brugger's mill 100
Masonic Temple............. 212
Mechanics' Row............. 100

Fire at Patten's block......88, 99, 222, 255
Piscataquog steam-mill....... 99
Print-Works................ 97
Stark mills.... 96
state reform school........... 100
town-house................... 195
Fire department...................... 85
engine, first.................. 26
on Chestnut street............ 100
on Elm street near Lowell.... 99
on Hanover street..... 98, 99, 100
on Manchester street...98, 99, 100
wards........................ 26
Fire King steamer company......... 86
Firemen's Relief Association........ 87
Fires.................................. 95
First board of engineers............. 29
of health................... 26
building on west side of Elm street..................... 27
city election................. 31
cotton-mill........ ....23, 267
court held.................. 29
engine-house................ 26
fire-engine................... 26
inhabitants.................. 11
land sale..................... 25
large fire..................... 95
mayor....................... 31
meeting-house........ 12
completed... 137
now standing.............. 130
mill.......................... 12
murder............ 24
newspaper................26, 323
police....................... 26
private house on Company's land....................... 25
representative, classed....... 19
unclassed...... 24
school-house................. 19
schools...................... 109
teacher...................... 109
town-meeting.... 15
in new village............. 27
Fish, at Amoskeag................... 11
John B.................... 320
Fisk, James......................... 240
Flanders, George M................. 74
Isaac C...........31, 251, 261, 270
Flannels, made..................283, 305
Fliers, made........................ 312
Fling, Daniel W...................... 201
Flint, C. A.......................... 318
Ford, Elbridge..................... 26
Forest cemetery...................75, 129
Former associations................. 246
manufacturers................ 319
Forrest Dramatic Association........ 246
Forsaith, Hiram..................... 312
Samuel C............ 314
Fort Constitution.................... 345
Independence................ 343
near Nutt's pond............. 69
Sumter...................... 339
Forum, Public....................... 337
Foss, Andrew T..................... 143
Foster, Herman...................... 406
Foster's Democrat................... 337
Foundry, D. B. Varney's..........96, 316
Fountains......... ....44, 73
Fradd, Horatio....................... 87
Francestown mountains............. 372
Franklin hall........................ 136
telegraph.................... 79
Free church......................... 176
French and Indian War............. 13
Roman Catholics.........195, 200
Walter....................... 31
Freshets............................ 78
Fuller, Margaret.................... 163
Fulton Works....................... 320
Fusileers, Granite.. ....95, 237

Gage, George W..................... 74
Gale, Amos G....................... 320
Gamble house....................... 81
Gas, made........................... 310
Gas-Light Company, Manchester.... 309
Gay, Alpheus....................91, 345
Ira...................24, 268, 269
Gazette, New Hampshire............ 334
Winnipesaukee.... 335
Gerrish, George A............... 343
Gillis, David.................. 31, 89, 98
Jotham..................... 268
Gilmore, George..................17, 128
George C................... 341
Gingham, made............. ....283, 305
Glancy, Thomas F................... 318
Gleaner..... 328
Globe, New Hampshire Sunday...... 337
Goddard, George W................ 314
Goffe, John.....................11, 15, 70
Goffe's Falls..11, 70, 249, 254, 306, 318, 320
cemetery at................. 75
Gooden, Daniel...................... 173
John V...................... 173

Good Templars........ 234
Goodwin, Ichabod........ 339
Richard J. P........ 345
Gorges, Sir Ferdinando........ 9
Gould, Baldwin, —— & Company... 316
D. C........ 289
Government, city........ 83
Grain, ground........314, 317, 318
Grand Army of the Republic........ 241
Grange, Amoskeag........ 243
state........ 244
Granite........ 68
bridge........ 77
Farmer........331, 332, 333
& Visitor........ 334
File Works........ 312
Fusileers........95, 237
Lodge........221, 230
State Council........ 243
State Lodge........ 245
street........ 78
Temple of Honor........ 233
Grants of land........10, 12
Gray, F. L........ 318
Green, Stephen D........ 173
Guard, Abbott........339, 340
Guards, Head........ 240
Martin........345, 366
National........237, 344, 366
Sheridan........ 240
Stark........236, 342
Union........ 339
Gymnasium, Manchester........ 245

Haines, Joseph A........ 99
Rifles........ 240
Hale, Camp........ 343
Hall, city........29, 82
John........ 15
Joseph B........ 70
Marshall P........ 89
Samuel........ 252
Hallsville........70, 321
Hammer-handles, made........ 313
Hanover square........72, 73
street society........ 165
Haradon's Weekly Spy........ 331
Hardy, Orison........ 200
Harriman, Walter........ 342
Harrington, E. W........391, 408
steamer company........ 86
Harris, Dunn, —— & company........ 321
estate........ 96
Mary P........ 185
Harrytown........11, 12, 13
Hartshorn & Darling........ 316
Harvey, Matthew........ 80
Haseltine House........ 80
Hatchet-handles, made........ 313
Hatchets, made........ 308
Hayes, S. Dana........ 83
Head—Guards........ 240
Natt........ 410
Healey, Daniel F........ 82
Heavy Artillery........345, 364
Henrysborough........ 13
Henrysburg........13, 19
Herald, People's........ 324
Hero, Old........ 330
Herrick, H. W........ 242
Heyes, Anna........ 25
Hibernians, Ancient Order of........ 244
High school........ 44
cadets........ 241
debating club........ 246
Highway districts........21, 68
Hildreth, Ephraim........ 12
Hill, Charles H........ 318
Hills, Gilbert........ 82
Hillsborough county........17, 18
Earl of........ 17
Lodge........221, 224
History of Manchester........44, 92
Hobbs, Edwin H........276, 343
Hodge, Jeremiah........ 317
Holt, H. C........ 316
J. S........ 316
W. S........ 316
Holmes, William F........ 318
Hook & ladder company, Excelsior.. 86
house........ 28
Hooksett brick........ 20
Manufacturing Company........ 270
Mills........274, 293
road........ 28
Horr, Charles........ 99
Horse railway........ 76
Horses, value of........ 66
Hose........ 87
carriage, at Amoskeag........ 87
at Goffe's Falls........ 87
Pennacooks'........ 86
Hose Company, new........ 87
Pennacook........ 86
Hosley, John........ 413
Hospital, Webster........ 345
Hotels........ 79
Houghton, George C........ 345

House of correction.............. .. 28
Hoyt, D. J.......................... 30
John......................... 314
W. J......................... 315
Hubbard, George H............ 318
Thomas R.................... 317
William W................... 313
Hughes, Aaron P., Lodge............ 212
Hunt, J. T. P....... .... 271, 320
Nathan P.................89, 271
Hurlburt, W. Henry.................. 77
Huse, cemetery...................... 75
Isaac......................... 27
Hutchinson, Charles................. 271
Hydrants............................ 87

Incidentals.............. 79
Independence, Fort.................. 343
Independent Democrat............30, 329
Statesman.................. 326
Ingham, Edward..................... 81
Insurance companies................. 265
Insurance Company, Amoskeag Mutual Fire.................. 265
City Fire.................... 266
Manchester................. 266
City Fire and Marine....... 266
Fire and Marine 266
Mutual Fire 265
New Hampshire Fire......... 266
Odd Fellows' Mutual Life.... 224
State Fire................... 266
Iris & Souvenir...................326, 327
Iris & Literary Record............. 326
Iron Company, Manchester...... 319, 320
ore 13
work, made................. 315
Island mill.......................... 95
pond........ 69
House 80
Isle of Hooksett Canal Company..... 270

Jackson, Albert...................44, 249
Samuel P. 249
Jail, county......................... 81
keepers of..................... 82
James, Jacob F................. 90, 414
Janesville.....................70, 99, 314
Joe English hill..... 372
Johnson, Jeremiah, murder of....... 26
Thomas........ 318
Jones, Isaac H...................... 81
Seth K...................... 253
Josselyn, L. H...................... 316
Journal, Labor...................... 337
Merchants' Own............ 331
of Agriculture, N. H.....332, 334
Dollar Weekly Mirror & 332, 334
of Education, N. H.......... 335
of Medicine, N. H............ 353
of Music, N. H......... ..80, 337
Judkins, George F.................. 271
Junto Organ......................... 335
Justices of police court............32, 42

Keeley, P. C........................ 198
Keeney, Hudson...................... 314
Kelly, John L.............. 339
Kendall, B. C....................... 87
Rodney 247
Kennedy, John L.................... 82
Kent, Moody........................ 81
Kidder, Benjamin................... 11
John S...............74, 318, 319
Joseph...............28, 44, 344
Samuel B............20, 252, 271
Samuel P.................... 268
Killey, Walter S..................... 302
William L................... 302
Kimball, John D..................... 271
Orrin E..................... 314
William H.................. 28
Kinsley, Mrs. Benjamin............. 232
Knights of Pythias.................. 229
Knitting machines, made............ 316
needles, made............316, 317
Knowles, Mary J.................... 345
Know-Nothing movement......... ... 335

Labarum Council................212, 220
Labor Journal....................... 337
League...................... 229
Ladies' Enterprise.................. 335
Lafayette 214
Lodge............... ....211, 213
Lake Village Times..................336
Land and Water-Power Company, Amoskeag.....................274, 275
Land sale,..........25, 26, 29, 30, 271, 272
Lane, Daniel W...............67, 251, 315
Thomas W.................. 86
Warren L................84, 416
Langdon Mills 302
Langley, John.............. 213
Latitude of Manchester.............. 65
Lawyers............................. 80
League, Labor....................... 229
Women's Temperance........ 236

Leather, dressed..................314, 317
tanned........................ 314
Ledge, Amoskeag Company's........ 287
Leland, Crain, —— and Moody..... 100
Letter-carrier system................ 251
Lewis, Winslow, Lodge of Perfection 212
Lexington, news of battle of.......... 18
Library, public..................43, 44, 88
burned...................... 88
removed to new building... 88
Social......................20, 88
Lieutenant-colonels.................. 369
Lieutenants.......................... 370
Lincoln, Abraham..................... 339
George F..................306, 318
Line officers......................... 369
Lingfield, Edward..................... 11
Liquor-agent.......................... 28
Litchfield, classed with Derryfield.... 19
Literary Record, Iris &.............. 326
Souvenir..................... 326
Visitor....................... 336
Loan associations.................... 248
Lobdell & Russell.................... 270
Locks on Cohas brook................ 21
on Merrimack river.......... 278
Locomotive Works, Manchester..306, 320
Locomotives, made 272, 285, 306, 307, 311
Lodge, Aaron P. Hughes............. 212
Barbarossa................... 245
Benevolent................... 214
Bible......................... 213
Blazing Star.................. 214
Granite.....................221, 230
Granite State................ 245
Hillsborough...............221, 224
Lafayette...................211, 213
Mechanics'................... 227
Merrimack...........230, 231, 234
of Perfection, Winslow Lewis 212
Rising Sun................... 230
Stark......................... 234
Swamscott................... 230
Union Degree...............224, 235
Washington.................212, 219
Wildey....................... 228
Londonderry — Presbytery.......132, 184
settlers of.................... 10
Long, Joseph A. E................... 214
pond......................... 69
Longitude of Manchester............ 65
Loom harness, made................. 312
Lord, John P......................... 321
Lowell, Albion H..................... 315
Luce, Charles A....................... 44
Lyceum, Manchester..............28, 247
Lyons, Michael....................... 344

Mace, William........................ 232
Machine-Card Factory, Manchester.. 312
Machinery, made....284, 285, 312, 315, 317
Machine Company, Manchester...... 320
Machinists and Blacksmiths' Union.. 235
Magazine, Manchester............... 325
New Hampshire............. 327
Operatives' —— and Lowell Offering.................... 329
Majors............................... 369
Mammoth road...................25, 250
Manchester — Academy............. 247
& Keene railway............. 76
& Lawrence railway......... 75
Allodium.................... 326
American.................... 30
& North Weare railway ..75, 101
Aqueduct.................... 89
Aqueduct Company.......... 89
Art Association.............. 242
Atheneum.................... 29
a town....................... 23
Bank......................... 255
Bleachery.................... 319
Car and Machine Works...... 320
Centre.........15, 70, 130, 137, 249
Choral Union.................245
Chorus and Glee Club........ 248
City Fire and Marine Insurance Company............. 266
City Missionary Society...... 176
Daily American.............. 325
Mirror..................... 331
News....................... 336
Union...................80, 333
Democrat........324, 325, 327, 332
District Medical Society...... 246
Division No. 3............... 232
No. 19.................... 233
Engine...................... 326
Fire and Marine Insurance Company.................. 266
Five Cts. Savings Institution 263
Gas-Light Company......... 309
Gymnasium.................. 245
history of.................... 44
House.....25, 80, 100, 163, 271, 309
in the Rebellion.............. 339
Insurance Company.......... 266
Iron Company............319, 320

Manchester, latitude of.............. 65
Literary Association......... 248
Locomotive Works.......306, 320
longitude of.................. 65
Lyceum...................28, 247
Machine-Card Factory....... 312
Machine Company........... 320
Magazine.................... 325
Mechanics' Phalanx......339, 340
Memorial.................... 324
Mercantile Advertiser........ 329
Mesmeric Institute........... 246
Mills.....................272, 293
manufacturing department, 298
printing department....... 300
Musical Education Society... 248
Mutual Fire Insurance Co. . 266
named....................... 21
National Bank............... 256
National Guards..........344, 366
Oil Cloth Carpet Factory..... 321
Operative.................... 328
Palladium................... 328
Paper-Works................ 314
Printers' Literary Association 246
Print-Works................. 294
fire at...................... 97
Print-Works and Mills...294, 296
Representative............26, 323
Republican.................. 336
Rifle Company............26, 236
Saturday Messenger......... 329
Savings Bank................ 256
Section...................... 233
settlement of................ 10
Shoe and Leather Company.. 315
Social Union................. 246
soldiers, list of.............. 347
welcomed home............ 346
Spy.......................... 331
Telescope.................... 330
Transcript.................... 327
Veterans..................... 240
Women's Aid and Relief Soc. 207
Workman.................27, 325
Manufactures.....................78, 267
summary of.................. 311
Manufacturers, former.............. 319
miscellaneous................ 311
Maple Falls brook.................. 92
Marines............................ 368
Marshal, city.....................85, 102
first.......................... 32
tax-collector................. 42
Marshall, Charles H................. 89
Dustin........................ 341
Marston, C. L....................... 316
Martin, B. F.........197, 314, 372, 417
Guards...................345, 366
J. P.......................... 316
Mason, Capt. John...............9, 13
Masonic relief association............ 212
Temple....................... 212
burned................101, 212
Masons, Free....................... 211
Massabesic lake............65, 69, 90, 93
House........................ 79
Mast road.......................... 18
Mathes, Tucker &................... 320
Maynard, John H...............173, 271
Mayor, election of...............42, 43
first.......................... 31
votes for..................... 60
McAlpine, William J................ 91
McCrillis, John A................... 314
John B........................ 314
McDonald, William................. 120
McDowell, Alexander............16, 127
McGaw place...................... 213
McGregor, Robert.................. 19
McGregor's bridge...............19, 278
McMurphy, Alexander.............. 77
John.......................... 13
McNeil, John....................... 12
McQueston, David.................. 268
Means, William G.................. 136
Mechanics' — Lodge................ 227
Row.........79, 272, 311, 317, 321
fire at...................... 100
Medicine, New Hampshire Journal of 335
Meeting-house, built by town..16, 17, 128
made into a dwelling-house.. 129
made into a town-house...... 25
first....................12, 129
completed.................... 137
in Piscataquog village... 129, 176
Meeting-houses, barns used for....... 127
Memorial.......................... 27
Amoskeag.................... 323
Manchester.................. 324
Mercantile Advertiser, Manchester... 329
Merchants' — Exchange, fire at....... 98
Own Journal................. 331
Merrill, Anson S.................... 82
cemetery..................... 75
Henry C...................... 320
J. E.......................... 87
S. C.......................... 100

Merrill, Thomas D. 179
Merrill's Falls 77
Merrimack — House 79
Mills 294
Lodge 230, 231, 235
River Bank 262
River Savings Bank 264
square 44, 72
Steam and Gas Pipe Co. 319
Water Power Company 319
Mesmeric Institute, Manchester 246
Messenger and American 324, 327
City — and Republican 336
Saturday 30, 324, 329
Methodist chapel, Second 27, 28, 152
church, Elm-street 153
First 28, 137
North Elm-street 153
Second 152, 175, 221
St. Paul's 154
Wesleyan 175, 184
parsonage, First 138
Sunday-school, First 138
St. Paul's 154
Mile brook 69, 73
Military associations 236
Mill, first 12
cotton, first in Manchester, 23, 267
first in the state 267
Millstone brook 69
Mirror and American 80, 332
and Farmer 332
Daily 99, 331
Dollar Weekly 332, 334
and New Hampshire Journal of Agriculture 332, 334
Miscellaneous manufacturers 311
societies 211
Mission church 180
Sunday-school 180
Missionary, city 176
Society, City 176
Mitchell, Retyre 341
Moderators of town 38
Moldings, made 313, 318
Moody, Crain, Leland & 100
Moor, John G. 21, 268
Moore, Hannah G. 345
Ira 250
John P 19
L. P. 77
Samuel 70
Moore's Musical Record 336
village 70
Morrison, Charles R. 67
George W. 341, 344
Mosquito pond 69
Moulton, S. S. 270
Mount Horeb Encampment 217
Horeb Royal Arch Chap. 211, 215
St. Mary's Academy 121
Washington Encampment 228
Murder of Anna Ayer 24
Jeremiah Johnson 26
Jonas L. Parker 30
Musical Record, Moore's 336
Music — Hall 181
New Hampshire Journal of 337
Myers, W. H. 372

Namaoskeag 11
Namaske Mills 287, 304
Narragansett townships 12
War 12
Nashua Telegraph 336
National Guards 237, 366
Hotel 80
Naturalization in police court 42
Navy, soldiers in 368
Needles, knitting, made 316, 317
Nelson, David B. 343
Newburyport Veteran Artillery Association 240
Newell, John P. 419
William P. 89, 91
New England—Agricultural Society 80
Cavalry 363
Excelsior Company 321
New Hampshire — Agricultural Society 80, 331
a royal province 12
Cavalry 363
Central railway 75
Fire Insurance Company 266
Gazette 335
Journal of Agriculture 332, 334
Dollar Weekly Mirror & 332, 334
of Education 335
of Medicine 335
of Music 80, 337
Magazine 327
Poultry Society 80
settlement of 9
State Teachers' Association 335
State Temperance Society 330, 334
Sunday Globe 337
Temperance Banner 330
News, Manchester Daily 336

Newspaper, first.................... 26
Newspapers........................80, 323
Niagara Division.................... 233
Nuns, teachers in public schools..... 120
Nutfield.......... 10
Nutt's pond.......................13, 69

Odd Fellows........................ 221
building association.......... 223
Mutual Life Insurance Co.... 224
relief association............ 224
Offering, Lowell, Operatives' Magazine and 329
Officers, field, staff and line.......... 369
of city.....................33, 83
of schools.................... 122
of town....................... 33
Offutt, E. P......................... 99
Oil Cloth Carpet Factory, Manchester 321
Olzendam, A. P.................313, 421
Onward Council...................... 244
Operative, Manchester............... 328
Operatives' Magazine and Lowell Offering............................. 329
Organ, Junto........................ 335
Orphan Asylum, Roman Cath..26, 195, 277
Orpheus............................. 245
Owl 326

Paige, J. W. & Company........... 289
Warren....................... 271
Palladium, Manchester............... 328
Paper—Company, Blodget........... 319
Eagle..................... 321
hangings made............... 319
made.....................315, 321
Mill, Amoskeag.... 314
Uncanoonuc............... 315
Works, Manchester.......... 314
Park square.......................72, 73
Parker, Henry E.................... 136
James........................ 268
Joel.......................... 42
Jonas L., murder of.......... 30
Nathan..........153, 164, 320, 422
William..................183, 185
William M.................. 44
Parsonage, Episcopal............... 159
First Methodist............... 138
St. Ann's..... 195
St. Augustine's............. 195
St. Joseph's................. 195
Passaconnaway.....................9, 10
Pastor, longest term of service in Manchester....................... 133
Patrons of Husbandry............... 243
Patten, William..................99, 201
Patten's block, fire in..............88, 99
Patterson, John..................... 86
Payson, S. R........................ 306
White, —— & Company...... 297
Pennacook Hose Company...... 86
Indians..................... 371
People, Concord..................... 327
People's Herald..................... 324
Manchester Memorial and.. 325
Savings Bank............... 265
Perry, William G.................... 276
Pest-house... 83
Pettee, Holmes R.................... 314
Horace.......... 314
Peuple, La Voix du................. 336
Phalanx, Manchester Mechanics'.339, 340
Putnam....................... 240
Pherson, John F...... 86
Philbrick, Albinus.................. 312
Phœnix............................. 335
Pickels, William.................... 129
Pickers, power-loom, made.......... 312
Picks, made................ 308
Pierce, Franklin.................... 239
Nathan H 82
Thomas P...............261, 341
Pinkerton, George W............... 320
Piper, Benjamin H.................. 313
Piscataquog Aid Society............ 206
river.................18, 183, 318
Sunday-school.............. 185
village, 12, 42, 70, 99, 111, 176, 182, 183, 184, 204, 206, 214, 245, 249, 252, 297, 318.
academy.................. 184
Pitcher, Larned..............23, 268, 269
Police.............................. 84
first......... 26
court, allowed to naturalize.. 85
clerk of..................42, 85
justices of.........32, 42, 84, 85
Polls..............................32, 66
Ponds..............................69, 92
Population......................27, 32, 65
Porter, Alfred...................... 318
Portsmouth & Concord railway...... 75
Post, Louis Bell.................... 241
office........................ 249
Potter, Chandler E.........44, 84, 92, 424
Pound.............................20, 83
Preaching maintained by town....16, 17
Presbyterian—Board of Missions. ... 184
church at Bedford Centre.... 183

Presbyterian church at Manchester
Centre.................... 130
at Piscataquog village...... 182
doctrine taught.................. 183
settlers.......................... 10
Presbytery, Londonderry........132, 184
Prichard, Benjamin...........23, 267, 268
Print-cloths, made.................. 300
printed..................302, 321
Print-Works, Belmont.............. 321
Manchester................ 294
fire at.................... 97
Protestant churches................ 130
Providence Light Infantry........... 240
Veteran Association.......... 240
Public buildings.................. 81
Forum...................... 337
library.................43, 44, 88
Pumping-station at water-works...92, 94
Putney, P. B...................... 261
Pythian relief association............ 231
Pythias, Knights of................. 2 9

Quartermasters...................... 369
Quimby, Thomas L.................. 77

Railway, Concord.................... 28
horse........................ 76
Suncook Valley............66, 76
Railways.......................... 75
Rand, Jonathan..................... 109
Rangers, of Derryfield............ 15
Rifle........................ 342
Ray—brook......................... 69
cemetery..................... 75
John C....................... 81
Reading-room, in public library..... 89
Young Men's Christian Association.............. 204
Young Women's Christian Association................ 205
Real estate, value of................ 66
Rebellion, Manchester in the......... 339
Soldiers of the............... 347
War of the.................. 339
Record, Literary, Iris &............ 326
Moore's Musical............. 336
Reeds, made........................ 312
Reform school, state................ 80
Regiment, N. H.V., First, 240, 340, 341, 347
Second............... 340, 347
Third...............342, 344, 349
Fourth.........241, 342, 346, 351
Fifth......................... 353
Regiment, N. H. V., Sixth........... 354
Seventh.................343, 354
Eighth...................343, 355
Ninth....................343, 357
Tenth.............343, 344, 346, 358
Eleventh..................... 360
Twelfth..................346, 361
Thirteenth................345, 346
Fourteenth................... 362
Fifteenth.................... 362
Sixteenth.................... 362
Seventeenth.................. 345
Eighteenth................... 362
Unknown..................... 368
Irish......................... 343
H. A., First.............345, 364
U. S. A., First............... 368
U. S. S., First............... 367
Second..................... 368
Religious societies.................. 127
Representative, Amoskeag.......... 323
first, from Manchester by itself....................... 24
classed with Litchfield..... 19
Manchester..............26, 323
men......................... 373
Republican, City Messenger &....... 336
Manchester.................. 336
True........................ 336
Reservoir, Amoskeag Company's..93, 286
city's...................... 93
Reservoirs for fire purposes..28, 29, 44, 87
Residence of B. F. Martin........... 372
of Frederick Smyth.......... 371
of Waterman Smith.......... 372
Reynolds, Henry C..............308, 313
Richardson, Charles L.............. 276
E. P......................... 341
William..................... 90
Riddell, John....................... 12
Riddle, George W.................. 67
Isaac...........31, 32, 84, 320, 341
William P............213, 214, 426
Rifle Company, Manchester.......... 236
Rangers...................... 342
Rifles, Amoskeag................... 342
Haines...................... 240
Smyth....................... 237
Straw....................... 240
Rising Sun Lodge.................. 230
Robinson, Olney..................23, 268
Rock Raymond..................... 68
Rimmon..................... 68
Rogers, Bryant &................... 371

Rogers, Robert 15
Rolfe, William M 74
Rolls, made 313
Roman-Catholic—cemetery 75
churches 130
convent 195
French 195, 200
Orphan Asylum 26, 195, 277
property 196
schools 120
temperance societies 236
Rowell, Joseph M 30, 252
Roland C 85
Rundlett, Thomas 213
Russell, Barr & Company 270
Lobdell & 270
Ryan, John 164

Salaries of—city officers 83
clerk of the police court 85
engineers 86
justice of police court 85
librarian of public library 89
police 85
school committee 117
superintendent of schools 118
teachers 118
Sanborn, Alden W. 314
Seth J 200
Sargent, Levi 271
Sashes made 313, 320
Saturday Messenger 30, 324, 329
Night Dispatch 80, 337
Sawyer, J. B 90
J. C 315
pond 92
Sayles, Willard 23, 268, 269
Scales made 320
School, Amoskeag grammar 116
Ash-street grammar 114
bell, first rung from city hall, 29
committee 112, 117, 122
salary of 117
districts 19, 25, 27, 109
consolidated 43, 112
East grammar 114
evening 119
high, 44, 112
house, Falls 111
first 19
in districts six and nine 28
in districts three and four 27
old high 27
intermediate 116
School, Lincoln-street 115
North grammar 114
Park-street grammar 115
Piscataquog grammar 115
property 111
South grammar 113
state reform 80, 100
Wilson-hill 114
Schools 109
first 109
Roman Catholic 120
superintendent of 43, 44, 112, 117, 122.
Scotch Irish settlers of Londonderry 10
Seamless bags 293
Seccomb, Rev. Mr 127
Section, Manchester 233
Selectmen of town 33
Self-propellers, made 285
Settlement of—Londonderry 10
Manchester 10
New Hampshire 9
Settlers of Londonderry, Scotch Irish 10
Sewers 29, 31, 44, 68, 71
Sewing-machine attachments, bobbin-winders and thumb-screws, made 318
Shackburg, Dr 15
Shannon, Josiah 297
Sharpshooters, U. S., First regiment 367
Second regiment 368
Shattuck, Amos B 84
Brooks 81
Shaw, Edward 29
William M 319
Sheep, value of 66
Sheetings made 269, 283, 292, 304
Shepherd, Samuel 320
William 31, 271
Shepley, John 12
Sheridan Guards 240
Shirtings, made 269, 283, 304
Shoddy, made 306
Shoe and Leather Company 315
Shoes, dressing for, made 316
manufacture of 100, 316, 321
Shuttles, made 312
Sidewalks 44
Silesias, made 304
Simmons, George R 86
Slack, R. H 197
Slade, James 71
Slater, Samuel 23, 268, 269
Small-pox 19, 25, 27

Smith, Isaac W....................67, 84, 89
John A. V.................... 312
Joseph L.................... 315
Waterman..89, 98, 164, 320, 372 428
Smyth, Frederick 66, 80, 201, 340, 342, 346, 371, 430.
Rifles........................ 237
Smyth's block, built.................. 201
trees in front of.............. 68
Societies, miscellaneous.............. 211
musical...................... 245
of different kinds. 243
temperance.................. 231
Society, Antiquarian Sacred Musical, 248
Baptist, First................ 145
Merrimack-street.......... 174
Second.................. 189
Christian.................. 193
Congregational, First. 134, 136, 165
Franklin-street............ 167
Second.................... 165
Domestic Benevolent........ 194
Freewill Baptist, Elm-street.. 190
First...................148, 187
Merrimack-street........ 190
Pine street................ 187
Randall.................... 190
Manchester District Medical., 246
Manchester Musical Education.................... 248
Manchester Women's Aid & Relief...................... 207
New Hampshire Agricultural......................80, 331
New Hampshire State Temperance.................... 330
Piscataquog Aid.............. 206
St. Jean Baptiste.......... 245
Unitarian.................... 160
Universalist, Elm-street. .. 181
First...................... 139
Second..................... 180
Soda, made...... 318
Soldiers, Manchester, list of.......... 347
welcomed home.............. 346
Solicitors of city.................... 59
Sons of Temperance................. 232
Southwark, Jane.. 70
Taylor M.................... 70
Souvenir, Iris &..................326, 327
Literary...................... 326
Sovereigns of Industry.............. 244
Spear, Justin........................ 341
Spofford, John T..................... 251
Spokes, made......................... 313
Spooner, Harrison.................... 306
Spy, Haradon's Weekly............ . 331
Manchester.................. 331
Squares.............................44, 72
St. Ann's church.................120, 194
parsonage.................... 195
St. Augustine's church.............. 195
parsonage.................... 195
St. Jean Baptiste Society............. 245
St. John's Total Abstinence Society.. 236
St. Joseph's church.............121, 195
parsonage 195
St. Michael's church..........28, 156, 196
St. Patrick's Mutual Benefit and Protective Association......... 244
St. Paul's Total Abstinence Society.. 236
Staff officers.......................... 369
Stages................................ 76
Stanley, Clinton W................67, 433
Stanton Ben: F...................... 89
Stark, Archibald......... 11
Frederick G. 82, 268, 321
Guards...................236, 342
house........................ 81
John................15, 18, 24, 80
Lodge........................ 235
Mills.................271, 272, 287
agent's house.............. 26
counting-room............. 270
fire at. 96
place......................... 24
Veterans....... 237
William....................... 44
Stark's tomb.......................... 24
Star of Bethlehem................... 325
Stars and Stripes..................... 335
State Fire Insurance Company....... 266
Statesman, Independent.............. 329
Station, passenger...... 76
pumping...................... 92
Stationary engines made............. 285
Steam & Gas-Pipe Company, Merrimack.............................. 319
Steam fire engines, made............. 285
Stevens, Aaron F.................... 346
A. G......................... 271
Daniel L..................... 271
David 23, 267
Ephraim...............23, 82, 267
G. W 271
Josiah........................ 77
Phinehas.................... 271
pond.......................69, 29

Stevens, Robert....................23, 267
Stickney, Thomas.................... 21
Stock in trade in city, value of........ 66
Stockings, made.................... 313
Stocks in banks in city, value of..... 66
Stokes, Benjamin S................. 312
Stone, Eliza P....................... 345
Joseph....................... 297
Straw, E. A..66, 89, 90, 91, 275, 305, 320, 434
Herman F.................. 275
Rifles........................ 240
Streets.............................. 67
lighted........................ 44
superintendent of............ 68
Sullivan, Camp 342
Sulloway, Cyrus A.................. 67
Sumter, Fort........ 339
Suncook Valley railway...........66, 76
Sunday-school, Baptist, First........ 145
Merrimack-street.......... 174
Christian..................... 194
Congregational, First........ 133
Franklin-street............ 170
Episcopal.................... 159
Freewill Baptist, Merrimack-street...................... 191
Pine-street.......... 186
Methodist, First.......... ... 138
St. Paul's.................. 154
Mission...................... 180
Piscataquog................. 185
Second Advent.............. 192
Unitarian.................... 164
Universalist, Elm-street..... 182
First....................... 142
Superintendent of schools. 43, 44, 112, 117
salary of................... 118
of state reform school........ 81
of streets.................... 68
Surgeons............................ 369
Swamscott Lodge..................... 230

Tasker, J. C.......................... 320
Taxes.............................34, 66
collector of.................. 42
Taylor, Joel.......................... 251
Teacher, first........................ 109
Teachers, salaries of................. 118
state — association........... 119
Telegraph, fire alarm................ 87
Franklin..................... 79
Nashua...................... 336
Western Union.............. 79
Telescope, Manchester............... 330
Temperance Banner, New Hampshire......................... 330
cadets.......................... 236
Cadets of...................... 233
Daughters of................... 233
League, Women's............. 236
Society, New Hampshire State, 330
societies....................... 231
Sons of........................ 232
Templars, Good..................... 234
Temple, Cold Water................. 235
hall...................... .. 173
Masonic....................... 212
fire in..................101, 212
of Honor.................233, 235
Tenney, Franklin.............. ...101, 277
Tickings, A. C. A..................96, 269
made......................269, 283
Tiffany, Lyman.............. 23, 268, 269
Tillotson, B. M.................... 44
Times, Lake Village................ 336
Tools, made......................... 285
Topliff, Elijah M....................67, 84
Torrent, White Mountain.. 328
Towelings, made.................292, 318
Towle, Hiram......................... 70
Towlesville.........................70, 316
Town—clerks........................ 39
farm........................28, 82
house, built.. 27
burned.............. 29, 95, 167
converted from meeting-house.................... 25
re-built..................29, 167
hundredth anniversary of.... 44
incorporated................. 13
meeting, day of.............. 20
first........................ 15
first in new village......... 27
vacated..................16, 128
moderators of................ 38
officers..... 33
selectmen of................. 33
Transcript, Manchester.............. 327
Treasurers of city.................. 59
of public library............. 89
Tremont square................44, 72, 73
Trinity Commandry..............212, 216
Encampment............216, 217
True Republican..................... 336
Trustees of public library..........88, 89
Tubbee, Okah......................... 215
Tubbs, E. M.....................277, 315
Tucker & Mathes..................... 320

Tucker, Rev. Mr.................... 207
Turnverein.......................... 245
Turbine wheels, made............... 285
Tyng, William...................... 12
Tyngstown.......................... 12
Uncanoonuc mountains............. 372
Paper-Mill................... 315
Union—Association..........151, 164, 187
Blackmar................... 233
Degree Lodge...........224, 235
Democrat............80, 327, 332
Grand....................... 233
Guards...................... 339
Machinists & Blacksmiths'... 235
Manchester, Choral.......... 245
Daily...................80, 333
Social...................... 246
National Catholic Total Abstinence.................... 236
Number Six.................. 233
Weekly...................99, 333
Unitarian chapel......28, 29, 152, 164 187
church..............111, 162, 199
society...................... 160
Sunday-school............. 164
reduced to one class........ 163
Universalist church, Elm-street...... 182
First 27, 139, 141, 148
Second.................... 139
society, Elm-street.......... 181
First...................139, 180
Second.................... 180
Sunday-school, Elm-street... 182
First....................... 142
Upjohn, Richard.................... 197
Upton, Samuel....................84, 342

Valley cemetery..................... 27
Valuation of city.................... 66
of town...................... 32
Value of—city property............. 66
cows......................... 66
factories and machinery...... 66
horses....................... 66
polls........................ 66
real estate.................. 66
school property............. 111
sheep....................... 66
stock in trade............... 66
stocks in banks............. 66
Varick, John B..................... 112
Varney, D. B................96, 316, 438
James M.................... 341
Veteran Reserve Corps.............. 366
Veterans, Amoskeag................. 237
Manchester.................. 240
Stark........................ 237
Vickery & Company................. 318
W. H......................... 86
Village, Amoskeag..12, 42, 70, 100, 111, 130, 131, 139, 141, 143, 183, 249, 253, 273, 315, 321.
Moore's...................... 70
Piscataquog..12, 42, 70, 99, 111, 176, 182, 183, 184, 185, 204, 206, 214, 245, 249, 252, 297, 318
Villages............................ 70
Visitor, Farmers' Monthly...331, 332, 333
Granite Farmer &............ 334
Literary..................... 336
Voix, La—du Peuple............... 336
Votes for mayor at each election..... 60
Vulcan Works....................... 306

Walcott, Philemon................... 268
Wallace, A. C.....91, 99, 315, 317, 318, 341
C. W..............31, 44, 136, 439
William...................... 268
War, French and Indian............ 13
Narragansett............. 12
of 1812...................... 24
of the Rebellion............. 339
Revolutionary............17, 18
Seven Years'............... 15
Wards...........................42, 43
Warren, C. F....................... 310
S. D......................... 314
Washington, George................ 219
Lodge.................. 212, 219
Waste, made......................... 315
Watch, captain of the............... 85
Watchmen........................... 85
Water-Power Company, Amoskeag Land and.............274, 275
Merrimack.................. 319
Water-Works...............29, 43, 44, 90
commissioners of........... 91
engineer of................. 94
Watson, Alexander T............... 345
Watts, Horace P.................... 318
Webber, Samuel.................341, 342
Webster, John....................... 19
United States General Hospital......................... 345
William A................... 345
William B................... 305
Webster's Mills...................... 13
Wells, Charles...............30, 222, 250

Wentworth, Asa 30
Benning 13, 18
Henry T. 30
Horace 30
Wesleyan Methodist church 176
Western Union Telegraph 79
Weston, Amos 21
farm 129
James A. 21, 67, 76, 90, 440
Jason 251
Wheelwright, John 9
Whipple, Thomas J. 346
White, D. K. 100
Mountain Torrent 328
Payson & Company 297
Whitney, Henry S 271
Whittle, William 297
Wiggin, John S. 31
Wildey Lodge 228
Wilkins, James McKeen 81
Wilson hill 372
Wilson hill school 114
Wilson, H. T. 129
Newton, H. 84, 85
Winch, Isaiah 221
Window—frames, made 317
sashes made 318
Winnipesaukee Gazette 335
Women's Aid & Relief Society, Manchester 207
Temperance League 236
Wonolanset Encampment 225
Wooden wares, made 312
Wool pulled 314
Workingmen's associations 247
Workman, Manchester 27, 325
Worsted goods, dyed 302
made 300

Yankee Doodle 15
Young, John C. 345
Youngsville 70

BUSINESS DIRECTORY.

BILLIARD HALLS.

"Phenix," 1296 Elm st., Gaffney & Stowe. Residence, National Hotel.

BAKERY.

C. C. Fisk, 99 Hanover st. Residence, 322 Park st.

BOOKS AND STATIONERY.

E. R. Coburn, 16 Hanover st. Residence, Hall st.
A. Quimby, 7 Hanover st. Residence, 43 Hanover st.
Wm. H. Fisk, No. 4 Methodist Church Block. Residence, Manchester House.
C. E. Nutting, No. 2 City Hall, Elm st. Residence, 301 Amherst st.

BOOTS AND SHOES.

Frederick C. Dow, Merrimack Block, 832 Elm st. Residence, 263 Hanover st.

COAL AND ICE.

Dickey, Young & Co., 690 Elm st.

COUNSELORS.

John H. Andrews, Patten's Block, north entrance. Residence, 136 Myrtle st.
William R. Patten, Patten's Block, north entrance. Residence, Haseltine House.
Henry E. Burnham, Patten's Block. north entrance. Residence, 407 Hanover st.
Isaac L. Heath, Patten's Block, south entrance. Residence, Haseltine House.
Frank Hiland. Patten's Block, north entrance. Residence, Haseltine House.
David Cross, Patten's Block. Residence, 1552 Elm st.
S. D. Lord, 2 Union Building, 898 Elm st. Residence, 341 Hanover st.
N. P. Hunt, Patten's Block. Residence, No. 38 Ash st.
C. A. O'Conner, 801 Elm st. Residence, Haseltine House.
C. A. Sulloway, Patten's Block. Res., 324 Manchester st., cor. Manchester and Maple.
A. C. Osgood, Granite Block. Residence, 281 Central st.
Samuel Upton, Merchants' Exchange. Residence, Concord st., cor. Beech st.
J. W. Fellows, Merchants' Exchange. Residence, cor. Pearl and Union sts.
Henry W. Tewksbury, Towne's Block. Residence, 95 Harrison st.
Charles H. Bartlett, Riddle's Block. Residence, cor. High and Pine sts.
James F. Briggs, Patten's Block. Residence, 148 Concord st.
Henry S. Clark, 859 Merchants' Exchange, Elm st. Res., cor. Pine and Lowell sts.
Henry H. Huse, Patten's Block. Residence, Walnut st., cor. Bridge st.

CLOTHING.

John Lee, 7 Patten's Block. Residence, 311 Manchester st.
Cumner & Co., 888 Elm st. B. G. Cumner, N. W. Cumner.
A. H. Weston, 836 Elm st. Residence, cor. Chestnut and Prospect.
Folsom & Son, No. 3 City Hall Building. J. S. Folsom, J. A. Folsom.
Edwin Kennedy, 946 Elm st.
J. W. C. Pickering, 994 Elm st. Residence, Harrison st., cor. Union st.
Joseph Freschl, 770 Elm st.
John D. Bean, 1005 Elm st. Residence, cor. Pine and Concord sts.
Plumer, Chandler & Co., 897 and 899 Elm st.
P. K. Chandler, 930 Elm st. Residence, 143 Myrtle st.

CROCKERY, CHINA AND TABLE CUTLERY.

Chas. A. Smith, No. 3 Patten's Block. Residence, 593 Beech st.

CIVIL ENGINEERS.

Ellis & Patterson, Riddle's Block, 885 Elm st.

CARRIAGE MANUFACTURERS.

J. Wilson M. Hunt, No. 51 Lowell st. Residence, 20 Ash st.
A. W. Sanborn, No. 1168 Elm st. Residence, cor. Bridge and Beech sts.
J. B. McCrillis & Son, cor. Bridge and Wilson sts. Residence, 520 Beech st.

CIGAR MANUFACTURER.

Geo. H. Hubbard, 12 Hanover st , opp. P. O.

CLOAK MANUFACTURER.

W. P. Rundlett & Co., Cloak Rooms 49 Hanover st.

DRY GOODS.

Barton & Co., 849 and 851 Elm st
G. H. Tanswell, 29 Hanover st. Residence, 241 Central st.
Waite Bros., No. 1 Masonic Temple, Hanover st.
Holton & Sprague, 855 Elm st., Merchants' Exchange.
George S. Holmes, No. 3 Globe Block, Hanover st. Residence, 294 and 296 Hanover st.
S. P. Jackson, Jackson & Co., 861 Elm st.
A. Jackson, Jackson & Co., 861 Elm st.

DRUGGISTS.

Z. F. Campbell, cor. Elm and Amherst sts. Residence, 474 Pine st.
Chas. M. Jones, 1133 Elm st. Residence, 29 Ash st.
John R. Hanson, 1167 Elm st. Residence, Lowell st., cor. Beacon st.
G. E. Hall, cor. Elm and Hanover sts.

FRUIT, CONFECTIONERY AND TOYS.

E. O. Abbott, 989 Elm st. Residence, 43 Walnut st.

FANCY GOODS.

James Holmes, 860 Elm st. Residence, Chestnut st.

FURNITURE.

Wm. Parker, jr., 984 Elm st. Residence, 253 Central st.
Parker & Gordon, 824 Elm st. Residence, 361 Hanover st.
John E. Bennett, 732 Elm st. Residence, Manchester House.

FLOUR AND GRAIN.

H. & H. R. Pettee, 754 Elm st. Residences, 362 Hanover st. and 448 Amherst st.
Watts & Holmes, 698 Elm st., cor. of Central st.

GROCERS.

Henry C. Merrill, 928 Elm st. Residence, 119 Myrtle st.
A. M. Eastman, 850 Elm st. Residence, 275 Hanover st.
Eager & Robinson, 776 Elm st. J. Q. A. Eager, Fred A. Robinson.
J. M. Chandler & Co., 983 Elm st. J. M. Chandler, G. B. Chandler.
Andrew McNab, 750 Elm st. Residence, 368 Manchester st.
John Sweeney, 687 Elm st. Residence, cor. Elm and Central sts.
Locke & Demick, 71 Hanover st. R. M. Locke, L. B. Demick.
F. M. Boire & Co., 1076 Elm st. Residence, 512 Chestnut st.
O. Burpee, 1139 Elm st. Residence, 15 Laurel st.
D. M. Poore, 1163 Elm st. Residence, 85 Blodget st.
Moody & Co., 1217 Elm st.
B. P. Burpee, 744 Elm st. Residence, Merrimack st.
Octave L. Messier, 982 and 988 Elm st. Residence, 192 Manchester st.
Daniel Connor, 611 and 613 Elm st.
Flanders & Benson, 820 Elm st.
Stearns & Farmer, City Hall building, Elm st. Geo. H. Stearns, C. W. Farmer.
E. L. Gauvreau & Co., Connor Block, Elm st., opp. National Hotel.
A. Mallard & Son, 129, 131 and 133 Merrimack st.

HARDWARE, AGRICULTURAL IMPLEMENTS, ETC.

Daniels & Company, No. 1 Patten's Block, 938 Elm st.
W. C. Rogers, 1006 Elm st. Residence, Haseltine House.
John B. Varick, 809 and 811 Elm st. Residence, 537 Union st., cor. Concord st.

HOTELS.

P. W. Haseltine, Haseltine House, Manchester st.
John H. Willey, National Hotel, Elm and Granite sts.
F. A. McLaughlin, City Hotel, Elm st.

HARNESS AND CARRIAGE MART.

Edwin Branch, opp. City Hotel. Residence, 130 Pearl st.

INSURANCE AGENTS.

John C. French, 589 Elm st.
G. M. Sanborn, Towne's Block. Residence, 318 Manchester st.
Clarence M. Edgerly, 991 Elm st., Duncklee's Block.
W. G. Everett, 859 Elm st. Residence, River Road, north.

JEWELERS AND WATCH-MAKERS.

Dunlap & Baker, 959 Elm st., cor. Amherst st.
Langdon Simons, 1019 Elm st., Mercantile Block. Residence, 16 High st.

LIVERY STABLES.

Raymond & McLaughlin, 23 Lowell st. W. A. Raymond, Fred A. McLaughlin.

LUMBER.

A. Dinsmore, cor. Elm and Summer sts. Residence, cor. Beech and Pearl sts.

LEATHER AND SHOE FINDINGS.

Jeremiah Stickney, 1070 and 1072 Elm st. Residence, cor. Chestnut and Harrison sts.

MUSIC AND MUSICAL INSTRUMENTS.

I. S. Whitney, 866 Elm st., Ferren's Building. Residence, 241 Central st.
Baldwin & Batchelder, 9 Hanover st., over Post-Office.

MARBLE WORKERS.

Palmer & Garmon, 604 Elm st. I. D. Palmer, W. G. Garmon, C. D. Palmer.

MILLINERY.

Thomas Morgan, No. 13 Central Block.

MINERAL AND SODA WATER.

F. L. Gray, 868 Elm st. Residence, 143 Pearl st.

PHYSICIANS.

W. F. Byrns, M. D., Brown's Building, Elm st. Residence, Haseltine House.
James G. Sturgis, M. D., Office, 712 Elm st. Residence, 148 Pearl st.
C. A. Manning, M. D., Office, 10 Towne's Block. Residence, 431 Manchester st.

PHOTOGRAPHERS.

Stephen Piper, No. 905 Elm st. Residence, ditto.
S. D. Quint, No. 939 Elm st. Residence, 550 Chestnut st.
A. H. Sanborn, No. 996 Elm st. Residence, 11 Towne's Block.

PLUMBER AND GAS-FITTER.

Thos. A. Lane, 1 and 2 Wells' Block, Spring st. Residence, Clay st., near Elm st.

PAINTERS.

Joel Daniels, Smyth's Block, Elm st. Residence, 32 Ash st.

RESTAURANTS.

Leander Pope, 622 Elm st.
Barrett & Hunt, 1143 Elm st. Residence of J. W. Barrett, 332 Merrimack st.

STEAM-HEATING APPARATUS.

J. Q. A. Sargent, Haseltine House. Residence, 499 Beech st.

SPORTING GOODS.

Vickery & Stevens, 1043 Elm st.

STOVES.

Sullivan Bros., cor. Elm & Concord sts. and Brown's Block, south end Elm st.
Pike & Heald, 972 Elm st., Central Building. R. H. Pike, C. N. Heald.
D. Milton Goodwin, 710 Elm st. Residence, Park st., Hallsville.
Fairbanks & Folsom, 762 Elm st. H. B. Fairbanks, W. T. Folsom.

TOBACCONISTS.

J. B. Scott & Co., 796 and 798 Elm st. Residence, 362 Merrimack st.
A. D. Hunkins, 875 Elm st.

UNDERTAKERS.

Pearson & Wallace, opp. Hanover st. Church.
Hamilton Melendy, 93 Hanover st.

UPHOLSTERY GOODS.

Robert D. Gay, No. 1 Masonic Temple. Residence, 86 Prospect st.

WINES, LIQUORS, ETC.

Hayes & Co., 15 and 17 Concord st., Mercantile Block. Res., Harrison st. cor. Oak st.
Patrick Fahey & Co., 734 Elm st.

WOOD DEALERS.

G. A. Clarke, 374 Chestnut st.

WOOD WORKERS.

J. Hodge, Elm st., cor. Auburn st. Residence, 454 Amherst st., cor. Hall.

WOOD AND COAL.

E. P. Johnson & Co., 668 Elm st.

www.ingramcontent.com/pod-product-compliance
Lightning Source LLC
LaVergne TN
LVHW021226110826
845150LV00002B/256

* 9 7 8 1 4 2 5 5 6 3 6 5 3 *